The Internet of Things

T0144407

The Internet of Things
Enabling Technologies, Platforms, and Use Cases

Pethuru Raj

Anupama C. Raman

CRC Press
Taylor & Francis Group
Boca Raton London New York

CRC Press is an imprint of the
Taylor & Francis Group, an **informa** business

AN AUERBACH BOOK

CRC Press
Taylor & Francis Group
6000 Broken Sound Parkway NW, Suite 300
Boca Raton, FL 33487-2742

First issued in paperback 2022

© 2017 by Taylor & Francis Group, LLC
CRC Press is an imprint of Taylor & Francis Group, an Informa business

No claim to original U.S. Government works

ISBN-13: 978-1-498-76128-4 (hbk)
ISBN-13: 978-1-03-233971-9 (pbk)
DOI: 10.1201/9781315273095

This book contains information obtained from authentic and highly regarded sources. Reasonable efforts have been made to publish reliable data and information, but the author and publisher cannot assume responsibility for the validity of all materials or the consequences of their use. The authors and publishers have attempted to trace the copyright holders of all material reproduced in this publication and apologize to copyright holders if permission to publish in this form has not been obtained. If any copyright material has not been acknowledged please write and let us know so we may rectify in any future reprint.

Except as permitted under U.S. Copyright Law, no part of this book may be reprinted, reproduced, transmitted, or utilized in any form by any electronic, mechanical, or other means, now known or hereafter invented, including photocopying, microfilming, and recording, or in any information storage or retrieval system, without written permission from the publishers.

For permission to photocopy or use material electronically from this work, please access www.copyright.com (http://www.copyright.com/) or contact the Copyright Clearance Center, Inc. (CCC), 222 Rosewood Drive, Danvers, MA 01923, 978-750-8400. CCC is a not-for-profit organization that provides licenses and registration for a variety of users. For organizations that have been granted a photocopy license by the CCC, a separate system of payment has been arranged.

Trademark Notice: Product or corporate names may be trademarks or registered trademarks, and are used only for identification and explanation without intent to infringe.

Publisher's Note

The publisher has gone to great lengths to ensure the quality of this reprint but points out that some imperfections in the original copies may be apparent.

Library of Congress Cataloging-in-Publication Data

Names: Raj, Pethuru, author. | Raman, Anupama C., author.
Title: The Internet of things : enabling technologies, platforms, and use cases / Pethuru Raj and Anupama C. Raman.
Description: Boca Raton : Taylor & Francis, CRC Press, 2017.
Identifiers: LCCN 2016035997 | ISBN 9781498761284 (hardback : alk. paper)
Subjects: LCSH: Internet of things.
Classification: LCC TK5105.8857 .R35 2017 | DDC 004.67/8--dc23
LC record available at https://lccn.loc.gov/2016035997

**Visit the Taylor & Francis Web site at
http://www.taylorandfrancis.com**

**and the CRC Press Web site at
http://www.crcpress.com**

Contents

Foreword

Articulating technology trends, its potency, and impact is truly one of the most difficult tasks for a practitioner. It is not because there are so many points of view nor is it because the mortality rate here of an "idea or breakthrough" is high. The former is made tougher as there are no true experts (technologists, consultants, users, or analysts) who have gotten it right every time. On the mortality rate, it is important to appreciate that an idea or trend is made irrelevant as something else took over or was eclipsed by a series of changes that can be likened to nuclear reactions where an idea is either split into many ideas (fission) or when two or more smaller ideas fuse together, creating a larger, bigger trend (fusion).

In such a backdrop, it is imperative that we look at internalizing the trend appropriately aligned to business outcomes and appreciate its potency and power, all at the speed of thought. This book precisely attempts this in a rather focused and appreciative way.

At the start of this millennium, we started looking at the inevitable digitally connected world. The pace and potency of connecting computing devices grew exponentially as we, the citizens of the world, are wired to the world omnipotently present everywhere. The power of this connectivity has, in many ways, been prophesied long ago by those who set forth to define the meaning of telecommunications. However, the sheer pace at which the Internet of Things (IoT) paradigm is moving is truly amazing. Every common, casual, and cheap thing in our everyday environments gets systematically digitized through the lustrous use of edge/fog technologies (disposable, diminutive yet smart sensors, bar codes, microchips and controllers, RFID tags, specks, phones, etc.) to be elegantly sensitive, perceptive, reflective, and responsive, plus reliable.

All kinds of physical, mechanical, electrical, and electronic objects are thereby instrumented and interconnected with others in the vicinity as well as with remotely held software applications and datasets. With the addition of a bevy of devices (for smarter homes, smarter buildings, and smarter everything), the number of software services getting developed and deployed in central application repositories is growing rapidly. In short, by the year 2020, there will be billions of software applications and trillions of connected devices and digitized entities on this planet. The possible impacts are really mesmerizing for consumers and organizations, let alone for technologists. To us, this is no longer science fiction because it is truly *the art of the impossible*. The implications, impact, and imperative of this trend are truly irreversible, and the momentum is truly nuclear.

This book presents all the enabling technologies and tools for setting up and sustaining IoT applications and environments through a well laid out flow that is focused at the start on getting us to appreciate the nuances and nitty-gritty of the IoT concept. As we internalize this, the book moves seamlessly into defining the importance of the imperatives for the sustenance of the IoT ecosystem, and the need of the day is to devise protocols and technologies that are customized for their operations. These protocols and technologies are covered in Chapters 2–4 with an increased focus on IoT device connectivity and data transmission, nay telecommunication.

To realize the maximum value from IoT as a technology, we have to necessarily leverage and integrate programs with other underlying technologies such as cloud and analytics. Chapter 6 describes the unique capabilities of next-generation cloud infrastructure for hosting IoT platforms and applications. The data analytics chapter throws light on the IoT data collection, ingestion, storage, translation, real-time processing, mining, and analysis techniques that are required to squeeze out actionable insights from the data that are collected from IoT applications. This book also contains a dedicated chapter on edge/fog computing. The prominent IoT application enablement platforms (AEPs) and data analytics platforms in the marketplace are also covered in this book not just in passing but to the point of being a useful run book.

The second half of the book highlights the prominent use cases of IoT across the two main groups: consumer-centric IoT and Industrial IoT. The prominent examples that come under each of these categories are very well articulated. Some of the prominent use cases discussed are as follows:

■ Smart cities
■ Smart airports
■ Smart industry
■ Smart healthcare

The latest topics of study and research, such as cognitive clouds and cognitive IoT, are also discussed in detail, so that the journey to "the art of the impossible" can begin now. There are widely expressed concerns about IoT security, and this, too, has been explained by discussing in detail the various security breaches and the viable solution approaches to surmount them comprehensively. This is an area that will see even more action, as technology is quite secular and its power is harnessed by every section of society for all types of uses.

Welcome to the IoT journey. As you go through these pages, I am sure you will emerge with a bagful of ideas for your workplace, home, or society in general.

S. Premkumar
Executive Vice Chairman & Managing Director, HCL Infosystems Ltd.
Chief Mentor, HCL Talent Care Private Limited.

Preface

The recent announcements and articulations clearly show that there is a greater awareness and overwhelming acceptance that the future undoubtedly belongs to the Internet of Things (IoT). Hence university professors and IT industry professionals are in unison in unearthing pioneering technologies and toolsets to set everything right for the dreamed IoT era. A variety of concerted endeavors by different stakeholders is to substantially speed up the establishment and sustenance of the IoT-inspired smarter planet vision in a systematic and streamlined manner. In worldwide academic institutions and research labs, IoT has become the subject of deeper study and intensive research to explore and experiment any IoT-associated concerns and challenges and to expound viable and venerable solutions to boost the confidence of end users. There are conferences and confluences aplenty across the globe in order to accentuate and articulate the grandiose distinctions of the fast blossoming concept of the IoT.

This book has been consciously crafted with the sincere intention of telling all about the proven, promising, and potential IoT realization technologies and tools. A couple of chapters have been specially incorporated for clearly decoding and describing some of the prominent and dominant use cases across different industry verticals. Security, being brandished as the most inhibiting factor for IoT, is given extra thrust in this book in order to explain the nitty-gritty of security risks and vulnerabilities and to detail the path-breaking solution approaches, algorithms, and accomplishments.

Chapter 1 is exclusively written to decisively decipher the IoT conundrum. The IoT journey has been enumerated with finer details in order to empower prospective readers with the right and relevant knowledge so that they can easily understand the subsequent chapters without much difficulty. All the trends and transitions happening in the IoT space are illustrated in this chapter to showcase how the disruptive and transformative IoT notion is to significantly enhance the care, choice, comfort, convenience, and connectivity of people in the days to unfurl.

Chapter 2 is titled "Realization of IoT Ecosystem Using Wireless Technologies." In the first half of this chapter, we have discussed some of the key wireless technologies that have evolved or are evolving in order to support the requirements that are specific to an IoT system. Some of the protocols and technologies that we have discussed in this section are 5G, NFC, UWB, and ISO 18000 7 DASH7. In the second half of the chapter, we have tried to focus on low power wide area networking (LPWAN) technologies that are prominently used for interconnection of devices and applications in the IoT ecosystem. Some of the prominent ones discussed in this chapter are Sigfox, Weightless, Nwave, Ingenu, and LoRa.

Chapter 3 is titled "Infrastructure and Service Discovery Protocols for the IoT Ecosystem." In this chapter, we have elucidated reference architecture for the IoT ecosystem. Based on this reference architecture, we have explained the various IoT infrastructure protocols, including RPL, IEEE 802.15.4, 6LoWPAN, Bluetooth Low Energy, EPCglobal, LTE-A, Z-Wave, and ZigBee.

In the second half of the chapter, we have explained the various service discovery protocols, including DNS Service Discovery (DNS-SD), multicast Domain Name System (mDNS), and Simple Service Discovery Protocol (part of UPnP).

Integration and orchestration (Chapter 4) are the key tasks for the attainment of originally envisaged benefits of the IoT idea. There are innumerable innovations, disruptions, and transformations in the information and communication technologies (ICT) space these days. The prominent ones include digitization, distribution, industrialization, consumerization, and compartmentalization (virtualization and containerization). The result is that there are trillions of miniaturized sensors, billions of connected devices, and millions of software applications and services. Further, with the number of data sources climbing and device ecosystem growing rapidly, there are highly synchronized and integrated platforms for design, development, debugging, deployment, delivery, and even for decommissioning. The cloud movement has brought in a bevy of advancements in order to have highly optimized and organized IT environments. In such a highly distributed and decentralized environment, integration middleware standards and solutions become handy in seamlessly and spontaneously integrating all kinds of sensors, actuators, instruments, appliances, machines, equipment, utensils, tools, and so on along with remotely held software applications and data sources.

Chapter 5 is for the erudition of the freshly crafted and intelligent platforms for quickly and easily implementing IoT services and applications. All kinds of integration, orchestration, access, security, governance, enrichment, intermediation, and connectivity services are being given a part of the platform in order to lessen the developers' workloads. A single click then takes any implemented application to be executed to the deployment environment. Thus, IoT application enablement platforms (AEPs) are an essential thing for the forthcoming IoT-induced knowledge era. Similarly, IoT data analytics platforms help extract hidden patterns, pragmatic tips, useful associations, fresh possibilities and viable opportunities, actionable insights, possible risks, and so on out of accumulated IoT data.

There is no doubt that cloud environments emerge as the one-stop IT infrastructures for hosting, managing, and delivering business and IT workloads. For anytime anywhere any device any network any media access of IoT applications, services, and data, clouds are being positioned as the best environment. In this chapter, we have explained the uniqueness of cloud infrastructures for the ensuing era of IoT. The cloud journey is discussed in detail with all the appropriate information in order to enhance the understanding of the key contributions of the cloud paradigm for the intended success of the IoT to our readers.

Data analytics is the most important aspect of any industry vertical to be steered in the right direction to the desired destination. Data are a strategic asset. Any organization has to take data capture seriously and on subjecting the collected data into a variety of investigations in order to squeeze out usable and useful information that in turn enable decision makers and business executives to make correct decisions in time. IoT data originating from sensors and actuators have to be gathered, cleansed, processed, queried, analyzed, and mined in order to retrieve beneficial knowledge that can be given to IT and business entities to take appropriate decisions to automate most of the manual tasks. This chapter is specially crafted to express and expose all that can be accomplished through analytics platforms that can be cloud-hosted.

Chapter 8 introduces the fog or edge computing model. With the realization that faster response and real-time insights are two essential things for realizing highly competent and cognitive environments, the idea of edge computing is flourishing and is being continuously nourished by various product vendors, including IBM. There are different techniques and edge platforms for accentuating the new concept of fog computing. We have illustrated how edge clouds are being formed out of reasonably powerful edge devices in order to do service integration and orchestration. Further, how a large amount of IoT device data can be partitioned into smaller and easily manageable data modules to be allocated to those devices participating and contributing for the device cluster/cloud is discussed.

Chapter 9 is titled "Envisioning Futuristic Smart Airports Using IoT Integration." In this chapter, we have focused on the usage of the IoT concept to build futuristic intelligent airports. Various components of the IoT ecosystem that form the core pillars of the intelligent airport are the following: mobile devices, mobile technology, wearables, RFID/sensors, and beacons. The integration of each of these components into the airport ecosystem is examined in detail in this chapter. Ample use cases and real-life examples are provided in this chapter in order to provide an interesting reading experience for the readers.

Chapter 10 is titled "Envisioning Smart Health Care Systems in a Connected World." In this chapter, we have focused on the IoT use cases for the health care industry. The foundation technologies that are required for using IoT in the health care sector, challenges posed by the use of IoT for the health care sector, and the future promises of IoT for the health care sector are also discussed in detail in this chapter. In the second half of the chapter, we have focused on how the IoT supporting technologies, that is, cloud computing and big data analytics, are used in the health care industry.

Chapter 11 is titled "Smart Use Cases of IoT." In this chapter, we have uncovered three broad categories of use cases pertaining to the IoT ecosystem: industrial use cases, consumer use cases, and governance use cases. Under industrial use cases, we have mainly focused on two broad use cases: smart energy and smart transportation systems. Under consumer use cases, we have mainly focused on the following: smart homes, smart buildings, and smart education systems. Under governance use case, we have mainly considered smart cities.

Chapter 12 is titled "Security Management of an IoT Ecosystem." In this chapter, we have examined the various security requirements of the IOT infrastructure. We have also discussed the security threats that exist in each IoT component. Starting with the cloud platform, the threats that exist for each of the underlying platforms such as big data and mobile devices are examined in detail. The various ways and means to tackle the security challenges are also discussed elaborately in the chapter. The different types of use cases that form a part of an IOT ecosystem are smart buildings, intelligent transportation systems, smart water systems, smart grids, and so on. The security threats for some of these applications and the techniques to safeguard them are also discussed in this chapter. This chapter concludes with a framework that can be adopted in order to build and maintain a safe and secure IT framework.

Hopefully, this book is an informative and inspiring one for our readers.

Acknowledgments

I express my sincere gratitude to Mr. John Wyzalek, the senior acquisitions editor, for immensely helping us from the conceptualization to the completion of this book. The reviewing and publishing teams at CRC Press/Taylor & Francis Group have been very prompt on this book project. Thanks a lot. I wholeheartedly acknowledge the fruitful suggestions and pragmatic contributions of my colleague (Anupama C. Raman) to this book.

I remember my supervisors, Prof. Ponnammal Natarajan, Anna University, Chennai; Late Prof. Priti Shankar, Computer Science and Automation (CSA) Department, Indian Institute of Science (IISc), Bangalore; Prof. Naohiro Ishii, Department of Intelligence and Computer Science, Nagoya Institute of Technology, Japan; and Prof. Kazuo Iwama, School of Informatics, Kyoto University, Japan, for shaping my research life. I express my heartfelt gratitude to Thomas Erl, the world's top-selling SOA author, for giving me a number of memorable opportunities to write book chapters for his exemplary books. I thank the IBM managers for extending their moral support in granting the required approval in time to go ahead with this book writing.

I also recollect and reflect on the selfless sacrifices made by my parents in shaping me up to this level. I expressly thank my wife (Sweetlin Reena) and sons (Darren Samuel and Darresh Bernie) for their perseverance as I have taken the tremendous and tedious challenge of putting this book together. I thank all the readers for their overwhelming support for our previous books. I give all the glory and honor to my Lord and Savior, Jesus Christ, for His abundant grace and guidance.

Pethuru Raj

I express my heartfelt thanks to John Wyzalek, the senior acquisitions editor, for helping us at each stage for the completion of this book. I also express my sincere thanks to the reviewing and publishing teams of CRC Press/Taylor & Francis Group. My wholehearted thanks to Dr. Pethuru Raj for his constant support, guidance, and insights that helped me craft various chapters of this book.

I thank IBM management for their wholehearted support in the successful completion of this book project. I also sincerely acknowledge the sacrifice of my parents, who made me what I am today. A special note of thanks is to my husband (R. Murali Krishnan) and daughter (Aparna) for their constant support and motivation. I acknowledge the support given to me by my parents-in-law, my sisters, and their families. I thank all my friends who have constantly helped and supported me to complete the book successfully. I would like to thank my friend and team member, Narendranath, for helping me with the graphics creation of this book.

A final note of thanks is to Siddharth Purohit, CTO—Global System Integrator labs, IBM, who consented to write the foreword of this book.

Anupama C. Raman

About the Authors

Pethuru Raj, PhD, has been working as a cloud infrastructure architect at the IBM Global Cloud Center of Excellence (CoE), IBM India, Bangalore. He finished the CSIR-sponsored PhD degree in Anna University, Chennai, and continued the UGC-sponsored postdoctoral research in the Department of Computer Science and Automation, Indian Institute of Science, Bangalore. He was also granted a couple of international research fellowships (JSPS and JST) to work as a research scientist for 3.5 years in two leading Japanese universities. He has been contributing book chapters to a number of technology books that are being edited by internationally acclaimed professionals. The CRC Press/Taylor & Francis Group had also released his first solo book, *Cloud Enterprise Architecture*, in the year 2012. He has edited and authored a book titled *Cloud Infrastructures for Big Data Analytics* published by IGI International in March 2014. In association with another IBMer, he finished a book, *Smarter Cities: The Enabling Technologies and Tools*, published by the CRC Press/Taylor & Francis in 2015. He has also authored a book on the Docker technology, and it is being published by Packtpub, the United Kingdom, in 2015. He has also published a book entitled *High Performance Big Data Analytics* by Springer-Verlag in 2015.

Anupama C. Raman is currently working as a curriculum architect for the Smarter Cities Brand of IBM and is a member of the Business Analytics team of IBM. She is a certified storage area networking expert and is also a certified data center architect. She is also certified in cloud infrastructure and services management. Apart from these technical certifications, in the field of writing, she is a certified information mapping professional and in the field of project management, she is a certified scrum master. She holds an MTech degree in computer science and engineering and is currently pursuing an MBA in IT management. She has presented and published more than 20 research papers in various national and international conferences, and has also written numerous book chapters with various national and international publishers. She has authored a book, *Intelligent Cities: Enabling Technologies and Platforms*, which was published by CRC Press/Taylor & Francis Group in June 2015. She has also written a book on big data analytics, which will be published by Springer-Verlag in December 2015. She is a regular columnist of *Forbes* and has authored several articles for *Forbes India*.

Chapter 1

Demystifying the IoT Paradigm

Abstract: The future Internet will comprise not only millions of computing machines and software services but also billions of personal and professional devices, diminutive sensors and actuators, robots, and so on, and trillions of sentient, smart, and digitized objects. It is an overwhelmingly accepted fact that the fast-emerging and evolving Internet of Things (IoT) idea is definitely a strategic and highly impactful one to be decisively realized and passionately sustained with the smart adoption of the state-of-the-art information communication technology (ICT) infrastructures, a bevy of cutting-edge technologies, composite and cognitive processes, versatile and integrated platforms, scores of enabling tools, pioneering patterns, and futuristic architectures. Industry professionals and academicians are constantly looking out for appropriate use and business and technical cases in order to confidently and cogently proclaim the transformational power of the IoT concept to the larger audience of worldwide executives, end users, entrepreneurs, evangelists, and engineers.

A growing array of open and industry standards are being formulated, framed, and polished by domain experts, industry consortiums, and standard bodies to make the IoT paradigm more visible, viable, and valuable. National governments across the globe are setting up special groups in order to come out with pragmatic strategies, policies, practices, and procedures to take forward the groundbreaking ideas of IoT, and to realize the strategic significance of the envisioned IoT era in conceiving, concretizing, and providing a set of next-generation citizen-centric services to ensure and enhance people's comfort, choice, care, and convenience. Research students, scholars, and scientists are working collaboratively toward identifying the implementation challenges and overcoming them through different means and ways, especially through standard technological solutions.

In this chapter, we provide a broader perspective of what exactly is the brewing idea of IoT as well as the tickling trends setting the stimulating stage for the IoT realization and demonstration: Why it has to be pursued with all seriousness and sincerity? What are the prickling and prime concerns, changes, and challenges associated with it? Where it will be applied extensively and expediently? What are the near- and long-term future, the key benefits, nightmares, risks, and so on? The primary focus is on corporate and consumer IoT besides semantic and cognitive IoT domains.

Why the IoT Is Strategically Sound

Information technology (IT) has been in the forefront in precisely and perfectly automating and accelerating a variety of business tasks in order to immensely empower businesses, partners, employees, and consumers to accrue the widely circulated and IT-enabled business benefits. IT is being positioned as the best business enabler. IT is constantly evolving to do better and bigger things. These days, IT, apart from being the greatest enabler of simple as well as complicated business operations, is penetrating powerfully into every tangible industry segment in order to proactively ensure newer and nimbler customer-centric business offerings. In short, IT is able to both simplify and amplify business outputs and outlooks significantly. It is absolutely clear that the strategically sound association and alignment between business and IT are on the consistent rise to create and sustain real-time, adaptive, composable, and instant-on enterprises. Having comprehensively understood the outstanding contributions of IT in keeping up the business expectations in the cut-throat competitive marketplace, business executives and entrepreneurs are striving hard and stretching further to put in more money to conceive, concretize, and deliver next-generation IT-enabled business services and solutions to their worldwide clients and consumers, to devise workable and well-intended mechanisms and methods to understand people's needs, and deliver them with all the quality of service (QoS) and quality of experience (QoE) attributes embedded in through the smart adoption and adaption of all kinds of exquisite advancements in the hot and happening IT field. Decision makers and other stakeholders are constantly looking out for fresh avenues for more revenues.

With businesses achieving the desired success on various fronts, there is a tectonic shift in IT being intrinsically leveraged for empowering people in their daily activities. That is, the movement toward consumer-centric IT is on the fast track with the emergence of innovative, transformative, and disruptive technologies.

IoT Leads to Smarter Computing

How human life will be on this planet in and around the year 2025? What kind of lasting impacts, cultural changes, and perceptible shifts will be achieved in the human society due to the constant and consistent innovations, evolutions, and inventions in information, communication, sensing, vision, perception, knowledge, engineering, dissemination, and actuation technologies? Today this has become a dominating and lingering question among leading researchers, luminaries, and scientists. Many vouch for a complete and comprehensive turnaround in our social, personal, and professional lives due to a dazzling array of technological sophistications, creativities, and novelties. Presumably computing, communication, perception, and actuation will be everywhere all the time.

It is also presumed and proclaimed that the ensuing era will be fully knowledge backed. It is going to be a knowledge-driven society. Databases will pave the way for knowledge bases, and there will be specialized engines for producing and persisting with self-managing systems. Knowledge systems and networks will be used for autonomic communication. Cognition-enabled machines and expert systems will become our casual and compact companions. A growing array of smarter systems will surround, support, and sustain us in our classrooms, homes, offices, motels, coffee houses, airport lounges, gyms, and other vital junctions, eating joints, and meeting points in big numbers. They will seamlessly connect, collaborate, corroborate, and correlate to understand our mental, social, and physical needs and deliver them in a highly unobtrusive, secure, and relaxed fashion. That is, the right information and rightful services will be conceived, constructed, and delivered to the right person, at the right time, and at the right place. Extensively physical artifacts and assets, mechanical and electrical machines, instruments, equipment, utensils, and wares, electronic devices, communication gateways, and IT systems will become the major contributors for this tectonic and tranquil modernization and migration. Every common, casual, and cheap thing will join the mainstream computing toward the world of cognizant, connected, and cognitive computing.

IoT Delivers Smarter Environments

Our living, relaxing, and working environments are envisioned to be filled up with a variety of electronics including environment monitoring sensors, actuators, monitors, controllers, processors, tags, labels, stickers, dots, motes, stickers, projectors, displays, cameras, computers, communicators, appliances, robots, gateways, and high-definition IP TVs. Apart from these, all the physical and concrete items, articles, furniture, and packages will become empowered with computation and communication-enabled components by attaching specially made electronics onto them. Whenever we walk into such kinds of empowered and augmented environments lightened up with a legion of digitized objects, the devices we carry and even our e-clothes will enter into a calm yet logical collaboration mode and form wireless ad hoc networks with the inhabitants in that environment. For example, if someone wants to print a document in his or her smartphone or tablet, and if he or she enters into a room where a printer is situated, the smartphone will begin a conversation with the printer automatically and send the document to be printed.

Thus, in that era, our everyday spots will be made informative, interactive, intuitive, and invigorative by embedding and imbedding intelligence into their constituents (audio or video systems, cameras, information and web appliances, consumer and household electronics, and other electronic gadgets besides digitally augmented walls, floors, windows, doors, ceilings, and any other physical objects and artifacts). The disappearing computers, communicators, sensors, and robots will be instructing, instigating, alerting, and facilitating decision making in a smart way, apart from accomplishing all kinds of everyday needs proactively for human beings. Humanized robots will be extensively used in order to fulfill our daily physical chores. That is, computers in different sizes, looks, capabilities, interfaces, and prizes will be fitted, glued, implanted, and inserted everywhere to be coordinative, calculative, and coherent, yet invisible for discerning human minds. In summary, the IoT technologies in sync up with cloud infrastructures are to result in people-centric smarter environments. Context awareness is the key motivator for business and IT systems to be distinct in their operations, offerings, and outputs. The days of ambient intelligence (AmI) are not far away as the speed and sagacity with which scores of implementation technologies are being unearthed and nourished by product vendors and system integrators.

IoT Prescribes the Shift toward People IT

According to IT experts, there will be a seamless and spontaneous merger of everyday technologies to create a kind of technology cluster to fulfill our personal as well as professional requirements instantly and instinctively. That is, there comes the possibility of the transparent merging of our minds with machines. Learning will be an everywhere and every time affair because we will have intimate and real-time access to the world's information assets and knowledge base using any of our accompanying electronic gizmos, and on the reverse side, we will have an unfailing backup of our brains on massive-scale digital storages. Massive research endeavors and efforts are concertedly put into these seemingly magical and leading-edge technology themes, which will let to connect our nervous systems to computers beneficially.

Disruptive and transformative technologies with the smart synchronization of a galaxy of information and communication technologies will emerge to realize revolutionary applications and to accomplish hitherto unheard social networking and digital knowledge societies. Auto-identification tags carrying our personal profile and preferences digitally will map, mix, merge, and mingle with others in the realization of novel human aspirations. Our daily tools and products can be converted into smart products by attaching ultrasmall computers. For example, our coffee cups, dinner plates, tablets, and clothes will be empowered to act smart in their operations and interactions with other products in the vicinity or even with the human beings. Finally, all the tangible and worthy things, objects, materials, and articles will be transitioned into smart and sentient digital artifacts. This will result in the IoT in the decades to come. There is hence no doubt that future generations will experience and realize complete and compact digital and technology-driven, -enabled, -sponsored, and -flourished living. The impact of IT in our life becomes bigger, deeper, yet calmer as days go by.

Having contributed to the unprecedented uplift of business-operation productivity and for composable businesses, IT is turning toward the people productivity. There are several noteworthy advancements in the IT landscape as listed later. Therefore, the shift toward people empowerment is on the right track. That is, not only business services and applications but also there will be conceptualization, best-of-breed implementations, and maintenance of people-centric services. There are best practices, patterns, platforms, processes, and products being unearthed and built to silken the route toward the envisioned people-centric IT. There are a series of delectable and desired developments in the IT landscape. You can find them in an orderly manner in this chapter.

The Brewing and Blossoming Trends in IT Space

We all hear and read that the IoT is very hot. Everyone from chip makers to software companies to retailers is getting in on the act and strategizing the ways and means of capitalizing on the IoT, which is being touted and termed as the next big thing. The twentieth century belonged to electricity, and it is being projected that the twenty-first century belongs to the IoT. There are a number of powerful trends and transitions consistently occurring in IT space helping directly and indirectly realize the originally envisaged benefits of the IoT.

The Key Drivers for the IoT Discipline

Worldwide enterprises yearn for remarkable and resilient transformations on two major aspects: business operation model and business information leverage. Another vital point not to be taken lightly is to sharply enhance the user experience of business offerings. It is an overwhelmingly accepted fact that the desired enterprise transformation happens by doing the following five things:

1. Infrastructure optimization
2. Process excellence
3. Architecture assimilation
4. Technology adaption and adoption
5. Leverage data (internal as well as external) toward actionable insights

At the fundamental and foundation level, a variety of nimbler technologies, techniques, tools, and tips are emerging and evolving in order to bring in delectable transformations in data virtualization and capture, representation, transmission, enrichment, storage, processing, analysis, mining, and visualization tasks. Other prevailing and promising trends include the following:

The device ecosystem is rewardingly embracing a host of miniaturization technologies to be slim and sleek, yet smart in their operations, outlooks, and outputs.

Digitization and distribution are gaining plenty of ground nowadays, thereby all kinds of tangible items in our home, social, and office environments are getting transfigured to be sensing, perception, communication, and actuation enabled, display attached, and so on. That is, ordinary articles become extraordinary, common, casual, and cheap objects, and our working, walking, and wandering places become connected and cognitive to seamlessly and spontaneously join in the mainstream computing process. In short, everything gets emboldened to be smart, every device becomes smarter, and every human being is smartest in his or her actions, reactions, and decision-making portions of his or her earthly living with the pervasive, unceasing, and unobtrusive assistance of service-oriented, sustainability-insisted, and smartness-ingrained devices, systems, applications, and networks.

Extreme and deeper connectivity is another well-known phenomenon in order to establish and sustain ad hoc connectivity among different and distributed devices and digitized objects at the ground level and with off-premise, on-demand, and online applications. That is, the ensuing era is that everything gets instrumented, interconnected, and intelligent.

Everything Gets Service-Enabled

A family of futuristic and flexible architectural paradigms, patterns, and principles such as service-oriented architecture (SOA), event-driven architecture (EDA), model-driven architecture (MDA), resource-oriented architecture (ROA), and microservices architecture (MSA) is emerging to present every important and tangible thing in our midst as a usable and workable resource to the outside world. That is, everything has its own service interface expressed and exposed. In addition, the service implementation of any sensor, device, machine, and so on gets hidden from the service requester.

Big Data Becomes Big Insights

All kinds of interactions, collaborations, and compositions among the connected entities lead to massive volumes of multistructured data. The machine-generated data are far larger than man-generated data. The data volume, velocity, and variety are seeing a remarkable rise. With innumerable devices, tags, stickers, sensors, appliances, machines, instruments, gadgets, and so on getting fervently deployed in a distributed and decentralized fashion in increasingly significant locations such as homes, hospitals, and hotels, the tasks including data collection, classification, cleansing, fusion, and transition to information and knowledge have to be accomplished in real time using a series of greatly sophisticated and dependable technologies.

Real-time analysis results in a nice and neat realization of timely and actionable insights and faster responses.

Envisioning Software-Defined Clouds

The cloud paradigm started with server virtualization, and now every component of IT infrastructure gets virtualized to substantially improve IT inflexibility, portability, replacement and substitution, and extensibility. The brewing trend is ticking toward converged, centralized, automated, shared, optimized, virtualized, and even federated cloud infrastructures.

The Diversity of IoT Data Sources

Types and numbers of data sources are exceedingly rising. With billions of connected devices and the projected trillions of sensors, the data size is going to be tremendously massive. The different data sources are summarized as follows:

- *Data from passive sources*: These are less powerful and low-energy sensors and must be activated before they can capture and transmit data, and they only produce data when asked to do so. For example, a sensor that measures ground-water saturation only produces current data when the application program interface (API) is duly invoked. These are typically sensors that are diminutive, long lasting, and getting deployed in risky, remote, and rough locations.
- *Data from active sources*: These sensors are typically active and continuously streaming data, such as those from a jet engine. Thus, there is a need to have data capture, processing platforms, and infrastructures in place to readily receive and extract insights out of data streams.
- *Data from dynamic sources (fog devices)*: These are physical, mechanical, electrical, and electronics systems attached with sensors. These sensors are for enabling data transmission with IoT devices such as a smart thermostat. These sources have the inherent capacity and capability to carry out conversations with enterprise, web, and cloud-based IoT applications with all kinds of IoT devices at the ground level. We have talked about the encouraging roles and responsibilities of fog devices extensively in Chapter 8.

The veritable trend is that with the stability and maturity of the service paradigm, everything is being presented as a service providing, brokering, and consumer entity. Data, applications, platforms, and even infrastructures are being consciously codified and comingled as publicly discoverable, remotely accessible, autonomous, highly available, usable, reusable, and composable services. The vision of *everything is a service* is seeing a neat and nice reality. The service enablement delicately hides the implementation and operational complexities of all kinds of IT resources and only exposes the functionality and capability of those resources in the form of public interfaces in order to be dynamically found and bound.

In summary, the advancements are compartmentalized as follows.

The Technology Space

There is a cornucopia of disruptive, transformative, and innovative technologies such as connectivity, miniaturization and instrumentation, sensing, fusion, perception, actuation, and real-time analyses that result in actionable insights, knowledge engineering, dissemination, interfacing, and so on.

The Process Space

With new kinds of sophisticated technologies, services, and applications, big data, converged, elastic and instant-on infrastructures, and trendy devices joining into the mainstream IT, fresh process consolidation and orchestration, process innovation, control, and reengineering, process governance, and management mechanisms are emerging and evolving.

Infrastructure Space

The emerging infrastructure consolidation, convergence, centralization, federation, automation, and sharing methods clearly indicate that the much-maligned infrastructure landscape is bound to reach greater and greener heights in the days to unfold. Compute, communication, storage, analysis, and presentation infrastructures are trekking toward a bevy of exemplary transitions. Physical infrastructures are turned and tuned to be network discoverable and accessible, loosely coupled yet cohesive, programmable, and remotely manageable virtual infrastructures.

- *System infrastructure*: Hardware infrastructures (servers, storage, network solutions, specific appliances, etc.).
- *Application and data infrastructure*: Development, deployment, execution containers and consoles, databases, and warehouses.
- *Middleware and management infrastructure*: There are integration buses, backbones, fabrics, messaging brokers, and containers. With the intensifying complexity of IT space due to uninhibited complicity and heterogeneity of technologies, products, programming languages, design approaches, protocols, data formats, and so on, the importance of introspective middleware goes up considerably.

Infrastructures are becoming lean, mean, and green. Further, with IT agility getting operationalized as IT infrastructures become dynamically programmable, autonomic, auto-provisioning, on demand, and online, the goal of business agility is steadily seeing the neat and nice reality. These are possible due to integration brokers, execution containers, and messaging middleware, event capturing and processing engines, development, deployment and delivery platforms, analytical software, management solutions, and so on.

Architecture Space

Service-oriented architecture (SOA), event-driven architecture (EDA), model-driven architecture (MDA), service component architecture (SCA), resource-oriented architecture (ROA), and so on are the leading architectural patterns simplifying and streamlining the enterprise, mobile, embedded, and cloud IT. With the unparalleled and surging popularity of the service-orientation paradigm, everything is being presented and prescribed as a service. That means everything is given its functional interface so that other systems and services can find, bind, and leverage the distinct capabilities and competencies of one another.

Envisioning the Internet of Things Era

Owing to digitization, distribution, and decentralization, there is a renewed focus on realizing a legion of digitized objects, which are termed and touted as sentient materials or smart objects that are being derived out of ordinary and everyday objects. That is, common and casual things are being empowered or modernized to possess some of the IT capabilities such as computing, networking, communication, sensing, actuation, and display. That is, not only computers and electronic devices but also everyday articles and artifacts in our midst join the mainstream computing. In short, minimization, integration, federation, consolidation, virtualization, automation, and orchestration technologies are fast maturing toward producing disappearing, disposable, affordable, connected, dependable, people-centric, and context-aware devices. These are service-enabled to form high-quality device services. Actually, the web journey has been very much to appreciate.

The initial web (web 1.0) was just for reading (simple web), then web 2.0 has emerged for not only reading but also writing (social web), now it is being expected to have web 3.0 for reading, writing, and for linking multiple web content, applications, services, and data (semantic web), and the future is definitely web 4.0 for the envisioned era of knowledge (smart web). That is, every important thing in our environment is web-enabled to interact with cloud-based data, applications, services, content, and so on. Further, everything is connected with entities in the vicinity. Cloud infrastructures are being continuously enhanced to be a centralized and core platform for the smart web. The future Internet is, therefore, IoT.

IoT is all about enabling extreme connectivity among various objects across the industry domains. In this book, we would like to focus on the following themes and titles. We would like to write all about the key drivers for the IoT vision, the enabling technologies, infrastructures and platforms, prominent solutions, facilitating frameworks and tools, enabling architectures, business and use cases, concerns and challenges, and so on. As mentioned earlier, a string of promising and positive trends in IT space have laid a strong and sustainable foundation for the out-of-the-box visualization of the future prospects of the raging IoT idea. In a nutshell, the prevailing trend is all about empowering all kinds of casual and cheap articles and artifacts in our everyday environments to be IT-enabled, networking them in an ad hoc manner using a variety of communication technologies on a need basis to leverage their distinct capabilities individually as well as collectively in order to decisively and concisely understand the various needs of the people in that particular environment, and deciding, disseminating, and delivering the identified services and information unobtrusively to the right people at the right time and at the right place.

Deeper Digitization toward Smart Objects or Sentient Materials

Every tangible thing is getting digitized with the aim of attaching the much needed sensing and communication capabilities so that each and everything in our midst is capable of participating and contributing for the mainstream computing. There are multiple ways for empowering ordinary objects to become useful, usable, and extraordinary artifacts. The minuscule tags, stickers, chips, sensors, motes, smart dust, actuators, LED displays, and so on are the most common elements and entities for the speedy, simpler, and copious realization of smart objects. As a prime example, we all are increasingly and intimately connected to the outside world for outward as well as inward communication through slim, sleek, handy, and trendy smartphones. The ubiquity and utility of multifaceted phones are foretelling a lot of positives for humans in the days to unfold. In the same way, each and every item commonly found in our environment becomes connected and smart in their operations, outlooks, and outputs. The smartness derived via such internal as well as external enhancements enables them to be elegantly and eminently constructive, cognitive, and contributive. The maturity and stability of mesh network topology and technologies ensure these empowered and emboldened materials find and bind with other similarly enabled articles (local as well as remote) to leverage their unique functionalities and features in order to fulfill the varying needs (information, transaction, and physical) of people.

Such a long-standing empowerment goes a long way in unearthing a host of nimbler business and IT models and services, fresh possibilities and opportunities for businesses and people, scores of optimization methods for swiftly heading toward the vision of people IT, the solid and sharp increment in the user experience of diverse business and IT offerings, and so on.

The Connected Devices

The device space is fast evolving (implantable, wearable, mobile, portable, nomadic, fixed, etc.). The rough and tough passage from the mainframe and the pervasive PC cultures to trendy and handy portables, handhelds and wearables, disappearing implantables, invisible tags, stickers, labels, and chips, and versatile mobiles subtly and succinctly convey the quiet and ubiquitous transition from the centralization to the decentralization mode. This positive and pathbreaking trend, however, brings the difficult and dodging issues of heterogeneity, multiplicity, and incompatibility. That is, all kinds of participating and contributing devices, machines, instruments, and electronics in our personal as well as professional environments need to be individually as well as collectively intelligent enough to discover one another, link, access, and use to be competent and distinctive to accomplish bigger and better things for humans.

The end result is that constructing and managing cross-institutional and functional applications in this sort of dynamic, disparate, decentralized, and distributed environments is laced with a few unpredictable possibilities. That is, there are chances for risky interactions among varied services, sensors, and systems resulting in severe complications and unwanted implications for the safety and security of the human society. Also, it is envisioned that the future spaces will be highly digitized environments with a fabulous collection of digital devices and digitized artifacts; each is distinct in its face, feature, and functionality. Figure 1.1 succinctly illustrates the prevailing IT trends. The IT evolutions and revolutions are categorized as follows.

This compendium of devices will be increasingly interlinked to local as well as the global network transparently. With this sophisticated, yet complicated scenario brewing silently and strongly, it is logical to think about the ways and means of ably and autonomically utilizing, managing, and extracting their inherent capabilities (specific as well as generic) and capacities for

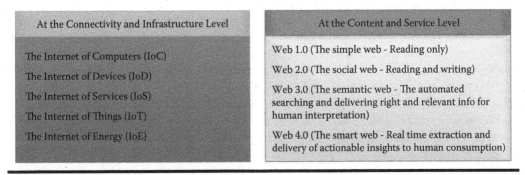

At the Connectivity and Infrastructure Level	At the Content and Service Level
The Internet of Computers (IoC)	Web 1.0 (The simple web - Reading only)
The Internet of Devices (IoD)	Web 2.0 (The social web - Reading and writing)
The Internet of Services (IoS)	Web 3.0 (The semantic web - The automated searching and delivering right and relevant info for human interpretation)
The Internet of Things (IoT)	
The Internet of Energy (IoE)	Web 4.0 (The smart web - Real time extraction and delivery of actionable insights to human consumption)

Figure 1.1   The evolution of the Internet paradigm.

arriving at a horde of people-centric, pioneering, and premium services. As we are keenly waiting for the paradigm of *computing everywhere every time* to cherish and flourish, it is imperative to nourish and nudge any variety of participating devices to be extremely agile and adaptive and to empower them to proactively, preemptively, and purposefully collaborate, correlate, and corroborate to figure out the user(s)' contextual needs by dynamically connecting, complementing, and sharing the dynamic resources with one another accordingly and unobtrusively. At the other end, there are a wider variety of input and output devices such as tablets and smartphones to assist people to finish their personal as well as professional assignments effectively and efficiently. That is, devices are becoming device ensembles and clusters through internal as well as external integration.

Adaptive Applications

The sensor and device data are scientifically captured, cleansed, and crunched to produce pragmatic insights that are in turn supplied to enterprise, web, mobile, transactional, cloud, operational, and analytical applications to be dynamically adaptive in their decision making, deals, deeds, and deliveries. Thus, digitized objects, connected devices, and adaptive applications will form the major chunk of the forthcoming knowledge era.

In summary, there are a wider variety of machines, appliances, consumer electronics, instruments, smartphones, tablets, notebook computers, sophisticated, specific as well as generic robots, personal yet compact and multipurpose gadgets and gizmos, kitchen utensils, and so on. On the other hand, there are resource-constrained, low-cost, low-power yet multifaceted smart and semantic elements, and entities such as miniaturized yet multifunctional sensors, actuators, microcontrollers, stickers, and tags. The real beauty here is that all these are getting connected with one another in their vicinity as well as with the remote cloud platforms and infrastructures. Connected, context-aware, and cognitive services will become the normal thing in that perceived era.

Illustrating the Device-to-Device/Machine-to-Machine Integration Concept

The pervasiveness of ultrahigh communication (wired as well as wireless) technologies facilitate the important and long-standing goal of enabling devices to seamlessly and spontaneously interact with one another to share their potentials. The communication field is going through a stream of praiseworthy transformations. There are new paradigms such as autonomic, unified, and ambient communication. With the maturity and stability of adaptive communication platforms and infrastructures, there arises a bunch of highly beneficial communication features and models. Even business processes are tightly coupled with communication capabilities so that more intimate and intensive processes are bound to erupt and evolve fast toward the neat and nice fulfillment of peoples' aspirations.

This newly found ad hoc connectivity capability among a whole lot of devices ranging from invisible and infinitesimal tags, smart dust, stickers, and sparkles in our daily environments to highly sophisticated machines on the manufacturing floors and hospitals has resulted in a series of people-centric and premium applications and services. Several industrial domains are very optimistic and looking forward to this paradigm shift in conceptualizing and concretizing a growing array of creative and cognitive applications for their user community. Telecommunication service providers are the very vital partners for the unprecedented and inhibited success of *device-to-device*

(D2D) integration. A bevy of next-generation applications is being conceived and constructed based on this grandeur transformation brought in by the D2D integration idea.

There are a number of noteworthy use and business cases escalating the gripping popularity of the idea of *machine-to-machine* (M2M) communication. The prominent ones among them include home integration solutions (proprietary as well as standardized) that are in plenty these days in order to simplify and streamline the rough and tough tasks associated with home networking and automation. This has led to innumerable smart or intelligent homes at least in the advanced countries. Again smart metering of all the modules and devices of electricity grids results in scores of smart grids across the globe. The seamless communication among the various components of classic cars has resulted in connected or smart cars. This goes on and on. Fueled by such an abundant enthusiasm and optimism among product and platform vendors, telecom companies, IT service providers, system integrators (SIs), government departments, standard bodies, and research labs in academic institutions and business organizations, the idea of deeper and extreme connectivity among all kinds of devices of varying sizes, scopes, and structures is to produce a multitude of robust and resilient services.

The Popular M2M Applications

With the growing stability and maturity of M2M standards, platforms, and infrastructures, inspired innovators, individuals, and institutions could bring forth a number of unique use cases for strengthening and sustaining the M2M technology campaign.

Smart Energy

Energy has become a scarce commodity, and hence its preservation is very much obligatory. Also, more energy consumption means more heat dissipation into our fragile environment. That is, with efficient usage of precious power energy, the much-feared environmental degradation and global warming can be grossly minimized to achieve environmental sustainability.

Smart metering solutions (this is an M2M solution connecting every energy-gobbling device in a network with the centralized smart meter) are very much accepted and used in advanced countries in order to accurately understand the usage. In other words, smart electricity meters help energy consumers to decode how energy savings can be achieved based on the readings and alerts being rendered by smart meters. The advanced metering infrastructure (AMI) is an active and ongoing research area to generate solutions for energy efficiency.

Smart Health Care

Health care is turning out to be a huge industry in the years to unfold. There are a number of specific devices for measuring and managing a number of health parameters of humans. M2M solutions are capable of reminding the patient and their family members as well as the doctor in case of any emergency arising out of any abnormality in any of the health readings.

Smart Home Security

Sophisticated home networking, integration, automation, security, and control mechanisms are hitting the market very frequently. M2M solutions for home security are merging with energy management to provide remote alarm controls as well as remote heating, ventilation, and air conditioning (HVAC) controls for homes and businesses through mobile phones.

Smart Cargo Handling

M2M solutions are being manufactured into a variety of storage or handling containers including cargo containers, money and document bags, and nuclear waste drums. The real-time location of the container, whether it has been opened or closed, and how containers are being handled through motion sensors, can be easily obtained to prevent any possible security and theft risks and to increase recovery capability of stolen or lost material.

Smart Traffic Management

M2M solutions are able to provide real-time road traffic information to vehicles' drivers via automobile GPS devices to enable them to contemplate better alternatives.

Smart Inventory and Replenishment Management

M2M solutions can be integrated into the sensors measuring the amount of bulk product in a storage bin. This information can be made available to both the supplier and the user, so proactive reorders can be initiated when inventories reach a predetermined level. This is very beneficial for the manufacturing process that does not consume a consistent and predictable amount of product or the transport time of the bulk product results in product run-out.

Smart Cash Payment

M2M solutions allow mobile credit or debit card readers to provide secure and encrypted data transmissions at the transaction and ticketing counters in hyper malls, hotels, movie theaters, food joints, and so on. Retailing becomes a smooth affair without standing in the queue for cash payment. The seamless connectivity between tags, tag readers, cash cards, merchant banks, retailers, and so on goes a long way in considerably enhancing the customer experience.

Smart Tracking

M2M solutions allow parents to track their children very precisely sitting from the office and empower caregivers to remotely track those with disabilities as well as independently living, disease-stricken, debilitated, and bed-ridden people. Managers can monitor their employees performing duties in rough and tough places. Especially those who work in oil wells, fight a forest fire, help out in disaster-struck places, battle in war zones, hike in mountains, and so on are to be immensely benefited through such kinds of technological innovations.

The items inside vending machines can connect with their suppliers and provide all the relevant information about the number of bins and bottles inside and how much more are needed to fill up the vending machine. This is definitely a sharp improvement over the current practice.

Smart Displays

All kinds of machines such as ATMs, vending machines, television sets, security video cameras, sign posts, and dashboards can be intertwined together at strategic locations. With such intimate integration through a competent M2M solution, customized video, as well as static images, can be dispatched to these machines to flash time-sensitive and preferred details and displays. A hungry person could order his pizzas on his mobile phone yet see the pizza details and pictures on the larger screen of any one of these machines or with connected projectors showing the images on a white wall to give a clear vision.

Smarter Manufacturing

A car is driven back to its home garage for the night, and its data port is plugged in. Then, some exciting things start to happen. First off, the car sends diagnostic information back to the manufacturer to cross check against any system that requires repair, maintenance, or replacement. The manufacturer then downloads a selection of new driver experiences, including a different acceleration style (choice of sporty or smooth), improved navigation and mapping software, and new stay-in-lane safety features.

From an outside perspective, the IoT offers an unlimited selection of innovations, ranging from an electric toothbrush that monitors correct brushing style through to tire pressure sensors in truck fleets to geolocation sensors attached to livestock. The potential for their use is limitless, and this includes on the factory floor. Connected manufacturing is the IoT. Proactive analytics helps a device identify future needs, such as the case when a part might fail, when it requires service, or when supplies need to be ordered. When the machine itself can dispatch the appropriate commands to a human or another machine, it ensures smooth, safe, and economical operation.

Smart Asset Management

Every industry has its own set of specific assets. For example, hospitals should have a number of scanning machines, diagnostic equipment, health care monitors, robots, and other instruments. That is, there are a variety of devices both small and large. The real challenge lies in their effective location identification in case of any emergency, upkeep, management, monitoring, inventory, security, and so on.

There are several unique benefits of an M2M solution in this complicated scenario. An advanced M2M solution sharply reduces the time consumed by employees to pinpoint the assets' exact location, considerably increases their utilization, and provides the ability to share high-value assets between departments and facilities. With every asset in a hospital environment integrated with one another and with the remote web or cloud platforms via the M2M product, remote monitoring, repairing, and management are being lavishly facilitated. Through the connectivity established with cloud-hosted health care applications, every machine could update and upload its data to the centralized and cyber applications, thereby getting a number of activities fully automated by avoiding manual intervention, interpretation, and instruction.

Professionals and experts are exploring, experimenting, and expounding an increasing array of value-added business and use cases for a variety of industry segments to keep the momentum on the M2M space intact. There is another trend fast picking up these days with the active participation of academicians and industry veterans. Cyber-physical systems (CPS) are the new powerful entities gaining momentum. That is, all kinds of physical systems at the ground level are being empowered with scores of generic as well as specific cyber applications, services, and data. That is, not only connectivity but also software-inspired empowerment is being ticked as the next-generation evolution in the machine space.

Smarter Retailing

McDonald's has gone for a unique experiment in user engagement. A blend of IoT devices and contextual promotions have allowed the restaurant operator to tailor its mobile application offers and advertising to information such as location, weather, purchase habits, and response to promotions. For example, if someone is moving quickly on a hot summer day, the application, which runs on a Vmob contextual analytics platform, shows an offer for a soda at a nearby drive-through. This has received a rousing welcome from customers.

For retailers, using the IoT for marketing and sales comes down to creating meaningful experiences in order to increase loyalty and customer engagement. Starbucks, the coffee chain, chose to launch a number of remote beacons in its Seattle establishments. For customers with the Starbucks app, the beacons push notifications on the freshest brews and personalized promotions. The idea is to transition the casual customer to premium blends that are offered at Starbucks.

Facilitating customer transactions and rewarding brand interactions are effective ways to strengthen customer loyalty. Home Depot is leveraging IoT to increase customer engagement on the second dimension, providing personalized service and information to their customers to help them in their decision-making process. Their mobile app allows shoppers to locate inventory, compare shops, ask experts about projects, and see how products would look in their homes. Once inside the store, the app can guide them through aisles to find the products.

The IoT has exciting propositions for different industry verticals including retailers. Interactive touch screens, contextual advertising, geotargeted promotions, personalized in-store environments, and augmented reality are just the beginning. However, it is important to remember that the value of IoT does not lie in technological advances but instead in improving and creating immersive customer experiences.

Explaining the Aspect of Device-to-Cloud (D2C) Integration

As discussed earlier, the device ecosystem is growing rapidly. There are myriads of embedded devices for different purposes and places. Embedded devices are increasingly networked to enable device-to-device interactions. Now devices are service-enabled to express and expose their functionality via one or more service interfaces. That is, devices are seen as service-providing entities. The advantage here is that all kinds of device heterogeneities and complexities are hidden behind the service interfaces. Any device can connect with any other devices over any network and team up for doing better and bigger things. Now devices are also web- and cloud-enabled. That is, devices can be remotely monitored, measured, managed, and maintained. With the cloud enablement, devices can connect with cloud-based applications and data sources to be empowered accordingly. The OSGi (Open Service Gateway initiative) modular and dynamic model reduces operational costs and integrates multiple devices in a networked environment, tackling costly application development, maintenance, and remote service management. Dynamism is the key to the unprecedented success of the OSGi idea. We have talked about the unique contributions of the OSGi concept in Chapter 4.

The Internet has global-scale, open, public, and cheap communication infrastructure. Devices are able to communicate with the faraway clouds through the Internet. Dedicated networks too can be established and used for mission-critical requirements. There are device-specific clouds emerging these days. The iDigi device cloud (http://www.idigi.com/) is an infrastructure service designed to empower different devices and their networks. The iDigi device cloud solves the challenges of massive scalability and service reliability while meeting the requirements for utmost security and privacy. It is also indicated that the iDigi connector is the appropriate bridge for integrating client's applications with the iDigi device cloud. The cloud paradigm has grown enormously, and its grip on several business domains is simply incredible. There are specific cloud infrastructures emerging. That is, we often hear about sensor cloud, device cloud, knowledge cloud, mobile cloud, science cloud, and so on. The pervasiveness and popularity of the cloud technology are surging ahead with enhanced awareness about its strategic contributions to the whole humanity.

Clouds Infrastructures for Next-Generation Device Applications

As we all know, the much-dissected and discoursed cloud paradigm has laid a stimulating foundation for compactly fulfilling the grand vision of IT infrastructure optimization through a seamless synchronization of several proven, enterprise-scale, and mission-critical technologies such as compartmentalization (virtualization and containerization), grid, on-demand, utility, and autonomic computing models, service orientation, and multitenancy. This groundbreaking evolution and elevation in the IT field have brought in innumerable and insightful impacts on business as well as IT domains these days. Clouds are being positioned and proclaimed as the highly consolidated, converged, virtualized, shared, and automated IT environments for hosting and compactly delivering a galaxy of diverse IT solutions and business services. The cloud technology ensures anytime, anywhere, any network, and any device access to information and service. That is, the much-anticipated ubiquitous service delivery is being fully facilitated with the arrival, articulation, and adoption of the powerful cloud idea. The trend is that all sorts of business and IT services, applications, and data are now being modernized accordingly and adroitly migrated to cloud platforms and infrastructures in order to reap all the originally envisioned benefits (technical, user, and business cases).

The cloud paradigm has become a versatile IT phenomenon and a fabulous fertile ground that has inspired many in the world to come out with a number of newer cloud-centric services and platforms that facilitate scores of people-centric, multifaceted, and rich cloud applications to reach out to many in this connected world. Besides, there have been a variety of generic as well as specific innovations in the form of pragmatic processes, patterns, best practices, key guidelines, metrics, and so on for moderating the rising IT complexity, for enhancing IT agility, autonomy, and affordability, and for heightened IT productivity. The robust and resilient cloud model is directly helping out worldwide business enterprises to achieve the venerable mission of *more with less*. Thus, cloud as the core, central, cheap, and cognitive infrastructure for implicitly taking care of all kinds of business changes, concerns, and challenges portends and portrays a brighter and blissful future for business organizations in order to surge ahead and to keep up their edge earned in their offerings, outputs, and outlooks.

With a legion of resource-constrained, embedded, and networked devices joining in the IT landscape and with the seamless synchronization with the remote, on-demand, and elastic clouds (generic clouds such as public, private, and community or specific clouds such as storage, knowledge, science, data, sensor, device, and mobile), there abound hordes of real-time and sophisticated applications and services.

Cloud Infrastructures for IoT Data Analytics

We have seen how the new-generation devices work as the input or output entities for accessing cloud-based software and data for composing powerful applications. Now with millions of interoperable, interactive, and insightful IoT devices, the data getting generated by IoT devices is reaching terabytes and petabytes of data. There are requirements for capturing and crunching IoT big data.

There are special appliances and cloud-based analytics solutions for doing real-time analytics on big data. Thus, public, private, and hybrid clouds are being touted as the one-stop IT infrastructure solution for doing batching, real-time, streaming, and IoT data processing. Distributed intelligence allows for greater degrees of personalization. In health care, medical device dashboards can reflect an individual patient's information and requirements. At home, an intelligent refrigerator can automatically add needed items to a grocery list or grocery delivery service. In manufacturing, greater capacity opens up for customized production according to an individual customer's requirement without extensive retooling or downtime. The machines themselves can decide how best to approach the project and self-organize to get each job done.

Cloud Infrastructures for Smartphone Services

Every business-class application is mobile enabled to enable them to be accessed and used by mobile devices on the go even at the vehicular speed. The mobile interfacing is being mandated widely. There are human–machine interfaces (HMIs) for activating a plethora of machines. There are a number of mobile technologies and tools facilitating the leverage of all kinds of applications while on the move. With the explosion of smartphones and tablets, every kind of cloud and enterprise application is being provided with mobile interfacing. There are several operating systems such as Android, iOS, Windows Phone, and BlackBerry OS for powering up smartphones. On the other hand, there are mobile and device clouds (say, iCloud is the mobile cloud for iOS phones, etc.). These clouds are being set up in order to host and store all kinds of smartphone services, multistructured data, and so on. That is, cloud connectivity is essential for devices and phones to be relevant for users in the days ahead. In short, an integrated network of disparate and distributed resources, assets, and articles is the principal need for the eulogized smart world.

The Emergence of the IoT Platform as a Service (PaaS)

Cloud-based integrated platforms are very vital for crafting IoT applications. The generic PaaS solutions are being extended to be IoT optimized to enable building next-generation IoT solutions. In this section, the specific extensions to the general PaaS solutions are presented.

Device Management

The ensuing era is termed as the connected one. Everything gets instrumented and interconnected to exhibit intelligent behavior. All kinds of devices are getting connected with one another and with remotely held applications. The devices through their purpose-specific interactions generate a lot of data to be captured and castigated at cloud infrastructures to emit out insights. Thus, IoT platforms are to have the inherent functionality and feature to intelligently manage all kinds of connected devices. The device authentication, authorization, audibility, integration, orchestration, security, and so on need to be guaranteed through the device management capabilities.

The Real-Time Analytics of IoT Big Data

In industrial IoT deployments, systematic processing of high volumes of sensor and machine data in real time to extract actionable insights is essential for providing true business value. The IoT platform has to have event processing engines.

The testing features include capabilities such as dynamic message simulation, throughput generation, and the ability to record and replay message traffic under specific conditions.

Integration with Enterprise Systems

Integration with all kinds of external and enterprise-scale systems is mandatory for any standard IoT platform to bring forth sophisticated applications. For example, manufacturing machines at the manufacturing floors are integrated with enterprise resource planning (ERP), customer relationship management (CRM), supply chain management (SCM), and knowledge management (KM) applications in order to ensure utmost automation. The results and outputs are simply the aggregated ones. Any event information gets instantaneously captured and processed in order to activate appropriate systems in time. Any slight delay may lead to destruction. The much needed integration gets fulfilled through a host of integrators, connectors, drivers, and adaptors.

Thus, next-generation IoT platform has to enable a kind of special linkage among IoT applications, services, devices, data, and other resources. One set of these will act as data sources, whereas some others contribute as data crunchers and the remaining go as real actuators. There will be more additional features being meticulously embedded and etched in order to tackle future needs.

Digging into the Cloud-to-Cloud (C2C) Integration Paradigm

There are cloud service providers (CSPs) setting up their cloud centers in geographically distributed locations in order to serve worldwide customers differently. Some offer only cloud infrastructures, whereas others provide platforms and applications as well. There are cloud management platforms such as OpenStack distributions, VMware solutions, and even proprietary platforms for establishing and sustaining cloud centers. A growing array of technologies and tools keep up the cloud idea. That is why we often hear and read about software-defined clouds, federated clouds, edge clouds, hybrid clouds, science clouds, storage clouds, and so on. The cloud movement with the smart application of a suite of promising and pioneering technological advancements is still on the fast track. The continuously changing IT requirements of worldwide enterprises are being powerfully supported by the geographically distributed cloud centers. Traditional data centers are being modernized to be cloud centers through the leverage of cloud-centric practices, platforms, and patterns. The arrival of templates-driven cloud orchestration tools simplifies operating multiple cloud centers remotely in a policy-aware manner. There are a number of noteworthy innovations in the cloud landscape. Real-time cognitive analytics of cloud data goes a long way in keeping up the clouds. The cloud performance will be kept while keeping up the cloud utilization. Automated and faster responses will be the principal key for cloud centers, which emerge as the most crucial ingredient for businesses behemoths.

Due to the enhanced heterogeneity and multiplicity-induced complexity, the goal of cloud interoperability has become a tough challenge for cloud users. Cloud brokers, procurers, and auditors are therefore emerging and joining in the already complicated cloud ecosystem. Even cloud consumers are afraid of the vendor lock-in issue as there are manifold barriers being erected around cloud infrastructures and platforms.

There are a couple of well-known trends gripping the cloud landscape. First, geographically distributed and differentiating clouds are being established and sustained. Second, institutions, individuals, and innovators are eyeing cloud software, platforms, and infrastructures for reaping the originally postulated and pronounced benefits. The same cloud services are being provided by multiple providers with different service level agreements (SLAs) and operational level agreements (OLAs). Incidentally, business processes that span across several clouds and services of multiple clouds need to be found, bound, and aggregated to build composite data, services, processes, and applications. All these clearly insist on the urgent need for competent federation techniques, standards, patterns, platforms, and best practices for a global network of clouds. IBM cloud orchestrator (ICO) is a leading product suite for enabling cloud orchestration.

Intra as well as interenterprise integration has to happen via cloud integration services and solutions. Service organizations and system integrators are embarking on a new fruitful journey as cloud brokerages in order to silken the rough edges; therefore, distinct and distributed clouds can be identified and integrated seamlessly and spontaneously to work collaboratively to achieve bigger and better things. Cloud service brokers (CSBs) are a kind of new software solution for cloud integration.

An IoT Application Scenario

In an extended enterprise scenario, all kinds of functional divisions are interconnected with one another via the cloud-hosted middleware suite. Clearly cloud occupies the prime spot in any integrated environment. All the common services are getting deployed in network-accessible cloud platforms. Only specific functionalities are being maintained at the edges. The CSB plays a stellar role in streamlining and simplifying the complex integration hurdles and hitches as shown in Figure 1.2.

There are cloud integration appliances and solutions in plenty in order to effortlessly integrate date across clouds (private, public, and hybrid clouds). In short, CSBs are very relevant for distributed computing. There are federation approaches for realizing the vision of the Intercloud. Standards are being formulated to establish run-time linkage between geographically distributed clouds in order to attend some specific scenarios. There are cloud orchestration platforms for purposely uniting clouds. Cloud interoperability is vehemently insisted as clouds are very vital for the success of the IoT concept. Both generic and specific clouds need to be integrated in order to fulfill the unique demands of any IoT applications and hence cloud integration, orchestration, and

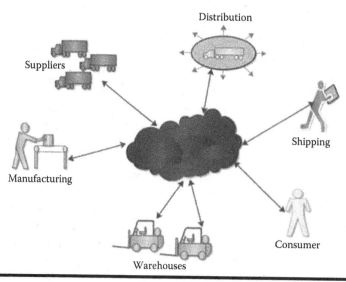

Figure 1.2   A cloud-based integrated environment.

automation is essential for the projected and promised success. At different levels and layers, the much needed linkage is being tackled and treasured. There are integration appliances, hub and bus-based middleware, event processing engines, service repository, and scores of tools for enabling cloud connectivity and interactions. Like system integrators, we will hear more about cloud integrators or brokers in the days to emerge for providing next-generation connected applications to people. Clouds integrate multiple entities and clouds are too integrated toward the IoT era.

Describing the Sensor-to-Cloud Integration Concept

As indicated earlier, every empowered entity in our environments is further strengthened by getting integrated with local and remote IT environments. As sensors are being prescribed as the ear and eye of the futuristic digital world, sensor networking with nearby sensors as well as with far-off applications needs to be facilitated. There are frameworks and middleware platforms for enabling need-based networking of diverse sensors within themselves as well as with distant software components.

In the past few years, smart sensor networks (SSNs) have been gaining significant traction because of their potential for enabling very intimate and interesting solutions in areas such as smart homes, industrial automation, environmental monitoring, transportation, health care, and agriculture. If we add a collection of sensor-derived data to various social networks or virtual communities, blogs, musings, and so on, then there will be fabulous transitions in and around us. With the faster adoption of micro and nanotechnologies, everyday things are destined to become digitally endowed to be distinctive in their actions and reactions. Thus, the impending goal is to seamlessly link digitized objects or sentient materials with our physical environments. Other frequently used and handled devices such as consumer electronics, kitchen utensils and containers, household instruments and items, portable, nomadic, and mobile gadgets and gizmos, and so on are also integrated with remote cloud-based applications via middleware solutions (message-oriented, event-driven, etc.). That is, cyber systems are being inundated with streams of data and messages from different and distributed physical elements and entities. Such an extreme and deeper connectivity and collaboration is to lead to cool, classic, and catalytic situation-aware applications.

Clouds have emerged as the centralized, compact, and capable IT infrastructure to deliver people-centric and context-aware services to users with all the desired qualities entrenched. This long-term vision demands that there has to be a comprehensive connectivity between clouds and billions of minuscule sensing systems.

Google cloud platform (GCP) provides the infrastructure to handle streams of data fed from millions of intelligent devices. The architecture for this type of real-time stream processing must deal with ingest, processing, storage, and analysis of hundreds of millions of events per hour. The architecture in Figure 1.3 depicts such a system. Devices or things are physical devices that interact with the world and collect data. These may be able to communicate only via networks that are unable to reach the cloud platform directly (e.g., over Bluetooth low energy, or BLE). The standard devices (IoT gateways, smartphones, routers, consumer electronics, etc.) can route data directly over networks to the cloud platform.

Cloud pub or sub is a shock absorber for both incoming data streams as well as application architecture changes. Even standard devices may have limited ability to store and retry sending telemetry data. Cloud pub or sub provides a globally durable message ingestion service. It scales to handle data spikes that can occur when swarms of devices respond to events in the physical world and buffers these spikes from applications monitoring the data. By using topics and subscriptions,

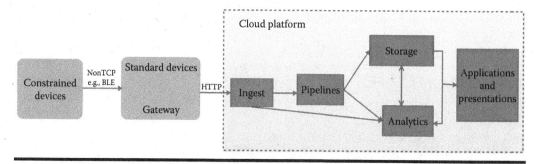

Figure 1.3   Google cloud platform architecture for stream processing from millions of intelligent devices.

you can allow different functions of your application to opt-in to device-related streams of data without updating the primary ingest target. Cloud pub or sub also natively connects to other cloud platform services, gluing together ingest, data pipelines, and storage systems.

Pipelines manage data after it arrives on the cloud platform. This includes tasks such as:

■ *Transform data*: This can convert the data into another format, for example, converting a captured device signal voltage to a calibrated unit measure of temperature.
■ *Aggregate and compute data*: By combining data, it is possible to add checks such as averaging data across multiple devices to avoid acting on a single and spurious device, or ensure we have actionable data if a single device goes offline. By adding computation to the pipeline, it is possible to apply streaming analytics to data while it is still in the processing pipeline.
■ *Enrich data*: This can combine the device-generated data with other metadata about the device, or with other data sets, such as weather or traffic data, for use in subsequent analysis.
■ *Move data*: This can store the processed data in one or more final storage locations.

Google cloud dataflow (Figure 1.3) is built to perform all of these pipeline tasks on both batch and streaming data. With native connectors to cloud pub or sub and a variety of eventual storage destinations or sinks, cloud dataflow is a fully managed Swiss Army knife for data processing.

Storage

Data from the physical world comes in various shapes and sizes. Cloud platform offers a wider range of storage solutions from unstructured blobs of data, such as images or video streams from connected cameras, to structured entity storage and high-performance time-series databases.

Analytics is all about extracting the hidden insights, associations, opportunities, patterns, tips, and so on from the raw or processed data. Often the value of IoT analytics comes from combining data from the physical world with data from other sources such as social sites and business applications such as CRM, SCM, and KM.

Azure IoT Hub Device Management

IoT solutions are typically comprised of many types of devices with different software, firmware, connectivity, and security capabilities. For many businesses, it is a challenging affair to keep the software, firmware, and configuration of new devices up to date. This is an issue that is often compounded as IoT devices are geographically dispersed and huge in numbers. In addition, many businesses now need to connect older or legacy devices they invested in years ago, some of which are not capable of communicating directly to the cloud, and need an intermediary to establish the cloud linkage. With new device management capabilities in Azure IoT Hub, administrators can enroll, view status and health, organize, control access, and update the software, firmware, and configurations of millions of geographically dispersed IoT devices. Customers can realize significant time and resource savings by removing the burden of developing and maintaining custom device management solutions.

Azure IoT Hub scales to manage millions of devices supporting the LWM2M protocol, the leading standard from the Open Mobile Alliance (OMA) for IoT device management. The key APIs are the following:

- *Device Registry Manager API*: This provides a first-class device object for working with IoT devices in your cloud solution. Through this device object, your cloud solution can interact with device and service properties. Device properties are used by the device for configuration or to inform the IoT solution of device state (e.g., firmware version, OEM name, serial number, etc.). Service properties, such as tags, are reference data needed by the IoT solution, and not by the device.
- *Device groups API*: This works with your fleet of devices in groups and controls access in a way that maps to your solution topology.
- *Device queries API*: This finds a flurry of devices in your IoT solution, based on tags, device, or service properties.
- *Device models API*: This refines the information model for the devices and entities in your IoT solution.
- *Device jobs API*: This runs and monitors simultaneous device orchestrations on your global fleet of devices across a heterogeneous device population.

SensorCloud (http://www.sensorcloud.com/) is a unique sensor data storage, visualization, and remote management platform, leveraging powerful cloud computing technologies to provide excellent data scalability, rapid visualization, and user programmable analysis. SensorCloud's core features include FastGraph, MathEngine, LiveConnect, and the OpenData API. LORD MicroStrain's wireless and inertial sensors allow instant uploading of their data to SensorCloud. Third party devices and other data sources can also push data to SensorCloud via the OpenData API or via the provided CSV uploader. Once uploaded, your data are securely stored in the cloud and can be accessed from anywhere or downloaded for offline use. Alerts are provided to help notify you of real-time events in your data. MathEngine analytics allow you to perform both simple and complex mathematical operations on your data, all in the cloud.

Any sensor-centric cloud platform allows building connectors between any service, any sensor, any software, and any hardware. Through the multiprotocol support, routing, and API adaptors, it is being made easy to securely connect to any cloud or any device. It is possible to quickly and effectively build and launch powerful applications that can manage entire factories and supply chains or build operating environments for worldwide cities that manage sensors from different vendors.

The final outcome of these delectable and desirable trends and technologies is the Internet of devices and services that in turn leads to smarter applications for humans. That is, with self-, surroundings-, and situation-aware devices along with cloud infrastructures and the Internet as the communication infrastructure, people-centric services can be precisely and perfectly decided, developed, and delivered to humans in real time.

Homeland Security and the Sensor Cloud

The sensor cloud takes the cloud concepts and applies it to sensor networks (The Sensor Cloud the Homeland Security 2011). That is, intelligent wired or wireless sensors store their data in the cloud, subscribers are allowed to view and analyze the data, and administrators carry out remote management of the sensors. The concept of the sensor cloud has caught on because of the ubiquity and utility of sensors. We all know that the latest smartphones carry a number of sensors such as an accelerometer, cameras, microphone, GPS, compass, proximity, and ambient light. Similarly, specialized sensors are being embedded in most of the electronic and electrical equipment. Defense weapons carry a bevy of specific sensors. Robotics, avionics, electronics, mechatronics, and other engineering fields rely heavily on sensors and actuators to bring forth more automation, acceleration, and augmentation. Thus, sensors occupy a prominent spot in everything these days as the digitization is increasingly penetrative, pervasive, and persuasive. Owing to the massive volumes of sensors being attached to all kinds of physical, electrical, mechanical, and electronics, the amount of sensor data is growing exponentially.

Companies are now building clouds to store the data captured by such sensors. There are several surveillance sensor networks in place throughout the world. Local as well as national governments are responsible for setting up and running their own surveillance sensor networks considering the rise of man-made and natural disasters. Smarter cities across the world establish and run their own networks (city surveillance, traffic management, VIP security, critical infrastructure, coastal surveillance, border control, etc.). Thus, worldwide countries, counties, and cities are showing exemplary interest in sensing and responding to various needs and events proactively and preemptively. In addition, other homeland security agencies have their own networks and infrastructures. That is, best-in-class connectivity and cyber infrastructures are being placed in order to annihilate any kind of attacks on people and properties. Each network of surveillance and security cameras (CCTVs) and other types of sensors has its own infrastructure for video or content management and storage. There are technologies and tools for real-time video capture, processing, and analytics. Thus, sensor-enabled homeland security is on the fast track.

The problem with the current decentralized architecture is that many of the agencies do not have the required resources for managing the infrastructure. Older sensor data are not properly archived or are misplaced. Further, silos of surveillance sensor networks prevent the emergence of an integrated command center at a global level. One solution that would address the above issues would be to build a homeland security sensor cloud that services all web-connected surveillance sensor networks: video, audio, radar, trace detectors, access control, motion detectors, and so on. The sensor cloud will store the sensor data and allow authorized users to view and analyze the same. Agency-specific applications can be developed based on the needs of the user agencies.

The sensor networks will need to conform to a common standard (either by upgrading the hardware or by plugging in a gateway) to ensure that they connect to the cloud and that the data streams for each type of sensor can be stored in a common database. The owners of the data will have to be agreeable to share their data (in combination with data from other owners) for exemplary analysis, data mining, and other information-extraction techniques.

On concluding, the phenomenon of sensor-cloud integration is to grow and glow in the days to unfurl. The cloud-based sensor platforms are to play a very vital role in shaping up the next-generation digitized and intelligent applications.

The Prominent IoT Realization Technologies

Information technologies are coming and going. Many have arrived with much fanfare but could not survive the onslaughts and faded away into the thin air silently without making any substantial contributions to the human society. Some have withstood due to their inherent strengths and copiously contributing toward business innovation, disruption, and transformation. In this section, you can find a number of influential technologies for the IoT realization:

- *Computing paradigms*: Service, social, cluster, grid, on-demand, utility, mobile, autonomic, trustworthy, cloud, and fog or edge computing.
- *Communication*: Unified, ambient, and autonomic communication models providing standards-compliant 3G, 4G, and 5G communication capabilities.
- *Context-aware computing*: Ubiquitous sensing, vision, perception, and actuation methods, edge or fog clouds, etc.
- *Middleware solutions*: Integration, intermediation, aggregation, fusion, federation, transformation, arbitration, enrichment, and composition mechanisms.
- *Digitization and edge technologies*: Tags, stickers, smart dust, motes, LED, specks, beacons, chips, microcontrollers, invisible sensors, implantables, wearables, portables, etc.
- *Sensing, perception, and vision*: These are very mandatory for establishing IoT environments.
- *Miniaturization*: Micro- and nanoscale electronics product design techniques and tools.
- *Knowledge engineering and enhancement*: Data to information and to knowledge transition through data mining, analytics, processing, and so on, event processing engines, knowledge discovery and dissemination, knowledge correlation, corroboration techniques, and so on. Dashboards, report-generation tools, knowledge visualization platforms, and so on play a very vital role in presenting the extracted knowledge in a preferred format.
- *Interfacing*: Natural and adaptive, intuitive, and informative interfaces.
- *Real-time insights* through in-memory computing and in-database analytics, appliances for real-time processing of IoT big data.
- *Compartmentalization through virtualization and containerization*: The software engineering technique (divide and conquer) is being replicated on hardware resources to bring in the much needed flexibility, extensibility, and maneuverability and ultimately for hardware programming. The hardware components, hitherto black boxes, are being turned and tuned through the smart application of the premier compartmentalization techniques to be white box modules.

The good news is that there are several powerful, proven, potential, and promising technologies and tools erupting fast to facilitate the right tasks with ease. These days, technologies comingle to form technology clusters to fulfill hard-to-crack problems. The much-discussed and dissected cloud technology actually represents a smart collection of several enterprise-scale, mission-critical, and accomplished technologies to bring in the much needed elasticity in IT infrastructures. That is, the prevailing trend is to leverage potential technologies individually or collectively toward specific business efficiency and resiliency. With the commendable advancements in infrastructure optimization, process excellence, state-of-the-art platforms (development, debugging, administration, management, and delivery), and architecture flexibility, the right and cutting-edge technologies need to be understood and used rightfully to realize the IoT vision.

The IoT: The Key Application Domains

The arrival of the IoT paradigm foretells a variety of applications for the envisioned smarter planet. The resultant applications out of all the developments in the IoT space are a string of intelligent and interactive workspaces and smarter environments such as smarter homes and offices. For example, the Japan Railways (JR) is setting up smarter railway stations to enhance the convenience, choice, comfort, and freedom of travelers. A smarter environment typically comprises a dazzling array of infinitesimal and intelligent electronic gizmos that can perceive the context, act, and react based on the happenings in it. Further, the goals of seamless mobility, interoperability, and connectivity are achieved among the participating devices in the environment dynamically. In addition, the stationed and positioned devices can connect and collaborate with any other devices entering into the environment by forming small-scale, on-demand, purposeful, and ad hoc networks toward achieving specific tasks.

Therefore, hitherto unknown and unforeseen applications through a judicious mix of shrewd systems and sensors can be created dynamically at real time and granted to any user on demand. The exceptional characteristics of these devices are self-organizing, self-adapting, self-repairing, self-optimizing, self-configuring, and self-recovering. Precisely speaking, they can bounce back to the original state if there is any kind of serious obstruction, disturbance, or disaster, and capable of forming insightful networks with others in the vicinity automatically. Other critical assets and artifacts are various types of high-end server machines, storage appliances, and network solutions. The renowned ingredients in any intelligent zones include physical assets, mechanical, electrical, and electronics luxuriously fitted with smart labels, barcodes, pads, tags, stickers, dots, motes, dust, specks, beacons, LED lights, and so on. Market watchers, analysts, and researchers have come out with the following opportunities for businesses in the years ahead:

- *New business possibilities*: The IoT-inspired agility, affordability, and adroitness will have a perpetual and paramount impact on business establishments and how they are being run. The IoT idea will help companies create new value streams for customers, speed up time to market, and respond more rapidly to customer needs. The productivity of corporate resources goes up sharply, whereas more premium services can be realized and supplied to consumers. Business processes can be highly optimized to make money out of technological innovations in the IoT landscape.
- *Tending toward the insights as a service (IaaS) era*: The amount of IoT data becomes humungous, and with the faster stability and maturity of IoT data analytics products and platforms, the new service model of IaaS is bound to flourish. That is, the idea of insights everywhere every time becomes a common and casual thing. The goal of ambient intelligence (AmI) will see the light sooner than later. It is possible to make sense out of data heaps to take correct and timely decisions. IoT data becomes a strategic asset for any organization to journey in the right direction.
- *Fresh revenue opportunities*: The IoT can help companies ensure additional services on top of traditional lines of business. Newer market avenues will open up in order to substantially raise the company's revenues.
- *Automation at its peak*: With every tangible thing in an enterprise environment getting empowered and connected, there will be a fresh wave of compelling automation. With clouds emerging as the one-stop IT infrastructure for hosting platforms and workloads, the aspect of deeper and exciting automation is very near. Business operations get substantially accelerated and augmented. That is, businesses become IT-driven and consumer-centric.

Precisely speaking, the extreme connectivity of important things is to bring a paradigm shift in the way people live, work, interact, think, decide, act, and react. Hitherto unforeseen applications can be built and delivered to people with the stabilizing and scintillating maturity of the IoT concept. Especially insights-driven, situation-aware, and physical services can be supplied to people. Take the scenario of ambient assisted living (AAL). Diseased and debilitated people can order their coffee maker to make a cup of coffee and a humanoid robot can bring the coffee from the kitchen to the bedside. Viable and venerable business and operational models need to be worked out collectively by product vendors, IT and telecommunication service providers, cloud integrators, end users, and national governments to bring forth intelligent devices and services for the impending knowledge era.

The IoT, however, comes with its own challenges, including a lack of standards, the ability to scale globally, security concerns, and an immature ecosystem. For vendors, there is no homogeneous IoT market—each industry and application is different. For users, especially IT organizations, there can be issues of managing operational systems in an organization that might be culturally designed as a support organization, as well as dealing with the real-time demands of many IoT applications. With the overwhelming acceptance of cloud as the most valuable technology for quickly and easily achieving the long-standing goal of infrastructure optimization, there will be more consolidation in the IT landscape with cloud occupying the prominent and dominant place. Figure 1.4 vividly illustrates the rising significance of cloud in the IT domain.

The future seems to be very bright. With consumers' expectations consistently climbing to newer heights, the need for unearthing pathbreaking ideas, concepts, and techniques in the IT industry is being insisted very feverishly. As indicated in the beginning, IoT is definitely a powerful and pioneering idea to be taken very seriously toward its implementation. As Figure 1.5 illustrates, there will be many distinct spaces emerging and evolving with different kinds of applications, multistructured data, services, and devices.

The real complication lies in the seamless and spontaneous integration of heterogeneous systems, sensors, services, and data embedded inside. Further, it is essential to extract actionable insights out of streaming data from different and distributed sources in real time in order to be hugely beneficial for knowledge workers and decision makers. Knowledge engine is the appropriate platform that internally comprises an open and industry-strength integration container for

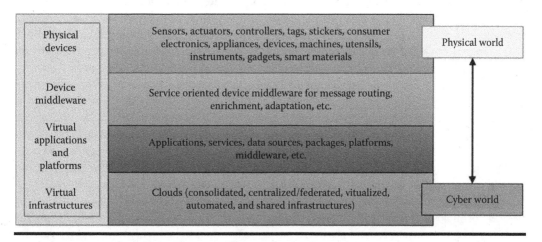

Figure 1.4   The integration of cyber and physical worlds.

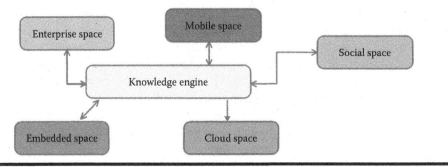

Figure 1.5   The futuristic integrated environments.

flawlessly aggregating all kinds of data (business, government, social, machine, personal, etc.), processing, mining, and analyzing them smartly, and finally disseminating the extracted knowledge to the concerned in time. Not only knowledge services but also the large-scale accumulation of actuators such as the famous humanoid robots in our midst, IT-enabled, knowledge-encapsulated, and insightful physical services will be developed and delivered to the needy.

Primarily there will be clouds as the centrally managed policy-based infrastructure (cyberspace), wherein resilient platforms, adaptive applications, and services are hosted, versatile knowledge engines with integration and dissemination capabilities can be at cyber or intermediate level (middleware space), and service-enabled devices and sensors are deployed and energized at the ground level (physical level). That is, the cloud is the virtual IoT infrastructure and other prime participants include low-cost, low-power yet networked and smart devices at the physical level. Extreme and deeper connectivity among diverse and distributed infrastructural systems and ground-level data-capturing, brokering, transmitting, and persisting devices and sensors via introspective middleware software solutions are for understanding people's requirements and act on this instantaneously.

The IoT Challenges and the Research Domains

With the projection of extreme data, billions of devices, and trillions of digital entities, the challenges on IT are bound to rise up sharply. The current IT environments are bound to face a variety of shortcomings for storing the massive amount of IoT data and for subjecting the collected IoT data appropriate analytics to extract timely and actionable insights. International Data Corporation (IDC) has clearly visualized and portrayed the following critical and crucial challenges for IT for the envisioned IoT days. We need elastic compute servers, storage appliances, and network connectivity solutions on the infrastructure front. On the platform side, we need highly synchronized platforms for simplifying data cleansing, translation, aggregation, mining, and processing. Further, knowledge discovery and dissemination platforms are insisted on sharing what is extracted out of IoT data.

Data centers are transitioning toward cloud centers (cloud 1.0) and the next evolution is cloud-enabled data centers (cloud 2.0) through the incorporation of powerful concepts such as software-defined compute, storage, and networking. That is, future data centers will be software-defined, automated, optimized, and virtualized. The containerization concept being expounded by the Docker technology is another interesting thing to watch for in the years to unfold. Thus, the traditional IT infrastructures and platforms are being tweaked to be highly right and relevant for the projected IoT era.

The Research Domains

There are conferences and confluences fostering the deep discussion on IoT-related issues focusing on technical enablers of the next-generation IoT applications. The first and foremost thing is to establish and sustain seamless and spontaneous connectivity between multiple and heterogeneous elements and entities. The connectivity with remote applications and data sources too has to be realized for physical devices to be intelligent. The other principal requirement is the service enablement as every important thing is being expressed and exposed as a service through one or more interfaces for the outside world. Any service requesters and users can easily find and send out requests to services-providing devices. The key research topics include:

1. *Energy-efficient device architectures*: Energy conservation and preservation occupy an important research topic due to the fact that any environment or physical asset comprises a variety of sensors and actuators attached to it. Owing to the multiplicity of devices, the energy need is bound to zoom up and hence energy optimization turns out to be an important topic for study and research. Energy harvesting and novel hardware designs are being given extra thrust considering the faster stabilization of the IoT days.
2. *Elastic IoT infrastructures*: There can be an unexpected spike in the number of devices and people participating in any IoT environment and applications. Thus, IoT platforms and infrastructures need to be highly adaptive and accommodative to have a large number of communicating devices and digitized objects.
3. *Highly optimized communication protocol*: There are a massive number of resource-constrained, networked, and embedded devices in an IoT environment. Further, there is an emerging phenomenon of edge or fog computing devices such as IoT gateways, smart meters and appliances, smartphones, data aggregators, and so on. For transmitting data and document messages within themselves as well as with remote control or analytical application packages, a suite of pioneering protocols is being insisted across. Standard protocols are being tweaked to be highly beneficial for specific application domains.
4. *Data deduplication and compression mechanisms*: These are all very important in restricted environments.
5. *Data reliability* is another important criterion for the IoT era to succeed immensely. That is, the timeliness and trustworthiness of IoT data need to be guaranteed in order to arrive at correct decisions. Any kind of ambiguity, internal misrepresentation, external manipulation, and so on of data lands in irreparable risks. There are evidence and belief theories extensively discussed and discoursed for enhancing the quality of captured sensor data.
6. *Device security* is emerging as a top trend for researchers to unearth groundbreaking inventions and innovations for ensuring foolproof, impenetrable, and utmost security for devices and their data.

Thus, there are innumerable fresh opportunities and possibilities with a comity of interesting and inspiring upgrades in the IoT technology and tool landscapes.

The Emerging IoT Flavors

The IoT paradigm is on the fast track. In simplified terms, the IoT represents the future Internet of comprising not only computers and communicators but also empowered sensors and actuators. All kinds of software components (homegrown, off-the-shelf, packaged, etc.) are also web or cloud- and mobile-enabled. This hitherto unseen enormity of the future Internet opens up a growing array of game-changing use cases for people, business behemoths, governments, individuals, innovators, and institutions.

Enterprise IoT adoption has entered a new phase, with global product brands applying IoT to manage anything from hundreds-of-thousands to hundreds-of-millions to billions of digitally enabled products, each driving real-time applications and services. As enterprises turn their physical products into digital assets, they face extraordinary new challenges of real-time data scale and connectivity that demand a best-in-class IoT smart product platform to manage billions of software identities in the cloud for these products. Global product manufacturers, retailers, and service providers have to be capable of working with a diversity of different device and connectivity technologies, enabling digital applications to be built quickly and easily in an increasingly dynamic environment while at the same time protecting enterprise integrity and data with rigorous security. In this section, we explore and expound the various flavors of the raging IoT domain.

The Industrial Internet of Things (IIoT)

Multinational companies are examining the benefits of using the embedded intelligence and network connectivity of IoT devices to improve their own systems and products. Companies are most interested in instrumenting their operations, looking for events that are a warning of impending failure in systems, or squeezing additional efficiency out of their operations. These are instances of simply upgrading or enhancing existing hardware in factories, refineries, office buildings, and other physical plants with IoT goodness. Manufacturing companies have been among the earliest adopters of IoT. General Electric (GE) has pushed forward its own massive internal investment in IoT technology to collect analytic data from everything from gas turbine engines to locomotives. IoT is also part of the *factory of the future* concept embraced by aircraft manufacturer Airbus, where National Instruments is helping the company put smart IoT technologies into their smart tooling and robotics systems that work alongside human operators.

The IIoT will transform companies and countries, opening up a new era of economic growth and competitiveness. We see a future where the intersection of people, data, and intelligent machines will have far-reaching impacts on the productivity, efficiency, and operations of industries around the world. The major beneficiary is the industry segments that are showing exemplary interest and involvement in exploring and embracing the IoT idea literally. All sorts of manufacturing machines are getting connected with one another as well as with the cloud-based business, monitoring, measurement, and management applications. Forward-thinking manufacturers are standing out from their competitors by building connected and cognitive machines. Businesses also gain a competitive advantage by enabling their existing products through a host of technologically sound and strategic solutions in order to capture the necessary intelligence in time to offer their customers new sets of premium services illustrated as follows:

- *Improving operational efficiency*: Enhanced productivity through optimal and smart utilization of industry equipment, machinery, and so on, the condition monitoring toward predictive maintenance, and so on. Operational analytics is the emerging analytical field for significantly improving the operational condition.
- *Optimizing assets*: Enhanced utilization of industry assets, utensils, wares, and so on, the remote and continuous health check of assets and so on, to avoid any kind of slow-down, break-down, and even let-down.

- *Envisioning next-gen services*: The connected machines are being empowered with additional capacities, capabilities, and competencies such as machine learning and natural language processing (NLP) to substantially enhance user experience.
- *Exploring fresh avenues for higher revenues*: The smart monetization of connected products is seeing the reality through fresh business and operational models. Usage-based and real-time dynamic pricing is another option wide open for industries to leverage the power of the IoT idea.

The sample IIoT use cases (Intel) are the following:

Software and sensors are controlling more of what once was done by humans, often more efficiently, conveniently, and cheaply. This practice is changing how we interact with the physical world. We talk to our televisions and they listen, thanks to embedded sensors and voice processing chips that can tap into the cloud for corrections. We drive down the road and sensors gather data from our cell phones to measure the flow of traffic. Our cars have mobile apps to unlock them. Health devices send data back to doctors, and wristwatches let us send our pulse to someone else. By some estimates, by 2025, the number of devices connected to the Internet will outnumber the people on the planet. That is, there will be 50 billion connected machines ranging from networked sensors to industrial robots. Here are a few sectors wherein the IoT is bound to make waves of distinct automation:

- *Automotive industry*: Consumers want the digital experiences in their vehicles to align with the ones they enjoy everywhere else. When tied to the IoT, the car is an integral part of the interdependent web of information flow, turning data into actionable insight both inside the car and in the world around it.
- *Energy industry*: Through the IoT, the power grid's countless devices can share information in real time to distribute energy more efficiently. Consumers, businesses, and utility providers get the information they need to better manage their energy-connected things to consume less energy.
- *Health care*: The IoT is transforming remote patient monitoring, personalizing treatment, improving outcomes, and lowering health care costs. For instance, wearable ultrasound-based sensors enable senior citizens to live independently longer by monitoring their activities and detecting falls.
- *Industrial*: Manufacturers are harnessing ever-increasing amounts of data from equipment and suppliers. The ability to analyze data from every link of the manufacturing value chain helps companies increase efficiency, keep production running smoothly, and reduce costs.
- *Retail*: Retailers use the IoT to provide personalized and immersive experiences that keep shoppers coming back. Gathering and organizing data is the only part of the challenge. Intel and its ecosystem of collaborators are leading the effort to analyze, understand, and extract value from that data.
- *Smart buildings*: The IoT is enabling a transformation in building efficiency and management. Intel and its ecosystem deliver building automation solutions optimized for scalable Intel architecture to reliably interoperate with the full building ecosystem.

There are other industry verticals gaining immensely and immeasurably with all the decisive advancements in the IoT field. For example, GE is fitting their aircraft engines with a number of smart sensors in order to minutely monitor, measure, and manage them. The sensor data are being systematically subjected to purpose-specific investigations to showcase their performance levels to perspective buyers.

Autodesk SeeControl is an enterprise IoT cloud service that helps manufacturers to connect, analyze, and manage their products. It virtualizes machines, links them with reporting devices, and through analytics, unlocks the data trapped inside utilizing the unlimited computing power of cloud IT. The SeeControl platform offers a no coding and drag-and-drop approach to IoT that enables users to innovate fast and without teams of programmers. It

1. Generates real-world product performance data to improve future designs
2. Predicts when products might fail and perform maintenance
3. Creates new service revenue and product upgrade opportunities
4. Optimizes field supply chain and material replenishment costs

AWS IoT (https://aws.amazon.com/iot/how-it-works/) is a managed cloud platform that lets connected devices easily and securely interact with cloud applications and other devices. AWS IoT can support billions of devices and trillions of messages, and can process and route those messages to AWS endpoints and to other devices reliably and securely. With AWS IoT, your applications can keep track of and communicate with all your devices, all the time, even when they are not connected. AWS IoT makes it easy to use AWS services like AWS Lambda, Amazon Kinesis, Amazon S3, Amazon Machine Learning, Amazon DynamoDB, Amazon CloudWatch, and Amazon Elasticsearch Service with built-in Kibana integration to build IoT applications that gather, process, analyze, and act on data generated by connected devices, without having to manage any infrastructure.

AWS IoT (Figure 1.6) allows you to easily connect devices to the cloud and to other devices. AWS IoT supports HTTP, WebSockets, and MQTT, a lightweight communication protocol specifically designed to tolerate intermittent connections, minimize the code footprint on devices, and reduce network bandwidth requirements. AWS IoT also supports other industry-standard and custom protocols, and devices can communicate with each other even if they are using different protocols.

The era of IIoT has been heralded primarily as a way to improve operational efficiency. But in today's environment, companies can also benefit greatly by seeing it as a tool for finding growth in unexpected opportunities. In the future, successful companies will use the IIoT to capture new growth through three approaches: boost revenues by increasing production and creating new hybrid business models, exploit intelligent technologies to fuel innovation, and transform their workforce. IoT has opened up a new, virtually inexhaustible source of technical innovations, which are equally valuable for a broad variety of industries. By applying smart connected devices, sensors, and gateways to control each part of the production process, manufacturing, and infrastructure, companies are dramatically increasing their operational efficiency.

Figure 1.6   Device-to-cloud integration by AWS IoT.

Consumer Internet of Things (CIoT)

The IoT is changing how consumers interact with consumer electronics, enabling greater convenience for a better experience, access to data that enables them to optimize their usage, and increasing control they have over their devices. With IoT, the world is at their fingertips. Wearables, gadgets and gizmos, portables, implantables, handhelds, consoles, appliances, instruments, and utensils are the fast-emerging and evolving IoT products. The number of connected devices in the hands of people in their everyday works and walks is definitely soaring. Examples include fitness trackers, smart home thermostats, Wi-Fi connected cameras, virtual reality headsets, smart refrigerators and toasters, alarm panels, and smart glasses. The connection between all of them is that they are often controlled by apps.

Consumer devices like Nest's Internet-connected learning thermostat, Nest Cam surveillance camera, and Protect networked smoke alarm promise a more energy-efficient and safer home. Wearable IoT devices are just starting to take off. Within the next two to three years, it is predicted that wrist-based devices will lose the need to be tethered to a smartphone. At the same time, interactions between wearables and nearables (e.g., beacons, Amazon Echo, connected cars) will grow.

The health field is the most immediate fit for wearables because they can gather data that have a benefit without conscious human action. Governments are especially interested in the analytical powers of IoT-collected data for all sorts of reasons, from tuning services at the most basic levels to understanding how to respond to emergency as well as collecting revenue. Traffic lights and even pedestrian crossing buttons could be used as networked sensors. The AppCarousel (http://appcarousel. com/) features and services designed especially for the Consumer IoT market are as follows:

- Revenue generation solutions
- An ecosystem of developers to create great apps
- Help at the design stage to make apps an integral part of a manufacturer's IoT strategy
- A global highly scalable cloud platform to handle connections with millions of connected devices
- Security solutions for authentication and data protection
- Compelling on-device and companion app store experience
- Web stores for ease of viewing IoT app catalog on regular devices
- Software updating and management solutions
- An app supply chain compatible with, and tested for, each device
- Integrations with the device and the manufacturer's back-end systems
- Support for the lifecycle of the device software

There is a renaissance waiting for the Internet. With the surging popularity, penetration, pervasiveness, and persuasiveness of the most grandiose and glamorous IoT idea, we are now steadily entering into the connected era. Devices communicate with themselves in the vicinity, with remotely held devices, applications, and platforms over any network, and with humans through HMIs. This development has resulted in a myriad of such connected devices. A kind of middleware solution is mandatory for binding heterogeneous devices from different manufacturers.

Kaa (http://www.kaaproject.org/) is an open-source IoT middleware platform for managing, collecting, analyzing, and acting on every aspect of communications between connected devices. Kaa offers a range of pluggable features that allow building killer apps for consumer products in days instead of weeks. Out of the box, Kaa is compatible with virtually any modern consumer product or microchip—smart TVs, smart home appliances, HVAC systems, wearables, and microcomputer boards. Taking advantage of highly programmable and feature-rich interoperability enabled by Kaa, consumer IoT products will allow for hassle-free remote monitoring and control, event-driven operations, user context awareness, and even autonomous cross device collaboration on specific tasks.

The IoT is changing the game for consumer electronics manufacturers, enabling new revenue opportunities, providing new insights into consumer usage, and bringing true interoperability with other connected consumer products. Leveraging proven technology, consumer electronics manufacturers can get products to market quickly that consumers will love.

Social Internet of Things (SIoT)

Social web (web 2.0) sites such as Facebook, Google+, and LinkedIn are very popular these days. People are getting connected with one another for different purposes across the globe through these web-scale social platforms. The social sites extract our likes, dislikes, updates, and interactions. Digital communities are being formed for sharing their expertise and experience through these platforms. For example, LinkedIn is specific for knowledge workers. There is a bevy of advantages through people's participation. Product vendors gain the viewpoints of their esteemed customers. Outside-in think is all set to flourish. Advertising through these social sites is gaining a lot of momentum. Further, there is scientific evidence that a large number of individuals tied to a social network can provide far more accurate answers to complex problems than a single individual or a small group of even knowledgeable individuals.

The SIoT is defined as an IoT where things are capable of establishing social relationships with other objects, autonomously with respect to humans. In this way, a social network of objects is created. The adoption of the SIoT paradigm presents several advantages:

- The resulting structure of the things' social network can be shaped as required to guarantee network navigability so as to effectively perform the discovery of objects and services and to guarantee scalability as in human social networks.
- A level of trustworthiness can be established for leveraging the degree of interaction among things that are friends.
- Models can be designed to study social networks to be reused to address IoT-related issues.

Social messaging apps are where many of us spend most of our smartphone time. By integrating with the devices and things in our lives, this bond will likely grow stronger only. It also positions the social app as not only the main communication interface but as our alert and device control interface as well.

Context awareness features have become critical for social applications, and as it turns out, the things in our lives can provide an amazing amount of information about both us and our surroundings. By integrating with sensors in our homes, the wearables on our body and with the car we drive, these services will have a better understanding of where we and those in our network are, as well as a better contextual understanding of what we are doing. The social sites are capable of connecting people to the things in our lives. So it is not a surprise if one day you find yourself chatting with or at least controlling your garage door using your favorite social messaging app.

There is no doubt that many applications and services should be associated with groups of objects, whose individuality will be *sacrificed* to the overall interest of providing services to users. This is the case of applications involving the use of swarm intelligence and swarm robotics. IoT objects should start establishing social relationships on the basis of the object profile, activities (such as movements), and interests (applications deployed on the object and services it implements). These relationships can also be categorized according to the events that trigger their establishment. A *colocation* relationship may be established among objects (either homogeneous or heterogeneous) used always in the same place; a *cowork* relationship may be established whenever objects collaborate to provide a common IoT application (as in case of objects that come in touch and cooperate for applications such as emergency response, telemedicine, etc.).

Social objects are expected to take a central role in the deployment of applications that rely on opportunistic and loosely coupled interactions among objects and whose value is in their capability of dynamically discovering key information and services from *unknown* communities of objects.

Alice has just arrived in Beijing for the first time without having planned the journey in advance so finding the right way to get to her hotel is not easy. Alice starts her SocialMobility application to find the best options currently available. On arrival at the airport, her smartphone had already established a new social relationship with the touristic totem, through which it could reach the bus station information terminals and the taxi control units. SocialMobility forwards queries following colocation and social relationships to collect information about available transport services, relevant prices, and expected time schedules from various objects directly or indirectly connected to Alice's device. Queries and responses are handled hop-by-hop in the social object network and finally processed at Alice's smartphone. She takes a look at the results that are already ordered on the basis of her preferences and selects her preferred solution, that is, the bus service. SocialMobility then issues a request to buy a ticket and the bus terminal (or another friend object) redirects the application to the mobile ticketing service so that Alice receives the ticket on her smartphone.

To make such applications a reality, each object should be equipped with social functionalities to discover other social objects in the surroundings and establish social relationships, and to search for services and information of interest by crawling the object social network.

Semantic Internet of Things (SIoT)

The promise of the IoT is that the lights, the thermostat, and the garage door can all collaborate to make our house more comfortable. Land use and transportation could be more efficient if cars and parking spaces or people needing a ride could find one another. Electrical supply and demand could be matched better if the different electrical appliances could talk to each other reliably to smooth consumption. Thus, device integration and orchestration are being presented as the absolute necessity for the IoT paradigm to succeed. With the continued expansion of the IoT, the interoperability requirement for all the participating devices and objects gains significance. Standards-developing organizations have done a tremendous amount of work to standardize and solidify protocols to simplify implementation and to lower the cost of IoT products. Several efforts by individuals as well as agencies are underway in order to guarantee seamless and spontaneous interactions among local as well as remote objects and devices without any constraints. There are adaptors, connectors, and drivers to facilitate devices to find and talk with one another on a need basis. Figure 1.7 clearly depicts how different networks of devices cooperate with one another in deciding things dynamically and plunging into the implementation with all the clarity and confidence.

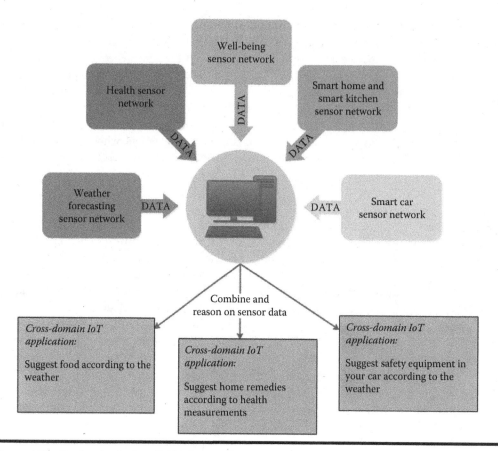

Figure 1.7   Device-to-device (D2D) integration.

By providing network connectivity to embedded devices, everyday objects will be able to inter-act with each other, introducing new services and opportunities to end users. For example, a typi-cal home area network (HAN) can connect a set of devices such as computers, printers, streaming clients, and set-top boxes. Similarly, smart energy devices such as refrigerators, thermostats, and smart meters enter the market; the proliferation of heterogeneous technologies pose serious chal-lenges for interactions among devices following different specifications. However, the real benefits of the IoT paradigm happen only through meaning-based interactions.

IoT devices are quite diverse and measure different parameters and with different conventions and units of measure. Due to the increasing heterogeneity and multiplicity of devices participat-ing in IoT applications and environments, the device complexity is to abound sharply in the days ahead. Context awareness is a prime property for IoT devices to act distinctly. Providing interop-erability among the *things* on the IoT is the most fundamental requirement to support object addressing, tracking, and discovery as well as information representation, storage, and exchange. Applying the powerful, proven, and potential semantic technologies to IoT promotes the real-world interoperability among different, decentralized and distributed IoT resources, informa-tion models, data providers, and consumers. This much-anticipated feature facilitates effective data access and integration, resource discovery, semantic reasoning, and knowledge extraction. Semantic technology is, therefore, emerging as a necessary building block for the IoT future.

Otherwise, the billions of connected devices do not talk with one another meaningfully. The suite of semantic technologies includes ontologies, resource description framework (RDF), linked open data, semantic annotation, and so on, and these are all going to be game-changing in realizing the semantic IoT. With semantics-enabled devices, we get semantic data that in turn assist in dynamically crafting semantic IoT services.

Why Semantics for the Interoperable IoT

The semantics technologies and tools are emerging as the viable and venerable approach for fulfilling the meaning-based IoT interoperability. First, semantics brings forth an explicit description of the meaning of IoT data in a structured and simplified way so that different and distributed IoT devices could understand and work together in a meaningful manner. Typically heterogeneous IoT data becomes homogeneous as the same vocabulary is used for understanding. There are semantic reasoning techniques and engines fast emerging, and hence the era of semantic IoT is to see the light soon.

Junwook Lee and the team have come out with a research paper titled "Semantic WISE: An Applying of Semantic IoT Platform for Weather Information Service Engine." The WISE semantic IoT platform (Figure 1.8) consists of five main modules: semantic ontology, semantic processor, semantic query engine, semantic repository, and semantic open API.

Based on the semantic platform, disaster management service was improved using the functionalities of user context detection and prediction.

READY4SmartCities is a project to reduce energy consumption and CO_2 emission in smart cities by using ontologies and linked data. This project provides guidelines to help data providers to generate energy-related data as linked data. It introduces the concept of cross domain data such as climatic, occupation, pollution, traffic, and activity. It builds a data set with 50 domain ontologies specific to smart cities and smart home. The STAR-CITY project uses semantic web technologies to diagnose and predict road traffic congestions. There are a number of initiatives

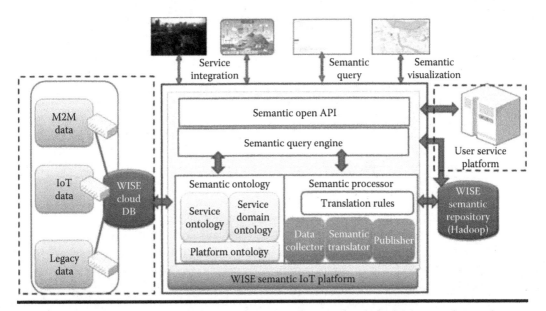

Figure 1.8   The semantic IoT platform architecture for weather information service engine.

across the globe for leveraging the fast-maturing and stabilizing semantic technologies in order to bring in the true interoperability among various participants in any environment.

Cognitive Internet of Things (CIoT)

The traditional approach to the programmable computing is the one in which data are shepherded through a series of predetermined and if/then processes to arrive at expected outcomes. This paradigm simply does not possess the wherewithal to process the IoT data, which are massive in volumes and multistructured. Besides, the velocity, variability, and viscosity of IoT data are varying.

Programmable systems thrive on prescribed scenarios using predictable data. And this rigidity limits their usefulness in addressing many aspects of the increasingly complex and fast-paced world. Rather than being explicitly programmed, cognitive systems learn from varied interactions with humans and leverage their experiences with their environments. They intelligently model, train, hypothesize through evidence, learn, and answer from IoT data. Cognitive systems are not deterministic and instead are probabilistic. And this cognition capability enables them to keep pace with the volume, complexity, and unpredictability of IoT data.

Cognitive systems can also make sense of the 80% of the world's structured data (images, videos, and audio files, machine and sensor data, social data, tweets, blogs, etc.). That means businesses are now able to illuminate the distinct aspects of the IoT that were previously invisible. That is, actionable patterns and insights culled from disparate IoT data sources come handy for businesses to make informed decisions in time.

Envisioning Cognitive IoT

To bring ambitious IoT applications into being, we need powerful and sophisticated ways of processing, mining, and analyzing IoT data quickly and easily (www.ibm.com). Cognitive systems have the inherent potential to do so. Hence, the term of cognitive IoT has emerged and the newly incarnated topic is bound to be nourished through appropriate technologies and tools.

By translating massive amounts of unstructured data into meaningful outputs, IBM Watson IoT platform helps identify trends, anomalies, probabilities, and patterns that otherwise might go unseen. IBM is bringing the power of cognition to the IoT data by making available new Watson APIs as part of its new IBM Watson IoT Foundation Analytics offering. In a physical world, in which devices and systems are becoming highly digitized, the capabilities provided by these APIs aim to give IBM clients, partners, and developers an ever fuller sense of the data on which they rely:

■ *The natural language processing (NLP) API family* enables users to interact with systems and devices using simple, human language. Natural language processing helps solutions understand the intent of human language by correlating it with other sources of data to put it into context in specific situations. For example, a technician working on a machine might notice an unusual vibration. He can ask the system "what is causing that vibration?" Using NLP and other sensor data, the system will automatically link words to meaning and intent, determine the machine he is referencing, and correlate recent maintenance to identify the most likely source of the vibration, and then recommend an action to reduce it.

■ *The machine learning Watson API family* automates data processing and continuously monitors new data and user interactions to rank data and results based on learned priorities. Machine learning can be applied to any data coming from devices and sensors to automatically understand the current conditions, what's normal, expected trends, properties to monitor, and suggested actions when an issue arises. For example, the platform can monitor incoming data from fleet equipment to learn both normal and abnormal conditions, including environment and production processes, which are often unique to each piece of equipment. Machine learning helps understand these differences and configures the system to monitor the unique conditions of each asset.

■ *The video and image analytics API family* enables monitoring of unstructured data from video feeds and image snapshots to identify scenes and patterns. This knowledge can be combined with machine data to gain a greater understanding of past events and emerging situations. For example, video analytics monitoring security cameras might note the presence of a forklift infringing on a restricted area, creating a minor alert in the system. Three days later, an asset in that area begins to exhibit decreased performance. The two incidents can be correlated to identify a collision between the forklift and the asset that might not have been readily apparent from the video or the data from the machine.

■ *The text analytics API family* enables mining of unstructured textual data including transcripts from customer call centers, maintenance technician logs, blog comments, and tweets to find correlations and patterns in these vast amounts of data. For example, phrases reported through unstructured channels—such as *my brakes make a noise, my car seems to slow to stop,* and *the pedal feels mushy*—can be linked and correlated to identify potential field issues in a particular make and model of car.

Thus, the incorporation of the cognitive capability of IoT applications and platforms is all set to bring in the much needed revolutions and revelations in the days ahead.

Conclusion

One workable view frames IoT as the use of network-connected devices embedded in the physical environment, to improve some existing processes, or to enable a new scenario not previously possible. These devices and things are adequately empowered to collect data from their environments and assets, and pass them to control and analytical systems to extract insights hidden inside the data sets. This breakthrough transition brings on the necessary foundation for various businesses to think about new kinds of premium services to their consumers, partners, employees, and other stakeholders.

With business functionalities being fully automated with the careful usage of all the matured and stabilized developments in the IT field, it is expected and expressed that there has to be a tighter alignment between IT and the consumer in the days to unfold. Every kind of our daily life requirements (personal, professional, and physical) need to be identified in time with ease. Every mandated requirement has to be translated into a deliverable service dynamically. That is, IT has to touch every tangible part of our life proceedings in this temporary and transient life on this planet. In short, people-enablement is the next target for the fast-growing IT. The distinct capabilities such as self-, surroundings-, and situation-awareness are very important for accurately deciding our requirements in time, and such a correct and concise understanding goes a long way in coolly facilitating the required services for us. As enunciated in this chapter, the mandated transformation happens with a series of highly competent and cognitive technologies.

It is widely opined that the IoT technologies are capable of realizing the desired and drastic expectations quiet efficiently toward providing a cornucopia of context-aware, real-time, dynamic, insights-encapsulated, and knowledge-centric services to make people smarter. In this chapter, you can find the key improvements and improvisations in the IoT technology space, how technologies voluntarily cooperate with one another in perfectly and precisely identifying and understanding of our needs, and how they cognitively connect, coordinate, and complement in accomplishing and delivering the right and relevant services to the right people at the right place at the right time.

Bibliography

A Simplified TOGAF Guide for Enterprise Architects, www.peterindia.net.

An Information Technology (IT) Portal, http://www.peterindia.net.

Cloud Enterprise Architecture, CRC Press, Boca Raton, FL, http://www.crcpress.com/product/isbn/9781466502321, October 2012.

Cloud Infrastructures for Big Data Analytics, IGI Global, Hershey, PA (The chief editor and the author of four chapters), http://www.igi-global.com/book/cloud-infrastructures-big-data-analytics/95028, 2014.

Hassan, M. M., B. Song, and E.-N. Huh, A Framework of Sensor- Cloud Integration Opportunities and Challenges, *ICUIMC*, 2009.

High-Performance Big Data Analytics: The Solution Approaches and Systems, Springer-Verlag, London, http://www.springer.com/in/book/9783319207438, November 2015.

Intelligent Cities: The Enabling Technologies and Tools, CRC Press, Boca Raton, FL, http://www.crcpress.com/product/isbn/9781482299977, June 2015.

Learning Docker, Packtpub, Birmingham, https://www.packtpub.com/, July 2015.

Next-Generation SOA, Prentice Hall, Upper Saddle River, NJ, http://www.amazon.com/Next-Generation-SOA-Introduction-Service-Orientation/dp/0133859045, 2014.

The Sensor Cloud the Homeland Security, http://www.mistralsolutions.com/hs-downloads/tech-briefs/nov11-article3.html, 2011.

Chapter 2

Realization of IoT Ecosystem Using Wireless Technologies

Abstract: Machine-to-machine (M2M) services have revolutionized the wireless world leading to the evolution of a plethora of technologies and services to support M2M. M2M services are closely tied to the IoT device world, and hence the mobile technologies and services that have evolved to support M2M are part of IoT ecosystem as well. In the first half of the chapter, we have discussed some of the key wireless technologies that have evolved or are evolving in order to support the requirements that are specific to IoT systems. Some of the protocols and technologies that we have discussed in this section are the following:

- 5G
- UWB
- NFC
- ISO 18000 7 DASH7

One of the key challenges of the IoT world is power management, that is, how to provide power to the billions and trillions of devices that are a part of the IoT ecosystem. A new technique called energy harvesting holds a lot of promises to solve this power problem, which is present in the IoT ecosystem. Details of this energy conservation approach are discussed at length in this chapter.

Low-power wide area networking (LPWAN) technologies are prominently used for interconnection of devices and applications in the IoT ecosystem. Details of the LPWAN technology and the LPWAN topologies are discussed in this chapter. Some of the prominent LPWAN protocols that are used in the market are also discussed in this chapter. The protocols that are discussed in this chapter are the following:

- Sigfox
- Weightless
- Nwave
- Ingenu
- LoRa

Introduction

Mobile networks already offer connectivity to a wide range of devices that has opened up new realms of service and connectivity options both for the service providers and for the end users. One type of service that has significantly created an impact in the day-to-day lives of people is M2M service. M2M is a term used to describe solutions that focus on remote collection and transfer of data from embedded sensors or chips placed on remote assets that are fixed or mobile. Smart mobile devices nowadays are used extensively to interact and control various machines, and hence they are excellent candidates to perform communication with remote devices using M2M technology.

M2M connections as a share of total mobile connections is a strong indicator of M2M market maturity. The percentage of M2M in the total mobile connections in the leading mobile markets is depicted in the graph of Figure 2.1.

Market predictions indicate that by the year 2020, the number of connected devices in the world will be roughly about 25.6 billion, which is almost three times more than the present status of connected devices. Out of these, 10.5 billion will be e-connected using mobile technology and mobile networks. Rest of the devices will use other technologies such as wide area network (WAN) and short-range radio to establish connectivity. In this chapter, we will cover in detail all these interconnecting technologies that constitute the IoT ecosystem.

The stupendous growth of IoT ecosystem, which is fueled by the M2M services, is expected to drastically increase the service revenue of M2M services using mobile devices and networks as depicted in the graph of Figure 2.2.

For the mobile operators to support M2M services, it is necessary to introduce a radical change in the operational approach used by them. For example, the customer tariffs for traditional mobile communication services are typically based on usage of the various services. In case of IoT or M2M based services, tariffs will be linked to service value. To be clearer, consumers of e-reader service may pay for the device up front and then pay separately for each book download. In most of the cases, mobile service operators who offer IoT services will not be visible to the end customer. The change in the operational approach of the mobile service operators is depicted in Figure 2.3.

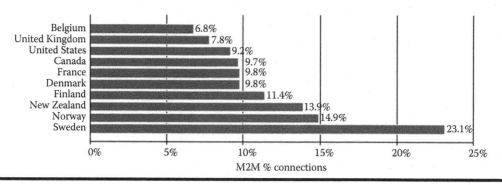

Figure 2.1 Percentage of M2M connections.

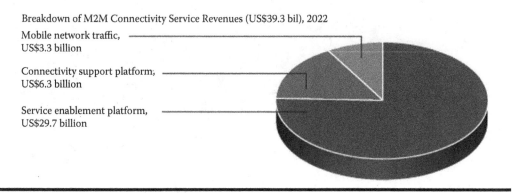

Figure 2.2   M2M service revenue.

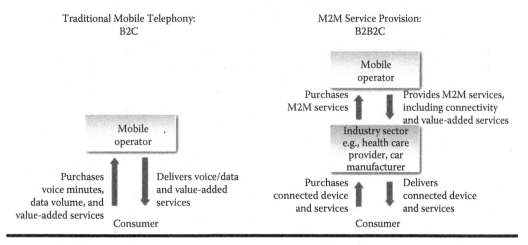

Figure 2.3   Traditional mobile versus M2M.

Architecture for IoT Using Mobile Devices

An architecture for IoT services using mobile devices is depicted in Figure 2.4.

The main components of the diagram are as follows:

1. Data are collected from a wide range of sources and equipment using mobile phones. These data include data from remote sensors and other electronic devices, data which are generated by various infrastructure components such as buildings, water networks, and transportation systems.
2. These data are transferred using the various wired and wireless networking options. They are then collected and stored in some kind of a database or a data warehouse. Analytics is applied to these data in order to derive meaningful insights that define the future course of action.
3. These data are used as an input for service delivery platform (SDP) that runs several IoT application services. These services span across all domains like transportation, health care, water networks, and so on. These SDPs will provide open APIs that will help the developers to design new value-added services.

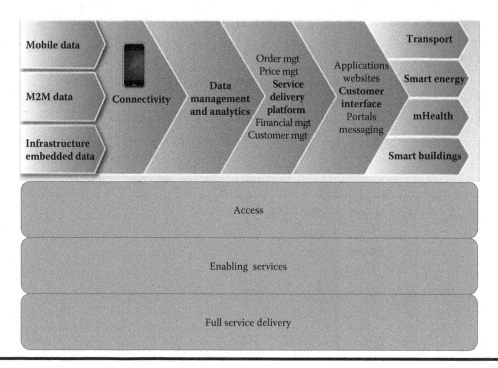

Figure 2.4   Architecture for IoT using mobile devices.

The use of mobile devices for IoT services will also impose varying demands on mobile networks. For instance, services pertaining to public safety will have low latency and bandwidth requirements in contrast to surveillance services that will require high bandwidth as well. Location-based and proximity services offered by the mobile devices will also play a crucial role in the IoT ecosystem. The graph given in Figure 2.5 depicts the latency and bandwidth requirements of various types of IoT services.

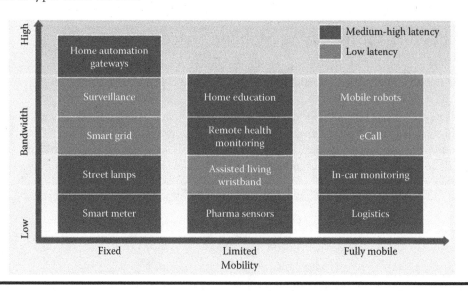

Figure 2.5   Latency and bandwidth requirements of various types of IoT services.

A conscious choice of wireless technology should be made as per the IoT application and the use case. Some of the prominent wireless technologies in the IoT industry are described in this chapter.

Mobile Technologies for Supporting IoT Ecosystem

5G Technology

The main requirements of a mobile network to support IoT devices are the following:

■ Support for massive number of devices (10–100 times more device support than the existing networks)
■ Support for high data rate (increase the existing data rate 10–100 times)
■ Reduce the latency between end-to-end devices; ideally, the latency should be less than 5 ms
■ Provide consistent quality of experience (QoE)
■ Reduce capital and operations cost

The key features that are used in 5G networks in order to cater to the above-mentioned requirements are as follows:

■ Software-defined networking (SDN)
■ Network functions virtualization (NFV)

Software-Defined Networking

SDN is a paradigm in which network control is decoupled from the underlying network devices and is embedded into a software-based component called SDN controller. This separation of control enables the network services to be abstracted from the underlying components and helps network to be treated like a logical entity. The high level architecture of SDN is depicted in Figure 2.6.

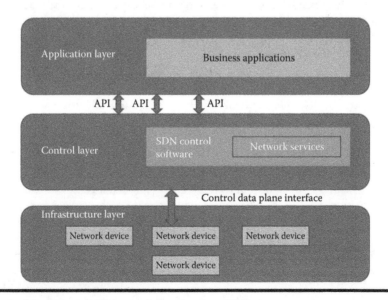

Figure 2.6   Architecture of software-defined networking.

All the business applications that run in the network are a part of the applications layer. All the components of the network are a part of the infrastructure layer. The SDN software component resides in the control layer and interacts both with the applications and with the infrastructure components.

The core of the SDN is the software component that is called the SDN controller. The entire network can be controlled by means of the SDN controller, and the SDN controller appears to all other components of the network as a logical switch. SDN controller can be used to monitor and control the operations of the entire network. This greatly eliminates the hassles of configuring hundreds of network devices. The network administrators can now change network settings dynamically using SDN programs. SDN controller interacts with the business applications using SDN APIs. SDN controller interacts with infrastructure components of the network using some control protocols such as open flow. Open flow is one of the most prominent protocols used in SDN, though there are many other protocols as well for SDN. SDN helps intelligent orchestration and provisioning of the network quickly using software programs that are written in the control layer. The development of open APIs is in progress for SDN architecture, and this will give a great deal of vendor independence for the SDN architecture. As of now, all the vendor devices that use a common SDN protocol for communication can be controlled centrally from the SDN controller.

Following are the benefits of SDN:

- *Centralized control of multivendor network equipment*: All network equipment that use a common SDN protocol for communication can be controlled centrally using an SDN controller irrespective of the vendors who have manufactured the equipment.
- *Reduced complexity through automation*: SDN framework provides features to automate and manage several network related functions that are otherwise time consuming when done manually. This automation will bring down operational cost and also reduce the errors that are introduced due to manual intervention.
- *Improved network reliability and security*: Network policy implementation that used to take months together previously can now be accomplished in a matter of few days. SDN framework eliminates the need to configure each network device individually, and this in turn reduces the possibility of security breaches and other noncompliance aspects, which may arise during policy implementation.
- *Better user experience*: SDN architecture provides flexibility to dynamically change configuration as per the user requirements. For example, if a user requires specific level of QoS for audio data streams, it can be configured to happen dynamically using SDN controller. This offers better user experience.

Network Functions Virtualization

NFV is a concept that uses virtualization technologies to provide specific network related services without the necessity to have custom hardware appliances for each network function. This is the main value proposition offered by NFVs. Some examples of NFVs are virtual firewalls, load balancers, WAN accelerators, and intrusion detection services. NFV can be visualized as a combination of virtualization and SDN, and the relationship is depicted in Figure 2.7.

It is not necessary to use SDN to implement NFV. Present day virtualization techniques are robust enough to build NFVs. However, the orchestration and management capabilities of SDN greatly enhances the capabilities of NFV, and hence the use of SDN is being advocated during

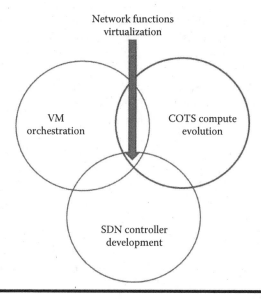

Figure 2.7   Network functions virtualization (NFV).

the development of NFVs. Virtualization of network services does not necessarily mean separate hypervisor partitioned virtual machines (VMs) that contain each service instance; instead, it could also mean the following (Egli 2015):

- Services that are implemented in a machine that has multiple or compartmentalized OS(s)
- Services that are implemented within a single hypervisor
- Services that are implemented as distributed or clustered as composites
- Services that are implemented on bare metal machines
- Services that are implemented in Linux virtual containers

These techniques may use some kind of storage device like NAS to share their state.

NFVs are still an evolving area; however, following are some of the concerns that should be kept in mind during design of NFVs (Egli 2015):

- The use of hypervisor and delivering virtualized services using the same underlying physical hardware can lead to a conflict for physical resources. This may cause a performance drop in the delivery of services, which are related to that specific component. NFV orchestration system should monitor such performance degradation very carefully. The NFV orchestration system should also keep track of the hypervisor and the physical resources so that any contention for resources can be carefully sorted out without any drop in performance.
- The virtualized services are hosted on the hypervisor component, which could become a single point of failure. This failure will impact all the VMs that are running on that server and will also disrupt the services that are offered by those VMs.
- The virtual switch that is present in the hypervisor can get overloaded in an attempt to serve multiple vNICs of the various VMs that are running on it. The hypervisor should have some mechanism to identify and prioritize traffic control in so that application and management failures can be avoided.

■ The hypervisor has the capability to keep the applications unaware of the changes in physical machine state like failure of an NIC port. SDN controller and orchestration cooperation should bridge this awareness gap and perform timely actions.

In some cases, VMs can be migrated from one server to another as a part of a high-availability (HA) strategy. This migration can impact a service delivery in several ways. So appropriate steps need to be taken to ensure that no disruption of services happens.

5G Architecture

High frequency bands suffer from huge amounts of propagation loss, and this severely limits the coverage area. Hence, cells that work at high frequency bands have small coverage area and are called small cells. In order to boost mobility performance, small cells are overlaid on the coverage of macro cells that operate in low frequency bands that leads to the formation of heterogeneous networks. As deployment becomes dense, an increased control signaling interaction comes into picture on account of frequent handovers between small and macro cells, which in turn reduces the efficiency of heterogeneous networks.

In order to boost the performance of heterogeneous networks, control plane (C-plane) and user plane (U-plane) decoupled architecture is planned to be used by the 5G wireless networks. In this decoupled architecture, crucial C-plane is expanded and placed at low frequency bands in order to guarantee reliability of transmission. The corresponding U-plane is moved to the available higher frequency bands in order to increase the capacity of 5G architecture. With significant coverage of macro cells, very less handovers happen to the C-plane when compared to the existing coupled architecture of heterogeneous networks. Hence, in the new 5G architecture, under a macro cell, the handover process is just simplified to the U-plane handover, which reduces a lot of control signaling interaction. This in turn boosts the performance of 5G networks. The salient features of the proposed 5G architecture vision are the following:

■ *Presence of 2 logical network layers*: a radio network layer that provides minimum functionalities of layers 1 and 2 and a network cloud that provides functionalities of all the other higher layers.
■ Dynamic deployment and scaling of network functions of the network cloud using SDN and NFV that was explained earlier.
■ A lean protocol stack by eliminating redundant functionalities.
■ Separate provisioning of capacity and coverage in the radio network (RN) by using the C or U plane split architecture and by using different frequency bands for capacity and coverage.
■ Presence of data-driven network intelligence to optimize usage of network resources and to ensure appropriate planning.

Ultra Wide Band Technology

Ultra wide band (UWB) is a technology that is used for communication among low-range and low-power sensors and mobile devices that require very low power and high bandwidth. UWB has a lot of features that make it suitable for IoT communication. They are as follows:

■ Possibility of high accuracy transmission even indoors
■ Resistance to multipath fading

- Good scalability in dense deployment
- Low-power consumption
- High bandwidth transmission

UWB acts as a complementing technology to other existing wireless radio technologies such as Wi-Fi and WiMax. UWB provides very cost-effective, power-efficient, and high bandwidth solution for data communication among devices that are within a distance of 10 m or 30 ft.

How UWB Works

UWB works differently from conventional narrowband radio frequency (RF) and spread spectrum technologies (SS) such as Bluetooth* Technology and 802.11a/b/g. The UWB transmitter works by sending billions of pulses simultaneously across a wide range of frequencies that are several GHz in bandwidth. The UWB receiver that receives these pulses then translates these pulses into data by listening to a familiar sequence of pulses sent by the UWB transmitter. UWB's combination of larger spectrum, lower power, and pulsed data improves speed and reduces interference with other wireless spectrum. The high level architecture of UWB is depicted in Figure 2.8.

The key technology that is used in UWB is multiband orthogonal frequency division multiplexing (MBOA). The benefits of MBOA are the following:

- Flexibility to configure spectrum using software-configurable emissions
- Capability to adapt easily to different worldwide regulatory bodies
- Future scalability and backward compatibility
- Use of standard CMOS technology that helps to speed up development and also provides advanced performance
- Very robust in multipath environments

ISO 18000 7 DASH7

This standard was developed by DASH7 Alliance. This is a low power, low complexity radio protocol for all sub-1 GHz radio devices. It is a nonproprietary technology for an open standard, and the solutions that use this protocol may contain a pool of technologies that operate in their

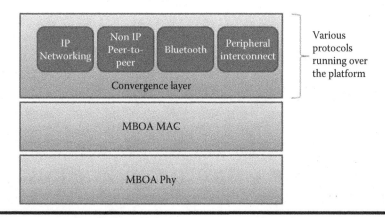

Figure 2.8   Layered architecture of UWB.

own ways. Common for these technologies are that they use a sub-1 GHz silicon radio as their primary communicating device. The main application use cases of DASH7 are the following:

- Supply chain management
- Inventory or yard management
- Warehouse optimization
- Smart meters
- Commercial green building development

Near Field Communication Technology

Near field communication technology (NFC) is a combination of radio frequency identification (RFID) and networking technologies. It is a unique wireless technology that enables easy and convenient short-range communication between electronic devices. It connects all types of consumer devices and facilitates easy communication among them. It acts as a secure gateway and allows consumers to use NFC enabled mobile devices to store and access all kinds of data. If two NFC enabled devices are brought closer to one another, they can automatically initiate network communication without the need for any preconfiguration or setup.

NFC enabled consumer devices can be used to store and exchange any types of personal data like messages, photographs, MP3 files, and so on. Following features of NFC make it very suitable for IoT communication:

- Ease of use
- Instant natural connectivity
- Zero configuration
- Smart key access

ROLE OF NFC IN MOBILE E-TICKETING—A REAL LIFE CASE

An e-ticket is a token or pass that is used by the consumers for various purposes like travel on public transportation, gain entry to various entertainment or sports venue. With the help of NFC, e-ticket process just takes matter of seconds for completion. It also provides plenty of convenience for the consumers. After completion of payment information, the purchased e-ticket will be transferred to consumer's mobile. NFC technology will enable consumers to use their mobile device as contactless payment and ticketing device.

MOBILE PAYMENT AND E-TICKETING IN PRACTICE

The Cityzi project is a large-scale precommercial roll-out of mobile contactless services. French mobile operators will market the first NFC handsets for use by several thousand customers. Customers will be able to discover, for the first time in France, a multiservice offer of mobile contactless services, delivered through the support of mobile operators. The first commercial mobile NFC handsets were marketed to 500,000 residents in the Nice metropolitan area along with a set of mobile NFC applications. In the summer of 2010,

Orange sold the phone at its nine stores in Nice and nearby Manton and Beau Soleil, with approximately 30 retailers selling the NFC enabled phones. The scope of the initiative covers the entire urban community of Nice, including the city as well as the 24 neighboring communes. The first services on offer within the framework of *Mobile Contactless Nice* will include the following:

- *Public transport*: Ticketing, passenger information
- *Promotion of local heritage and education*: e-campus project
- *Trade and retail*: Local bank transactions, mobile loyalty, and couponing programs
- *Cultural/tourist information*: Museums, the Nice transport company, Lignes D'Azur, which operates buses and trams in the city, has an NFC option similar to Oyster in London or Octopus in Hong Kong. Cityzi customers can load up the Bpass Java application resident on the phone with credit to make journeys through an over-the-air transaction. Tickets can be bought at €1 each, or for €2 with parking, or in packs of €10. Each tram journey costs €1, and users can have credit of up to €19 on a phone at any one time. The price of the tickets is charged to the subscriber's phone bill, and the mobile operator runs a revenue share with Lignes D'Azur. The phone can be used to take the tram or bus for journeys even if the phone's battery is flat, although you need a connection to add a ticket to the phone. Perhaps the most powerful part of the technology is the use of NFC tags with a link to the phone's web browser. Waving the phone over a tag takes the browser straight to a preprogrammed page, providing access to real-time tram and bus times, TV listings, news, weather, restaurant booking, and directory enquiries. The scheme has been a huge success with other locations anxious to replicate the program (https://www.globalplatform.org/industryinterviewscityzi.asp).

Energy Harvesting for Power Conservation in the IoT System

In an IoT ecosystem, there will be millions and trillions of devices that are connected and are communicating with each other using some form of wireless technology. This raises a concern about the power generation mechanisms that should be employed for maintaining this huge device ecosystem. Millions and trillions of devices will amount to the purchase of millions and trillions of batteries that should be maintained and disposed of as well. This poses a tough energy problem to the whole concept of IoT. Energy harvesting provides a direct solution for providing power to these huge numbers of devices using clean energy.

Energy harvesting technologies refer to the use of power generating elements such as solar cells, piezoelectric elements, and thermoelectric elements, in order to convert various types of energy such as light, vibration, and heat energy into electricity. This electricity is then used efficiently to supply power to IoT devices.

Power generation using one of the above-mentioned methods can be used mainly because of the fact that semiconductors have now reached a balanced state between improving performance of power generating elements and falling power consumption of active devices. That is why, nowadays, there is plenty of focus and attention on the energy harvest technology that can solve the dissemination problem in wireless sensor terminals as part of the IoT ecosystem.

Architecture of an Energy Harvesting Terminal for a Wireless Sensor Network

A wireless sensor terminal generally consists of a sensor that is used for sensing the surroundings and a master control unit (MCU) for processing the collected data and for performing other system control activities. A wireless chip is also present for providing support for wireless communications. Instead of a dry cell battery, a power IC that is matched to the power-generating element in the wireless sensor network (WSN) is present in the wireless sensor network node. These components are depicted in Figure 2.9.

The power generating element used should be carefully selected after taking into consideration the type of energy that is collected from the surrounding environment, that is, whether it is vibration, light, or heat. The most common elements which are used are as follows:

- Solar
- Piezoelectric
- Thermoelectric

It is also necessary to ensure that the power IC to be used with the power-generating element should be able to efficiently collect the power from that element without loss, and that it is capable of supplying the stabilized power to a later stage IC. The generated power for each WSN changes as per the size and the generating environment. When integrating energy harvester into a device, it is necessary to identify the following carefully:

- What type of energy will be obtained
- What size of an energy harvester can actually fit on a device
- What will be the balance present in the device between consumption power and the generation power

Another important aspect to be considered for choice of power IC is that it should match the power generating element present in the WSN. To be specific, the voltage or current output characteristics of the power generating element will vary according to the element, and it is mandatory to choose a power IC that will provide optimal results.

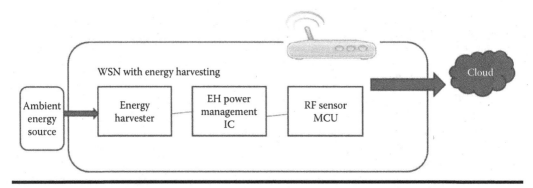

Figure 2.9   Energy harvesting in WSN.

It is also very important to ensure correct choice of wireless communication mechanism for a WSN terminal. Following are the key parameters to be kept in mind for choice of wireless communication channel:

- Communication distance
- Type of network that is going to be built
- The amount of data which are transmitted
- The type of application under consideration
- Power consumption requirements

Out of the parameters listed above, in the context of energy harvesting, the critical aspect to be considered is to reduce power consumption. So the wireless technologies that are commonly used are ZigBee and Bluetooth low energy (BLE).

One important aspect to be considered for energy harvesting is striking a balance between generated power and consumed power. This is critical mainly because of the fact that the device will not work if the power generated is lesser than the power consumed. Although the power generating features of power generating elements are continuously improving, it is challenging to continuously supply power to a device. One approach is to collect and store the generated power in a capacitor and then supply the power for sensor operation at regular time intervals. This will help to provide a method to balance power generation with power consumption.

In order to balance the generated power to the consumed power, developers need to correctly calculate factors such as:

- Power collection time for power collecting element
- Usable electric load

This calculation requires trial and error even when generated power and estimated power can be calculated accurately. When the values of generated power and consumed power are not accurate, it is a good practice to calculate optimal values in each instance. Implementing this estimation effort is highly challenging in a real-time scenario. There is a component called energy harvesting starter kit that helps speed up development of energy harvesting for a WSN. This kit has an RF component that typically works at 2.4 GHz, and the component also contains a protocol implementation that is customized for low-power consumption. It is also possible to change the protocol to ZigBee or BLE by replacing the corresponding chip.

Development of devices that use energy harvesting power ICs are growing in a quick paced manner and has found diverse applications in diverse fields. In some situations, energy harvesting provides battery free WSN terminals, whereas in other cases, energy harvesting extends battery life.

Mobile Application Development Platforms

Mobile application development is the process of developing application software for mobile devices. These application software are mostly installed on the phones at the time of manufacturing or they can be downloaded by the consumers from various mobile software distribution centers. Mobile application software developers have various design considerations like the screen size of the mobile devices, hardware and software requirement specifications, and so on, as there are a vast variety of mobile platforms that are available. There are many mobile application development platforms that are available in the market. Each of them will have an integrated development environment (IDE) that provides all tools that are required for a mobile application developer to write, test, and deploy applications into the target platform environment. Some of the key mobile platforms are Android, iOS Windows mobile OS, and the Symbian OS.

As there are many mobile platforms that are available, it has always been a matter of concern for the mobile application developers about the target mobile platforms for which each mobile application should be built. This has led to the evolution of cross OS platforms for mobile application development. These platforms offer an excellent alternative to ignoring one mobile OS in favor of another and offer platforms that provide support for developing mobile applications that work across multiple mobile application development platforms. Some of the key cross OS platforms available in the market are discussed below:

1. *RhoMobile*: RhoMobile provides Rhodes, which is an open source, Ruby-based framework. It helps development of many native mobile applications for a wide range of smart phone devices and operating systems. The operating systems that are supported include iOS, Android, Windows Mobile OS, RIM, and Symbian.

   This framework has capabilities that allow you to develop your source code once and use it too quickly to build application for all major mobile platforms. Native applications that are developed using this framework have the capability to use the mobile device's hardware, including GPS, camera, as well as location data to further enhance the application capabilities. In addition to Rhodes, RhoMobile also provides RhoHub, which is a hosted development environment, and RhoSync, which is a standalone server that keeps application data current up to date on end user's mobile devices.

2. *Appcelerator*: This belongs to free or open source software (FOSS) framework. Titanium development platform offered by it allows the development of native mobile, tablet, *and* desktop applications through typical web development languages such as JavaScript, Hyper Text Markup Language (HTML), and so on. Titanium users will also have access to more than 300 social and other APIs and their associated location information. The native applications that are developed using this platform can be stored either in cloud or in the mobile device. They are designed to take full advantage of the mobile device hardware, especially the camera and the video camera.

3. *WidgetPad*: It is a collaborative, open-source mobile application development environment. It can be used for creating smart phone applications using standard web technologies like CSS3, HTML5, and JavaScript. This platform provides features like project management, source code editing and debugging, collaboration, versioning, and distribution. It can be used to create mobile applications that work on iOS, Android, and WebOS.

4. *PhoneGap*: It won the winning pitch at Web 2.0 Expo San Francisco's 2009 Launch Pad event. It is a FOSS framework that helps you develop mobile applications for iOS Android, Symbian, and BlackBerry platforms using web development languages such as JavaScript and HTML.

5. *MoSync*: MoSync is another FOSS cross platform mobile application development software development kit (SDK) that supports common programming standards. The SDK includes tightly integrated compilers, runtimes, libraries, device profiles, tools, and utilities. MoSync provides an eclipse-based IDE for C/C++ programming. It is expected to provide support for JavaScript, Ruby, PHP, and Python languages soon. This framework supports a large number of operating systems like Android, Symbian, and Windows mobile.

Mobile Use Cases for IoT

Some examples of mobile use cases of IoT are summarized in Table 2.1.

Low Power Wide Area Networking Technologies

Low power wide area networking technologies (LPWAN) technologies are used extensively for communication in the IoT ecosystem. LPWAN technologies are superior when compared to Bluetooth and BLE for M2M communication because of their cost effectiveness and low-power consumption. LPWAN technology is ideal for connecting devices that send small amounts of data over a long range with battery efficiency. An ideal example of devices that fall under this category are sensors, which are used for transmitting data within smart homes, buildings, parking systems, and so on.

Table 2.1   Low power wide area networking technologies (LPWAN)

Mobile Use Cases for IoT	Challenge	Mobile-Based Solution
Intelligent energy conservation	• Access to electricity for development of cities • High levels of electricity theft • Inefficiencies of traditional grid • High levels of electric vehicle charging • Inability to track energy consumption and usage in real time	A mobile-based energy management service that helps consumers track and manage energy consumption in real time, pay bills using mobile devices, track energy theft, and identify energy leakage
Wireless fleet management	• Inefficiencies in supply chains	A mobile-based intelligent fleet management solution for mobile tracking of fleet and routing using embedded telematics
Remote health care monitoring	• Reliance on costly health care models • Aging infrastructure and outdated technology • Limited real-time data about patient's body parameters	Remote patient monitoring and health care solutions using mobile devices
Mobile payments and ticketing	• Cost of maintaining multichannel ticketing systems • Inconvenience for the consumers	A mobile ticketing platform that uses the NFC technology to provide end-to-end ticketing solutions for the customer
Analytics and commercial insights	• Disconnected data sets in silos • Inability to track and derive useful insights about various aspects pertaining to citizens in diverse city domains	Mobile business intelligence platforms that provide real-time insight for the city government

The key features of LPWAN that make it suitable for IoT ecosystem are the following:

■ *Long-range communication*: Ability to support nodes that are greater than or equal to 10 km distance from the gateway. However, the correct distance is based on the LPWAN technology that is used.
■ *Low transmission data rate*: Less than 5000 bits of data are sent per second. Often only 20–256 bytes per message sent several times a day.
■ *Low-power consumption*: This provides very long battery life for the devices. Many times, the battery life may last up to 10 years.

LPWAN technology is ideally suited for the following two types of applications:

1. *Fixed, medium-to-high density connections*: This is mainly used in cities and for buildings as an alternative option for cellular communications. Some common examples are smart grids, GPS-based asset tracking systems, and smart lighting systems.
2. *Long life, battery powered applications*: For applications that need a long range. Some examples are water meters, gas detectors, smart agriculture systems, and so on.

The bandwidth and the range requirements of various wireless networking technologies are summarized in Figure 2.10.

The needs of IoT and M2M applications have given rise to some specific requirements on LPWAN technologies as compared with other wireless technologies. This is depicted in Figure 2.11.

For LPWAN technology, a star-topology network is preferred instead of a mesh-topology network. The endpoints of star networks are connected directly to access points. Repeaters can be used to fill in gaps in coverage areas so that there is no drop in transmission power. LPWAN technologies operate with 140–160 decibels that can provide several miles of range. In order to accomplish high miles, highly sensitive receivers are employed in LPWAN

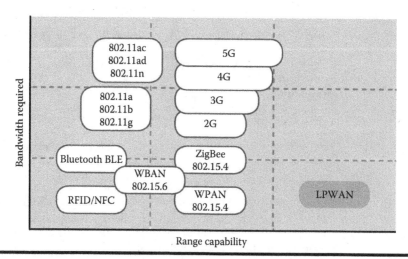

Figure 2.10   Bandwidth requirements of LPWAN technologies.

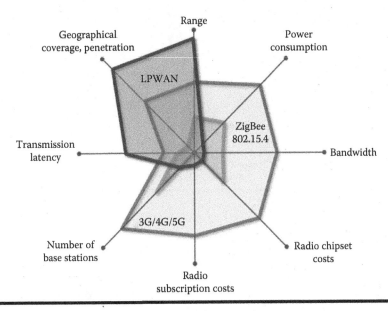

Figure 2.11   Requirements of LPWAN technologies.

technologies. The following are the most important parameters to be considered while choosing a LPWAN technology:

- Capacity
- Quality of service
- Range
- Reliability
- Battery life
- Security
- Cost
- Proprietary versus standard

LPWAN Network Topologies

LPWAN has two network topologies:

- Direct device connectivity (base station)
- Indirect device connectivity through an LPWAN gateway

Direct Device Connectivity Topology of LPWAN

This topology is depicted in Figure 2.12.

- The base station that is present in the network provides connectivity to a large number of devices.
- The traffic is sent to servers (cloud) through TCP or IP-based networks (Internet).
- The base station is responsible for translation of protocol from IoT protocols such as MQTT or CoAP to specific device application protocols.

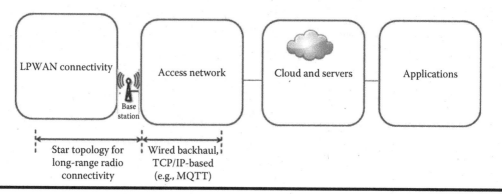

Figure 2.12   Direct device connectivity topology of LPWAN.

Indirect Device Connectivity through an LPWAN Gateway

This topology is depicted in Figure 2.13.

In certain networks where it is not possible to connect devices directly to LPWAN, a local gateway is used to bridge LPWAN connectivity to some short-range radio (SRD) technology like ZigBee or BLE. This gateway generally runs on mains power as it has to support a large number of devices. The gateway should also have the capability to perform protocol conversion from SRD radio technologies to LPWAN technology. Gateways also provide more security to IoT ecosystem as they offer options to implement powerful security algorithms.

Sigfox

Sigfox is very popular in the LPWAN industry. It has partnership with a lot of vendors in the radio space such as Texas Instruments, Silicon Labs, and Axom. Sigfox does not support bidirectional networks and offers support for uplink only sensor applications. This imposes a restriction on the end user to transfer only 15 bytes of traffic at a time with an average of only 10 messages per day. This limits the usability of this technology only for very simple devices.

Sigfox uses antennas that are set up on towers in order to receive data from devices such as parking sensors and water sensors. Data transmissions using Sigfox technology happen in 868 or 915 MHz frequency bands.

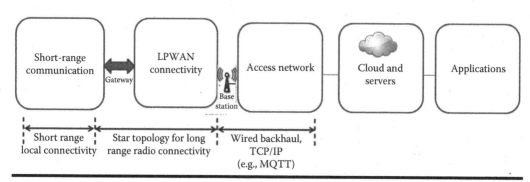

Figure 2.13   Indirect device connectivity through an LPWAN gateway.

Sigfox's wireless systems send data in very small quantities very slowly using a mobile technology called binary phase shift keying (BPSK). Data transmissions for long ranges are done with the help of long and short messages.

Binary Phase Shift Keying

Phase-shift keying (PSK) is a modulation technique that transmits data by changing the phase of the reference signal, which is called carrier wave. This technique is widely used for data transmission RFIDs, wireless LANs, and Bluetooth. Binary phase shift keying (BPSK) is the simplest form of PSK. It uses two phases that are separated by an angle of 180°. Since there are two phases, this technique is also called 2-PSK.

Sigfox is widely used for applications that send small, infrequent bursts of data. Some examples of application domains are alarm systems, location monitoring systems, and simple metering systems. In these systems, signal data are sent few times to ensure that the data gets transmitted. The downside of this approach is shorter battery life for battery powered applications.

Weightless

Weightless is an open LPWAN standard. It operates in sub-1 GHz unlicensed spectrum. Weightless has three open standards:

- Weightless-P
- Weightless-N
- Weightless-W

Weightless-P

This standard offers bidirectional communication. It uses a narrow band modulation scheme in order to provide bidirectional communications capability. This standard provides very high quality of service (QoS) parameter that is the best in class offered in the IoT sector.

Weightless-P will offer the committed performance rate, network reliability, and security parameters that are given by 3GPP carrier grade solutions. This standard also provides substantially lower costs when compared to other LPWAN technologies. This standard has less than 100 uW power consumption in an idle state. This power consumption rate is low when compared to 3 mW, which is used by other best cellular technologies that are available in the market.

Weightless-N

This standard offers one-way communication. They have a long battery life of about 10 years and have a low network cost. The Weightless-N standard uses star network architecture. It works in sub-GHz spectrum using ultra narrow band (UNB) technology. This standard offers a range of several kilometers even in urban environments. This standard offers very low power consumption, which in turn provides a long battery life for devices. This standard requires small conventional cells, minimal hardware, and incurs less network costs. This standard uses differential binary phase shift keying (DBPSK) digital modulation scheme to transmit using narrow frequency bands. This standard uses a frequency hopping algorithm in order to reduce interference.

This standard provides support for encryption and implicit authentication using a shared secret key regime in order to encode transmitted information via a 128-bit AES algorithm. This standard offers support for mobility as the network can automatically route terminal messages to the correct destination. Using this standard, multiple networks that are operated by different companies are enabled and can be colocated as well. Each base station that operates using this standard queries a central database in order to determine which network the terminal is registered to in order to decode and route data correctly.

Weightless-W

This standard is the most extensively used option as it runs in the unused TV spectrum. Data rates from 1 Kbit/s to 10 Mbit/s are possible based on the link budget with the size of data packets starting from 10 bytes. There is no upper bound on packet size. The overhead is extremely low, for example, 50 byte packets have less than 20% overhead. Both acknowledged and unacknowledged message transmission modes are supported. The multicast call feature allows messages to be sent to multiple devices. Interrupt feature supported by this standard allows devices to raise alarms in order to notify specific events that need attention such as power outage.

Service provision layering features provide worldwide contracts and automated change of network provider capabilities. Terminals can run multiple applications at the same time, and the mobility is fully supported. This standard provides an ultra secure 128-bit encryption and authentication model, which is based on a shared secret key. This standard has an extremely low complexity architecture. This type of architecture facilitates low-cost implementation using minimal memory and processor power in order to further extend battery life.

At the network level, careful scheduling features enable transmissions to be planned well ahead of time. The capability to plan ahead of time provides very high loading efficiency. The frequency hopping and intelligent frequency planning features help to maximize throughput on congested networks.

This standard offers wide range of modulation schemes and spreading factors, which in turn offers flexibility in network design. The range is about 5 km in indoor terminals. The entire core network runs as a software service that enables cloud hosting of this service.

NWave

NWave operates in UNB radio spectrum, which runs in sub-1 GHz ISM bands. They use a star networking topology for their operation. This allows direct communication with base stations. NWave uses advance demodulation techniques that help this standard to coexist with other radio technologies without causing any additional noise or distortion in transmission.

Ingenu

Ingenu uses a technology called random phase multiple access (RPMA).

Random Phase Multiple Access

Random phase multiple access (RPMA) technology is a combination of technologies that are designed exclusively for wireless M2M communication. RPMA supports large coverage area due to the high sensitivity levels of its receivers. High levels of receiver sensitivity provide good levels of signal power while maintaining significant capacity levels. RPMA also operates in 2.4 GHz band that provides greater transmission power for this technology. All these factors are responsible for the great signal strength and more coverage area offered by this technology. An RPMA access point can also support hundreds and thousands of endpoint devices with various data rates.

Access points and endpoints of RPMA are synchronized in such a way that endpoints send signals that fall inside predefined frame sizes. Endpoints transmit their signals with a delay in such a way that it does not exceed the frame size. The access point despreads the signal and checks it for errors using cyclic redundancy check. Endpoints send their signals with a delay that is planned in such a way that it does not exceed the frame size. While receiving a signal, RPMA endpoints are aware of the conditions that exist in the channel and also about the local interference levels of signals. A combination of all these techniques combined in a specific and unique way gives RPMA the capability to support simultaneous demodulation of up to 1200 fully overlapping signals.

LoRa

LoRa Alliance12 promotes use of an open standard for LoRa-based networks called LoRaWAN. This standard was developed by Semtech, IBM research, and Actility. Following are the main features of LoRaWAN:

- They have three open standards that provide various types of options for end users.
- Since it is an open ecosystem, there are a lot of software and vendors that are available in the market for supporting this standard.
- This standard lacks many features like support for roaming, packetization, firmware upgrades over air, and so on.
- In order to use this standard, the network server software should be run in the cloud that mandates subscription from a network server vendor.
- Semtech is the only vendor that manufactures the chips that may impact the scale of production and adoption of this standard.

Conclusion

M2M services have revolutionized the mobile devices segment. The wireless operators are on the lookout for different ways to improve and expand their services in order to support M2M services. M2M services are very closely linked to IoT ecosystem. Use of wireless networks and devices for M2M-based services makes them an important component of the IoT ecosystem as well. Several technologies are emerging in the wireless domain in order to accommodate the requirements of the IoT system. Some of the prominent networking technologies that were discussed in this chapter are the following:

- 5G
- UWB
- NFC
- ISO 18000 7 DASH7

One of the key challenges that exists in the IoT domain is the power challenge, that is, how to supply power to all the trillions of interconnected devices. One new technique that holds a lot of promises for solving this problem is called energy harvesting. The concept of energy harvesting has been discussed at length in this chapter.

LPWAN technologies are nowadays becoming very popular with the IoT devices. The concepts of LPWAN and the LPWAN topologies are discussed in this chapter. Some of the prominent LPWAN vendors in the market are also discussed in this chapter. The LPWAN products that are discussed in this chapter are as follows:

- Sigfox
- Weightless
- Nwave
- Ingenu
- LoRa

Bibliography

Egli, P. R. 2015, http://www.slideshare.net/PeterREgli/lpwan.

Keita Sekine. Energy-harvesting devices replace batteries in IoT sensors. http://core.spansion.com/article/energy-harvesting-devices-replace-batteries-in-iot-sensors/#.VoJtEUal0Rk.

Ultra-Wideband (UWB) Technology. http://ecee.colorado.edu/~ecen4242/marko/UWB/UWB/wireless_pb.pdf.

Understanding the Internet of things, a white paper by GSM association, July 2014.

Chapter 3

Infrastructure and Service Discovery Protocols for the IoT Ecosystem

Abstract: There is no standard architecture for the IoT ecosystem. In this chapter, we have defined a reference architecture, and we have used this architecture throughout this chapter. It is a five-layered architecture and the different layers are as follows:

- Objects layer
- Object abstraction layer
- Service management layer
- Application layer
- Business layer

In the rest of this chapter, we have attempted to define the protocols that are used in the infrastructure layer and service management layer. For ease of definition and reference, we have combined the objects and the object abstraction layer and referred to it as the infrastructure layer.

The main protocols that we have tried to define for the infrastructure layer are the following:

- RPL
- IEEE 802.15.4
- 6LoWPAN
- Bluetooth low energy
- EPCglobal

- LTE-A
- Z-Wave
- ZigBee

Service discovery is very important for an IoT ecosystem as it is very important for IoT devices to advertise and use the services of other devices that are present in the Internet of Things (IoT) network. In the rest of this chapter, we have tried to elaborate on three prominent service discovery protocols that are used for IoT devices:

- DNS service discovery (DNS-SD)
- Multicast domain name system (mDNS)
- Simple service discovery protocol (part of UPnP)

Introduction

IoT should have the capability to connect and transfer data among billions and trillions of devices. For this to happen seamlessly, it is critical to have a layered architecture in place. The architecture should be highly scalable and flexible to accommodate the wide gamut of components and technologies that form a part of the IoT ecosystem.

Layered Architecture for IoT

The layered architecture that we are going to use as a reference in this chapter is given in Figure 3.1.

The different layers are as follows:

- Objects layer
- Object abstraction layer
- Service management layer
- Application layer
- Business layer

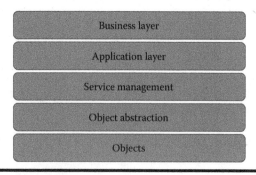

Figure 3.1   Layered architecture for IoT.

Objects Layer

Objects layer, also known as devices layer, comprises the physical devices that are used to collect and process information from the IoT ecosystem. Physical devices include different types of sensors such as those that are typically based on micro-electromechanical systems (MEMS) technology. Sensors could be optical sensors, light sensors, gesture and proximity sensors, touch and fingerprint sensors, pressure sensors, and more. Standardized plug and play mechanisms should be used by the objects layer in order to integrate and configure the heterogeneous types of sensors that belong to the IoT device ecosystem. The device data that are collected at this layer are transferred to the object abstraction layer using secure channels.

Object Abstraction Layer

This layer transfers data that are collected from objects to service management layer using secure transmission channels. Data transmission can happen using any of the following technologies:

- RFID
- 3G
- GSM
- UMTS
- Wi-Fi
- Bluetooth low energy
- Infrared
- ZigBee

Specialized processes for handling functions such as cloud computing and data management are also present in this layer.

Service Management Layer

This layer acts as middleware for the IoT ecosystem. This layer pairs specific services to its requester based on addresses and names. This layer provides flexibility to the IoT programmers to work on different types of heterogeneous objects irrespective of their platforms. This layer also processes the data that are received from the object abstraction layer. After data processing, necessary decisions are taken about the delivery of required services, which are then done over network wire protocols.

Application Layer

This layer provides the diverse kinds of services requested by the customer. The type of service requested by the customer depends on the specific use case that is adopted by the customer. For example, if smart home is the use case under consideration, then the customer may request for specific parameters such as heating, ventilation, and air conditioning (HVAC) measurements or temperature and humidity values.

This layer provides the various types of smart services, which are offered by various IoT verticals. Some of the prominent IoT verticals are as follows:

- Smart cities
- Smart energy
- Smart health care

- Smart buildings or homes
- Smart living
- Smart transportation
- Smart industry

Business Layer

This layer performs the overall management of all IoT activities and services. This layer uses the data that are received from the network layer to build various components such as business models, graphs, and flowcharts. This layer also has the responsibility to design, analyze, implement, evaluate, and monitor the requirements of the IoT system. This layer has the capability to use big data analysis to support decision-making activities. This layer also performs a comparison of obtained versus expected outputs to enhance the quality of services.

Protocol Architecture of IoT

The various protocols used for communication in the various layers of the IoT ecosystem are categorized as shown in Figure 3.2.

The various protocols that come in each category are summarized in Figure 3.3.

All the application layer protocols were covered in Chapter 2. In this chapter, we will focus on protocols that work in other layers of the IoT ecosystem starting with infrastructure protocols.

Infrastructure Protocols

Routing Protocol

RPL stands for routing protocol for low power and lossy networks. It is an IPv6 protocol. Low-power lossy networks include wireless personal area networks (WPANs), low-power line communication (PLC) networks, and wireless sensor networks (WSNs). These networks have some characteristics:

- Capability to optimize and save energy
- Capability to support traffic patterns other than unicast communication
- Capability to run routing protocols over link layers with restricted frame sizes

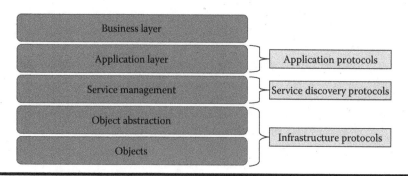

Figure 3.2   Protocol architecture of IoT.

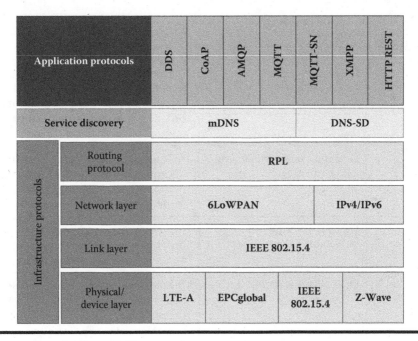

Figure 3.3 Categorization of IoT protocols.

RPL was designed to support minimal routing needs by building a highly robust topology over lossy networks. This protocol provides support for various types of traffic models: multipoint-to-point, point-to-multipoint, and point-to-point. Devices in the network that use this protocol are connected to each other in such a way that no cycles are present in the connection. In order to achieve this, a node called destination oriented directed acyclic graph (DODAG), which is routed at a single destination, is built initially. RPL specifications refer to DODAG as DODAG root. Each node that is a part of DODAG knows its parent node but does not have any information about its child nodes. RPL maintains at least a single path from each node to the root and the preferred parent. This is done in order to increase performance by pursuing a faster path. The DODAG topology used in RPL is depicted in Figure 3.4.

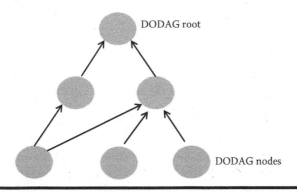

Figure 3.4 DODAG topology.

Table 3.1 DODAG control messages

Serial Number	Name of the Message	Description
1	DODAG information object (DIO)	This message is used to keep the current rank (level) of the node, determine the distance of each node to the root based on some specific metrics, and choose the preferred parent path.
2	Destination advertisement object (DAO)	This message is used to unicast destination information toward selected parents of a node. This control message helps RPL to maintain upward and downward traffic.
3	DODAG information solicitation (DIS)	This message is used by a specific node in order to acquire DIO messages from another reachable adjacent node.
4	DAO acknowledgment (DAO-ACk)	This message is used as a response to a DAO message and is sent by a DAO recipient node like a DAO parent or DODAG root.

The four important types of control messages are used by RPL to maintain routing topology and maintain the updated routing information. These control messages are summarized in Table 3.1.

A DODAG will start its formation when the root node starts sending its location information using DIO message to all low-power lossy network (LLN) levels. Routers that are present at each specific level register the parent path and participation paths for each node. Each node propagates its DIO message, and the DODAG gets built gradually. When a DODAG is constructed, for each node, the preferred parent obtained by the router is set as a default path toward the root.

The root also has the capability to store the destination prefixes obtained by DIOs of other routers in its DIO messages to have upward routes. To provide support for downward routes, the routers should emit and propagate DAO messages to the root by unicasting through parents. These messages will be able to identify the corresponding node of a route prefix as well as the crossing route.

RPL routers work under one of the two modes of operation (MOP): nonstoring or storing modes. In *nonstoring* mode, RPL route messages move toward lower levels based on IP source routing, whereas in *storing mode*, downward routing is based on destination IPv6 addresses.

IEEE 802.15.4

This protocol was created in order to specify a sublayer for the medium access control (MAC) and physical layer primarily for low-rate wireless private area networks (Figure 3.5).

On account of diverse benefits offered by this protocol such as low power consumption, low-data rate, and low-cost and high-message throughput, it is very suitable for use in IoT systems as a communication protocol. This protocol also provides reliable communication and can handle a huge number of nodes (approximately about 65K nodes). This protocol is ideal for secured

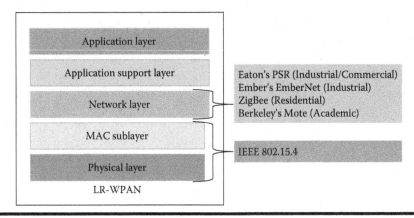

Figure 3.5   Architecture of IEEE 802.15.4.

communication as it provides high levels of security, encryption, and authentication services. The only negative side of this protocol is that it does not provide any quality of service (QoS) guarantees. This protocol forms the basis of ZigBee and other protocols that are used in IoT communication.

IEEE 802:15.4 supports transmission at three frequency bands using a direct sequence spread spectrum (DSSS) method. On the basis of frequency channel, data transmission happens at three data rates:

- 250 kbps at 2.4 GHz
- 40 kbps at 915 MHz
- 20 kbps at 868 MHz

This protocol supports two types of network nodes:

- Full function devices (FFD)
- Reduced function devices (RFD)

FFDs can act as personal area network (PAN) coordinator or as just a normal node. The coordinator has the capability to create, control, and maintain the network. FFDs can store routing table within their memory and can implement a MAC. They can also communicate with other devices using one of the following topologies:

- Star
- Peer-to-peer
- Cluster-tree

RFDs are very simple nodes, and they have constrained resources. They can only communicate with a coordinator node using only the star topology.

- Star topology: This contains at least one FFD and a few other RFDs. The FFD that is designated to work as a PAN coordinator should be located at the center of the network. This FFD has the responsibility of managing and controlling all other nodes that are a part of the network (Figure 3.6).

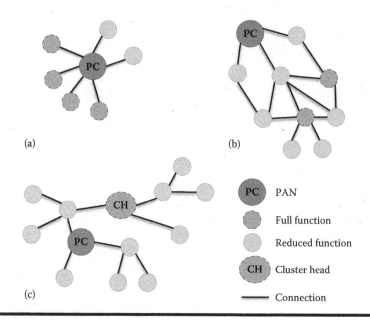

Figure 3.6 (a–c) **Different types of star topologies.**

- Peer-to-peer topology: This contains a PAN coordinator and other nodes communicate with each other in the same network or through intermediate nodes to other networks.
- Cluster-tree topology: This is a special kind of the peer-to-peer topology. It consists of a PAN coordinator, a cluster head, and normal nodes.

IPv6 over Low-Power Wireless Personal Area Networks

6LoWPAN stands for IPv6 over Low-Power Wireless Personal Area Networks. It is an open standard defined in RFC 6282 by the Internet engineering task force (IETF). The key feature of 6LoWPAN that makes it suitable for IoT communication is that though it was originally designed to support IEEE 802.15.4 low-power wireless networks in the 2.4-GHz band, it now supports a wide range of networking media such as sub-1 GHz low-power RF, Bluetooth smart, power line control (PLC), and low-power Wi-Fi.

Network Architecture of 6LoWPAN

The architecture of 6LoWPAN mesh network is depicted in the diagram that is given in Figure 3.7. The uplink to the Internet is provided by the access point (AP), which in this case is an IPv6 router. Different types of devices such as PCs and servers could be connected to the AP. The components of the 6LoWPAN network are connected to the IPv6 network using a 6LoWPAN edge router. Following are the functions performed by the edge router:

- It enables exchange of data between 6LoWPAN devices and the Internet (or other IPv6 network).
- It enables exchange of data among devices that are part of 6LoWPAN network.
- It helps to generate and maintain the 6LoWPAN network (Figure 3.7).

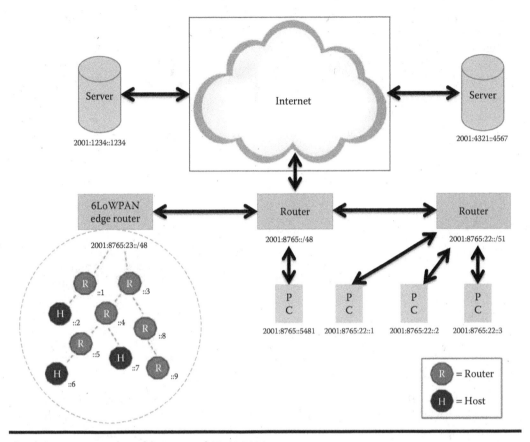

Figure 3.7   Network architecture of 6LoWPAN.

As 6LoWPAN networks can communicate natively with IP networks, they are connected to IP networks simply using IP routers. In general, 6LoWPAN networks will typically act as stub networks as they always operate on the edge.

The edge routers that are used to connect 6LoWPAN networks to other IP networks forward IP datagrams between different media that are used in IP networks. The media used in IP network could be Ethernet, Wi-Fi, 3G, or 4G. As the edge routers used in the 6LoWPAN network forward datagrams to other IP networks using network layer, they do not maintain the state of application layer. This in turn lowers the workload on the edge router in terms of processing power, which makes it possible to use low cost embedded devices with simple software as edge routers.

The devices that are present in a 6LoWPAN network can be classified into two categories:

- Routers
- Hosts

Routers are devices that route data to other nodes in the 6LoWPAN network. Hosts are also known as end point devices, and they do not have the capability to route data to other devices in the network. Host could also be a sleepy device that could check the routers at regular intervals for data.

Protocol Stack of 6LoWPAN

The protocol stack of 6LoWPAN is shown in Figure 3.8.

Many protocols such as ZigBee require complex application layer gateway in order to connect to the Internet. 6LoWPAN solves this issue with the help of an adaptation layer that is present in between the IP stack's data link and network layer. The adaptation layer allows transmission of IPv6 datagrams over IEEE 802.15.4.

Now let us compare the features of OSI layer protocol stack to 6LoWPAN protocol stack.

Physical layer: This layer in the OSI model is responsible for the conversion of data bits into signal that can be transmitted through air. In 6LoWPAN, IEEE 802.15.4 is used as physical layer.

Data link layer: This layer ensures that a reliable connection or link is established between two nodes by correcting the errors that occur in physical layer during data transmission. The media access control (MAC) layer that provides access to the media is also present in the data link layer. In 6LoWPAN, IEEE 802.15.4 is the MAC layer. The adaptation layer of 6LoWPAN that provides adaptation from IPv6 to IEEE 802.15.4 is also present in the data link layer.

Network layer: This layer is responsible for routing of data in the network. This layer ensures that data or packet from a source device is delivered to the correct destination device. The devices are identified using their IP address, which is assigned by using the Internet protocol (IP). In 6LoWPAN, IPv6, or RPL, is used in the network layer.

Transport layer: The transport layer helps ensure that multiple applications running on each device have their own communication channel and can start sessions between applications running on other end devices. Transmission control protocol (TCP) is the prominent transport layer protocol used in the Internet. However, as TCP is a connection oriented protocol, it incurs significant overhead and may not be suitable for all devices especially for devices that have low power consumption. In such scenarios, user datagram protocol (UDP) which is a connectionless protocol with a lower overhead could be a better choice.

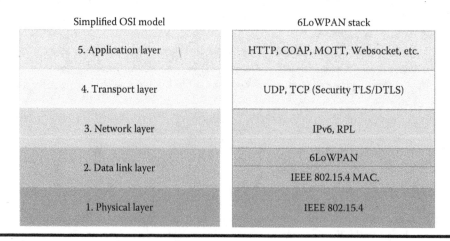

Figure 3.8   Protocol stack of 6LoWPAN.

Application layer: The main responsibility of application layer is data formatting. A popular application layer that is used in the Internet is HTTP that runs over TCP. HTTP uses XML that in turn is a text-based language with a large overhead. Hence, it is not suitable for 6LoWPAN systems that have low power consumption. As HTTP is not suitable for use in 6LoWPAN systems, several other alternatives like COAP and MQTT are used in 6LoWPAN systems.

In short, 6LoWPAN is very promising for use in the IoT market because of the following reasons:

- Support for IP communication
- Support for large mesh network topology
- Very low power consumption
- Robust communication capabilities

Bluetooth Low Energy

Bluetooth low energy (BLE) was started as part of the Bluetooth 4.0 core specification. BLE uses short-range radio with minimum power and operates for a long time. Its range coverage is about 100 meters, which is roughly about 10 times more than conventional Bluetooth. Latency of BLE is 15 times lesser than that of conventional Bluetooth. BLE operates using a power between 0.01 mW and 10 mW. These characteristics make BLE an ideal protocol for use by IoT devices.

The protocol stack of BLE is depicted in Figure 3.9.

Physical layer: This layer receives and transmits data bits.
Link layer: Following are the functions performed by the link layer:
    – Media access control
    – Error control
    – Connection establishment
    – Flow control

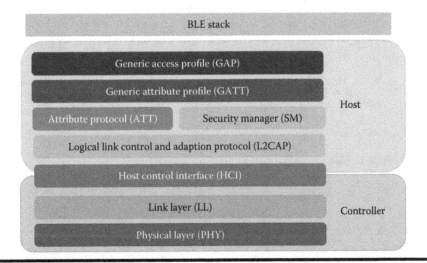

Figure 3.9   Protocol stack of BLE.

Host control interface (HCI): The HCI layer provides a command, event, and data interface that allows link layer to access the data from upper layers such as GAP, L2CAP, and SMP.

Logical link control adaptation protocol (L2CAP): This layer mainly performs multiplexing of data channels. This layer also does fragmentation and reassembly of larger packets.

Generic access profile (GAP): This layer defines processes related to the discovery of Bluetooth devices and also lays down link management aspects while establishing connection between Bluetooth devices. Following are the different types of roles defined by GAP when operating over low-energy (LE) physical channel:

- Broadcaster role: A device that operates in this role can send advertising events. The device that operates in this role is referred to as a broadcaster. The broadcaster has a transmitter and may have a receiver as well.
- Observer role: A device that operates in this mode can receive advertising events. The device is referred to as an observer. The observer has a receiver, and it may have a transmitter as well.
- Peripheral role: A device that is in the peripheral role accepts the establishment of an LE physical connection. A device that operates in the peripheral role will be in a slave role in the link layer connection state. A device that operates in the peripheral role is called a peripheral device. A peripheral device has both a transmitter and a receiver.
- Central role: A device that is in central role initiates establishment of a physical connection. A device that is operating in central role will be in a master role in the link layer connection. A central device has both a transmitter and a receiver.

Generic Attribute Profile

Generic attribute profile (GATT) specifies a framework using the attribute protocol (ATT) layer. This framework mainly defines services and their characteristics. GATT lays down various aspects of service such as service procedures, characteristics, and various aspects that pertain to the broadcast of service characteristics. The two roles that are specified by GATT profiles are the following:

- GATT client: Any device that wants data is called a GATT client. It sends requests and commands to the GATT server. A GATT client can receive responses and other notifications sent by the GATT server.
- GATT server: Any device that has the data and can accept incoming requests from the GATT client is called GATT server. A GATT server sends responses to a GATT client.

The BLE stack can support both the roles simultaneously for a custom profile use case if required.

Attribute Protocol

The ATT layer defines a client or server architecture above the BLE logical transport channel. The layer allows a GATT server to communicate with a GATT client by exposing a set of attributes and interfaces.

Security Manager Protocol

Security Manager Protocol (SMP) specifies the procedures and behavior to ensure security by managing pairing, authentication, and encryption between the devices.

EPCglobal

RFID (radio frequency identification) devices are wireless microchips used for tagging objects for automated identification. Electronic product code (EPC) is a unique identifier stored in an RFID tag that helps to identify and track items in a supply chain management scenario. EPCglobal is the organization that developed EPC, and EPCglobal also prepares and maintains standards that are related to RFID and EPC. RFID can be used as a key technology for IoT devices for the following reasons:

- Openness
- Scalability
- Reliability
- Support for object IDs and service discovery

The key components of EPCs are classified into four types:

- 96-bit
- 64-bit (I)
- 64-bit (II)
- 64-bit (III)

All types of 64-bit EPCs provide support for about 16,000 companies with unique identities and cover 1–9 million types of products and 33 million serial numbers for each type. The 96-bit type provides support for about 268 million companies with unique identities, 16 million classes of products, and 68 billion serial numbers for each class.

An RFID tag has two main components: an electronic chip to store the identity of the object and an antenna that allows the chip to communicate with the tag-reader system. The communication between the tag and tag reader happens with the help of radio waves. The two main components of an RFID system are:

- Radio signal transponder
- Tag reader

The tag reader generates a radio field that can identify objects using reflected radio waves of the RFID tag. RFID system works by sending the tag number to the tag reader with the help of radio waves. After that, the RFID tag reader passes on the tag number to a specific application which is called object-naming services (ONS). The ONS can perform a look-up operation to get further details of the tag such as the place of manufacture and the year of manufacture.

The working of the RFID system is summarized in Figure 3.10.

An EPC code has four parts as summarized in Figure 3.11.

The EPC id system connects the EPC identities to a centralized database using an EPC reader, which is implemented through middleware. The discovery service is a technique of EPCglobal to identify and track required data with the help of tags and ONS.

The different types of EPC tags are summarized in Table 3.2.

Long Term Evolution-Advanced

Long term evolution-advanced (LTE) also referred to as 4G LTE is a standard for wireless mobile network, and it provides high speed data transfer rates for wireless networks. It will provide

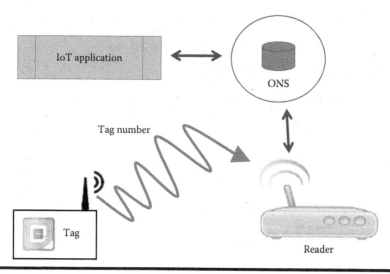

Figure 3.10   Components of RFID system.

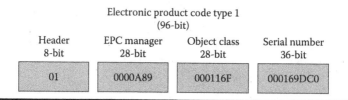

Figure 3.11   EPC code.

Table 3.2   Different Types of EPC Tags

EPC	Description	Tag Type	Functionality
0	Read only	Passive	Write once and read many times
1	Write once and read only	Passive	Write once and read many times
2	Read or write	Passive	Read or write many times
3	Read or write	Semipassive	Attached within sensor
4	Read or write	Active	Attached within sensor While providing a radio wave field to communicate with the reader

50 times performance improvement for existing wireless networks. LTE broadcast is a single-frequency network (SFN) that operates in a broadcast mode. It is a part of the series of standards known as evolved multimedia broadcast multicast service (eMBMS). There are several key use cases of LTE for IoT because of its service cost, scalability, and performance especially from a smart city or intelligent city perspective. Some of the key use cases are summarized in Table 3.3.

Table 3.3 Key Use Cases of LTE

LTE Service Offering	Usage for Intelligent Cities
Live event streaming	Live coverage of key events happening in a city such as sports, concerts, award ceremonies, elections, and so on.
Real-time TV streaming	Real-time delivery of important sports events, news channels, and other popular TV shows. This will enable entertainment amid work that will in turn go a long way in boosting the productivity. In contrast to a situation where an employee may be prompted to take a leave of absence or abstain from work in order to watch some key TV event.
News, stock market reports, weather, and sports updates	Provides news, stock market reports, weather, and sports updates several times during the course of a day with on-device caching features.

Z-Wave

Z-Wave is a low-power wireless communication protocol that is mainly used for home area networks (HAN). It has widespread applications in the development of remote control applications for smart homes as well as other small-sized commercial domains. Z-Wave was developed by ZenSys and later on improved by Z-Wave alliance. Z-Wave operates mainly in the sub-GHz frequency range that is typically around 900 MHz.

This protocol uses low-powered mesh networking topology. Each node or device that is a part of the network has the capability to send and receive control commands through walls and floors of a home, and they use intermediate nodes to route data around obstacles that might be present in the house.

Components of Z-Wave Network

The main components of a Z-wave network are the following:

- Controllers
- Slave nodes

Controllers

A controller is a device that has the capability to build a routing table for Z-Wave network. This device can also calculate the routes to different node. There are two types of controllers; they are:

- Primary controller
- Secondary controller

— *Primary controller*: It is the device that contains a description of the Z-Wave network and has the capability to control the outputs. This device assigns network or home ID and node ID to each Z-Wave node during the enrollment process. There will be only one primary controller in a network at a specific point in time. This node maintains information on which nodes can reach each other.

— *Secondary controller*: It is the device that contains the network ID like the primary controller. This device remains stationary in order to maintain the routing table.

Slave Nodes

Slave nodes are nodes that do not contain routing tables, but instead may contain a network map. The network map contains routes to different nodes that are assigned to it by the

- *Slave nodes*: They have the ability to receive frames from other nodes and respond to them if necessary.
- *Routing slave*: These nodes have the ability to provide several alternate routes for talking to other slave nodes and controllers.
- *Frequently listening routing slave*: This device or node is configured to wake up at the time of every wake-up interval.

ZigBee

ZigBee protocol was framed by the ZigBee alliance. Following features of ZigBee make it very suitable for IoT applications:

- Low power consumption
- Low cost
- Support for large number of network nodes (<=65K nodes)

Apart from the features listed above, ZigBee has a decentralized network topology that is very similar to that of Internet. This protocol has the capability which allows nodes to find new routes if one route fails in the network. This feature makes it a very robust wireless protocol.

ZigBee specification uses lower layers of IEEE 802.15.4 protocol stack and defines its own upper layers from network to application including application profiles as shown in Figure 3.12.

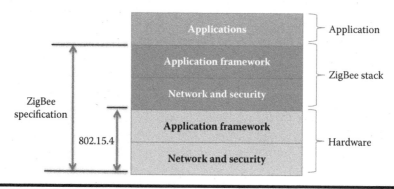

Figure 3.12 Protocol architecture of ZigBee.

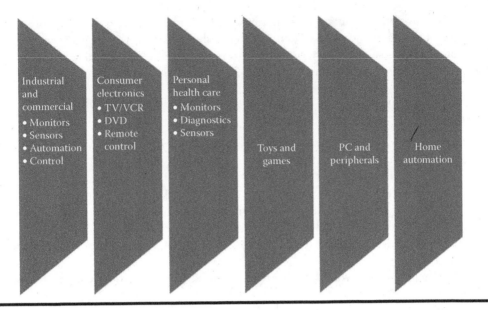

Figure 3.13   Main application areas of ZigBee.

Some of the main application areas of ZigBee protocol are summarized in Figure 3.13.

Device or Service Discovery for IoT

The high scalability and the huge number of devices, which form a part of the IoT ecosystem, mandate the presence of a resource management mechanism that has the capability to register and discover resources and services in a self-configured, dynamic, and an efficient way.

Some of the technologies that are currently available in the IoT device discovery space are discussed below.

Bluetooth Beacons

They have become very prominent in most of the smart phones and tablets nowadays. This is how they work:

- A beacon device sends out a signal consisting of a unique identifier, which belongs to that particular beacon. No response or signal is sent from the user's device back to the beacon.
- If a user has turned on Bluetooth in his mobile device, the mobile device can receive nearby beacon signals. When an app in the user's mobile device recognizes the ID of a beacon, it can trigger a notification or take any other course of action.
- If Bluetooth is turned off in user's mobile device, beacons are not detected.

Wi-Fi Aware

This is a planned update to Wi-Fi that would add all beacon-like features for discovering and establishing connection with nearby devices. This feature works very similar to a beacon and will allow a user's smart phone to act as both a broadcaster and a receiver by allowing other smart phone users to discover and connect to it in order to share updates, photos, play games, and for several other purposes. Wi-Fi alliance will start certifying devices for this new feature addition soon, and this feature is expected to be available in mobile devices by the year 2016.

Physical Web

This is a project that was started by Google's Chrome development team. This is how the product is expected to work on completion [1]:

- Devices broadcast beacon-like signals that contain a URL.
- The operating system of user's mobile device will have specific software that will have the capability to detect physical web signals that will appear in their mobile devices such as search results. Mobile device users can tap the link if they want to access content present in that device.
- User's mobile devices will be able to scan for physical web signals only when the device is in use.
- The physical web is protocol-agnostic. The current prototype implementation uses BLE signals, but it could be adapted to use Wi-Fi aware or other signal types as well.

Open Hybrid

With open hybrid, it is possible to directly map a digital interface to a physical object. By doing this, it is never required for a user to memorize any drop down menu or app. With the help of hybrid editor, it is possible to approach an object and interact directly with its mapped user interface. Using this feature, it is possible to interact with objects or spaces that you have never accessed before. It is never a requirement to memorize how things are connected or how an application runs using the various menu options present in it [1].

Shazam

Shazam was launched in 2002 and it was an automated, text message-based system. It is a mobile app whose main capability is to identify music by just taking over a device's microphone for few seconds. This concept is now being expanded to identify digital content that is associated with all types of real world objects and experiences. Following are some of the additional planned features to Shazam:

- Ability to identify audio content present in TV shows and movie theater
- Capability to connect to Bluetooth beacons
- Ability to detect ultrasonic signals from advertisement displays
- Ability to read tags that are embedded in print content

Chirp

Chirp is a software that allows devices to communicate with the help of brief melodic tweedles. Chirp app has a software development kit that allows it to run on Arduino and Spark Core apart

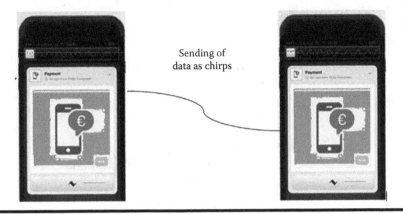

Sending of
data as chirps

Figure 3.14 Working of chirp.

from iOS and Android operating systems. Chirp allows devices that lack traditional network connections to create an Internet made of sound.

How Chirp Works

- Chirp contains a short string of data, which has been encoded using alphabets of electronic birdsong that includes 32 semitone pitches.
- Encoding and decoding of data are done locally by each mobile device, and hence it is not necessary to have an Internet connection for basic exchange. What is required is just a speaker to send data and a microphone to receive data.
- Instead of splitting huge amounts of data into chirps, there exists an option for the device to upload files to a cloud server and then tweet out a URL that will contain chirps.
- Chirps are highly reliable over short distances in locations that are quiet without much of background noise (Figure 3.14).

Protocols for IoT Service Discovery

The protocols that are prominently used in the IoT service discovery space are the following:

- DNS service discovery (DNS-SD)
- multicast domain name system (mDNS)
- Simple service discovery protocol (part of UPnP)

multicast Domain Name System (mDNS)

Multicast Domain Name System (mDNS) is a service that can work like a unicast DNS server. This approach is very flexible because of the fact that DNS namespace can be used locally without any additional configuration. mDNS is an apt choice for embedded Internet-based devices because of the following reasons:

- No manual configuration or administration is required to manage devices.
- It is possible to run this without any additional infrastructure.
- High level of fault tolerance because of the capability to function even if infrastructure failure happens.

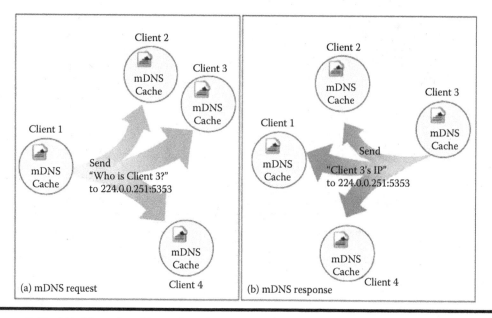

Figure 3.15 Working of multicast domain name system (mDNS).

A service of IoT that wants to use service discovery using mDNS first inquires names by sending an IP multicast message to all the nodes that are present in the local domain. This message is a query, using which the client asks the devices with a specific name to respond back. When the target device receives a message, which contains its name, it sends a multicast response message that contains its IP address. All devices that are a part of the network update their local cache with the target device's name and corresponding IP address that can be used for service request at a later point in time (Figure 3.15).

DNS Service Discovery

This protocol helps the clients to discover a set of desired services that are present in a network with the help of standard DNS messages. This protocol also helps to connect devices without any external administration or configuration. DNS service discovery (DNS-SD) typically uses mDNS to send DNS packets to specific multicast destinations using UDP. Service discovery is a two-step process:

1. Finding host names of required services (in the example given below, it is a printer service)
2. Pairing IP addresses with their host names using mDNS

It is very critical to find host names of devices because IP addresses may change, whereas host names will not change. The pairing function multicasts network related details like IP address and port number to each related host in the same network. With the help of DNS-SD, the host names of the devices in the network can be kept constant so that the same host name can be used later on without decrease of trust and reliability.

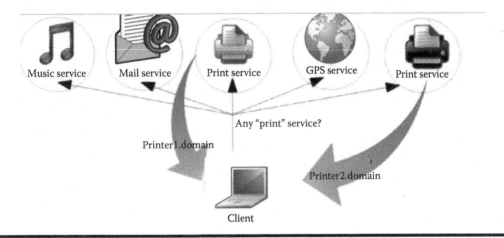

Figure 3.16 Service discovery of a printer service using DNS-SD protocol.

The example given in Figure 3.16 illustrates service discovery of a printer service using DNS-SD protocol.

Universal Plug and Play

Universal Plug and Play (UPnP) is a collection of networking protocols that was devised by UPnP forum. The main features of UPnP that makes it suitable for service discovery of IoT devices are the following:

- Capability of a UPnP device to join a network dynamically (automatically) and obtain IP addresses of other devices and at the same time convey its capabilities to other devices
- Zero configuration and administration

The three basic components of a UPnP network are the following:

- Devices
- Services
- Control points
    - *Device*: It is a container for services and other nested devices, which are part of the network. A service basically is the most granular unit of control that offers a set of actions.
    - *Control points*: This provides the feature of device discovery and control by receiving device and service descriptions and by invoking service actions.
    - *Services*: The set of services that are offered by UPnP devices.

The protocol that offers service discovery feature for a UPnP network is the simple service discovery protocol (SSDP). SSDP is based on multicast-based discovery of devices that form a part of the network.

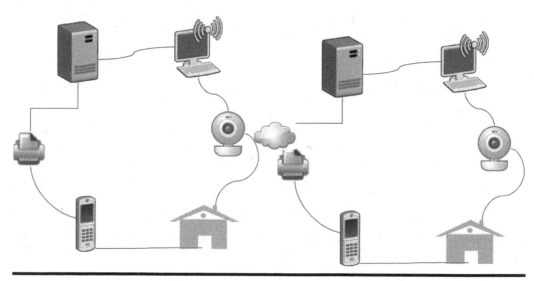

Figure 3.17   Working of UPnP.

The SSDP lets a control point look for devices and services, and it also allows a device to announce its availability. A UPnP control point sends an SSDP search request in order to discover devices and services that are available on a specific network. A UPnP device in turn listens to the multicast port.

Remote access feature of UPnP networks enables a remote UPnP device or UPnP control point to connect home or any other small business network to interact with a UPnP device or control point that is present in another home or small business network. This remote access support and flexible connectivity options offered by the UPnP make it very suitable for service discovery and interconnection of multiple IoT networks.

A typical example is depicted in the graphic shown in Figure 3.17 where two gateway devices connect two home or small business networks to the Internet through an access network and establishes a remote connection with a remote network using a public Internet backbone and through the gateway that is located in the remote network.

Prominent IoT Service Discovery Products Available in the Market

Bonjour

Bonjour is a suite of zero-configuration networking and service discovery protocols from Apple. Bonjour's networking architecture provides features that help to publish and discover TCP or IP-based services that are available in a Local Area Network and WAN. For example, Bonjour will help to connect a printer to a network without having to assign an IP address to it. Because of the zero configuration feature provided by Bonjour, computers can automatically discover the printer's IP address. Mobile apps can also leverage the services of Bonjour to detect presence of other app instance on the network. For example, two users who are using an iOS photo sharing app can share photos using Bluetooth without the need for manual configuration of IP addresses. Bonjour supports advertising and discovery services in a network using mDNS and link local addressing if required.

Consul

Consul is a service discovery product from Hashi Corp. Following are the key features of Consul:

- Health discovery of services
- Key or value store for dynamic configuration of services
- Support for multi data center integration with any additional layers of abstraction

Basic Architecture of Consul

Every node that is expected to provide Consul services runs a Consul agent. Consul agent is not required for service discovery; it is only required for health checking of services on the node. The consul servers store data. Components of an infrastructure that need to discover the services present in the network can query either consul servers or consul agent.

AllJoyn

The main challenge in the setup of IoT infrastructure is that many devices can communicate only with other devices from the same manufacturer or with only their manufacturer's private clouds. The AllSeen Alliance launched an open source framework called AllJoyn in order to overcome these challenges and limitations that are imposed by the IoT system. All the devices that are operating in the AllJoyn framework can share data irrespective of their manufacturer, brand, operating system, and other technical specifications. The AllJoyn framework helps devices and apps to advertise and discover each other in the network.

The two components of the AllJoyn framework are AllJoyn apps and AllJoyn routers (also called as apps and routers). Apps communicate with routers and vice versa. Apps can only communicate with other apps in the network by sending their request through a router (Figure 3.18).

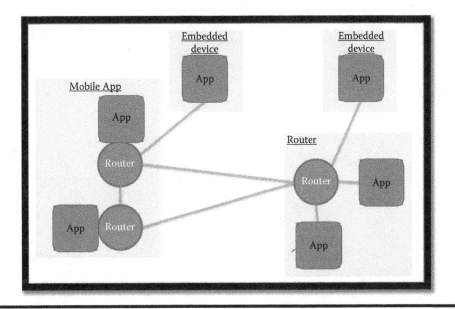

Figure 3.18   Communication of AllJoyn.

HUAWEI LiteOS

LiteOS is the world's most lightweight IoT OS that was announced in March 2015 by Huawei Technologies. It is extremely light weight in size (10KB) and provides zero configuration, autodiscovery, and autonetworking features to devices in the IoT ecosystem. It can be widely used and applied to various IoT application areas like smart homes, wearable, connected vehicles, and other IoT use cases. The LiteOS simplifies the development of hardware to enhance IoT connectivity [2].

Conclusion

There is no standard reference architecture for IoT. There are several architectures in place as perceived by different organizations. We have attempted to define architecture at the start of this chapter. The rest of this chapter uses this reference architecture to define the protocols that work in each layer of the IoT ecosystem. The architecture that was defined by us has five different layers:

- Objects layer
- Object abstraction layer
- Service management layer
- Application layer
- Business layer

We have tried to map the objects layer and object abstraction layer to the infrastructure layer of the IoT ecosystem. This layer contains the devices and other components that form a part of the IoT ecosystem. We have tried to define the key protocols that are used in the infrastructure layer.

It is very important for IoT devices to discover and talk to each other. This concept is called service discovery. The important service discovery protocols that are used in the IoT context are also explained in this chapter. Finally, we have tried to conclude the chapter by describing the service discovery products that are available in the market.

References

1. http://postscapes.com/iot-device-discovery.
2. http://pr.huawei.com/en/news/hw-432402-agilenetwork3.0.htm#.Vn-zsEal0Rl.

Chapter 4

The Integration Technologies and Tools for IoT Environments

Abstract: The technologically inspired capability of instrumenting and interconnecting computationally powerful as well as resource-constrained devices (physical, mechanical, electrical, and electronics) with one another in the vicinity as well as with cloud-hosted software applications and data sources over any network is to enable the devices to exhibit a kind of shrewdness in their operations and outputs. Not only everyday instruments, machines, appliances, wares, utensils, equipment, and so on but also common, cheap, and casual articles such as cots, chairs, cups, tables, pipes, doors, sofas, and windows in our personal, professional, and social environments are being technically tuned and turned to exhibit hitherto unforeseen smart behavior and to join in the mainstream computing. Further, the environments wherein those embedded yet empowered devices are being deployed in large numbers ultimately become smart in their contributions for the occupants and owners of the environment.

These transitions are being enabled through the systematic leverage of hugely powerful edge technologies such as disposable and diminutive sensors, actuators, chips, controllers, codes, stickers, pads, tags, labels, speck, and smart dust. That is, the aura and era of the Internet of things (IoT) have started to beckon and dawn on us powerfully with the overwhelming use of promising, proven, and potential technologies. Our living, working, social, edutainment, and entertainment places are being systematically decked and demonstrated to be lively and lovely. The methodical adoption and adaptation of scores of digitization and distribution technologies are to bring a series of disruptions and transformations in our lives. The much-anticipated digital living, economy, and world are bound to see the light at the end of the long tunnel.

The capabilities such as connectivity, networking, communication, integration, and orchestration of digital elements, devices, and IT systems are imperative to seamlessly share their unique capabilities and capacities. In this chapter, we are extensively covering the connectivity technologies, topologies and tools, and their contributions for setting up and sustaining smarter environments (smarter homes, hospitals, hotels, etc.), and ultimately the smarter planet.

Introduction

As per various reports being released by market watchers, analysts, and researchers, by the year 2020, the Internet is to host and deliver millions of software applications and services. Also, billions of connected devices and trillions of digitized entities are to get hooked with the Internet. It all began like this. Millions of computers (servers, desktops, and laptops) have been networked in a standardized manner to form the Internet for sharing each one's unique features and functionalities. Currently all kinds of handy and trendy, and slim and sleek, multifaceted devices such as smartphones, household utensils, consumer electronics, and machines are being attached to the Internet. With this continued addition, the size of the Internet is definitely bound to grow, but the significance of the present day Internet for the humanity is also steadily growing. The future is for web-enabling all kinds of concrete and tangible things. That is, the brewing trend is digitizing ordinary things in our daily environments to make them a valuable partner in the future Internet.

As a first step, all kinds of industrial machines, sensors, actuators, and controllers are attached to the Internet, thereby strongly kicking in the era of industrial Internet. Further, all kinds of personal, social, and professional gadgets and gizmos are accordingly empowered to join on the Internet. With the availability of deeper and extreme connectivity technologies and tools, every worthwhile thing in our midst is to get linked up with the Internet. The results are going to be simply mesmerizing for the whole world especially in sharply enhancing care, choice, convenience, and comfort for people. That is, the era of the IoT or the Internet of everything (IoE) or the industry Internet or the Internet of important things (IoIT) is to arrive soon in realizing a bevy of smart and sophisticated applications for people.

It is an overwhelmingly accepted statement that the fast-emerging and evolving IoT idea is definitely a strategic and highly impactful vision to be decisively and deftly realized and passionately sustained with the smart adaptation and adoption of cutting-edge technologies, the state-of-the-art infrastructures, synchronized processes, integrated platforms, enabling tools, enabling patterns, key metrics and guidelines, best practices, innovative products, industry-strength standards, and futuristic architectures. Industry professionals and academic professors are constantly looking out for appropriate use, business, and technical cases in order to confidently and cogently proclaim the transformational value and power of the IoT concept to the larger audience of worldwide executives, end users, entrepreneurs, evangelists, and engineers.

A growing array of open standards is being formulated, framed, and polished by domain experts, industry consortiums, and standard bodies to make the IoT idea more visible, viable, and valuable. National governments across the globe are setting up special expert groups in order to come out with pragmatic policies and procedures to take forward the solemn and sublime ideals of IoT, and to realize the strategic significance of the IoT paradigm in conceiving, concretizing, and providing a bevy of context-aware and citizen-centric services to ensure and enhance peoples' living. Research students, scholars, and scientists are working collaboratively toward identifying the implementation challenges and overcoming them via different means and ways, especially standards-sticking technological solutions. This chapter is specially crafted to throw light on the emerging integration tools and techniques in order to integrate and orchestrate digitized and connected entities and elements. You can find more details on the following integration scenarios:

1. Sensor and actuator networks
2. Device-to-device (D2D) integration
3. Cloud-to-cloud (C2C) integration
4. Device and sensor-to-cloud (D2C) integration

IoT Communication Protocol Requirements

One definition of IoT is connecting devices to the Internet that were not previously connected. A factory owner may connect high-powered lights. A triathlete may connect a battery-powered heart-rate monitor. A home or building automation provider may connect a wireless sensor with no line power source. But the important thing here is that in all the above cases the *thing* must communicate through the Internet to be considered an *IoT* node. Since it must use the Internet, it must also adhere to the Internet engineering task force (IETF) Internet Protocol Suite. However, the Internet has historically connected resource-rich devices with lots of power, memory, and connection options. As such, its protocols have been considered too heavy to apply wholesale applications in the emerging IoT.

There are other aspects of the IoT that also drive modifications to IETF's work. In particular, networks of IoT end nodes will be lossy, and the devices attached to them will be very low power, saddled with constrained resources, and expected to live for years. The requirements for both the network and its end devices might look like Table 4.1. This new model needs new, lighter weight protocols that do not require a large amount of resources.

Considering these unique needs, gaining a deeper knowledge of IoT connectivity and data transmission protocols is paramount. This chapter is specifically crafted for that.

Table 4.1 The IoT Devices Networking Requirements

IoT End Network Requirements	Networking Style Impact
Self-healing/scalable	Mesh capable
Secure	Scalable to no, low, medium, and high security without overburdening clients
End-node addressability	Device-specific addressing scalable to thousands of nodes
Device Requirements	*Messaging Protocal Impact*
Low power/battery-operated	Lightweight connection, preamble, packet
Limited memory	Small client footprint, persistant state in case of overflow
Low cost	Ties to memory footprint

The IoT Portion for Smarter Enterprises and Environments

The IoT concept is an intellectual and inspirational idea gaining immense momentum these days as it has the inbuilt power to bring pathbreaking benefits for us. With the implementation technologies and tools being unearthed and sustained by worldwide product vendors and research professionals collectively and cognitively, the days of the IoT era is all set to beckon the world decisively. Apart from the people empowerment, the raging IoT paradigm is gripping every kind of industry verticals. Industry experts and business executives are very keen to embrace the IoT advancements in order to be ahead of their competitors. The national governments are strategizing viable and value-adding strategies and plans in order to bring forth spectacular and sparkling benefits to their constituents and citizens. The social implications are being systematically expounded in order to articulate the IoT-sponsored advantages for the human society. Thus, every segment, sector, and situation in our everyday life is to get sagacious benefits with the faster maturity and stability of IoT technologies, platforms, infrastructures, and services. The personal as well as professional lives are to be impacted significantly in the days ahead with the surging popularity, pervasiveness, and persuasiveness of the IoT paradigm. All kinds of industry verticals are to be transformative and disruptive with the adoption of the pragmatic advancements and innovations happening in the IoT field.

Worldwide enterprises yearn for remarkable and resilient transformations on two major aspects: business operation model and business information leverage. Another vital point not to be lightly taken is to sharply enhance the user experience of business offerings. It is an overwhelmingly accepted statement that the desired enterprise transformation happens through the following five tasks:

- Infrastructure optimization
- Process excellence
- Architecture assimilation
- Technology adaption and adoption
- Leveraging data (internal as well as external) for deriving insights

For smarter enterprises and environments, the role and the responsibility of the IoT technologies and tools are really immense and incredible.

The Growing Importance of the IoT Paradigm

The ensuing era of IoT is to play a very stellar role in shaping up our everyday environments. The IoT concept is an engrossing and essential disruption for everyone in this extremely connected world. In this section, we are to discuss the prime and paramount shifts sweeping the entire human society. It is an important point to note that there are a number of noteworthy technology-induced transitions happening in the IT field.

The Meteoric Rise of Device Ecosystem

With innumerable devices, sensors, controllers, and actuators getting fervently deployed in distributed and decentralized fashion in important locations such as offices, manufacturing floors, retail stores, food joints, shopping plazas, nuclear installations, forest and border areas, critical junctions, malls, and entertainment centers, the amount of data getting generated and collected goes up tremendously. The machine-generated data are far larger than man-generated data.

The device ecosystem is embracing a bevy of miniaturization technologies to be slim and sleek, yet smart in their operations, outlooks, and outputs. That is, multifaceted devices are hitting the market in plenty. For example, highly miniaturized yet mesmerizing smartphones are being produced in millions these days. Smartphones are not only connecting people with people but also turning out to be capable of operating machines locally as well as remotely.

Digitization and distribution are gaining a lot of ground nowadays, thereby all kinds of tangible items in our home, social, and office environments are getting transfigured to be computational, communicative, sensitive, perceptive, capable of knowledge discovery and dissemination, decision-enabling, and accomplishing. That is, ordinary articles become extraordinary. Casually found objects in our working, walking, and wandering places become digitized. Thus, IT-enabled things are cognitive enough to seamlessly and spontaneously join in the mainstream computing process. In short, every tangible thing gets emboldened to be smart, every electronics becomes smarter, and every human being is set to become the smartest in his or her actions, reactions, and decision-making with the pervasive, unceasing, and unobtrusive assistance of service-oriented and smartness-ingrained devices, game consoles, media players, consumer electronics, business as well as IT services and communication networks.

Extreme and deeper connectivity is another well-known phenomenon in order to establish and sustain ad hoc connectivity among dissimilar and distributed devices to share their unique capabilities. Further, it is all about the purposeful integration with remote, off-premise, on-demand, and online applications. These days, devices are accordingly instrumented in the factory itself to collect or generate data from their environments and users to be transmitted to centralized control systems, that is, lately, devices are empowered by embedding a number of newer modules internally. In addition, devices are enabled to connect with outside world.

The Dazzling Growth of Operational and Transactional Systems

With the continued penetration of IT into every aspect of human living, the number of business and IT systems automating and accelerating business operations is growing steadily. This is bound to result in a huge amount of log, performance or throughput metrics, security attacks, and transaction data.

Deeper and Decisive Data Analytics

The above-mentioned fifth aspect is gaining a lot of ground these days with the faster maturity and stability of data management and analytics solutions and services. At the fundamental and foundation level, a variety of nimbler technologies and tips are evolving in order to bring in delectable transformations in data capture, representation, transmission, enrichment, storage, processing, analysis, mining, visualization, and virtualization tasks. The reasons for the swelling popularity of data science and engineering are articulated below for the benefit of readers.

Data become big, fast, streaming, and IoT data due to multiple transformations such as newer data sources are emerging. Data collection and transmission technologies are maturing, data storage and management systems are flourishing, and above all, there is a greater awareness and realization that data bring forth actionable insights. Not only the data volume but also the data velocity, viscosity, variability, and variety are seeing a remarkable climb. As the tactical as well as the strategical value of data is growing, the field of data science, engineering, management, and analytics has grown considerably nowadays.

The Emergence of Pioneering Analytics (*Generic as well as Specific*)

The IT infrastructures, platforms, processes, patterns, programming languages, middleware solutions, and databases are getting spruced up for the ensuing challenge of multistructured and massive data. There are deep learning and knowledge engineering algorithms coming up fluently to speed up the process of knowledge discovery and dissemination. With these advancements, there are newer analytical capabilities such as diagnostic, predictive, prescriptive, and personalized analytics. Real-time analysis is another interesting development enabling a variety of newer possibilities through a nice and neat realization of actionable insights in time with the emergence of centralized and even federated cloud infrastructures.

State-of-the-Art Data Science Tools

There are powerful algorithms and tools for empowering data scientists in scanning data and spitting out useful information quickly. The language R is turning out to be a powerful paradigm in helping data scientists immensely. Data mining and statistical computing algorithms, text analytics, natural language processing (NLP), deep learning, cognitive computing, and various mathematical concepts come handy in facilitating fine-tuned and personalized data analysis.

A family of futuristic and flexible architectural paradigms, patterns, and principles such as service-oriented architecture (SOA), event-driven architecture (EDA), model-driven architecture (MDA), resource-oriented architecture (ROA), and microservices architecture (MSA) has arrived to consume data-driven insights, and to build sophisticated systems.

The much-discussed and discoursed *cloudification* is bringing forth high optimization and organization to ICT infrastructures, thereby clouds are being touted as the one-stop IT solution for all the needs of people in the days ahead.

According to IT experts, there will be a seamless and spontaneous merger of everyday technologies to create a kind of technology cluster to fulfill our personal as well as professional requirements instantly and instinctively. That is, there comes the possibility of the transparent merging of our minds with machines. Learning will be everywhere and every time affair because we will have intimate and real-time access to the world's information assets and knowledge base using any of our accompanying electronic gizmos, and on the reverse side, we will have an unfailing backup of our brains on massive-scale digital storages. Massive research endeavors and efforts are concertedly put into these seemingly magical and leading-edge technology themes, which will let to connect our nervous systems to computers beneficially in the days ahead.

In summary, disruptive and transformative technologies with the smart synchronization of a galaxy of information and communication technologies will emerge to realize revolutionary applications and to accomplish hitherto unheard social networking and digital knowledge societies. Auto-identification tags carrying our personal profile and preferences digitally will map, mix, merge, and mingle with others in the realization of novel human aspirations. Our daily tools and products can be converted into smart products by attaching ultrasmall computers. For example, our coffee cups, dinner plates, tablets, and clothes will be empowered to act smart in their operations and interactions with other products in the vicinity and with the human beings. Finally, all the tangible and worthy things, objects, materials, and articles will be transitioned into smart and sentient digital artifacts. This will lead to the endearing IoT era in the decades to come. There is hence no doubt that future generations will experience and enjoy complete and compact digital and technology-enabled living. The impact of IT in our life becomes bigger, deeper, yet calmer as days go by. The IoT layered architecture is shown in Figure 4.1.

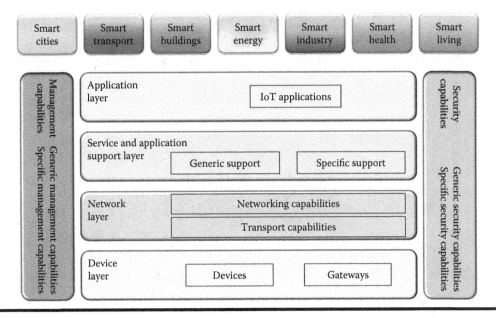

Figure 4.1 The IoT reference architecture. (From ITU Telecommunication Standardization Sector, http://www.itu.int/en/ITU-T/Pages/default.aspx.)

IoT has direct and decisive applications in fields such as home, building and industry automation, smarter health care, retail, government, energy, logistics, and cities. Every worthwhile industry domain is getting impacted immensely with the IoT adoption. Having understood that IoT opens up fresh possibilities and new opportunities, IT service providers, independent software vendors (ISVs), system integrators, product vendors, consulting organizations, standard agencies, governments, academic institutions, and other stakeholders are showing exemplary interests and involvements in promoting, proclaiming, and prescribing the IoT paradigm.

Sensor and Actuator Networks

Sensing is tending to be ubiquitous. Sensors are being touted as the eyes and ears of next-generation software applications. A number of technologies especially miniaturization, networking, communication, and so on are contributing immensely to the unprecedented success of the sensing paradigm. Sensors are becoming exceptionally tiny to be easily disposable, disappearing, and yet elegantly deft. Therefore, sensors, which are typically low-cost, power, and memory systems, are gradually and graciously penetrative, pervasive, and persuasive. Sensors are becoming smart in the sense that they are able to conserve and preserve their battery energy in order to prolong their lives. Smart sensors are capable of buffering and transmitting the data captured or generated. Sensors are increasingly complying with the mesh topology toward increased maneuverability and reliability. Sensors are mainly for environmental and asset monitoring. All kinds of physical, mechanical, electrical, electronics, and IT systems are being fitted with a variety of sensors for monitoring, measuring, and managing various aspects, conditions, and situations of the systems. For example, all kinds of vehicles and their body parts are being fitted with smart sensors in order to proactively and preemptively attend their needs in time so that any kind of collapse and failure can be prevented. Smartphones are being embedded with numerous sensors. Even large-scale IT

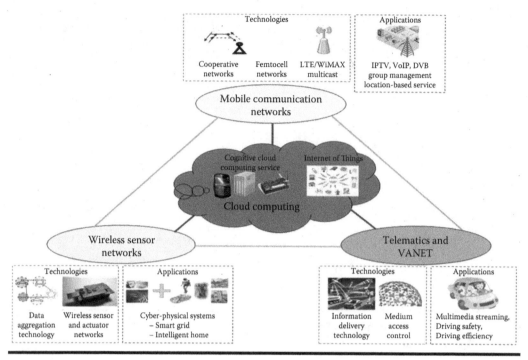

Figure 4.2 Networks of networks of sensors and actuators.

data centers and server farms are being sensor-enabled in order to capture their operational values. Figure 4.2 vividly illustrates how sensors, electronics, mobiles, and so on are being networked together to collect data to be deposited in central repositories for posterior processing.

Thus, sensors are very vital for our everyday environments especially rough and tough ones. Sensors are being networked toward taking data from sensors to remote control systems. There are data fusion algorithms in plenty in order to dynamically capture and aggregate various sensor values to come out with composite indicators. Further, there are ways and mechanisms being prescribed in order to eliminate all kinds of sensor data impurities, deviations, deficiencies, and disturbances so that the primary needs of data trustworthiness and timeliness are being fulfilled. Increasingly sensor data are subjected to a litany of investigations in order to squeeze out valuable intelligence for taking informed decisions in time. There is a growing array of sensor-centric data transmission protocols. Further, sensor data modeling is an interesting phenomenon.

There are industry-strength data formats for unique and unambiguous representation, exchange and persistence, and interpretation. The list of sensor-centric software services is steadily growing. Sensor gateways, middleware, brokers, adaptors, connectors, drivers, and controllers are being leveraged in order to collect and transmit sensor data. There are frameworks and platforms to speed up the process of sensor-cloud integration so that sensor data can be accumulated in one centralized place to enable cloud-based data analytics. Sensor data and the insights extracted out of it are tactically and strategically sound for various service providers. Thought-provoking industry, personal, and social use cases are being published with the continued growth and adoption of the sensor technology. Actuation is generally based on sensing, and hence, actuators and sensors go hand in hand. Actuators are the ones that accomplish the execution based on the sensor findings.

Sensors and actuators are therefore the essential ingredients for any environment to be smart. Actuators are designed in such a way to receive sensor values and act strictly based on that. Thus, networking of sensors and actuators turns out to be an important affair for setting and sustaining smarter environments. Clouds are the most sought-after IT infrastructures for hosting sensor-specific platforms and applications. As sensor data analytics is crucial for formulating sophisticated and people-centric applications, sensor data analytics platforms are increasingly deployed in clouds.

The pragmatic use cases out of sensor networks are emerging and evolving. A wireless sensor network (WSN) is a network formed by a large number of sensor nodes where each node is equipped with a sensor to detect different physical phenomena such as light, heat, pressure, presence, and gas. WSNs are regarded as a revolutionary information gathering method to build next-generation people-centric IoT applications. There are several research papers depicting the growing and glowing sensor applications in the peer-reviewed sensor journals (http://www.hindawi.com/journals/js/ and http://www.mdpi.com/journal/sensors).

Body sensor networks (BSNs) are also very popular challenges related to IoT. BSNs are to improve the quality of life and for providing ambient assisted living (AAL) facility. BSNs ensure improved health care of disabled, debilitated, and diseased people. Also, they improve our daily routines such as playing sports. The distributed and changeable character of BSNs introduces new concerns and challenges to solve. As per experts, the research in the area of BSNs must cover low-level hardware design to higher level communication and data fusion algorithms, up to top-level applications.

Sensor-to-Cloud Integration

Sensor and actuator data need to be taken to nearby or faraway clouds for storage and analytics. There are multiple cloud options ranging from off-premise, on-premise, and to edge clouds. Public clouds are typically for historical, comprehensive, and batch processing whereas interactive, stream, and real-time processing in a secure fashion are better accomplished by edge or fog clouds wherein proximate or local processing gets done comfortably. Edge or fog clouds are being formed dynamically by clubbing and clustering together several resource-intensive devices in the particular environment. Connected devices are bound to produce futuristic fog clouds as there is a lot of interest in real-time analytics for gathering tactical and timely insights. Figure 4.3 depicts the sensor-to-cloud integration through IoT middleware or gateway. Increasingly IoT application enablement platforms (AEPs) situated at cloud environments in association with IoT data analytics platforms are able to receive ground-level data and work on it to carve out pragmatic intelligence.

Typically there can be three layers and levels for enabling data to be carried over to clouds to be crunched accordingly as illustrated in Figure 4.4.

There are several unique advantages being associated with clouds these days. Cloud environments are being positioned and prescribed as the best-in-class IT infrastructure for sensor data storage and analytics. Cloud infrastructures inherently support IT resource elasticity, application or workload scalability, and so on through IT consolidation, centralization, federation, sharing, automation, and virtualization techniques and tools. Geographically established clouds are getting integrated through standards and brokers, thereby distributed resource and service orchestration get facilitated with just a single click. Data virtualization and information visualization platforms are seamlessly integrated with data analytics platforms to speed up the transition from data to actionable insights that get disseminated to machines as well as men in time to proceed with the accurate actuation and execution with clarity and confidence.

In summary, everyday objects are being equipped by embedding and imbedding sensors to gain the communication capability. This will create a range of potentially powerful and promising

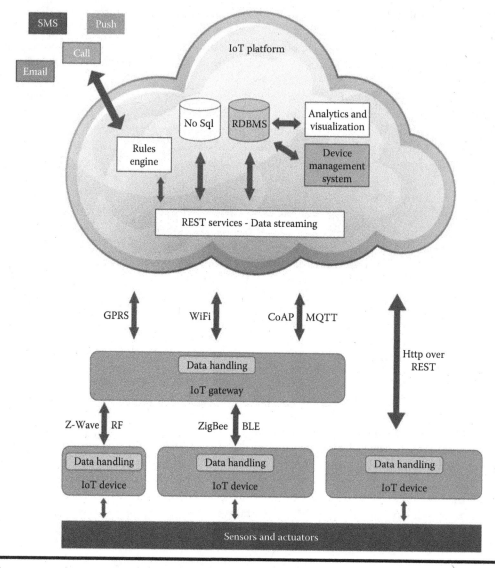

Figure 4.3 The passaging architecture for sensor and actuator data to cloud.

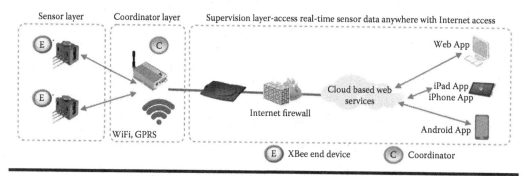

Figure 4.4 The layered architecture for sensor-to-cloud integration.

services in many different domains. Fire, flame, and fall detection procedures are automated through the employment of several sorts of sensors. Similarly, there are multiple scenarios being identified and articulated well for sensor and actuator networking. Thus, the fact that sensors are talking to local as well as remote sensors, actuators, and applications collectively as well as individually is going to be a real game-changer for the forthcoming IoT world.

The IoT Device Integration Concepts, Standards, and Implementations

There are several standards for device integration, especially for consumer and industry devices. That is, these standards are compactly and constantly optimized toward integrating a wide variety of distributed, decentralized, and disparate devices. However, the ultimate target is to establish smarter environments that readily link cross domain automation modules [home, building and industry automation, manufacturing execution systems (MES), cyber-physical systems (CPS), health care instruments, media players, Internet gateways, consumer electronics, kitchen utensils, appliances, manufacturing machines, defense equipment, vehicles, robots, sensor and actuator networks, personal digital assistants, energy grids, etc.]. Initially, industrial machinery was chosen for internal as well as external communication and integration considering their unique value propositions toward industry automation.

Machine-to-Machine Communication

Machine-to-machine (M2M) uses a device (sensor, meter, etc.) to capture an *event* (temperature, inventory level, etc.), which is relayed through a network (wireless, wired, or hybrid) to an application (software program) that translates the captured event into a meaningful information (e.g., items need to be restocked). With the availability of implementation technologies, a large number of intelligent machines sharing information and making decisions without direct human intervention is getting realized.

The M2M applications are varied and vast:

- Physical and homeland security through connected security and surveillance cameras, alarm systems, and access control
- *Object tracking and tracing*: Fleet management, supply chain management, order management, asset tracking and management, road tolling, and traffic optimization or steering
- Automated payment through the integrated point of sales (PoS), vending machines, gaming consoles, integrated dashboards, and so on
- Smarter health care through continuous monitoring vital signs, ambient assisted living (AAL), telemedicine, remote diagnostics, and so on
- Remote diagnostics or maintenance or control of machines, sensors, and actuators, lighting, pumps, valves, elevators, roadside vending machines, transport vehicles, and so on
- Advanced metering infrastructure (AMI) for power, gas, water, heating, grid control, industrial metering, and so on
- Industry automation through production chain monitoring and automation
- Home or building or campus networking and automation
- Mobile enablement for machine operations

There are a number of protocols for enabling machines connecting and corresponding with one another. Machine data are getting captured and communicated to centralized control and analytical systems to squeeze and spit out insights that can be used for subsequent decision-making and appropriate actuation. Cloud-based machine-centric services can be dynamically downloaded, installed on various ground-level machines to empower them to behave adaptively and adroitly. Thus, machine connectivity brings forth an assortment of newer capabilities and capacities for machines and people.

Service Oriented Device Architecture for Device Integration

SOA has been a successful and sagacious architectural style, approach, and pattern for designing and developing next-generation enterprise-scale distributed systems. SOAs are often used to improve flexibility and reusability of components in complex distributed applications. This is achieved by modeling functional blocks as independent and self-sufficient services. There are several standards fast emerging and evolving fully subscribing to the game-changing SOA paradigm. There are around 50 well-established web services (WS) standards to realize new-generation service oriented systems. Generally, the SOA idea is for partitioning monolithic enterprise applications into a dynamic set of easily identifiable, manageable, usable, consumable, and composable services. Every service is bound to expose one or more service interfaces and service implementations, which can be done using any programming language hidden behind interfaces.

Service interfaces are for enabling different services getting identified, matched for, and integrated with one another. Further, multiple services can be systematically composed to create business-aligned and process-aware composite services. Thus, service-based application and process integration is the new normal in enterprise and cloud IT environments. Similarly, there is an integration established between applications and various data sources. Thus, data, applications, systems, and networks are being integrated seamlessly and spontaneously through APIs being expressed and exposed by various services (IT and business).

This phenomenal success is getting replicated for the device space. That is, devices are hidden behind their service interfaces in order to decimate all kinds of barriers and to enable devices talking with one another programmatically. That is, the hugely successful SOA paradigm is being tweaked toward service-oriented device architecture (SODA) to enable service-based device integration. Devices and machines need to be instrumented and interconnected with one another in order to communicate and collaborate to showcase intelligent behavior. Device integration empowers devices to share their unique service capabilities with one another. Service requests and responses are getting fulfilled through SODA. Data and event messages can be transmitted over any network among devices to activate one another to accomplish the desired tasks. Further, devices can be linked up with applications and data sources hosted in web and cloud environments. Thereby devices can be activated over the Internet communication infrastructure remotely. Remote monitoring, measurement, management, and maintenance of various devices deployed in mission-critical and disaster-stricken environments get simplified and streamlined through software infrastructure solutions that are stringently complying with the SODA specifications and standards. That is, the Internet of devices (IoD) paradigm is steadily seeing the reality. Finally, web-enabled devices are being designed and manufactured in large quantities and sent out to the market. For example, web-enabled refrigerators are already hitting the market.

SODA is an emerging concept for the device world. There are several standards such as DPWS, OSGi, RESTful services, and OPC fulfilling the SODA idea.

An Illuminating Use Case

As expressly indicated above, the device variety and volume are on the consistent climb (Figure 4.5). Freshly designed devices are hitting the market in large quantities these days. A sample pictorial representation of smart homes illustrating different devices with specific capabilities is given below. A range of devices-enabled use cases is also indicated in the picture. For example, the use case of motion detection is for enabling lighting for people who are entering into a hall or room within the home. Similarly, if any unknown person enters into the house, immediately the security alarm will go off reminding the security personnel to plan and proceed with authority to mitigate any kind of incursion-induced damages to people as well as properties.

Let us start with the device profile for web services (DPWS) standard.

However, IoT systems containing a huge number of devices, in contrast to small numbers in industrial and home applications, cause some features of DPWS such as dynamic discovery and publish or subscribe eventing, impossible in a global and mass deployment of devices. It is, therefore, necessary to extend DPWS to fit IoT scenarios with several problems to be resolved before DPWS can successfully arrive in the IoT domain.

Use case: In the new ecosystem of networked devices, many IoT platforms are provided to build a new generation of web-based applications aggregating these services. Peter, an IoT user, chooses a DPWS platform for his web-based home automation system. He would like to make a module for controlling a newly purchased DPWS heater. The heater is equipped with a temperature sensor, a switch, memory, a processor, and networking media, and is implemented with a hosted heater service. Heater service consists of seven operations: (1) check the heater status (GetStatus), (2) switch the heater on or off (SetStatus), (3) get room temperature (GetTemperature), (4) adjust the heater temperature (SetTemperature), (5) add (AddRule), (6) remove (RemoveRule), and (7) get (GetRules) available policy rules for defining the automatic operation of the heater. Peter connects the heater to the network and tries to control it from his IoT application. We will follow Peter's development process to understand what challenges he can encounter when developing, deploying, and consuming the device from his IoT application and how the extended DPWS helps him to solve these problems. This use case illustrates a common case in several consumer applications when a new device joins the network.

Device Profile for Web Services

Services provide a standard and interoperable means for M2M communication. The two major classes of services are (1) representational state transfer (REST)-compliant services, in which resources are manipulated using a uniform set of stateless operations, and (2) arbitrary services, which expose an arbitrary set of operations and use SOAP messages. Both strictly go with the SOA architectural pattern.

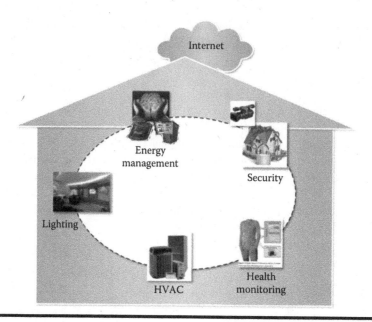

Figure 4.5   A smarter home use case.

DPWS is a device-specific (Lerche et al. 2011) and SODA-compliant standard that comprehensively addresses discovery, description, security, and control of devices and services on local as well as remote networks. Messaging is the connecting mechanism. DPWS defines a set of implementation constraints to provide a secure and effective mechanism for describing, discovering, messaging, and eventing of services for resource-constrained devices. There are two types of services in DPWS: hosting service and hosted service. The former is a special service representing a device to participate in discovery and to describe other services hosted in it. The latter present the functionalities of each device and are called hosted services. DPWS uses SOAP, WS-Addressing, and MTOM/XOP for messaging, and supports SOAP-over-HTTP and SOAP-over-UDP bindings. It uses WS-Discovery for discovering a hosting service (device) and WSDL to describe the hosted service (device service). It uses web services metadata exchange to define metadata about the device, web services policy to define a policy assertion to indicate compliance of the device with DPWS, and WS-Transfer to retrieve service description and metadata information about the device.

DPWS is based on several other WS specifications:

1. WS-Addressing for advanced endpoint and message addressing
2. WS-Policy for policy exchange
3. WS-Security for managing security
4. WS-Discovery and SOAP-over-UDP for device discovery
5. WS-Transfer or WS-Metadataexchange for device and service description
6. WS-Eventing for managing subscriptions for event channels

The widely articulated OSI model for the DPWS standard is given in Figure 4.6.

DPWS is evolving fast in order to facilitate developing device services and for orchestration of composite services that are more tuned to peoples' everyday needs. Not only service-oriented applications but also event-driven applications can be realized with the appropriate leverage of

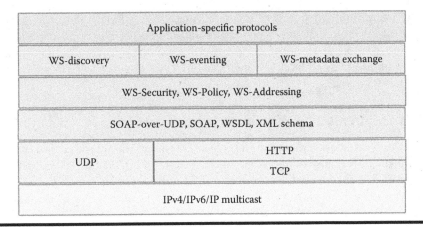

Figure 4.6 The DPWS OSI model.

any one of the DPWS implementations. DPWS is an important component in realizing and sustaining the ideals of the IoT goals.

The DPWS (feverishly promoted by OASIS [https://www.oasis-open.org/standards]) enables the realization of services leveraging both resource-constrained as well as intensive devices. That is, DPWS is contributing incredibly toward having connected devices and digitized objects that are the key causes for nourishing and flourishing the IoT idea. The widely accepted DPWS standard is being positioned as the cornerstone for the realization of service-oriented and event-driven IoT applications on top of any type of devices. Further, the DPWS standard takes care of the integration with web-based applications and services via the open and public Internet communication infrastructure.

About the DPWSim Development Toolkit

As indicated above, DPWS is a widespread standard for service design, development, deployment, and integration for all kinds of devices that are much deviated from typical compute machines. Due to its immensely surging popularity, there came a number of implementations. Especially the European consortium has invested heavily in this promising and potential technology in conceptualizing and concretizing a number of projects to promote the awareness and usage of device integration tools and tips. Those projects could solve many technical problems and successfully released several implementations of DPWS stacks for resource-constrained devices. DPWS is the key technology in several projects under European research and development (R&D) initiatives of Information Technology for European Advancement (ITEA) and Framework Programme (FP) such as ITEA SIRENA, ITEA SODA, FP7 SOCRATES, and FP7 IMC-AESOP. These projects have contributed to the standard specification and successfully released a number of DPWS implementations to foster the adoption of the DPWS technology.

DPWSim (http://sourceforge.net/projects/dpwsim/) is one such simulation toolkit to support building device applications that in turn use the distinctive services being offered by low as well as high-end devices. Devices can be collocated or distributed. There are networking topologies and communication technologies in plenty for the device ecosystem in order to enable different devices participating in constructing and deploying next-generation people-centric device-enabled applications.

DPWSim, which complies with the DPWS standard, allows application developers to prototype, develop, and test their IoT applications without the presence of physical devices. That is,

DOWSim is a simulation environment for mimicking various devices and their capabilities. It can also be used for the collaboration between manufacturers, developers, and designers during the new product development process. DPWSim mimics all the software and protocol features of DPWS under an intuitive graphical user interface (GUI) to provide an efficient way to simulate and manage DPWS devices.

The Reference Architecture for Smarter Hospitals

In this segment, we describe creating a prototype of a smarter hospital and simulating it using DPWSim toolkit. In this hospital design, we have an ICU and many hospital wards. If a critical patient is admitted to the hospital, he is taken to ICU and a request is sent to the head physician to attend the patient with all the urgency. Similarly, if a patient, who is not so critical, is admitted to a hospital, he is taken to a general ward, wherein a general practitioner is requested to attend the patient. Also, if the condition of a patient in general ward becomes critical, he is immediately shifted to an ICU, and an appropriate request is sent to the head physician. If any patient in the hospital needs special care, a nurse or caregiver is instructed to attend the medical needs of the patient. In case, there is a discharge of a patient from the hospital, the room in which the patient was admitted needs to be properly cleaned and janitor is ordered for room cleaning.

In this scenario, there are several devices and sensors talking with one or the other in order to sense what is happening and accordingly actuate other devices to do the right tasks in order to fulfill the health care process. We have published the implementation details via a research paper. DPWSim is the simulation toolkit.

Messaging Methods: Pub or Sub and Point-to-Point

The WS-Eventing specification is a *publish-subscribe (pub or sub)* event-handling protocol (Figure 4.7) that allows consumers to subscribe to one or more topics and be asynchronously

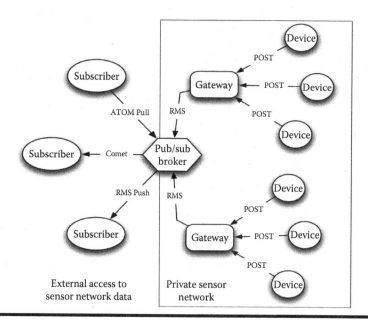

Figure 4.7 The role of pub/sub broker toward device integration.

notified of events generated by a service. This is a simple thing to implement in a service-oriented system. However, the resulting architecture is quite complex. On the other hand is the point-to-point (P2P) mechanism where producers insert their message in a queue, where it is read by only one consumer. A queue may contain more than one consumer, but the message is delivered to only one consumer. This has several advantages over pub or sub as it is more efficient, reliable, and scalable as load balancing between consumers is inherently taken care of. It is especially suitable to transmit large amounts of high-frequency data, and thus, the P2P mechanism is more appropriate to transmit sensor readings. The Java messaging service (JMS) standard specifications prescribe both pub or sub and P2P options for effective messaging. Unfortunately, DPWS does not use a queuing mechanism and supports WS-Eventing.

WS-Eventing is useful for sending data across very different hardware and software platforms. However, the pub or sub method is very inefficient method when implemented on low-power devices. A viable alternative is to use an intermediate machine that does the distribution of events to their subscribers. Any DPWS toolkit should support at least transmitting SOAP-over-UDP messages and support one-way, request-response, and solicit-response message exchange patterns. Further, the underlying Internet protocol (IP) stack must support IP multicast.

Thus, in short, DPWS is the device-centric SOA standard being prescribed for device integration and orchestration. Having stripped of all the flabs, the DPWS standard is made nimble and fit for the growing device ecosystem to build a growing collection of connected and embedded services. There are several DPWS standard implementations. We have talked about only one implementation (DPWSim), which is a simulation toolkit to support the development of next-generation people-centric applications. It has been shown that DPWS is a promising technology to seamlessly integrate device functionalities and events into plenty of services and applications on the web. DPWS thus far has been widely used in the automation industry, home entertainment, and automotive systems.

There are optimized implementations such as device service bus (DSB) for seamlessly integrating and composing different devices and services. That is, DSBs are the stripped down version of enterprise service bus (ESB) platforms. With the number of generic and purpose-specific devices going up remarkably, the device broker or bus or middleware or hub solutions are acquiring special status in establishing seamless linkage among devices to enable them to share their specific capabilities with one another, thereby better and bigger device-centric, cognitive, and context-aware services can be built and delivered to their users instantly.

Node.DPWS: Efficient Web Services for the IoT

Node.js handles network input or output (I/O) operations in an event and nonblocking fashion, whereas file I/O operations are handled asynchronously. In Node.js, each new connection requires only a small heap allocation. Moreover, its executing thread cannot be blocked. That is, in situations such as waiting for data from a remote database, the thread's runtime is smartly utilized for serving other requests. The above feature results in very fast applications, which also scale well, even in the case of resource-constrained devices.

As Node.js intrinsically addresses many of the issues associated with real-time and lightweight application communications, it has quickly gained the support of the worldwide developers' community. Node's characteristics are a good match for event-driven web services deployable on networked and embedded devices expected to be copiously present in our everyday environments in the years ahead. Thus, Node.js has emerged as an attractive solution for implementing the DPWS specification to potentially deliver highly scalable device services. Further, it can handle many clients concurrently, although consuming fewer resources.

Node.DPWS provides such an implementation of DPWS using Node.js. Developers are responsible for describing the device's attributes (e.g., manufacturer or device name), its supported services (e.g., temperature service), operations (e.g., get current temperature), and events (e.g., over-heating alerts). There are additional libraries to accomplish a bevy of supporting services. Libraries can properly advertise the details and match them to any kind of external requests. More complex operations can be performed through the library. For example, allowing clients to subscribe to temperature readings at set intervals or when certain events occur by adopting the WS-Eventing specification. Node.DPWS also supports autodiscovery by implementing WS-Discovery, which is a multicast discovery protocol to locate services. Apart from discovering devices, the developed library facilitates replies to discovery requests, forwarding the developer-defined device details to requesting nodes whose queries match the device.

The Open Service Gateway Initiative Standard

The Open Service Gateway Initiative (OSGi) (Dohndorf 2010) is an independent, nonprofit corporation working to define and promote open specifications for the delivery of managed services to networked environments, such as homes and automobiles. These specifications define the OSGi service platform, which consists of two pieces: the OSGi framework and a set of standard service definitions. The OSGi framework, which sits on top of a Java virtual machine, is the execution environment for services. The OSGi framework was originally conceived to be used in restricted environments, such as set-top boxes, and now the standard is being prescribed as the best course of action for all kinds of resource-constrained as well as heavy devices.

OSGi is an industry standard for building Java applications out of modular units loosely connected through services. OSGi brings in the built-in support for describing and handling modules and their dependencies. Traditionally, OSGi has been used to decompose and loosely couple Java applications into easily manageable software modules. These modules encapsulate different parts of the whole functionality, and their lifecycle can be individually controlled at runtime. For instance, each single functional module can be updated to a newer version without restarting the application. This key differentiation makes OSGi popular for developing long-running applications such as the firmware of hardware devices or extensible applications. Modules typically communicate through services, which are ordinary Java classes published under a service interface in a central service registry. Through the service registry, service consumers can retrieve a direct reference to the service object of interest. Hence, OSGi provides a very lightweight communication model that avoids performance-adverse indirections known from container systems such as EJB runtimes.

Universal Plug and Play (UPnP) and DPWS (Huang 2011) require devices to communicate using SOAP or other extensible markup language (XML)-based communication protocols, supporting nonbinary protocols on the device calls for adequate computational power, and this results in higher cost and power consumption. If it is feasible to implement the necessary functionality on the devices, they can be accessed directly by other network participants. For a device to participate in a Jini network, it needs to support Java, and to execute a JVM. This is not feasible for small devices. But as services provide a form of abstraction, we have a second possibility. Proxies can be used that implement the middleware-compliant services on behalf of a device and interact with the device using proprietary protocols. These proxies can be outsourced to network nodes with higher computational capabilities like PC, fixed devices (Wi-Fi gateway, etc.). Thus, even small devices can participate in a Jini network via their proxies. As the abstraction capability of services is inherent to every SOA middleware, UPnP and DPWS also allow the proxy-centric approach.

In the case of OSGi, all services need to be executed as Java bundles on the central gateway. The bundles then communicate to the devices using proprietary means. Thus, the proxy approach is mandatory in OSGi. The topology, which describes the network setup of a device-centric SOA, is another key characteristic to be taken into consideration. This results in a star topology. Such a topology is favorable, for example, in a home environment, where usually, at least, one full-featured device, for example, a laptop, phablet, tablet, or a Wi-Fi router, exists that acts as the connectivity gateway, to which all sorts of home appliances with relatively small computational capabilities are connected all the time.

For Jini and DPWS (in a certain mode), services can be distributed in the network, but need a central service registry to allow dynamic device discovery. This means that a far more open network topology is possible in comparison to OSGi, but still these networks rely on a central component to function. In UPnP and DPWS (in another mode), the network is created on a peer-to-peer basis without the need for any centralized responsibilities. Although Jini, UPnP, and DPWS favor a distributed network, it is still possible to use proxies that are executed on a single machine. This way, a star topology is possible for these SOA device middleware solutions as well. The chosen topology has a definite impact on the scalability and robustness of the system.

Scalability

Scalability refers to the capabilities of a system to compensate an increase or decrease in the number of participants in the network. In this respect, an OSGi network with only a central gateway is not able to scale with the number of participants. The gateway is a dedicated piece of hardware. When the number of services to be executed on the gateway exceeds its capacity, the typical compensation mechanism is not possible during runtime. The only chance to adjust to the needs is to shut down the network and to replace the current gateway with more powerful hardware. Or the OSGi software can be deployed in several commodity services in order to tackle the scalability goal.

For Jini, UPnP, and DPWS, this is different, as they inherently base on distributed communication. The scalability of these networks primarily relies on the scalability of the underlying physical network, for example, Ethernet and WLAN. Applying extensible network topologies including switches and routers allows company intranets to scale to the number of employees. Thus, Jini, UPnP, and DPWS are able to scale gracefully. One exception for Jini and DPWS (in a certain mode) is the central lookup registry. Just like in the case of the OSGi gateway, exceeding the capabilities of the registry is a problem. But unlike OSGi, the registry is only queried to look up a service and does not need to do the intensive processing. Thus, the extension of the network has less impact on the service registry than on an OSGi gateway.

Robustness

Here, we will take a look at what will happen if devices are not available to the system due to a component failure or outage. For the chosen SOA realizations, the failure of a single service has only to be compensated by depending services but has no effect on the SOA system as a whole. In OSGi, the necessary OSGi gateway is a single point of failure. As the services are executed on the gateway, a failure of the gateway will prevent any further system activity. The high-availability (HA) mode through the clustering of gateways is the appropriate way forward.

In Jini, a failure of the central service registry is less severe. Without service registry, it is no longer possible to find a new service. But as devices in a Jini network communicate directly with each other, already connected services can continue to interact without any disturbance, deficiency, or degradation. A DPWS network is even more fault tolerant, as mechanisms are defined by which it is dynamically decided whether to use a service registry or do decentralized look-up. Thus, failure of the service registry in DPWS can be compensated by the network. For a UPnP network, a failure of a service has no additional effects, as interaction is completely done on a peer-to-peer (P2P) basis.

Remote OSGi

Designing distributed applications, where no homogeneous devices are present and no centrally managed infrastructure is available, is a highly complex issue. Enabling everyday devices to connect to clouds as well as making them discoverable, linkable, and usable by means of common open standards is not sufficient. There is a strong need for modular, global solutions for applications that are based on reuse, seamless integration, and runtime composition of services provided by these devices. Running within a Java Virtual Machine (JVM), OSGi offers an in-JVM SOA. The self-contained SOA, the environment of OSGi extended to exceed JVM boundaries is a suitable technology for this purpose, whereas DPWS allows solutions for devices with constrained resources. A research paper by Oliver Dohndorf (Towards the Web of Things: Using DPWS to Bridge Isolated OSGi Platforms) defines the following key requirements for DPWS-OSGi mutual integration:

- *Location transparency*: The usage of local and remote OSGi and DPWS services must not differ for clients. Remote services are to be accessed as if they resided in the local framework.
- *Support of legacy services*: Providing services remotely should not require any modifications.
- *Fault transparency*: The communication faults specific to a distributed environment must be handled in the same way as the reliability aspect is addressed by OSGi.
- *Dynamics*: The continuous changes in the topology imply that services appear, disappear, or become temporarily unavailable all the time.
- *Manageability*: Local clients—DPWS as well as OSGi—should be able to access only those services that are intended to be remotely available. On the contrary, a mechanism should be provided to integrate only white listed remote services into a local OSGi framework.
- *Compatibility*: Only standard OSGi services can be used in the solution. Moreover, the solution must also be applicable to those OSGi implementations that are designed for resource constrained device.

Eclipse Kura

Eclipse Kura is an Eclipse IoT project that provides a platform for building IoT gateways (http://eclipse.github.io/kura/). It is a smart application container that enables remote management of such gateways and provides a wide range of APIs for allowing you to write and deploy your own IoT application. Kura runs on top of the Java Virtual Machine (JVM) and leverages OSGi, a dynamic component system for Java, to simplify the process of writing reusable software building blocks. Kura APIs offer easy access to the underlying hardware including serial ports, GPS, watchdog, USB, GPIOs, I2C, and so on. It also offers OSGi bundle to simplify the management of network configurations, the communication with IoT servers, and the remote management of the gateway.

Kura components are designed as configurable OSGi declarative service exposing service API and raising events. Although several Kura components are in pure Java, others are invoked through JNI, and have a dependency on the Linux operating system. Kura comes with a set of advanced support services.

openHAB

openHAB is a software for integrating different home automation systems and technologies into one single solution that allows overarching automation rules and that offers uniform user interfaces (http://www.openhab.org/). This means openHAB

1. Is designed to be absolutely vendor-neutral as well as hardware or protocol-agnostic
2. Can run on any device that is capable of running a JVM (Linux, Mac, and Windows)
3. Lets you integrate an abundance of different home automation technologies into one
4. Has a powerful rule engine to fulfill all your automation needs
5. Comes with different web-based UIs as well as native UIs for iOS and Android
6. Is fully open source
7. Is maintained by a passionate and growing community
8. Is easily extensible to integrate with new systems and devices
9. Provides APIs for being integrated with other systems

There are many home automation solutions and IoT gadgets on the market, which are all useful on their own. They come with their own way of how to set up and configure devices, and are perfect for their intended use cases. The problem with all of these systems and devices is that these use cases are defined by the manufacturer—but as a user, you will quickly come up with wishes that are not supported out of the box, or which require interaction between the different systems. openHAB fills this gap: It puts the user in the focus and allows him to do what he wants to do. It thus serves as an integration point for all your home automation needs and lets systems talk to each other across any vendor or protocol boundaries. The macrolevel architectural representation is given in Figure 4.8.

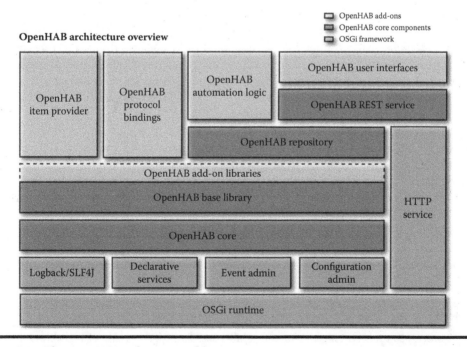

Figure 4.8   The openHAB reference architecture.

The REST Paradigm

Today everything is fitted with one or more APIs in order to connect and collaborate with everything else in the vicinity or with remote ones over any network. With the overwhelming success of APIs, these days APIs are penetrative and pervasive. Especially for the impending connected era, the rise and relevance of APIs are grandiosely significant. We have embedded, mobile, web, cloud, analytical, and enterprise applications and services in plenty, and all are fitted with apt APIs for enabling seamless and spontaneous integration and interactions. REST (representational state transfer), being synonymous with XML or JSON over HTTP, is the one standout for the forthcoming IoT (Han 2014; Cubo 2014) days. In the recent past, JSON has supplanted XML as the data format of choice for the web.

At its core, REST [1] is an architectural pattern for uniformly accessing and modifying a resource. One entity (the server) is the authority over the current state of an object. Other entities may request a *representation* of the current object and may also send requests to create, modify, or delete the object. The current popular REST model uses URIs to identify objects (*/lamp/1234*), HTTP verbs to specify an action, and JSON to represent the object. To fetch an object, a client may send an HTTP request to *GET /lamp/1234*. The server may respond with an HTTP 200 and a body containing JSON data.

With DPWS, it is possible to develop and deploy service-oriented device applications that are satisfying and sticking to the SODA (Lee et al. 2015) architectural pattern. However, it still has a big overhead due to many expensive bidirectional message exchanges and data representation in XML. Hence, there is a surging popularity for RESTful architecture, which complies with the resource-oriented architecture (ROA), a distinct architectural style. REST is a resource-oriented software architecture style for building Internet-scale distributed applications. Typically, the REST triangle defines the principles for encoding (content types), addressing (nouns), and accessing (verbs) a collection of resources using Internet standards. Resources, which are central to REST, are uniquely addressable using a universal syntax (e.g., a URL in HTTP) and share a uniform interface for the transfer of application states between client and server (e.g., GET/POST/PUT/DELETE in HTTP). REST resources may typically exhibit multiple typed representations using—for example—XML, JSON, YAML, or plain text documents. Thus, RESTful systems are loosely-coupled systems that follow these principles to exchange application states as resource representations. This kind of stateless interactions improve the resources consumption and the scalability of the system. Therefore, the implementation of a RESTful service can be more simple and lightweight compared to other similar architectures.

REST services can be developed and described using the web application description language (WADL). WADL is based on XML and describes applications based on HTTP. It supports the automatic description of RESTful services with machine-processable service descriptions. The SA-REST is an open, flexible, and standards-based approach for adding semantics to RESTful services. In the context of IoT, the RESTful services have many distinct advantages over arbitrary web services (i.e., SOAP) such as less overhead, low parsing-complexity, statelessness, and tighter integration with HTTP. In addition, applications supporting RESTful services perform better on wireless sensor network with limited resources. There are a few integrated frameworks to speed up the process of building and deploying a bevy of RESTful services across industry verticals.

The Device Connectivity via the OPC Standard

OLE for process control (OPC) is the interoperability standard for the secure and reliable exchange of data in the industrial automation space and in other industries. It is platform-independent and ensures the seamless flow of information among disparate devices from multiple vendors. The OPC foundation is responsible for the development and maintenance of this standard. The OPC standard is a series of specifications developed by industry vendors, end users, and software developers. These specifications define the interface between clients and servers, as well as between servers and servers, including access to real-time data, monitoring of alarms and events, access to historical data, and other applications.

When the standard was first released in 1996, its purpose was to abstract PLC-specific protocols (such as Modbus, Profibus, etc.) into a standardized interface allowing HMI or SCADA systems to interface with a *middle-man* who would convert generic-OPC read or write requests into device-specific requests and vice versa. As a result, an entire cottage industry of products emerged allowing end users to implement systems using best-of-breed products all seamlessly interacting via OPC.

Initially, the OPC standard was restricted to the Windows operating system. As such, the acronym OPC was born from OLE (object linking and embedding) for process control. These specifications, which are now known as OPC Classic, have enjoyed widespread adoption across multiple industries, including manufacturing, building automation, oil and gas, renewable energy, and utilities among others. With the introduction of SOA in manufacturing systems, there came new challenges in security and data modeling. The OPC foundation, therefore, developed the OPC UA specifications to address these needs and at the same time provided a feature-rich technology open-platform architecture that was future-proof, scalable, and extensible (https://opcfoundation.org).

Thus, for the foreseeable IoT era, every sort of physical assets, mechanical and electrical systems, consumer, medical, and industrial electronics, avionics, robots, security and surveillance cameras, personal and professional gadgets and gizmos, health care instruments, defense equipment, IT infrastructures, and other hardware modules need to be seamlessly integrated with one another through adaptive network topologies to empower each one of them individually as well as collectively to participate and contribute immensely and assertively for people. DPWS, OSGi, OPC, uPnP, Jini, and so on are the renowned service-oriented standards for hiding devices by presenting them as services for outside world. Device integration and orchestration are the principal goals of these integration methods.

Let us now plunge into the data transmission protocols that are part and parcel of the above device integration standards.

The Device Integration Protocols and Middleware

Edge technologies such as sensors and actuators are accurately inserted inside and outside all kinds of physical, mechanical, electrical, electronics, and IT systems in our everyday environments. The instrumentation technology domain has grown up powerfully in the recent past so that a number of minutely miniaturized, disappearing, and disposable edge technologies are able to be precisely embedded and imbedded onto all sorts of tangible and important elements and entities. The idea is nothing, but to empower common, cheap, and casual things in our midst to be digitized, smart, and sentient. With such kinds of instrumentation, interconnectivity is readily getting accomplished. Actuation devices are instrumented to be seamlessly integrated with one another in the vicinity and with remote ones over any network in order to sharpen and share their distinct capabilities. Ultimately everything becomes smart, every device becomes smarter, and every human, who is increasingly assisted by multiple networked and embedded devices, becomes the smartest in all activities he or she involves in.

The accordingly instrumented is to communicate their state and any state changes. Further, they can capture any kind of events and worthwhile data from their operating environments and pass them too. Sensor and device data are getting collected and aggregated by data aggregator devices and then are sent to the faraway control, analytics, and processing platforms and work-loads hosted in IT infrastructures. IT resources are very important to receive and subject the data to a variety of deeper and decisive investigations to emit out insights that in turn enable machines and men to take precise and perfect decisions. There is a growing array of data transmission protocols in the industry. The renowned protocols are as follows:

- *MQTT*: A protocol for collecting device data and communicating it to servers (D2S)
- *XMPP*: A best protocol for connecting devices to people, a special case of the D2S pattern, since people are connected to the servers
- *DDS*: A fast bus for integrating intelligent machines (D2D)
- *AMQP*: A queuing system designed to connect servers to each other (S2S)
- *CoAP* (Shelby et al. 2013): An optimized protocol

Message Queue Telemetry Transport

Message queue telemetry transport (MQTT) was originally developed and released by IBM (http://mqtt.org/). Over the past couple of years, the protocol has been moved into the open source community for further collaborative development. This has seen a significant growth in popularity as MQTT-enabled smartphone applications have taken off on a strong note.

The design principles and aims of MQTT are much more simple and focused. It provides publish-and-subscribe messaging. And it was specifically designed for resource-constrained devices and low bandwidth and high latency networks such as dial-up lines and satellite links. Basically, it can be used effectively in integrating embedded systems. One of the crucial advantages MQTT has over more fully featured *enterprise messaging* brokers is that it is intentionally low-footprint and hence is ideal for IoT applications. In fact, companies like Facebook are using it as part of their mobile applications because it has such a low power footprint and is extremely light on network bandwidth.

Some of the MQTT-based brokers support many thousands of concurrent device connections. It offers three qualities of service: (1) fire-and-forget or unreliable, (2) *at least once* to ensure it is sent a minimum of one time (but might be sent more than one time), and (3) *exactly once*. MQTT targets device data collection. As its name states, its main purpose is telemetry or remote monitoring. Its goal is to collect data from many devices and transport that data to the IT infrastructure. It targets large networks of small devices that need to be monitored or controlled from the cloud. Figure 4.9 vividly illustrates the uniqueness of MQTT.

MQTT implements the much-published hub-and-spoke model. It makes neither enabling D2D transfer nor fanning the data to many recipients. A hub-and-spoke architecture is naturally fit for the goals of MQTT. All the devices connect to a data concentrator server like IBM's new MessageSight appliance. As the protocol works on top of transmission control protocol (TCP), which provides a simple and reliable stream, the data loss is not there. Since the IT infrastructure uses the data, the entire system is designed to easily transport data into enterprise technologies like ActiveMQ and enterprise service buses (ESBs).

MQTT's main strengths are simplicity (just five API methods), a compact binary packet pay-load (no message properties, compressed headers, much less verbose than something text-based like HTTP), and it makes a good fit for simple push messaging scenarios such as temperature updates, stock price tickers, oil pressure feeds, or mobile notifications. It is also very useful for connecting

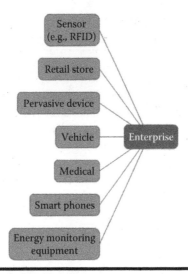

Figure 4.9   The MQTT-enabled device connectivity.

machines together, such as connecting an Arduino device to a web service with MQTT. MQTT enables applications like monitoring a huge oil pipeline for leaks or vandalism. Those thousands of sensors must be concentrated into a single location for analysis. When the system finds a problem, it can take action to correct that problem. Other applications for MQTT include power usage monitoring, lighting control, and even intelligent gardening. They share a need for collecting data from many sources and making it available to the distant IT applications, platforms, and infrastructures.

- *VerneMQ* (https://verne.mq/) is a high-performance distributed MQTT message broker. It scales horizontally and vertically on commodity hardware to support a high number of concurrent publishers and consumers while maintaining low latency and fault tolerance. As indicated above, the pioneering MQTT protocol connects virtually everything. Client libraries are available for most programming languages and environments. A built-in plug-in mechanism allows connecting custom message stores (SQL and NoSQL databases), rule engines, and complex logging, and event processing infrastructures. VerneMQ can be deployed on a wider variety of platforms for reliable and fault-tolerant operations. This platform is to access smart meters over a light-weight, secure, and bidirectional communication link. It is being positioned as the one for enabling connected cars, smarter lighting, public transportation, and smarter homes.
- *ThingMQ* (https://thingmq.com/) is a carrier-grade multiprotocol message broker for IoT that runs on the cloud. Any device can be easily connected to their cloud using MQTT, CoAP, REST, or WebSockets and ThingMQ handles the rest. To get started, one can use the free shared instance of ThingMQ. You simply connect your device to mq.thingmq.com using the M2M protocol of your choice. For higher security, you can connect your device to one of the dedicated instances. But here devices need to be authenticated. Once you are connected, you need to choose a unique identifier for your device, for example, my-thing-id. Data can be published under my-thing-id via MQTT, CoAP, REST, or WebSockets protocols using JSON, plain text, XML, BSON, MsgPack, or any other payload format.

Extensible Messaging and Presence Protocol

Extensible messaging and presence protocol (XMPP) is primarily for understanding the presence as articulated in Figure 4.10. That means humans are intimately involved here. The various flows are picturized in Figure 4.10.

XMPP uses the XML text format as its native type, making person-to-person communications natural. Like MQTT, it runs over TCP. Its key strength is a name@domain.com addressing scheme that helps connect the needles in the huge Internet haystack. In the IoT context, XMPP offers an easy way to address a device. This is especially handy if those data are going between distant and mostly unrelated points just like the person-to-person case. The most implementations use polling or checking for updates only on demand. A protocol called BOSH (Bidirectional-streams over Synchronous HTTP) lets servers push messages. XMPP provides a great way to connect your home thermostat to a web server so you can access it from your phone. Its strengths in addressing, security, and scalability make it ideal for consumer-oriented IoT applications.

ejabberd

ejabberd is an open source Jabber or XMPP server designed from the ground up to be the building bricks of highly critical messaging systems (https://www.ejabberd.im/). Written in Erlang programming language, ejabberd is cross platform, fault-tolerant, clusterable, very modular, and highly versatile. It can be extended to other programming languages, such as Elixir. Designed to be massively scalable, it is widely used to power web-scale deployments across many software industries: mobile messaging, social networks, gaming, IoT, and so on. ejabberd is taking great

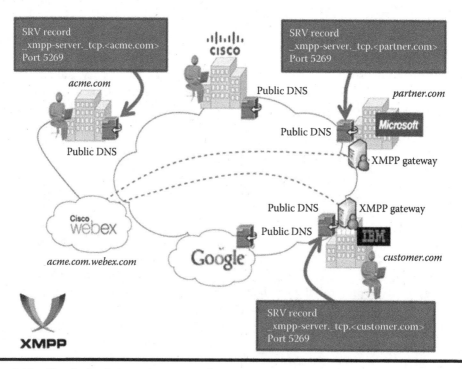

Figure 4.10   The device interactions scenario.

care of XMPP compliance, implementing most of the XMPP extensions published by the XMPP standard foundation.

Data Distribution Bus

Data distribution bus (DDS) (http://portals.omg.org/dds/) (Figure 4.11) is a middleware protocol and API standard for data-centric connectivity from the object management group (OMG). DDS targets devices that directly use device data. It distributes data to other devices. Although interfacing with the IT infrastructure is supported, DDS's main purpose is to connect devices to other devices. It is a data-centric middleware standard with roots in high-performance defense, industrial, and embedded applications. DDS can efficiently deliver millions of messages per second to many simultaneous receivers. DDS implements the pub or subpattern.

Devices need to communicate with many other devices, and TCP's simple and reliable P2P streams are far too restrictive. Instead, DDS offers detailed quality of service (QoS) control, multicast, configurable reliability, and pervasive redundancy. In addition, fan-out is a key strength. DDS offers powerful ways to filter and select exactly which data goes where, and *where* can be thousands of simultaneous destinations. Some devices are small, so there are lightweight versions of DDS that run in constrained environments.

The hub-and-spoke style is completely inappropriate for device data use. DDS implements direct D2D *bus* communication with a relational data model. Similar to the way a database controls access to stored data, a data bus controls data access and updates by many simultaneous users. This is exactly why many high-performance devices need to work together as a single system. High-performance integrated device systems use DDS that delivers the flexibility, reliability, and speed necessary to build complex, real-time applications. Applications include military systems, wind farms, hospital integration, medical imaging, asset-tracking systems, and automotive test and safety. DDS connects devices together into working and distributed applications at physics speeds.

It integrates the components of a system together, providing low-latency data connectivity, extreme reliability, and a scalable architecture that business and mission-critical IoT applications need.

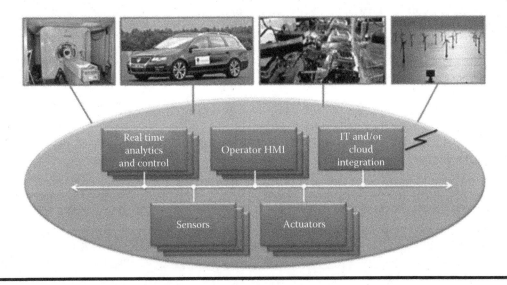

Figure 4.11   The reference architecture of DDS middleware.

Many real systems include devices, servers, mobile nodes, and more. They have diverse communication needs, but it is better and easier to use a single communication paradigm when possible. System designers should determine, which of the protocols meet the primary challenge of their intended applications. Then, if possible, extend that primary choice to all aspects of the system. For example, interdevice data use is a different use case from device data collection. Requirements for turning on your light switch (best with CoAP) are much different than the requirements for managing the generation of that power (best with DDS), monitoring the transmission lines (best with MQTT), or communicating power usage within the data center (best with advanced message queuing protocol [AMQP]).

Overall, DDS is the most versatile of these protocols. It can manage tiny devices, connect large, high-performance sensor networks, and close time-critical control loops. It can also serve and receive data from the cloud. DDS communication is peer-to-peer. Elimination of message brokers and servers simplifies deployment, minimizes latency, maximizes scalability, increases reliability, and reduces cost and complexity. Using DDS does require building a data model and understanding data-centric principles. It is ideal for IoT applications that require a lasting, reliable, and high-performance architecture.

Advanced Message Queuing Protocol

Advanced message queuing protocol (AMQP) was designed as an open replacement for existing proprietary messaging middleware (http://www.amqp.org/). Two of the most important reasons to use AMQP are reliability and interoperability. As the name implies, it provides a wide range of features related to messaging, including reliable queuing, topic-based publish-and-subscribe messaging, flexible routing, transactions, and security. AMQP exchanges route messages directly by topic and also based on headers.

There is plenty of fine-grained control possible with such a rich feature set. One can restrict access to queues, manage their depths, and more. Features such as message properties, annotations, and headers make it a good fit for a wide range of enterprise applications. This protocol was designed for reliability at the many large companies who depend on messaging to integrate applications and move data around their organization.

AMQP is a binary wire protocol, which was designed for interoperability between different vendors. Where other protocols have failed, AMQP adoption has been strong. Companies like JP Morgan use it to process one billion messages a day. NASA uses it for Nebula cloud computing. Google uses it for complex event processing. Here are a couple of additional AMQP examples and links:

1. It is used in one of the world's largest biometric databases India's Aadhar project—home to 1.2 billion identities.
2. It is used in the ocean observatories initiative—an architecture that collects 8 terabytes of data per day.

AMQP is all about queues. It sends transactional messages between servers. As a message-centric middleware that arose from the banking industry, it can process thousands of reliable queued transactions.

AMQP (Figure 4.12) is focused on not losing messages. Any communications from the publishers to exchanges and from queues to subscribers use TCP, which provides strictly reliable P2P connection. Further, endpoints must acknowledge the acceptance of each message. The standard also describes an optional transaction mode with a formal multiphase commit sequence.

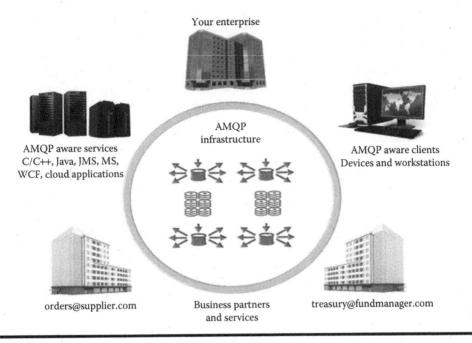

Figure 4.12   Internal and external interactions through AMQP.

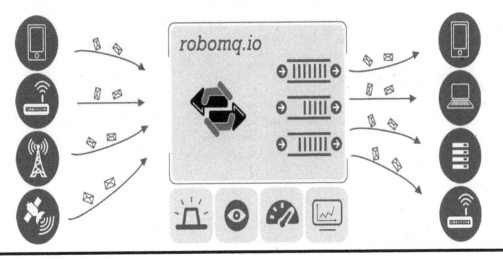

Figure 4.13   The robomq's queuing solution for device interactions.

True to its origins in the banking industry, AMQP middleware focuses on tracking all messages and ensuring each is delivered as intended, regardless of failures or reboots.

■ *robomq.io* (Figure 4.13) is an AMQP message broker connecting devices, systems, clouds, and things to create smart and context-aware applications. It provides cloud-hosted message queue as a service platform bundled with a management interface, dashboards, analytics, and software development kit (SDK). It is a highly scalable message queue cluster with built-in redundancy, failover, and elastic scaling to add resources as the message traffic increases.

- *robomq.io* brings the messaging platform in a fully managed and hosted message queue as a service SaaS model offering reliability, scale, and manageability required by today's cloud, mobile, M2M, and IoT applications. robomq.io is an end-to-end IoT middleware platform that can connect any device to any system, application, or cloud through its suite of connectors and adapters. It has an IoT gateway that allows devices and device mesh networks to connect to the cloud over cellular or wired connectivity. This also comes with real-time analytics engine, data-driven alerts, and device diagnostics and management capabilities to help you manage your IoT ecosystem effectively.
- *RabbitMQ* is an open source message broker. It receives and delivers messages from and to your applications. A message broker is (unlike databases and key-value store) purpose built to highly effectively and safely deliver information between your applications.
- *CloudAMQP* (Figure 4.14) is a hosted and managed RabbitMQ service in the cloud. Hosted message queues let you pass messages between processes and other systems. Messages are published to a queue by a producer. Then consumers can then get the messages off the queue when the consumers want to handle the messages. In-between, it can route, buffer, and persist the messages according to rules you give it. Messages can be sent across languages, platforms, and OS. This way of handling messages decouples your processes and creates a highly scalable system.
- *OpenAMQ* is a message broker plus client libraries for C or C++ and JMS. OpenAMQ gives you a simple and powerful C API called WireAPI as well as tools like PAL for easy scripting. It comes with remote admin tools, one-line failover, instant federation, and protection against slow clients, detailed logging, and other high-level features demanded by our largest and smallest users. OpenAMQ typically implements AMQP or 0.9 and AMQP or 0.9.1 (1.3x) versions.

Constrained Application Protocol

Constrained application protocol (CoAP) is a specialized web transfer protocol for use with constrained nodes and constrained networks in the IoT space. The protocol is designed for M2M applications such as smart energy and building automation. CoAP includes several HTTP functionalities, which have been redesigned for M2M applications over constrained environments on

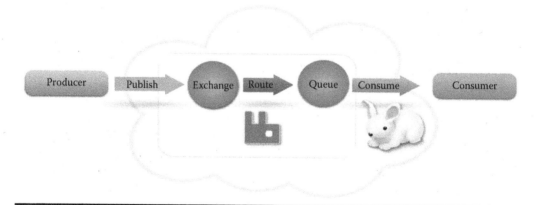

Figure 4.14   The end-to-end steps of cloud AMQP.

the IoT. That is, it takes into account the low processing power and energy constraints of small embedded devices, such as sensors. In addition, CoAP offers a number of features that HTTP lacks such as built-in resource discovery, IP multicast support, native push model, and asynchronous message exchange. There are many implementations of CoAP in various languages, such as libcoap1 (an open-source C-implementation) and Sensinode's NanoService2. The comparison of HTTP and CoAP stacks is pictorially indicated in Figure 4.15.

■ *Physical layer and data link layer*: Wireless networks are essential for the IoT. The IEEE 802.15.4 standard specifies the physical layer (PHY) and media access control (MAC) for low-rate wireless personal networks (LR-WPANs), which focuses on low-power consumption, low-cost, and low-rate data communication between constrained devices.

■ *Network layer*: IPv6 over Low-Power Wireless Personal Area Networks (6LoWPAN) standard defined by the IETF brings the IP to small embedded devices (e.g., sensors) in even the most constrained networks such as IEEE 802.15.4. In addition to 6LoWPAN, the IETF routing over low power and lossy networks (ROLL) working group has defined IPv6 routing protocol for low-power and lossy networks (RPL) for smart object Internetworking. Together these networking technologies provide means for small embedded devices to integrate into the Internet.

■ *Transport layer*: HTTP typically relies on TCP, which has performance problems over low-power and lossy networks (LLNs), is sensitive to mobility, does not provide multicast support, and has high overhead for short-lived transactions. CoAP, on the other hand, is built on top of the user datagram protocol (UDP), which provides significantly lower overhead and supports multicast.

■ *Application layer*: CoAP provides RESTful services optimized for resource-constrained networks and devices, and thus makes the protocol suitable to the IoT and M2M applications. In addition, it provides reliability (with default timeout and exponential back-off retransmission) mechanisms even without the use of TCP as the transport layer. One of the most important design goals of CoAP has also been to keep the message overhead as small as possible. HTTP can also be used over 6LoWPAN. However, the results

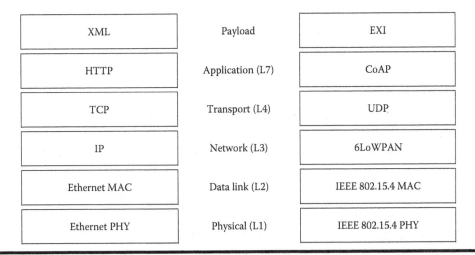

Figure 4.15   The comparison of HTTP and CoAP stacks.

show that the power consumption and bytes transferred per transaction are drastically lower when using CoAP over 6LoWPAN compared to HTTP over 6LoWPAN, and thus increasing the battery lifetime of constrained devices.

■ *Payload*: The W3C efficient XML interchange (EXI) format is a very compact, high-performance XML representation, which significantly reduces bandwidth requirements without compromising the efficient use of other resources, such as battery life, code size, processing power, and memory.

In summary, CoAP is a software protocol intended to be used in very simple electronics devices that allow them to communicate interactively over the Internet. It is particularly targeted for small low-power sensors, switches, valves, and other similar components that need to be controlled or supervised remotely, through standard Internet networks. CoAP is an application layer protocol that is intended for use in resource-constrained Internet devices, such as WSN nodes. CoAP is designed to easily translate to HTTP for simplified integration with the web, while also meeting specialized requirements such as multicast support, very low overhead, and simplicity. Multicast, low overhead, and simplicity are extremely important for IoT and M2M devices, which tend to be deeply embedded and have much less memory and power supply than traditional Internet devices have. Therefore, efficiency is very important. CoAP can run on most devices that support UDP or a UDP analog.

The Protocol Landscape for IoT

There are new protocols for enabling device integration. As the multiplicity and heterogeneity of devices are on the climb, the resulting complexity is to shoot up significantly. There are device middleware and a host of adaptors to translate between one protocol to the other in order to ensure unambiguous and uncluttered data consumption and processing of data being transmitted by devices. The matured OSI model is tweaked and twisted a bit for various device protocols. Here is a description for data-centric OSI layers:

■ *Connectivity layer*: RJ45 (the physical connector, usually for Ethernet), PLC, RS-232, RS-485, ModBus, USB (as a connector type, not the communication protocol), SPI, ODB2 (in Cars), and wireless (no connector!). There are gateways that will convert any of those physical connectors into wireless.

■ *Link protocol*: Ethernet 802.3, Wi-Fi 802.11a/b/g/n, Bluetooth, BLE, Dash 7, ZigBee, RFID, GSM, 6LoWPAN, and 802.14.5e are the widely used protocol to send data across. The last two are really focused on the IoT use case.

■ *Transport*: IPv4 and IPv6 are the ones for the transport layer. Due to the dazzling growth of devices, the adoption of IPv6 is accelerated.

■ *Session/communication*: MQTT, CoAP, a kind of REST protocol, but more efficient than HTTP, DDS, XMPP, and AMQP are the prominent ones in the IoT space today.

■ *Data aggregation/processing*: There are a number of data aggregation, transformation, and processing solutions. Apache Spark, Storm, Kafka, and so on are the most visible ones.

■ *Data storage/retrieval*: There are SQL, NoSQL, and NewSQL databases solutions to store IoT device data. Hadoop HDFS is the file system for IoT data.

Due to the burgeoning nature of devices and the data being generated by those devices, the IoT space needs many powerful data protocols. We have discussed the key protocols in Chapter 2.

Conclusion

Every kind of enterprise ranging from small to large in size is to be immensely benefited out of this game-changing concept. Smarter environments are to be realized with ambient intelligence in order to be situation-aware, people-centric, event-driven, and service-oriented. IT will be typically virtual, computing is set to be pervasive, goals such as activity and environment sensing are to be grandly ubiquitous, communication is unified and blessed with reliable and resilient connectivity, network topologies are varying and empowered by ultrahigh bandwidth, and knowledge extraction and engineering is common. Digitalization and distribution are set to be deeper in the sense that there will be billions of connected devices and trillions of digital objects. Every tangible thing in our homes, offices, hotels, hospitals, and manufacturing floors is enabled to be service-providing, consuming, and brokering in a purpose-specific manner. Ordinary things get digitized to exhibit adaptive behavior. The expected changes are really fascinating and fabulous with the adoption and adaptation of IoT platforms, patterns, processes, and practices.

The IoT conundrum is capable of touching every facet of our lives. It lays down a stimulating environment for conceiving and concretizing scores of smart and sophisticated applications for enabling knowledge workers, common people, decision-makers, scientists, and so on. Every kind of person is to be empowered with a lot of capabilities and competencies in order to shine in their daily works and walks. This chapter is being specifically planned and produced for expounding the connectivity approaches, device integration standards and implementations, and data transport protocols in the fast-evolving IoT space.

Bibliography

An Information Technology (IT) Portal, http://www.peterindia.net.

Cubo, J. 2014, A Cloud-Based Internet of Things Platform for Ambient Assisted Living, *Sensors*, 14, 14070–14105, doi:10.3390/s140814070.

Dohndorf, O. 2010, Towards the Web of Things: Using DPWS to Bridge Isolated OSGi Platforms.

Han, S. N. 2014, DPWSim: A Simulation Toolkit for IoT Applications using Devices Profile for Web Services, IEEE World Forum on Internet of Things (WF-IoT).

Hassan, M. M., B. Song, and E.-N. Huh, 2009, A Framework of Sensor-Cloud Integration Opportunities and Challenges, ICUIMC.

Huang, C.-M. 2011, Design and Implementation of a Web 2.0 Service Platform for DPWS-based Home-Appliances in the Cloud Environment, Workshops of International Conference on Advanced Information Networking and Applications.

Integration and IoT Resources, https://dzone.com/.

ITU Telecommunication Standardization Sector, http://www.itu.int/en/ITU-T/Pages/default.aspx.

Lee, N., H. Lee, and W. Ryu, 2015, Considerations for Web of Object Service Architecture on IoT Environment, *International Journal of Smart Home* 9, 1, 195–202.

Lerche, C., N. Laum, G. Moritz, E. Zeeb, F. Golatowski, and D. Timmermann, 2011, Implementing powerful web services for highly resource-constrained devices, in *2011 IEEE International Conference on Pervasive Computing and Communications Workshops*, pp. 332–335.

Moritz, C., D. Timmermann, R. Stoll, and F. Golatowski, 2010, Encoding and compression for the devices profile for web services, in *2010 IEEE 24th International Conference on Advanced Information Networking and Applications Workshops*, pp. 514–519.

The Open Service Gateway interface (OSGi), http://www.osgi.org/Main/HomePage.

Raj, P. 2012, *Cloud Enterprise Architecture*, CRC Press, Boca Raton, FL.

RESTful Services, https://docs.oracle.com/javaee/6/tutorial/doc/javaeetutorial6.pdf.

REST Without JSON: The Future of IoT Protocols, https://dzone.com/articles/json-http-and-the-future-of-iot-protocols.

Samaras, I., G. Hassapis, and J. Gialelis, 2013, A modified DPWS protocol stack for 6LoWPAN-based wireless sensor networks, *IEEE Transactions on Industrial Informatics*, 9(1), 209–217.

The Sensor Cloud the Homeland Security, 2011, http://www.mistralsolutions.com/hs-downloads/tech-briefs/nov11-article3.html.

Shelby, Z., K. Hartke, and C. Bormann, 2013, Constrained Application Protocol (CoAP), IETF Internet Draft, June 2013.

Yang, X. and X. Zhi, 2012, Dynamic deployment of embedded services for DPWS-enabled devices, in *2012 International Conference on Computing, Measurement, Control and Sensor Network*, pp. 302–306.

Chapter 5

The Enablement Platforms for IoT Applications and Analytics

Abstract: The Internet of Things (IoT) paradigm is definitely on fast track. There are a number of viable and value-adding business and technical cases being unearthed and articulated well by business as well as IT professionals for enabling worldwide governments and organizations to deeply focus on bringing forth a well-intended IoT strategy. However, any realistic IoT strategy in order to steer any kind of enterprises in a calculated fashion has to be stringently based on a solid foundation of pioneering processes, optimized and organized IT infrastructures, the state-of-the-art technologies, multifaceted architectures, and so on. In this book, we have discussed a variety of topics in the IoT field in order to empower the readers with sufficient amount of tips and insights. In this chapter, we would like to focus on proven and potential IoT platforms (applications and analytics), engines, middleware, gateways, communication protocols, and so on.

Researchers, visionaries, software architects, and evangelists are constantly producing a number of enabling IoT-centric patterns, products, and competent solutions for a variety of industrial as well as consumer requirements. Further, there are usable technical know-hows, evaluation metrics, and best practices. The idea is to enhance the awareness of IoT capabilities and competencies in guaranteeing the enhanced connectivity, care, choice, convenience, and comfort for knowledge workers and commoners. A number of manual, rough, tough, and time-consuming tasks in our everyday life are simply and systematically getting automated through the smart leverage of the powerful and pioneering contributions to the IoT concept, which has been meticulously nourished and nurtured through well-planned collaborative and concerted efforts by IT product vendors and service integrators, independent software vendors, academicians, communication and cloud service providers, and so on. Let us start with a few use cases.

Describing the IoT Journey

The IoT idea is percolating into every industry vertical. IT professionals and computer science professors are actively working on making it pervasive and persuasive. There are several forecasts from world-leading market researchers that by 2020, all kinds of tangible things in our everyday environments will be technologically modernized to be web-enabled. We are unequivocally reading a lot of distinct advantages of our ordinary articles getting hooked to the Internet. There are unique benefits for end users and technical professionals whereas newer business models are being talked about in order to explore fresh revenue-generating avenues through such kinds of web-enablement. For example, there is a news story about Samsung bringing forth Internet-enabled refrigerators. It can call up milk vendors to supply a few liters of milk when the amount of milk inside the fridge is going down below the threshold. The house owner can remotely see the food items that are not sufficient for next-day cooking and accordingly buy them from the hypermarket on the way back to home from the workplace in the evening. Even the enabled refrigerators can message to the owner about the quality and quantity of food materials. There are a lot of opportunities and possibilities with the technological advancements.

Due to the massive number of Internet-enabled things, the forthcoming era is being termed as the game-changing one for the total humanity. There are cloud infrastructures for hosting, delivering, and managing integrated IoT platforms. Further on, developers chip in with scores of things-centric applications and services. Industry-strength and open source platforms are being readied toward application construction, debugging, deployment, delivery, and even decommissioning. As an elevator pitch, even business managers can quickly bring up a few IoT applications with the support from these tools to showcase their uniqueness to their customers and clients.

Smartphones are already contributing immeasurably in connecting people everywhere every time. With the pervasiveness and persuasiveness of mobile phones, there are plenty of opportunities for enthusiastic software developers for developing powerful yet easy-to-use mobile-enabled applications. Today we have tens of thousands of smartphone-specific services getting accumulated and arranged in remote mobile clouds that emerge as a core and central location for smartphone users. Another noteworthy point is that mobile interfaces are established for empowering the business-critical software applications running in enterprise and cloud servers. That is, the ubiquitous access and operation of these mission-critical workloads are being facilitated through the mobile-enablement process.

Similarly, there will be specific and scintillating IoT devices for specific environments such as hotels, hospitals, homes, and so on. For example, home integration devices (HIDs) will become popular for smarter homes. The telling impact is that there will be thousands of newer applications that can be realized for smarter homes to be accessed and used through HIDs. Thus, it is indicated that by the year 2020, there will be millions of software applications when we sum up all device-specific and generic applications.

Machines and IT infrastructures are fitted with human–machine interfaces (HMIs), thereby people use their smartphones to interact with machines remotely. Besides smartphones, there are other input or output (I/O) devices garnering enough support in the marketplace in order to operate multiple applications and appliances individually as well as collectively. With these sweet and sparkling trends, apart from smartphones, phablets, and tablets, there will be implantable, wearable, and portable IoT devices in plenty to connect with remote applications and machines. Already standards-making organizations and agencies across the globe are going ahead at full speed to arrive at competent standards for enabling existing and emerging IoT devices to be the most convenient I/O entities to access faraway information and applications and to activate platforms and infrastructures. Thus, the interesting point is that all the contributing technologies, techniques, and tools are fast maturing and converging concomitantly to give the best-in-class environment for swiftly realizing the IoT vision. In this section, we are going to write about the well-known building blocks.

The IoT Building Blocks

The availability of myriad software infrastructure solutions to capture, ingest, and analyze IoT data has made IoT a hotbed of activity both in the consumer and the enterprise space. Many IoT use cases prompted the arrival of thousands of new start-ups that offer specific solutions. On the other hand, the emergence of IoT software solutions and services has led to the visualization of hundreds of new IoT applications. In this section, we are going to discuss the principal building blocks of futuristic IoT applications.

Digitized Entities and Connected Devices

As articulated in Chapters 1 and 4, all kinds of commonly found and cheap items need to be empowered with edge technologies in order to capture the various states of the particular item. For example, for a window in a home, the current state could be open or closed. Similarly, all kinds of ordinary yet tangible objects in a particular environment need to be enabled to be self- and surroundings-aware. Sensors can be attached to those casual articles in order to clinically and concisely capture their states. Different states can be sensed by deploying particular sensors on the physical entity in a particular location. For example, there are pressure, weight, gas, fire and fall detection, humidity, presence, and temperature sensors. The location is another decision-enabling state to be GPS sensors. For tracking inventory, the sensors can be deployed on each individual unit or they can be deployed on a pallet that uses a single sensor to monitor the weight of the pallet and track inventory. Thus, opportunities and possibilities are really immense. With such a methodical empowerment, our everyday objects in our midst turn out to be smart and sentient materials.

Not only casual items but also all kinds of physical, mechanical, electrical, and electronics devices in our personal as well as professional spaces are adequately enabled to be calculative, connected, sensitive, perceptive, and responsive. Thus, earthly artifacts are being pampered to be data capturing, crunching, and communicating to be self, surroundings, and situation-aware.

IoT or Sensor Data Gateway

Sensors and other edge technologies embedded with any object on the ground need to transmit the data captured. However, sensors typically do not have the power to send data to greater distances. Also, different sensors follow different data protocols and formats.

A gateway is responsible for accepting and aggregating data from all the digitized entities, sensor-attached physical assets, connected devices, instruments, machines, equipment, gadgets, and so on. Then this gateway passes on the data to analytics software solutions within the gateway (the chapter on fog or edge computing throws more light on this local or proximate processing), or to cloud-based and centralized controlling, and analytical software for data processing to extract actionable insights in time. In some cases, the gateway also filters, aggregates, or cleanses the incoming data to reduce the load on the network.

Application Enablement Platforms

There are powerful cloud-based platforms made available for worldwide developers to quickly come out with IoT applications based on the data shared by ground-level entities. There are application programming interfaces (mostly RESTful APIs) for passaging data from sensors and other devices in real time to the remotely held-up rapid application development (RAD) tools. Application enablement platforms (AEPs) facilitate the direct deployment of any built-in applications and services in cloud-based execution containers to be subscribed and used by other applications as well as humans.

Data Analytics Platforms

These are a bit complicated platforms directly attached with AEPs. There are powerful data mining, fusion, and processing algorithms getting implemented and incorporated in these platforms to elegantly draw knowledge out of data heaps. The insights extracted are then fed into AEPs to drive pioneering applications. The challenge with these platforms is that the amount of sensor and actuator data is becoming massive, and hence doing real-time analytics on big data is a bit difficult. There are technologically sound and solid solutions emerging in order to tackle this particular problem. The underlying IT infrastructures also need to be exceptionally elastic enough to cope with the big data challenges.

Increasingly data storage, processing, mining, and analyzing software solutions are being deployed in private, public, or even in hybrid clouds. Data are subjected to a variety of deeper and decisive investigations in order to extract pragmatic insights. There are big, fast, streaming, and IoT data whereas there are batch or ad hoc or historical or comprehensive processing apart from interactive and iterative processing. Thus, there are specific as well as integrated platforms on cloud environments for embarking on big and fast data analytics. Especially predictive, prescriptive, and personalized analytics domains are expected to be dominant in the years ahead.

Knowledge Discovery and Dissemination

At the end of the famous analytics process, we would have the appropriate knowledge to be leveraged with confidence. There is a bevy of correlation, corroboration, and collaboration mechanisms in plenty, in order to enable analytics solutions to emit highly beneficial insights. Also there are knowledge visualization tools apart from integrated dashboards in order to clearly articulate and accentuate the acquired insights to authorized men as well as machines. Based on the information availed, the actuation and execution systems proceed with the next set of activities with all the clarity. Information in multiple forms and formats can be displayed in smartphones. Natural interfaces will become more prominent. Further on, analytical platforms are seamlessly and spontaneously integrated with various I/O devices for sharing information in time.

Storage, Backup, and Archival

There are several reasons being quoted to have an effective data backup strategy. For doing historical and comprehensive analytics, IoT data has to be cautiously and consciously stored in easy-to-discover and access storage appliances, so that it can be found and retrieved later for fully complying with government regulations.

Cognitive Clouds

We have discussed IoT gateways, application-building, platforms, and so on. The crucial ingredient of the fast-growing IoT ecosystem is the cloud-enabled IT infrastructure. A number of grandiose automation and acceleration mechanisms are being passionately incorporated in enterprise and cloud IT environments to enable them to take on futuristic business evolutions and expectations with ease. There are open and industry-strength standards for simplified and streamlined cloud management. Besides, there is a host of configuration, delivery, deployment, and other automated tools to assist cloud administrators. On the implementation side, the aspect of resource utilization is being accentuated through consolidation, virtualization, containerization, automation, pooling, and sharing, and so on. Thus, there is a family of optimization methods being unleashed on IT resources and workloads (IT and business). Further on, the management of various IT resources and infrastructural modules is also methodically optimized to arrive at highly optimized and organized IT environment of servers, storages, and networking components.

These are all the major participants in envisioning and implementing next-generation IoT applications.

The Major Players in the IoT Space

The IoT also opens a range of new business opportunities for a variety of players. The first and foremost among them are the original equipment manufacturers (OEMs) producing huge volumes of multifaceted, multinet, multimedia, and multimodal IoT devices and edge technologies (sensors, actuators, codes, chips, controllers, LED lights, tags, stickers, and nano- and microscale entities for digitizing ordinary things, and so on). The idea is to empower physical assets and other everyday articles in our environments to be remotely monitored, measured, managed, and maintained. Google has recently bought a company *Nest* (https://nest.com/). This company produces three prominent products:

- The first one is the Nest Learning Thermostat. It is slimmer and sleeker with a bigger and sharper display. And it saves energy.
- The second one is highly advanced smoke alarms. It has an industrial-grade smoke sensor, tests itself automatically, and lasts up to a decade. It is also the first home alarm one can hush from his phone without any extra hardware required.
- The final one is the Nest Cam security camera that is designed to help you look after your home and family even when you are away. With 24/7 live streaming, advanced night vision, activity alerts, one app for all your Nest products, and a versatile magnetic stand, Nest Cam helps you keep an eye on what matters from anywhere.

ThingLogix Connected Water Management solution (http://www.thinglogix.com/) provides property managers and commercial landlords with the detailed insights to measure the usage of their tenants' water systems. Subscribers can easily track per unit water usage, monitor for leaks, and recognize broad patterns in water usage as well as provide remote and automated shut-off capabilities. ThingLogix Connected Car solution provides everything needed to integrate real-time automobile engine and location data into ServiceMax. This can help fleet managers easily track and maintain their vehicles, and make data available in real time to other employees to provide detailed insights to boost business efficiency and prevent maintenance issues. Similarly, there are hundreds of start-ups as well as established players investing their time, talent, and treasure in conceptualizing and concretizing a number of ground-breaking products for ensuring enhanced care, choice, convenience, connectivity, and comfort for people.

The second renowned player in the IoT ecosystem is the ones who produce IoT gateways, which are very vital for collecting and cleansing all kinds of data being emitted by vastly deployed IoT objects in a particular environment. These middleware solutions are being fitted with a number of features and facilities in order to establish a smooth linkage between IoT devices at the ground level with a growing array of software applications and databases at the cyber or virtual or cloud level. The IoT or sensor gateway is an important ingredient in order to achieve the much-needed translation and connectivity to remote control and cognitive applications.

The third player is the platform vendors. We need highly synchronized and syndicated platforms for data capture, cleansing, enriching, blending, mining, processing, and orchestration. IoT application enablement and IoT data analytics platforms are destined for powering up next-generation applications.

The fourth player is cloud service providers (CSPs) for fulfilling the IT infrastructure requirements. All kinds of IoT platforms (applications and analytics) are going to be ported and persisted on cloud infrastructures considering the fact that an extreme IT optimization is being guaranteed by cloud environments.

The fifth and final player is none other than the development community members. All the data, platforms, and infrastructures need to be smartly used for deriving pathbreaking and people-centric applications. With everything in place, innovators and individuals can simply focus on building and deploying smarter and sophisticated applications in clouds. These can be discovered and subscribed by worldwide users freely or for a small fee.

A Few Enthralling IoT Use Cases

There are industry-specific and generic use cases in plenty for galvanizing people in charge and command to spend their time, treasure, and talent in incorporating the IoT ideas and ideals in their enterprises and endeavors. The market watchers, analysts, and researchers are enthusiastically estimating and elaborating a staggering amount as IoT revenue, which is to be in the range of a few trillions of dollars, by the year 2020. IT companies are therefore seriously exploring different avenues to gain higher revenues. Powerful use cases are being typically captured and capitalized in two ways: the first one is through intense interactions with end users and the second is one is from inside experts, thought-leaders, visionaries, luminaries, and so on. And these are being put out in various public fora in order to revitalize peoples' enthusiasm for the fledgling IoT idea.

The automobile industry is awash with the distinct advancements toward designing, developing, and delivering smarter vehicles with the subtle and succinct incorporation of IoT technologies and techniques. The landscape of the auto industry is destined to change forever. The driving, traveling, and learning experiences of driver and occupants of vehicles are going to be altogether different. Vehicles-specific applications and real-time analytics being innately enabled through the extreme connectivity and service-enablement of IoT participants and constituents are going to be the real game-changer for the automobile industry.

However, there are several areas within the automotive industry that are facing the challenge of redefining business to keep up with the modern demands of an increasingly connected world. The IoT domain is all set to play a very vital and vast role in comprehensively and cognitively shaping up the struggling automobile industry. Without an iota of doubt, IoT-enabled automotive engineering is the principal find to speed up the launch of sophisticated vehicles that meet the mobility and sustainability demands of car manufacturers, buyers, as well as regulators.

■ *Smarter Supply Chain and Manufacturing Operations*: The industry keenly expects the next-generation automobiles to be the systems that think innocuously. The vehicles and the auto industry are generating a lot of useful and usable data. By seamlessly aggregating polystructured data from vehicle components, vehicles-centric software services in cloud environments, a litany of software applications such as driving and parking assistance systems, the roadside IT and communication infrastructures, faraway traffic servers, and so on, and then mining that data for actionable insights, it is possible to have a deeper and precise activity monitoring, granular performance management, supply chain optimization, and real-time decision-making.

■ *Connected and Cognitive Cars*: These days, we extensively hear and read about connected and driverless vehicles. That is, thousands of heterogeneous sensors and actuators are being imbedded and implanted on various vehicle components in order to capture and crunch various vehicle data points and performance pointers. The insights being squeezed out of the deeper analytics on the wealth of data captured, gleaned, and stacked are being used to automate a variety of vehicle operations that in turn facilitate the realization of bigger and better things. The idea is to build and market cognitive cars for the forthcoming era of knowledge-filled services.

In the remaining portions of this chapter, we have given a number of inspiring IoT business and use cases.

IoT Application Enablement Platforms

As the number of IoT devices explodes, we come across numerous IoT application development and deployment platforms, which contribute immensely to building pioneering IoT applications. Today there are several players in this arena and we are to discuss their products and solutions in detail in the subsequent sections of this chapter. We all know that machines were the first embracing the connectedness in order to be intelligent and useful for people. With connected machines pervading consistently, platform vendors came out with a number of integrated development environments (IDEs) and rapid application development (RAD) tools. There are agile programming platforms along with DevOps capabilities emerging in this game-changing space. Then with the growing complexity due to multiplicity and heterogeneity of devices, there came up powerful monitoring, measurement, management, and governance, security, and maintenance platforms. For composable businesses, disparate, distributed, and decentralized devices need to be found, integrated, and orchestrated. Thus, along with device composition device middleware or broker or hub or bus software solutions were built and released into the market. There are a number of convincing use cases why devices (personal, professional, and social) need to be meticulously integrated.

Characterizing IoT or Machine-to-Machine Application Platforms

It all started with the game-changing application platforms for connected machines. Originally machines were integrated with other machines in the vicinity and with remote machines, web-based business applications, and databases. For example, machines in the manufacturing floor were linked up with SAP application in the remote server machines with the idea of real-time information gathering, processing, analysis and knowledge discovery, and dissemination.

This technologically inspired integration goes a long way for business executives and decision-makers to take quick and informed decisions. Batch processing of industry data gets obviated and instead real-time processing to generate real-time insights gets the nod across the industry verticals. Machines internally have the required capacity and capability to establish a seamless and spontaneous linkage with others nearby as well as with faraway systems over any network. There are networking and communication technologies and topologies to facilitate this transition. To fulfill the device integration, Internet-of-Things/machine-to-machine (IoT/M2M) middleware solutions are therefore very essential. Besides integration, middleware infrastructure solutions are for accomplishing multiple tasks in an automated fashion.

For example, for diversified manufacturers, a common IoT/M2M platform can be set up to support machine applications across multiple divisions and business units. The software infrastructure utilization goes up steadily in this way. A chemical company could use a common platform to monitor tank levels, equipment utilization, vehicle location, and so on. Different tracking technologies (e.g., RFID, ZigBee, GPS, Wi-Fi routers, sensors, and so on) could be deployed in the same solution. With connected machines, companies can think of unearthing and expounding diverse functionalities. Corporations could provide excellent product support and care, perform remote diagnostics, and formulate a litany of value-added services. Machines capable of giving directly an indication of their functioning, performance, distinct features, and so on to people are to lay in a stimulating and scintillating platform for selling more products. In the recent past, GE has minutely embedded scores of sensors and actuators in their flight engines in order to extract every useful and usable data in order to boastfully convince their prospective clients. Through superior customer experience and delightful solutions, the much-wanted customer loyalty gets improved. These transitions remarkably increase customer retention and attract new users. Figure 5.1 succinctly explains how device data gets ingested and crunched by the cloud-based IoT platform to squeeze out hidden information and to make informed decisions.

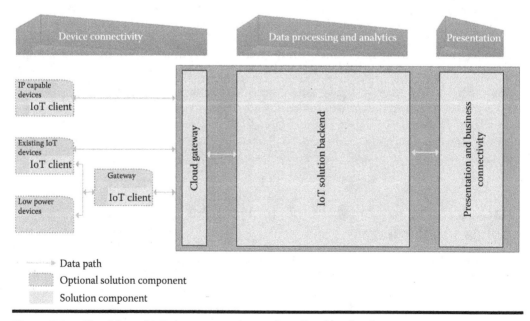

Figure 5.1   Cloud-based IoT data processing and application development.

The other advantages for a highly synchronized IoT/M2M AEP include the following:

1. Heterogeneous machines and devices can be integrated with one another in a hassle-free manner.
2. Fresh devices can be added to the environment or new firmware or software patches, revisions, and patches on currently running devices can be incorporated into the devices without any problem.
3. An integrated platform helps to future-proof a company's IoT/M2M investment. It can take care of device proliferation, performance, potentials, and so on.
4. IoT/M2M application platforms intrinsically take care of the *plumbing* so that the nonfunctional requirements (NFRs) and the quality of service (QoS) attribute such as the scalability, availability, security, pooling, and clustering needs is fulfilled. Substitution, replacement, and reusability of devices are graciously ensured. Application initiation and implementation get speeded up.
5. The application platforms are capable of scaling up to cover thousands of connected devices. A common foundation definitely enables efficient and cost-effective processing and storage of massive amounts of machines and their interaction data.
6. With the growing maturity of model-driven architecture (MDA) concept and domain-specific languages (DSLs), there are code cartridges and accelerators in plenty. By plugging them into the IoT/M2M application platform, it is possible to bring forth business logic without low-level coding and custom code. With DevOps tools, the software deployment too sees a kind of benevolent automation.
7. The platform approach allows companies to bring in new applications to market. The platform-provided services enable faster software development. Existing application components and services can be easily reused, thereby the time waste associated with rewinding the wheel gets avoided.
8. A platform-centric approach centralizes all the common services such as device discovery, the rules engine, alarm or exception handling, device management, and data management in one place and specific services to the connected devices.
9. A platform assists users and developers to offload application logic between the platform and the associated devices.
10. An M2M platform aids in the integration of devices and machines at the ground level to cyber applications such as ERP, CRM, SCM, and so on. There are several use cases for this feature. An alarm condition can trigger the automatic creation of a case (service request) in the CRM system for dispatching a field technician or the automatic generation of a replenishment order when consumables fall below a given level.
11. Multiple point solutions or machines or tools can be integrated with an ERP solution through the platform approach.

An IoT/M2M platform has to be a device, network, and protocol-agnostic. There are two main architectural approaches to IoT middleware. One type of IoT middleware platform follows the classic client or server architecture. One-half of the middleware is implemented on the central application server and the other half (the *agent*) is implemented on the remote device. The downside with this approach is that every device manufacturer has to implement the agent in order to be integrated with a centralized server. The other one centralizes the device translators on the server and allows several kinds of devices to communicate with the central server in their unaltered and native mode. This makes it easier to incorporate devices from many different manufacturers and to handle the manufacturers' upgrades to hardware and firmware.

The platform offers unlimited scalability and enterprise-grade performance through a comprehensive set of services. The other contributions are the best-in-class connectivity, protected data connections, secure storage in the cloud, and the easiest application integration, thanks to open APIs. With the growing array of platform services, every tangible thing becomes smart, every type of electronics becomes smarter, and finally, every human being is the smartest. Finally, IoT AEPs empower devices to be productive, useful for their owners, save resources, and open up new lines of business.

IoT AEPs—The Architectural Building-Blocks

Tangible things, at first, need to be digitized to be communicative so that their external connectivity is being simplified. Nowadays, our everyday devices are being instrumented and manufactured in such a way that they are intrinsically smart. So as far as the devices (personal, social, and industrial) are concerned, the connectivity capability is enshrined in the device itself. Now the differentiating role of any standard IoT platform is to connect digitized objects and devices with one another as well as with remote software applications, content, and databases. This strategically sound empowerment through any IoT platform is to result in scores of ground-breaking applications for the humanity. The IoT platform architecture may also consist of a software platform, an application development platform, or an analytics platform. In a more sophisticated form, a true end-to-end IoT platform comprises eight important architectural building blocks as vividly illustrated in Figure 5.2.

The job description of those eight components is as follows:

1. *Connectivity and normalization*: This is for connecting diverse and distributed devices through a host of device adapters. There are middleware solutions for unifying different protocols and data formats to make any device talking to any other device. A fine-grained interface is being provided in order to receive data and commands from devices as well as to devices.

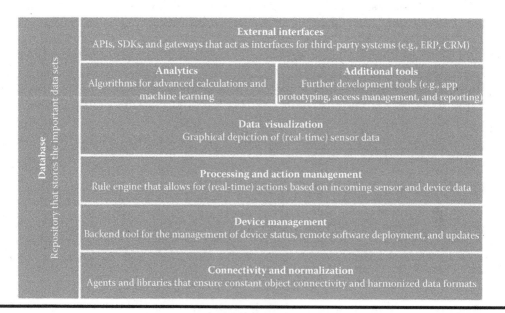

Figure 5.2   The principal building blocks of IoT AEPs.

2. *Device management*: This ensures that all the digitized entities and connected devices are working properly, seamlessly running patches and updates for software, and applications running on the devices or edge gateways.
3. *IoT database*: This is for the scalable storage of device or sensor data, which is becoming voluminous. With the growing number of connected sensors and devices, there is a need for big databases in cloud environments for data storage, processing, as well as analytics.
4. *Processing and action management*: Based on the captured sensor and actuator data, a bevy of advanced applications can be realized quickly and downloaded to ground-level devices dynamically to empower devices to behave differently. That is, devices are self, surroundings, and situation-aware.
5. *IoT data analytics*: Data becomes the most important asset for any system to be right and relevant to their users. All kinds of sensor and machine data are systematically gathered to perform a range of complex and composite analysis to make sense out of IoT data. There are simple data mining to powerful machine learning algorithms toward predictive, prescriptive, and personalized analytics.
6. *Information visualization*: There are dashboards and information visualization platforms to portray the knowledge discovered to various stakeholders in a more natural and intimate way. There are gadgets and gizmos for knowledge dissemination. The intelligence can be fed into various machines to behave differently.
7. *Additional tools*: IoT processes can be verified and automated through formalized workflow and data flow models. Modeling languages and process engines will be required to automate service orchestration to build process-aware and people-centric applications.
8. *External interfaces*: Any IoT platform has to be integrated with a variety of data sources and operational systems in order to receive data, and then there are multiple databases, data warehouses, and data lakes to store and subject them for deeper and decisive analytics. There are report-generation tools to be integrated. And a host of actuation systems needs to be stuffed with what is extracted to be multifaceted.

With the explosion of IoT devices and data, we need greatly competent and cognitive platform for connecting, configuring, operating, diagnosing, and managing of devices. The additional features include policy-based governance and security, service-enablement to be integrated, and orchestration of multiple devices and data capture, and storage and processing for application development. IoT data analytics capability is being deftly ingrained in IoT platforms for emitting pragmatic insights out of data heaps. The IoT platform has to be exceedingly modular as the analytics aspect is being recommended to be accomplished at online, off-site, and on-demand cloud environments and at on-site fog and edge device clusters. We have given more information on fog or edge analytics via the ad hoc formation of edge clouds in Chapter 8.

IoT and M2M Sensor Data Platform by AerCloud

AerCloud is an IoT cloud platform for collecting, managing, and analyzing sensor data for IoT and M2M applications. AerCloud enables applications to seamlessly scale up to millions of devices while ensuring bullet-proof reliability. The macrolevel architecture is given in Figure 5.3.

At the core of AerCloud is a highly scalable time-series database designed to meet the challenges of scale, speed, and rich analytics that innovative IoT applications demand. Delivered as a platform-as-a-service (PaaS), AerCloud offers a cost-effective, and pay-as-you-grow model that minimizes upfront expenses and enables nearly unlimited future growth. Unlike most

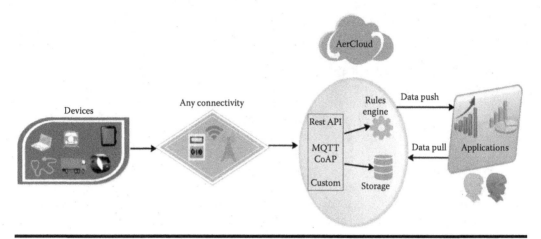

Figure 5.3 IoT and M2M sensor data platform by AerCloud.

AEPs, AerCloud can take an application from prototype to full-scale production. The key functionality is given as follows:

- Secure, reliable collection, storage, analysis, and publishing of M2M and IoT data that scales to millions of users and billions of devices as needed
- A rules engine that processes data in near real time that powers sophisticated alerting functionality in applications
- Industry standard protocols for collecting data from devices including CoAP and MQTT as well as support for custom protocols
- REST API that supports both pushing data to applications and applications pulling data on-demand

The Swisscom M2M AEP offers the following features:

- Comfortable remote management of device firmware with a centralized management platform
- Secure storage of all sensor and device data in the cloud
- Easy monitoring of saved data, reports, and warnings on the basis of graphical user interfaces (GUIs) or programming interfaces (by means of XML and JSON)
- An intuitive platform that allows to efficiently use already available applications and to quickly develop newer applications

ThingWorx IoT AEP

ThingWorx (http://www.thingworx.com/) is the industry's leading IoT technology platform. It enables innovators to rapidly create, debug, and deploy game-changing applications, solutions, and experiences. The IoT platform enables end users to connect, create, analyze, and experience their ordinary things in totally new ways. With ThingWorx, users can

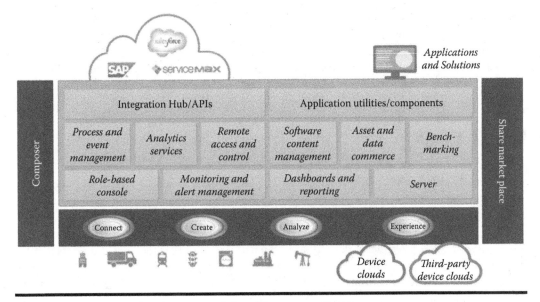

Figure 5.4 The system architecture of the ThingWorx IoT AEP.

■ Connect any device in the ecosystem to the IoT platform
■ Remove complexity and develop IoT applications and solutions
■ Quickly and easily automate complex big data analytics using integrated machine learning (ML) capabilities
■ Deploy solutions to meet the needs of the market—cloud, on-premise, and embedded options meet the needs of every use case

The system architecture is depicted in Figure 5.4.

ORBCOMM IoT Platform

Modern asset-tracking applications take the unique advantages of the cutting-edge identification, connectivity, sensing, tracking, orientation, and context-awareness technologies to remarkably improve visibility, return on investment (RoI), operational efficiency, and manage risk. But there are inherent challenges. The volume of data streamed is enormous. There is an integration need with new and evolving business systems. There are other practical challenges too. With iApp, enterprises can leverage ORBCOMM's scale and experience in a scalable and easy-to-use platform (http://www.orbcomm.com). iApp is a cloud-based IoT service platform that supports high-end IoT performance applications. iApp enables the rapid development, deployment, and management of sensor-based applications. iApp allows the creation of performance solutions that leverage identification tracking and GPS combined with local asset intelligence and monitoring for scalable, high ROI-based applications. iApp leverages satellite, cellular, BLE, RFID, barcode, and Wi-Fi communications technologies to provide the best solutions for customers.

■ *iApp for supply chain*: Track, optimize, and improve the integrity of the supply chain and logistic operations through complete, real-time, and transactional information
■ *iApp for inventory and warehouse management*: Improve the visibility, accuracy, and efficiency of inventory, high-value equipment, and work tools to improve ROI

- *iApp for cold chain and pharma*: Provide immediate *Time Out of Refrigeration* notifications throughout the supply chain by leveraging enterprise systems integration, sensors, and transportation infrastructure
- *iApp for energy*: Manage equipment, tools, people, and vehicles for complex applications involving oil and gas, pipeline, and offshore operations

Azure IoT Hub

The IoT Hub is the new entry in the Microsoft Azure cloud offering. It is a service that enables bidirectional communication between devices and Microsoft business engine in the cloud. The communication channel is reliable and secure and the authentication is per device using credentials and access control as pictorially represented in Figure 5.5.

Microsoft Azure IoT Hub is to easily and securely connect any IoT assets. People can use device-to-cloud (D2C) telemetry data to understand the state of their devices and assets and be ready to take action when a device needs the attention. In cloud-to-device (C2D) messages, it is possible to reliably send commands and notifications to any connected devices, and track message delivery with acknowledgment receipts and device messages are sent in a durable way to accommodate intermittently connected devices.

Azure IoT Hub has an *identity registry* where it stores all information about provisioned devices. This information is not related to devices' metadata but is related to identity and authentication. It provides *monitoring information* like connection status (connected or disconnected) and last activity time; people can enable and disable the devices using this registry. Further on, IoT Hub exposes another endpoint (*device identity management*) to create, retrieve, update, and delete devices.

Amazon Web Service IoT Platform

Amazon web service IoT (AWS IoT) is a platform that enables to connect devices to AWS services and other devices, secure data and interactions, process, and act on device data, and enable applications to interact with devices. The main concept in this IoT platform is the device *state*. The devices (named *things*) are able to report their state by *publishing messages* to the *message broker* through *topics*. The broker delivers received messages to all clients *subscribed* on the specific topics.

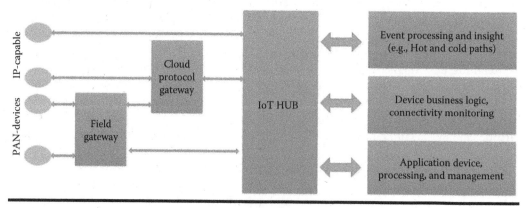

Figure 5.5   The system architecture for the Microsoft Azure IoT hub.

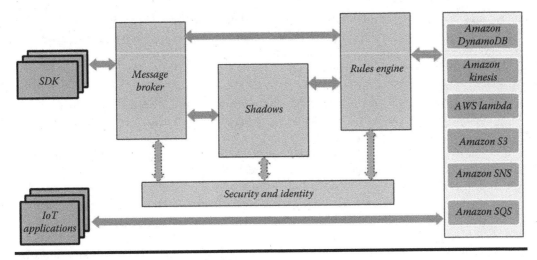

Figure 5.6   The AWS IoT platform architecture.

AWS IoT provides (Figure 5.6) the telemetry data to the system publishing states from devices to the cloud. The platform provides the command pattern changing the desired state for a thing shadow (of course changing the state for a device means to request an action).

AWS IoT has a *thing registry* that contains devices related information and allows adding custom attributes that are part of the devices metadata. The interaction with the thing registry to create, delete, and update things is enabled with the AWS CLI (command line interface) that provides all such operations.

The Axeda IoT Platform

As further described in Chapter 6, cloud technologies have brought about several noteworthy advancements on enterprise IT environments (data centers and server farms). The IT infrastructures are now automatically tuned to be workloads-aware. Based on varying user and data loads, the IT resources adapt themselves to be dynamically elastic to maintain the agreed service levels. Hardware programming and automation tools are the principal contributors for smarter IT. Thus, there is an undiminished rush toward cloud IT. Here too, IoT and M2M platforms are being tweaked to be hosted, delivered, and managed from cloud-enabled data centers (CeDCs). The pervasive and public Internet is the communication network infrastructure to establish connectivity to digitized entities and devices with the web.

There are several network technologies and topologies (WAN, MAN, LAN, CAN, PAN, BAN, and so on) for enabling devices talking with one another, in order to share their unique capacities and capabilities, through data and message communication. With the number of ergonomically designed devices going up considerably, there is a challenge of multiplicity, connectivity, and heterogeneity. With many devices joining in the mainstream communication and computing, the problem of big data raises its ugly head. Thus, devices are clubbed to form ad hoc and purpose-specific clusters to store and subject big data to derive insights in time. Thus, sophisticated platforms are very vital for surmounting the IoT-induced complications.

The Axeda Platform is a complete M2M data integration and application development platform with infrastructure delivered as a cloud-based service. With the highest levels of scalability and security as well as powerful development tools and flexible APIs, companies can quickly build and deliver custom M2M applications for the most demanding requirements and integrate M2M data into key enterprise applications and systems.

The Axeda Platform includes the following:

■ *M2M application services*: Allows developers to extend and customize the core platform functionality via a powerful embedded scripting engine and a rich set of web services for both SOAP and REST consumption
■ *M2M integration framework*: Accelerates integration with the Axeda platform and enterprise systems with standards-based message queue technology
■ *M2M data management*: Processes and stores incoming M2M data; manages device and asset types, data items, locations, alarms, and files; and includes built-in security for managing users, roles, user groups, and device groups

The readers can find the details about some of the renowned IoT or M2M platform vendors by clicking the links below:

1. WebNMS M2M Platform (http://www.webnms.com/m2m/)
2. ConnectM Yantra M2M Cloud (http://www.connectm.com)
3. M2M Platform: Everyware Cloud (EC) (http://www.eurotech.com)
4. Gemalto M2M Solutions (http://www.gemalto.com)
5. AirVantage M2M Cloud (http://www.sierrawireless.com/)
6. M2M Solution from Deutsche Telekom (http://m2m.telekom.com)
7. M2M Cloud Factory – The Open Source, Cloud-based Machine-to-Machine OEM Platform for Manufacturers and System Integrators (http://www.m2mcloudfactory.com/)
8. Connect Anything, Anywhere With Device Cloud (http://www.etherios.com)
9. The Nexus Industrial Internet of Things (IOT) platform makes it easy to launch connected services that reduce downtime and increase revenue (http://www.seecontrol.com/)
10. Telit M2m Platform Solution (http://www4.telit.com)
11. Sensors2Cloud is a specialized Internet of Things application-as-a-service company (http://www.sensors2cloud.com/)

We have discussed some of the IoT application platforms and their distinct capabilities. These platforms are for the capturing sensor, machine, and device data toward the realization of newer applications from the ground-up, or empowering existing applications to be smart. The next set of applications is none other than the analytics-attached and insights-driven applications.

The IoT Data Analytics Platforms

In the beginning, many people were using a single computer in a time-sharing mode for their IT needs. Today everyone has his own computing machine to fulfill his personal as well as professional needs. In the days to unfold, many types of computing, communication, storage, sensing, viewing, perception, knowledge-engineering, decision-making, and actuation devices will be there to collaboratively and cognitively probe and provide assistance to people in their daily chores with all perfection and precision. That is, there will be a bigger number of networked, embedded, and data-generating entities, and elements in and around us to be adroitly and adequately assistive.

The direct fallout is that the volume of data getting generated is bound to explode. With data emerging as the key for any system (simple and complex) to be smart, the aspects of data capture, storage, processing, and analysis are gaining immense momentum.

There are sparkling technologies and tools in plenty for consciously and carefully collecting and subjecting data into a variety of investigations to extract hidden patterns, tips, trends, associations, opportunities, and so on. In short, the process of transitioning of data into information and knowledge are being speeded up through automated tools and optimized processes. For example, consumers buy connected products and their usage in their customer locations, performance, and caliber data are being made available to product vendors. By leveraging product and consumer analytics methods on the gleaned data intelligently, product vendors think of bringing forth better products in their subsequent releases.

Thus, IoT device and thing data are very much indispensable to be systematically and semantically analyzed to squeeze out tactical as well as strategical insights in time. Highly integrated platforms are needed to extract intelligence out of IoT data. In this section, we are to look into some of the accomplished and renowned IoT data analytics platforms and their key differentiators.

IBM Watson IoT Platform

The IoT domain will soon be the largest single source of data on the planet, yet almost 90% of that data is never acted on. With the unique abilities of IBM Watson IoT platform to sense, reason, and learn, Watson opens the door for enterprises, governments, and individuals to finally harness this IoT data, compare it with historical data sets, and deep reservoirs of accumulated knowledge, and then find unexpected correlations that generate new insights to benefit business and society alike. When combined with the IBM Bluemix platform, Watson IoT platform provides simple, but powerful application access to IoT devices and data. Professionals can rapidly compose analytics applications, visualization dashboards, and mobile IoT applications. It helps in creating IoT applications that feed insights to backend enterprise applications.

IBM also will deliver Watson APIs and services on the Watson IoT cloud platform to accelerate the development of cognitive IoT solutions and services, helping clients and partners make sense of the growing volume, and variety of data in a physical world that are rapidly becoming digitized. With these moves, clients, start-ups, academia, and a robust ecosystem of IoT partners from silicon and device manufacturers to industry-oriented solution providers will have direct access to IBM's open and cloud-based IoT platform to test, develop, and create the next-generation cognitive IoT apps, services, and solutions. Leading automotive, electronics, health care, insurance, and industrial manufacturers that are at the forefront of the Industry 4.0 efforts are among those most expected to benefit. The four new API services include:

The Natural Language Processing (NLP) API Family enables users to interact with systems and devices using simple and human language. The NLP feature helps solutions understand the intent of human language by correlating it with other sources of data to understand the situation. For example, a technician working on a machine might notice an unusual vibration. He can ask the system "What is causing that vibration?" Using NLP and other sensor data, the system will automatically link words to meaning and intent, determine the machine he is referencing, and correlate recent maintenance to identify the most likely source and cause of the vibration, and then recommend an appropriate action to reduce it.

The Machine Learning Watson API Family automates data processing and continuously monitors new data and user interactions to rank data and results based on learned priorities. Machine learning (ML) can be applied to any data coming from devices and sensors to automatically understand the current conditions, what is normal, expected trends, properties to monitor, and suggested actions when an issue arises. For example, the platform can monitor incoming data from fleet equipment to learn both normal and abnormal conditions, including environment and production processes, which are often unique to each piece of equipment. Machine learning helps understand these differences and configures the system to monitor the unique conditions of each asset.

The Video and Image Analytics API Family enables monitoring of unstructured data from video feeds and image snapshots to identify scenes and patterns. This knowledge can be combined with machine data to gain a greater understanding of past events and emerging situations. For example, video analytics monitoring security cameras might note the presence of a forklift infringing on a restricted area, creating a minor alert in the system, three days later, an asset in that area begins to exhibit decreased performance. The two incidents can be correlated to identify a collision between the forklift and asset what might not have been readily apparent from the video or the data from the machine.

The Text Analytics API Family enables mining of unstructured textual data including transcripts from customer call centers, maintenance of technician logs, blog comments, and tweets to find correlations and patterns in these vast amounts of data. For example, phrases reported through unstructured channels—such as *my brakes make a noise, my car seems to slow to stop*, and *the pedal feels mushy*—can be linked and correlated to identify potential field issues in a particular make and model of car.

Cognitive computing represents a new class of systems that learn to scale, reason with purpose, and interact with humans naturally. Rather than being explicitly programmed, they learn and reason from their interactions with us and from their experiences with their environment, enabling them to keep pace with the volume, complexity, and unpredictability of information generated by the IoT. Cognitive systems can make sense of 80% of the world's data that computer scientists call *unstructured*, which means they can illuminate aspects of the world that were previously invisible, allowing users to gain greater insight, and to make more informed decisions.

There are more than 9 billion connected devices operating in the world today, generating 2.5 quintillion bytes of new data daily. IBM Watson, the world's foremost cognitive system, is capable of producing actionable insights out of IoT data. That is, accomplishing interactive and iterative processing on big data in order to spit out real-time insights is the essence of IBM Watson IoT platform.

ParStream IoT Analytics Platform

ParStream is the first platform built for IoT that provides immediate insights from big data volumes and high bandwidth data streams. ParStream delivers subsecond query response times even on hundreds of billions of data records while continuously importing new data at very high speed. Via a parallel streaming importer, ParStream enables ultrafast interface and fully flexible analytics to accelerate existing applications and to build new types of applications and business models in telecommunications, renewable energy, manufacturing, and many other industries.

The platform is powered by ParStream DB, a patented database that has consistently been recognized for industry-leading performance with subsecond query response times in analyzing billions of rows of data. It also includes innovative tools such as geodistributed analytics, alerts and actions, time series, advanced analytics, interfaces for the leading streaming or Extract, Transform and Load (ETL) technologies, and seamless integration of the leading visualization tools for IoT.

ParStream DB is a distributed, massively parallel processing columnar database based on a shared-nothing architecture. It was specifically engineered to deliver both big data and fast data, enabled by a unique high-performance compressed index (HPCI). This removes the extra step and time required for decompression of data. The ParStream platform contains a distributed columnar database that processes big data using massively parallel processing (MPP) on a shared-nothing architecture, which provides near-linear scalability on hundreds of terabytes of data. Querying and importing are executed in parallel to effectively use available computing resources.

The ParStream architecture leverages both in-memory processing and disk-based storage. Unlike typical in-memory databases, ParStream holds most of the data on disks and uses only a small amount of memory to hold patented compressed indices and hot data. Through a host of patented technologies, the ParStream IoT platform is able to do real-time analytics on big data. With the billions of connected devices and trillions of digitized objects, the IoT data are going to big data, and hence the platforms such as IBM Watson and ParStream are going to be right and relevant for the forthcoming era of knowledge-filled, service-oriented, and people-centric software applications.

Vitria IoT Analytics Platform

This popular paradigm provides deep and decisive insights in real time and helps to take timely intelligent actions to substantially transform business operations. This IoT analytics platform has a comprehensive set of unified capabilities for IoT applications delivered as a service offering. It includes a powerful set of self-service tools and a unique temporal analytics engine for accelerating IoT application development. The open design helps to leverage existing data, analytics, and tools to get better business outcomes faster. The key capabilities are as follows:

- *Streaming ingestion* leverages IoT communications and protocols to deliver fast ingestion of data.
- *Data warehouse/data lake* accesses historical data stored in various warehouses and databases.
- *Temporal analytics engine* provides faster analytics in real time by unifying across all types of analytics (i.e., streaming, historical, predictive, and prescriptive) to enable smarter actions and business outcomes.
- *Command center* provides a powerful set of self-service tools and dashboards with comprehensive business value indicators.

The platform architecture is depicted in Figure 5.7.

Pentaho IoT Analytics Platform

Sensor, M2M, and network data are expected to play a larger role in analytics as the originally envisaged goals of IoT become a reality. However, these data types present significant challenges related to data volume and variety, as well as predictive modeling. Pentaho provides the ability to blend operational data with data from IT applications and systems of record (SoR) and deliver intelligent analytics to those stakeholders who need them most.

Pentaho empowers organizations to integrate, transform, and orchestrate machine and sensor data in a big data environment as well as blend big data with data from traditional information systems.

- Ingest and process machine and sensor data in big data architectures from messaging services, web APIs, and data files
- Prepare, model, and explore semistructured and unstructured data sets

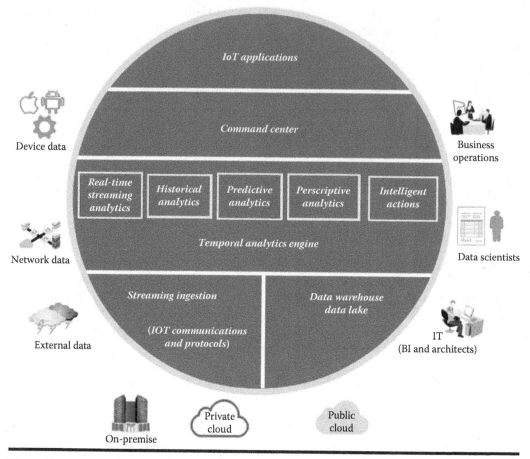

Figure 5.7   The vitria IoT analytics platform architecture.

- Native connectivity to leading Hadoop distributions, NoSQL stores, and analytics databases
- Blend sensor and machine data with data from data warehouses, enterprise applications, social media, and more
- Uncover meaningful patterns in equipment and device data with powerful machine learning and data mining tools

Pentaho's complete analytics solutions enable enterprises to provide customers and partners with equipment and device intelligence in the context of existing applications and business processes.

Splunk Software for IoT Data

Splunk software ingests, analyzes, and visualizes real-time and historical machine data from any source including industrial control systems and connected devices enabling businesses to improve their operations, ensure safety and compliance, perform preventative maintenance, and better manage the lifecycle of assets. The major contributions of Splunk software solutions are as follows:

1. Operations and troubleshooting
   - Measurement and verification
   - Root-cause analysis
   - Capacity planning
   - Anomaly and outlier detection

2. Cybersecurity, compliance, and safety
3. Business analytics
   - Customer intelligence
   - Device intelligence

Machine data, when captured and crunched through proven analytical algorithms, go a long way in safeguarding and shepherding machines. The operational, performance, and security analytics processes support preventive maintenance, ensure the utmost performance levels of machines, and secure the machines from any kind of internal as well as external attacks.

Guavus IoT Analytics Platform

Guavus provides a cloud-based IOT analytics platform that brings together network, machine, and a sensor generated data within the context of enterprise data to enable a new generation of vertically-specific IoT analytics applications. These analytics applications, which span complex data environments, provide contextually-aware insights that can be embedded into workflows and decision-support systems that significantly optimize business processes, resulting in increased value and new revenue streams. The key focus areas include

- Guavus fault management IOT analytics applications correlate and fuse data from smart devices such as alarms, motion sensors, drills, meters, and more to identify element issues, anomalies in traffic, trigger alarms, and automate corrective actions.
- Guavus smart metering IOT analytics applications enable enterprises to harness massive volumes of energy data and turn into valuable business insights. *What-If* scenario analysis and anomaly identification and notification enable businesses to achieve greater energy savings and carbon-emission targets.
- Guavus predictive maintenance IOT analytics applications allow enterprises to leverage advanced machine learning algorithms to identify early warning indicators of failing systems. It reduces unplanned downtime and provides confidence intervals for the time before failure of long lead-time components.
- Guavus service assurance IOT analytics applications bring together sensor, network, and business data to provide a single end-to-end view of any IOT network to enable the faster detection and response to service quality and delivery issues. It can fuse data from data transport systems, applications, and sensors and identify the factors that influence service quality, providing real-time alerts and automated corrective actions. It can also predict the QoS impact resulting from changes in configurations or network performance alerting operators immediately to service-impacting conditions. Finally, it can correlate and integrate historical data with real-time event data to provide go or no-go indicators for high-risk operational actions, for example, drilling wells.

- Guavus resource optimization IOT analytics enable enterprises to become more agile and competitive by maximizing the productivity of various resources in their supply chain.
- Guavus asset tracking IOT analytics applications allow enterprises to better track and manage physical assets and equipment performance.
- Guavus security IOT analytics applications correlate sensor, device, network and business data and apply anomaly detection algorithms to identify potential threat and conditions, breach indicators, and automatically mitigate in-progress attacks.

Thus, there are special-purpose IoT analytics platforms hitting the market so that none of the IoT data goes waste. Every bit gets collected and processed to spit up actionable insights.

Virdata IoT Analytics Platform

This is a highly scalable IoT and analytics cloud services platform with transparent pay-as-you-go pricing. The new platform is designed to monitor, manage, and analyze the hundreds of millions of endpoints and applications that must be networked effectively when offering IoT-based services. Through the integration of Spark and other major open source software, Virdata ensures that enterprises will continue to have the benefit of continuing market innovations. The Virdata platform can be deployed in the cloud, on-premises, or as a hybrid solution, to provide decision makers with actionable insights about how to optimize business operations, develop new revenue streams, and drive customer satisfaction.

Virdata provides enterprises and entrepreneurs in different industries with the necessary means to easily connect and monitor any type of device or application, to collect large amounts of data on a continuous basis, and with the APIs and tools to run actionable analytics in real time on the collected information. Virdata takes care of the following concerns: low-level device and operating system dependencies, NAT-and firewall-friendly connectivity, removing server infrastructure and hardware costs, scaling as the usage grows, data processing and storage, real-time status info and analytics, customized application-specific analysis, and reporting.

Virdata integrates lightweight program libraries into devices and applications for them to establish permanent publish-subscribe connections with the cloud platform. Taking advantage of the elastic nature of cloud environments, Virdata integrates distributed messaging, complex event processing (CEP), data processing, and big data analytics in one single platform that offers portal access, API access, and query capabilities to enterprises and application developers. Due to the simplified applicability across many industry verticals, the results of this unique platform are really fabulous. They are scalable connected car applications, the disruptive remote monitoring, and management of millions of consumer electronics devices, innovative health sensor use cases, and monetizable geomarketing applications for retailers.

Glassbeam is a new yet interesting machine data analytics platform for exceptionally mining machine data for license usage, performance and capacity, trends, and so on to gain valuable product and customer intelligence and to build better products. This can analyze all data including text from our everyday devices besides time series logs. The Glassbeam platform is to manage capacity, inventory, licenses and features, track replacements, view performance stats, and serviceable alerts. Several industries are using the Glassbeam platform to manage licenses, knobs and user profiles, *monitor network utilizations, crashes and reboots, and perform system health checks*. It is also doing a good job in maximizing the lifespan and performance of high-value medical assets, managing inventory, tracking replacements, and isolating facility-specific information including duration of the procedure, affinity to procedure type, and so on. With the machine-generated data projected to be around 80% of the total data being produced, the role, responsibility, and reward of Glassbeam are tending to be on the higher side.

General Electric (GE)'s Predix is the foundation for all of GE's industrial Internet applications providing powerful, consistent, secure, and scalable support for business optimization. GE aviation had analyzed 340TB of data from 3.4 million flights on 25 airlines to improve asset performance and minimize disruptions A truly global industrial IoT platform requires being able to connect a wide variety of machines, sensors, control systems, data sources, and devices. These can include building infrastructure, mining equipment, aircraft engines, health care devices, and even government systems. Predix can securely connect with multiple machines, old and new, from different vendors on very large industrial scales using a heterogeneous mix of data and communication protocols to aggregate data from these devices. The major advantages include:

- *Asset connectivity*: By 2020, around 50 billion assets and devices will be interconnected with one another as well as with the Web. Predix Cloud provides advanced connectivity-as-a-service for these industrial assets, combining proprietary technologies with global telecommunications partners to enable rapid provisioning of sensors, gateways, and software-defined machines.
- *Scalability for machine data*: Predix cloud was purpose-built to store, analyze, and manage machine data in real time. From capturing and analyzing time series data from a locomotive with thousands of sensors to delivering large object data like a 3D MRI image to a doctor for diagnosis, Predix cloud is built for the variety, volume, and velocity of industrial data.
- *Security + Compliance*: Predix cloud is designed with the most advanced security protocols available including customized, adaptive security solutions for industrial operators and developers.
- *Governance*: Predix cloud is designed to streamline governance and drive down compliance costs for each individual user while respecting national data sovereignty regulations globally.
- *Interoperability*: Predix cloud will operate seamlessly with applications and services running on a broad spectrum of cloud environments.

Thus, data is worthless unless it is cleanly gathered and put through a series of analytical processes to extract value-adding and decision-enabling intelligence.

The IoT Data Virtualization Platforms

Data being emitted and extracted by sensors and actuators deployed at various physical locations come in multistructured format. This diversity causes a lot of problems for analytical platforms to make sense out of it. Sensor data fusion is another task gaining importance to extract meaning and intelligence out of IoT data heaps. The data heterogeneity issue has to be surmounted to simplify the process of knowledge discovery and dissemination. There are technological solutions in the form of data adaptors and standards in order to bring in a semblance of sanity in any diverse and distributed data environment. Data virtualization is the new terminology for the age-old data integration. In this section, we are to see a few IoT data virtualization tools.

As per the Denodo website (http://www.denodo.com/en), data virtualization is synonymous with information agility. That is, it delivers a simplified, unified, and integrated view of trusted business data in real time or near real time as needed by the consuming applications, processes, analytics, or business users. Data virtualization integrates data from disparate sources, locations, and formats, without replicating the data to create a single *virtual* data layer that delivers unified data services to support multiple applications and users. The result is faster access to all data, less replication, and cost more agility to change.

Data virtualization is a kind of modern data integration. It performs many of the same transformation and quality functions as traditional data integration [ETL, data replication, data federation, enterprise service bus (ESB), and so on], but leveraging modern technology to deliver real-time data integration at lower cost, with more speed and agility. It can replace traditional data integration and reduce the need for replicated data marts and data warehouses in many cases, but not entirely.

Data virtualization is also an abstraction layer and a data services layer. In this sense, it is highly complementary to use between original and derived data sources, ETL, and ESB and other middleware, applications, and devices, whether on-premise or cloud-based, to provide flexibility between layers of information and business technology.

The Key Capabilities Data Virtualization Delivers

1. *Logical abstraction and decoupling*: Disparate data sources, middleware, and consuming applications that use or expect specific platforms and interfaces, formats, schema, security protocols, query paradigms, and other idiosyncrasies can now interact easily through data virtualization.
2. *Data federation on steroids*: Data federation is a subset of data virtualization, but now enhanced with more intelligent real-time query optimization, caching, in-memory, and hybrid strategies that are automatically (or manually) chosen based on source constraints, application need, and network awareness.
3. *Semantic integration of structured and unstructured*: Data virtualization is one of the few technologies that bridge the semantic understanding of unstructured and web data with the schema-based understanding of structured data to enable integration and data quality improvements.
4. *Agile data services provisioning*: Data virtualization promotes the API economy. Any primary, derived, integrated, or virtual data source can be made accessible in a different format or protocol than the original, with controlled access in a matter of minutes.
5. *Unified data governance and security*: All data are made discoverable and integratable easily through a single virtual layer, which exposes redundancy and quality issues faster. Although they are addressed, data virtualization imposes data model governance and security from source to output data services and consistency in integration and data quality rules.

The enterprise-scale data integration tools are being tweaked to have the inherent capability of capturing IoT data, cleansing, translating, and ingesting them into data storage and analytical platforms. With IoT sensor multiplicity and heterogeneity growing further, there will be more demands for highly powerful data-virtualization platforms.

IoT Data Visualization Platform

Finally, it is all about displaying the extracted in a preferred format. There are report-generation tools, integrated dashboards, and other information visualization platforms in plenty for the enterprise-scale business intelligence (BI) domain. For the raging IoT field, there are a few emerging for demonstrating and depicting the insights generated out of IoT data. Primarily visualization modules are embedded with the industry-leading IoT data analytics platforms whereas there are some detached yet easily attachable visualization tools. The open APIs are the dominant mechanism to integrate dashboards with mainstream analytics platforms to decision-makers to correctly visualize the right and relevant information and insights.

Bug Labs Freeboard (https://freeboard.io/) is a leading IoT data visualization platform. The following use cases definitely vouch for the need for competent visualization tool.

- *Air Quality*: In an effort to provide city bicycle riders with timely, relevant environmental data, Bug Labs teamed with a global wireless carrier to prototype a 3G-connected, GPS-enabled, and air-quality sensor that could be attached to city-sponsored rental bikes. When in use, these specially equipped bicycles provide real-time location-tagged air-quality data that is used to create a crowdsourced pollution index map for other bikers to use when planning their routes.
- *Distillery*: The Heising-330, from Bunker Stills, is a novel, modern, Internet-connected, and fully automated continuous still, built by and for the craft distillery. They use dweet.io + Freeboard to provide real-time remote monitoring and diagnostic information to still operators and maintainers.
- *Humidor*: The Humidor Sentinel is a small, Wi-Fi-connected sensor device that fits inside cigar humidors of all sizes and continuously measures humidity, temperature, and lid position information. Both Freeboard and dweet.io are used to provide real-time monitoring of these key quality metrics.
- *Residential*: More and more homeowners are installing a wide variety of sensors in their houses to provide remote monitoring capabilities of the important environment, security, and energy usage data. Freeboard provides a simple-to-develop way to build a single interface to multiple, disparate sensors from most popular manufacturers.

SenseIoT is a great sensor data storage platform. With SenseIoT, it is possible to easily store the data from heterogeneous sensors and devices safely and securely. SenseIoT also offers new-generation visualization tools, the possibility to set triggers, and manage data remotely. It supports any connected third-party IoT devices, sensors, or sensor networks through a simple open API.

- The city of London has already made a kick start with using the IoT concept. The sensors, which are embedded in the roads in London, help drivers to find parking spaces in busy London streets by creating a real-time map application, which also cuts pollution.
- Always knowing where our goods are is the key to good logistic leadership. Real-time insights and being able to act on this, through useful notifications and triggers, changes the service e-commerce and m-commerce service providers offer to their customers remarkably. SenseIoT also enables real-time visualization of the collected data.
- Energy is scarce. This basically forces us to deal with energy in a more sustainable and responsible manner. Efficient energy resource usage starts with good housekeeping. The records of energy consumption and usage patterns provide unique insights into the peaks of energy usage and the possibility of waste recycling.
- From smart blood pressure meters to smart patches, sensors are making a grand entrance in the world of health care. These devices monitor the health condition of patients on a 24/7 basis. Gaining this unique, real-time patient data can tremendously improve the quality of health care, which ultimately improves the quality of life.

ThingSpeak is another popular knowledge visualization platform gaining immense mind and market shares. This can collect and send sensor data to the cloud, analyze and visualize data, and accordingly trigger one or more actions to one or more recipients. There are several use cases publicly shared on the home page.

Car Counter

Using a webcam and a Raspberry Pi device, ThingSpeak has built a car counter and aimed it at a busy highway. The car-counting algorithm got implemented and deployed in the Raspberry Pi device and used the ThingSpeak platform and the MatLab tool to analyze and visualize the traffic patterns. Similarly, there are other real-world applications being realized through the convergence of IoT technologies and tools. ThingSpeak has the following properties:

- Real-time data collection and storage
- MATLAB analytics and visualizations
- Alerts
- Scheduling
- Device communication
- Open API
- Geolocation data

Thus, visualization platforms are essential for the intended success of the IoT idea. By accurately formatting the acquired knowledge in a visualized fashion, the visualization toolkits contribute immensely for the ensuing IoT era. With the mushrooming of smartphones, tablets, phablets, wearables, and portables, the visualization and knowledge dissemination domain is bound to see a number of delectable advancements in the days ahead.

The IoT Edge Data Analytics

We have seen IoT platforms for application-building and knowledge-extraction running on the enterprise as well as cloud servers. Considering the data volume, variety, velocity, variability, viscosity, and value, the contributions of these platforms are widely applauded and articulated. With the world leaning toward hybrid cloud solutions, there can be one or more channels being established in order to directly or indirectly connect on-premise and offshore IT environments (read cloud centers) to enable process, application, and data integration.

Now there is a twist. As there is an insistence for real-time analytics for bringing forth real-time insights and applications, there is a thought emerging toward local or proximate processing. That is, empowering devices themselves to be intelligent by putting the pioneering analytical capabilities into them. That is, devices are internally enabled to be analytical, articulative, and assistive. However, devices do not have sufficient memory and storage capacities and processing power to run any analytical software therein. Further on, collecting and crunching data using those resource-constrained devices is beset with several problems. For complex processing, several devices in the vicinity are selected to be formally clustered to form device clusters or clouds.

Predixion IQ enables advanced analytics on the edge, so any devices can deliver real-time results to the places they can be acted on. This is a powerful, edge, and cloud-based advanced analytics platform. Predixion IQ can be deployed onto edge devices, gateways, and in the cloud, fully integrated with your business applications. This supports complete end-to-end advanced analytics capabilities from data shaping to production deployment.

Predixion is broadly applicable across many industries including health care, manufacturing, energy, and transportation. Predixion and other companies like it are well positioned to capitalize on the growing adoption of advanced analytics by maintenance repair and operations (MRO) service providers who maintain industrial equipment for companies in a variety of infrastructure-intensive industries: aerospace and defense, general transportation, resource extraction, energy production and distribution, and continuous and discrete manufacturing. Most MRO providers have fixed-price support contracts, so their profit depends on service efficiency. To improve the MRO bottom line, service providers must optimize deployment location and timeliness of spares inventory, service facilities, and service personnel. Huge opportunities lie in the application of advanced analytics, using new big data sources and advanced predictive algorithms, to improve investments in working capital and maximize ROI.

Eclipse Kura is an open source incubator project aimed at providing an Open Service Gateway initiative (OSGi)-based container for M2M applications running in service gateways. Deploying and configuring one device to act as a node in IoT is relatively easy. Doing the same for hundreds or thousands of devices, supporting several local applications, is not so easy. This is where the new Eclipse project Kura comes in. Kura offers a platform that can live on the boundary between the private device network and the local network, public Internet or cellular network, providing a manageable and intelligent gateway for that boundary, capable of running applications that can harvest locally gathered information, and deliver it reliably to the cloud.

Kura can run on everything from general purpose devices, rugged mobile computers, wearable devices, service gateways and vehicle consoles, all the way down to the Raspberry Pi. Implemented as a Java-based platform, Kura can be installed on Linux-based devices and provides a remotely manageable system, complete with all the core services applications need and a device abstraction layer for accessing the gateway's own hardware. Through the Kura project, a set of common services including I/O access, data services, network configuration, and remote management are being provided to Java developers building M2M applications.

The technology proposed in the Kura Project is currently found in Eurotech's Everyware Software Framework (ESF), which, in conjunction with an application enablement platform like Eurotech's Everyware Cloud, can connect sensors, devices, or assets quickly to analyze data in real time for reliable, device-independent M2M applications.

Key Features and Highlights for Developers

Developers working with Kura will find that as it is an OSGi container, they will be working with a standard framework for handling events, packaging code, and a range of standard services. An application in Kura is delivered as an OSGi module and is run within the container along with the other components of Kura. Using the Eclipse Paho MQTT library, Kura provides a store-and-forward repository service for those applications to take the information gathered from the locally attached devices or network-attached devices sending that data onward to MQTT brokers and other cloud services.

Applications can be remotely deployed as OSGi bundles and their configuration imported (or exported) through a snapshot service. The same configuration service can be used to set up Kura's other OSGi compatible services—DHCP, DNS, firewall, routing, and WiFi—which can be used to manage the networking setup of a gateway and provision private LANs and WLANs. Other bundled services available include position, a GPS location service to geolocate your gateways; click, a time service to ensure good time synchronization; DB, a database service for local storage using an embedded SQL database and process; and watchdog services to keep things running smoothly.

To talk to network attached devices, applications can use Java's own networking capabilities (or optional support field protocols, such as Modbus and CAN Bus) to plug into existing device infrastructure. By abstracting the hardware using OSGi services for Serial, USB, and Bluetooth communications, Kura gives application developers portable access to a wide range of common devices though they can still use Java's own range of communications APIs when appropriate. An API for devices attached via GPIO, I2C, PWM, or SPI will allow a system integrator to incorporate custom hardware as part of their gateway.

The Kura package is completed with a web front-end, which allows the developer or administrator to remotely log in and configure all the OSGi-compliant bundles, and which developers can utilize to provide a web-facing aspect to their own application's configuration needs. Developers should find that the Eclipse IDE's OSGi tooling makes the route from code conception to installation on Kura an easily navigable path too. With a combination of an OSGi container, MQTT messaging, a rich range of network and local connectivity, remote web, and command-line control, and the familiar Eclipse tooling support, Kura is set to provide a compelling option for enterprise and IoT or M2M Java developers. We have written more on this emerging research topic in the chapter named as Edge or Fog Computing.

Conclusion

The IoT ecosystem is on the growth trajectory in order to fulfill the tactic as well as the strategic goals of the IoT paradigm. The contributions of the IoT technologies, tips, and tools for building and sustaining sophisticated software applications are overwhelmingly accepted as the most phenomenal aspect of the IT history. Professionals, as well as professors, are working in unison in order to substantially empowering the IoT landscape with a number of newer processes, patterns, platforms, products, practices, and so on. Information and communication infrastructures are being readied and remedied to be exceptionally ready for hosting IoT platforms and applications. In this chapter, we have given the leading platform players and their key differentiators for reaping the benefits being accrued out of the IoT advancements, disruptions, and improvisations. The gist is that how the IoT field facilitates data-driven insights and insights-driven institutions, innovators, and individuals.

The IoT Analytics Platforms—The Links

1. https://xively.com/
2. http://www.thingworx.com/
3. http://exosite.com
4. http://www.digitalservicecloud.com/
5. https://www.parstream.com/
6. http://www.kaaproject.org/
7. http://www.hivemq.com/

8. http://www.ilstechnology.com/devicewise-m2m-iot/
9. https://www.aylanetworks.com/
10. http://www.robomq.io/
11. http://www.ptc.com/axeda/product/iot-platform
12. http://www.cumulocity.com/
13. http://www.davranetworks.com/
14. http://www.platone.co/platform/
15. http://www.windriver.com/products/intelligent-device-platform/
16. http://www.stream-technologies.com/iotx/
17. http://www.kombridge.com/products/
18. http://www.arrayent.com/

Chapter 6

The Next-Generation Clouds for IoT Applications and Analytics

Abstract: The foremost objective of the hugely popular cloud paradigm is to realize highly organized and optimized IT environments for enabling business automation, acceleration, and augmentation. Most of the enterprise IT environments across the globe are bloated, closed, static, complex, and expensive. The brewing challenges are therefore how to make IT elastic, programmable, dynamic, modular, and cost-effective. Especially with the worldwide businesses cutting down their IT budgets, the enterprise IT team has to embark on a systematic and strategic journey to accomplish more with less through a host of pioneering technological solutions. Organizations are cogently leaning toward the view that business operations can run without any hitch and hurdle with less IT resources through effective commoditization, consolidation, centralization, compartmentalization (virtualization and containerization), federation, and rationalization of various IT solutions (servers, storage appliances, and networking components). Further on, the acts of simplification and standardization for achieving IT industrialization gain immense momentum these days. The various IT resources such as memory, disk storage, processing power, and I/O consumption are critically and cognitively monitored, measured, and managed toward their utmost utilization. The pooling and sharing of IT solutions and services are being given the prime importance toward the IT optimization.

Now with the sustained and solid projection by experts and visionaries across the globe that the era of IoT is strongly reckoning and beckoning on us, the paramount and predominant role of clouds as the most appropriate IT infrastructure for efficiently building, hosting, managing, and delivering IoT applications, databases, middleware, analytical platforms, and so on, is on the consistent rise. In this chapter, we talk about the trends and transitions happening in the cloud landscape in order to cope with the noteworthy advancements in the IoT space. Especially we would like to write about the powerful and pioneering cloud offerings:

- Hybrid and federated clouds
- Edge or fog clouds
- Software-defined clouds
- Cognitive clouds

Introduction

It is incredibly true that every common, casual, and cheap thing in our midst is becoming individually as well as collectively smart in their operations, outlooks, and offerings by implicitly yet systematically incorporating a host of technological advancements. Every kind of physical, mechanical, electrical, and electronic goods in our working, walking, and wandering environments are being increasingly instrumented in the design stage itself to exhibit a kind of intelligence in their actions and reactions. Especially instrumented devices, machines, utensils, robots, wares, equipment, sensors, actuators, beacons, bands, and so on are capable of interconnecting with one another in the vicinity as well as with remote ones over any network. Thus, anything meticulously instrumented and interconnected can demonstrate the intelligent behavior.

With the enhanced maturity and stability of smartness-enabling edge or fog technologies, best practices, design patterns, integrated platforms, and synchronized processes, every tangible thing in our personal, social, and professional environments is set to become smart. Ordinary things are becoming extraordinary ones. The digitization and distribution technologies are empowering every concrete thing in our midst to be smart. That is, they are becoming computational, communicative, sensitive, perceptive, and responsive. It is clear therefore that by the year 2020, there will be trillions of digitized entities and elements, billions of connected devices, and millions of software applications. With this unprecedented growth, the IT infrastructure has to be very pioneering, pathbreaking, and productive in order to be right and relevant for the forthcoming era of IoT.

Ultimately computing, communication, sensing, vision, perception, and intelligence have to be everywhere all the time. That is, the era of cognitive and collective computing is fast emerging. The software is to be embedded in everything; knowledge discovery and dissemination are all set to become common and cheap, decision-enablement is through data-driven insights. Knowledge engineering and enhancement are going to be influential through seamless and synchronizing collaboration, correlation, and corroboration. Self-, surroundings-, and situation-awareness are going to be automated to gain context awareness and activity recognition precisely and concisely. Actuation is simply people and precision-centric. Service-orientation is the primary underlying technique. Self-modeling, learning and reasoning, creating hypotheses, and adaptivity and dynamism are the core characteristics of the next-generation systems, networks, and environments, and so on. With all these capabilities meticulously established and entrenched, we will have a bevy of smarter environments such as smarter homes, buildings, grids, campuses, cities, and manufacturing floors.

The IoT technologies, techniques, tools, and tips are immensely and immeasurably contributing for realizing the envisaged smarter world. In short, every touchable thing will become smart, every kind of electronics will become smarter, and every human being is the smartest. Cognition will be the DNA of our everyday systems. The digital living will become contagious and capable of taking the quality of human lives to greater heights. Technologies will significantly enhance care, choice, convenience, and comfort for people. People will be ably assisted by multiple connected and coordinated devices and services. Technologies will play a decisive role in the total world in a silent and succulent manner. Smartphones have induced worldwide developers to come out with thousands of smartphone services for all kinds of people on the go. Similarly other purpose-specific devices for different environments such as hospitals, retail stores, railway stations, bus bays, airports, warehouses, conference halls, stadiums, entertainment plazas, eating joints, service stations, and educational institutions will enable software engineers and innovators to bring forth hundreds of thousands of hitherto unforeseen software applications to simplify and streamline human living across environments. In short, the IoT paradigm is the grandiose way for the future.

However, the crucial part is how to enable and empower our traditional IT infrastructure to easily and quickly fulfill the exponentially enlarging IoT-induced IT requirements. Cloudification is the best way as per the illustrious and industrious IT luminaries. That is why this chapter is earning an important portion and part of this book. We are to describe how cloud IT is playing a very vital and venerable role in shaping up the fast-emerging and evolving IoT-enabled knowledge era.

Reflecting the Cloud Journey

Cloud has become the mainstream concept in IT today, and its primary and ancillary technologies are flourishing and being nourished as described below.

About Technology Choice

There are several competent yet contrasting technologies in the IT space today and hence the selection of implementation technologies has to be strategically planned and carefully played out. The technology embarkation and usage have to be rolled out with all seriousness, otherwise even if the technologies chosen might be sound, yet projects would not see the originally envisaged success. Further on, the history clearly says that many technologies emerged and disappeared from the scene without contributing anything substantial due to the lack of inherent strengths and sagacity. Very few technologies could survive and contribute copiously for a long time. Primarily the intrinsic complexity toward technologies' all-round utilization and the lack of revered innovations are being touted as the main reasons for their abject failure and the subsequent banishment into the thin air. Thus, the factors such as the fitment or suitability, adaptability, sustainability, simplicity, and extensibility of technologies ought to be taken into consideration, although deciding technologies and tools for enterprise-scale, transformational, and mission-critical projects. The cloud technology is the best-in-class technology in the engrossing IT domain with the wherewithal, power, and potential for handsomely and hurriedly contributing for business disruption, innovation, and transformation needs. Precisely speaking, the cloud idea is the aggregation of several proven techniques and tools for realizing the most efficient and elastic IT infrastructure for the ensuing IoT era.

Software-Defined Clouds for IoT

Virtualization has put a firm foundation for the emergence of cloud computing. Especially server machines are being partitioned to carve out highly insulated virtual machines. Then a number of automation tools for resource provisioning, configuration, orchestration, monitoring, and management, software deployment, and delivery along with an integrated dashboard have been built to take the cloud idea to the next level. Most of the manual activities are being automated in the current cloud environments to reduce errors and to speed up the processes. The productivity of IT systems needs to be remarkably increased. There are standards such as OpenStack and their optimal implementations in order to enforce resource portability, interoperability, accessibility, scalability, live-in migration, and so on. That is, the distributed deployment of compute instances and storage appliances under the centralized management is the key differentiator for the prodigious success of cloud computing. The IoT era prefers this sort of IT arrangement in order to achieve what is set before it, and hence cloud is fast-stabilizing and maturing as the most appropriate IT infrastructure for the IoT era.

There are scores of IoT application enablement platforms (AEPs) being deployed on cloud environments. Then there are cloud storage, backup, and archival solutions in order to provide cloud-based IoT data storage and management. Cloud-based AEPs are specially used for simplifying and speeding up the application construction and subsequent hosting on clouds. Further on, as articulated in the IoT data analytics chapter, there are a few ground-breaking analytics platforms on cloud IT to facilitate the extraction of actionable insights out of IoT data, which is generally big in size and polystructured. Cloud networking is also on fast track.

The Enigma of Commoditization

The cloud paradigm is going through a number of incarnations. The future is to have software-defined cloud infrastructures comprising software-defined compute, storage, and networking modules. The crucial role of software on all kinds of our everyday systems is to go up sharply in the days to unfold. Even IT solutions are turning out to be software-intensive. There are proven and promising techniques such as the much-discoursed abstraction and encapsulation. These are mainly used for bringing forth simplicity by moderating complexity for deriving and sustaining software-defined systems. There are other complexity-moderation and mitigation techniques too.

Lately, the aroma of commoditization and compartmentalization is picking up. The tried and time-tested abstraction aspect is being recommended for commoditization. There is a technological maturity as far as physical or bare metal machines getting commoditized through virtualization and containerization. On the networking front, the propriety and expensive network switches and routers and other networking solutions in any IT data centers and server farms are consciously commoditized through a kind of separation. That is, the control plane gets abstracted out, and hence, the routers and switches have only the data forwarding plane. That means there is less intelligence into these systems, thereby the goal of commoditization of network elements is enabled. The controlling intelligence embedded inside various networking solutions is adroitly segregated and is being separately developed and presented as a software controller. This transition makes routers and switches dumb as they lose out their intelligence. Also, this strategically sound segregation comes handy in interchanging one with another one from a different manufacturer. The vendor lock-in problem simply vanishes with the application of the abstraction concept. Now with the controlling stake in pure software form, incorporating any kind of patching in addition to configuration and policy changes in the controlling module can be done quickly in a risk-free manner. With such a neat and nice abstraction procedure, routers and switches are becoming commoditized entities. There are fresh business and technical advantages as the inflexible networking in present-day IT environments is steadily inching toward to gain the venerable benefits of the software-defined networking (SDN) paradigm.

Such kinds of software-intensive systems are capable of guaranteeing the much-wanted IT flexibility. So it is anticipated that software-defined infrastructure (SDI) will be playing a bountiful and beautiful role in the forthcoming era of IoT-inspired knowledge services. Thus definitely, technologies are disruptive and transformative if selected properly and employed prudently. Such software-defined, sharable, composable, policy-aware, tools-assisted, configurable, and elastic environments are the most sought-after ones for the impending era of cognition-filled, context-aware, and connected services.

About the Cloud Technology

With the overwhelming acceptance of cloud concepts, there is a big turnaround and transformation waiting to happen for IT, the overwhelmingly accepted key enabler of business operations. Especially in the infrastructure front, there are possibilities and opportunities for dramatic and decisive optimizations. The cloud paradigm has also brought in newer service deployment, delivery, pricing, consumption, and composition models. Traditional customer-facing, enterprise-grade, and high-performance applications are systematically subjected to an affinity-checking process so that they can be adequately modernized and migrated to any cloud (public, private, and hybrid). These cloud-enabled applications are then hosted, managed, and maintained in centralized and converged infrastructures. Besides applications, all kinds of platforms (development, deployment, delivery, management, integration, and orchestration) are readied and remedied to run on cloud infrastructures without any friction. The Internet is being used as the open, cost-effective, and public wide area network (WAN) communication infrastructure for universal connectivity. That is, client-to-cloud and cloud-to-cloud integration are majorly achieved through the Internet. For specific and special clients, employing dedicated lines is also done toward great reliability, low latency, high throughput and performance enhanced security, and so on.

Before plunging into the cloud arena, there have to be deeper investigations toward gaining a greater understanding of its intrinsic capabilities besides any hidden charges and constraints. There are some scenarios wherein cloud is the best bet, whereas there are some other areas wherein cloud may be a laggard. There are a few well-known shortcomings such as security, controllability and visibility, performance, and so on, especially on faraway online, off-premise, and on-demand clouds. Generally speaking, the raging cloud idea is an amalgamation of a number of established technologies such as on-demand, utility, autonomic, cluster and grid computing models, virtualization and containerization, service-oriented architecture (SOA) and microservices architecture (MSA), multitenancy, and others. Network solutions such as firewall, intrusion detection and prevention, application delivery controllers (ADCs), switches, routers, load balancers, and WAN optimization solutions also play a solid role in assiduously propping up the cloud paradigm. Professors and pundits have come out with an assortment of enabling tools, best practices, design patterns, evaluation metrics, and key guidelines to make the cloud adoption simpler and faster. It is a fact that businesses are getting tangible benefits with the cloud movement at least in the long run. End users are being provided with the facility of anytime, anywhere, any network, and any device access to cloud resources, applications, and data.

Software developers and technical architects are gaining a lot of advantages with cloud-based software development platforms. There is a growing array of internal software libraries to be reused, a bevy of third-party software services, adaptors for files, database, and so on, a litany of connectors and drivers being made available in an integrated fashion in order to speed up the process of application construction. Application programming interfaces (APIs) especially RESTful APIs are copiously made available for any application to find, bind, and leverage appropriate services locally as well as remotely over any network. All kinds of web, mobile, IoT, analytics, cloud, and domain-specific applications can be easily designed, developed, debugged, deployed, delivered, and even decommissioned through cloud-based integrated development environments (IDEs), rapid application development (RAD) tools, and so on. Thus, the field of cloud-enabled software engineering is gaining a lot of momentum among software engineers. The renowned agile development models and methodologies are being meticulously tweaked to work handsomely even in clouds. IBM Bluemix is one of the leading cloud-based platforms for not only developing but also for deploying and delivering workloads to worldwide subscribers in an accelerated mode.

The once widening gaps between development and operational phases are getting closed down with the cloud embarkation and so on. The agile idea is to provide working software to businesses then and there in order to enhance business agility. But the recent DevOps phenomenon is for IT agility. The age-old complaint of software working in development environments is not working in testing, staging, and production environments on expected lines are getting solved through the usage of DevOps tools. With the heightened simplicity, ubiquity, universality, scalability, resiliency, availability, and consumability of cloud infrastructures, platforms, applications, and data, the cloud adoption and adaptation are definitely on the climb.

The Cloud Service Ecosystem

There are several cloud service providers (CSPs) such as IBM [1, 2], AWS, Google, and Microsoft, laying a strong and scintillating foundation for the IoT era. On the cyber side, the aspects such as provisioning, monitoring, and management of cloud infrastructures, methodically hosting an increasing array of cloud-enabled software platforms and applications, and keeping up cloud-resident data are becoming widespread through a variety of technologies and tools. At the ground level, a variety of input or output devices are emerging and captivating people ceaselessly. Slim and sleek, trendy and handy smartphones, tablets, wearables, and other personal and professional gadgets are flooding the market these days. Digital assistants come in various sizes, scopes, strengths, and structures to valiantly capture the market. Thus, IT industrialization at one end through the powerful position of cloud infrastructures and IT consumerization through a family of handhelds, portables, mobiles, pocketable, and so on at the other end are layout of a fruitful foundation for a growing array of smarter and sophisticated applications.

It is proven beyond any kind of doubt that cloud-based services actually have triggered greater business opportunities and possibilities for individuals, innovators, and institutions. The seamless connectivity and integration between physical devices with faraway as well as nearby cloud applications is to bring forth business, social, and personal benefits. Cloud infrastructures and platforms are extensively utilized for running numerous software applications for different industry sectors. For instance, home networking, integration, management, and automation software solutions are being taken to the cloud so that the creation and sustenance of smarter homes are getting simplified. Similarly, there are specific clouds such as sensor and device clouds, data, information and knowledge clouds, and science clouds for various industry verticals. Generic or horizontal application packages too are being modernized and migrated to cloud environments in order to reap all the originally envisaged benefits. Intelligent management solutions are deployed in cloud environments for equipment and devices' upkeep. As illustrated above, the integration between devices at the ground level with remote applications [device to cloud (D2C) integration] is easily fructified through a few pragmatic mechanisms such as open and industry-strength standards for resolving any sort of connectivity issues.

In the recent past, having well-intended RESTful APIs is the dominant factor for device integration. Whether it is installation, maintenance, or updates of device functionalities, the cloud-native as well as cloud-enabled systems come handy. Fresh bundles of functional modules can be dynamically downloaded, installed, and configured into devices to empower them to exhibit exemplary actions and reactions. Remote monitoring, management, repair, enhancement, replacement, substitution, and even decommissioning of several kinds of instruments, machines, ware, appliances, utensils, equipment, and instruments across various environments can be automated with just a few clicks. Automation is gearing and getting toward its peak in every aspect of our personal as well as professional lives.

For example, signage administrators used to send staff to regularly check digital signage equipment located in public places. But now with the surging popularity of clouds, that remote diagnostic, management, and enhancement applications are being taken to clouds, and with this transition, such equipment can be remotely operated and controlled over any network. Also, public institutions could authorize some of their management tasks such as traffic intersection monitoring to CSPs so as to optimize resources and achieve the operational efficiency.

The Key Motivations for Cloud-Enabled Environments

Once upon a time, IT was looked down as a cost center by businesses. Today that sentiment is fast changing, as IT is being increasingly recognized and repositioned as the biggest business enabler. However, with the topsy-turvy world economy, the budget getting allocated for IT department for bringing newer IT capabilities and competencies for continuously bolstering businesses to fulfill changing customers' expectations is increasingly flat and even sometimes lower than the previous years. In a nutshell, businesses want more out of IT investments. Thus, the motto of *more with less* has become a mantra for IT consultants, architects, and professionals to chalk out a viable and venerable IT strategy to support business activities without any lethargy and let up. IT luminaries and visionaries ceaselessly ponder about and work out robust and resilient mechanisms (competent technologies, process excellence, facilitating frameworks, futuristic and flexible architectures, highly optimized and programmable infrastructures, end-to-end platforms, reusable assets, etc.) to enable businesses in their long and illustrious journey. As a part of that IT rejuvenation and renaissance mission, a variety of IT concerns, constrictions, and challenges are being meticulously deciphered and articulated widely across.

IT departments of medium and big business organizations are stuffed and saturated with expensive IT resources. First, an indisputable fact is that across the globe, the IT utilization is very low in the range of 10–15%. That is, the expensive IT resources are sitting idle for most of the time. Therefore, there have been concerted and calculated efforts to enhance the purposeful utilization of all kinds of underutilized as well as unutilized IT infrastructures (servers, storage arrays and appliances, and network solutions) significantly. This assumes a bigger proposition for businesses especially in the context of continuously shrinking IT budgets. When the utilization goes up sharply, there can be substantial IT savings that in turn will lead to the addition of more right and relevant capabilities in the IT kitty without any additional capital investment. Resource pooling and sharing are interesting options for enhancing IT utilization. Thus, the aspect of IT optimization to take on business challenges and changes in a more compact and coordinated manner is the gist of the cloud paradigm.

Secondly, the need for programmability of IT infrastructures is being insisted these days, thereby their configuration, prognosis, performance engineering, governance, maintainability, and so on can be elegantly streamlined and spruced up. All sorts of IT resources enabling businesses are expected to be extremely lean, green, nimble, elastic, versatile, and above all workload-aware. That is, resources need to be aware of their workloads and their expected service qualities and ought to be intrinsically adaptive to meet them comfortably without any deviation, deficiency, and disturbance. The much-mandated capabilities such as resource discoverability and accessibility, maneuverability, consumability, and so on can be quite easily accomplished through the lavish incorporation of software into various IT resources. That is, the futuristic goal of attaining autonomic IT toward smarter computing can be achieved through software-defined environments (SDEs) that in turn comprise software-defined storage (SDS), SDN, software-defined computing (SDC), and so on. That is, IT is getting virtualized totally and the days of software-defined clouds are not too far away.

On summary, the above-mentioned aspects are the two top drivers for all the articulated advancements in the cloud landscape these days. All the traditional data centers are being systematically refurbished with a swarm of proven cloud technologies to be presented as highly elastic, elegant, and economical cloud centers. With this technology-driven cloud-enablement, the IT utilization has gone up to 50%. Still not satisfied with that, there are collective endeavors by thinkers and pundits to raise that value up through intimate and intense software-inspired automation and orchestration capabilities on various types of IT assets to make them grandly supple, smart, and sophisticated. It is being predicted that with this solid and sound enhancement, the IT utilization is bound to go up further remarkably.

A Look at Cloud-Inspired Enterprise Transformations

There are a few noteworthy transitions expected with the embracement of the cloud paradigm. Apart from a renaissance in the IT discipline, different cloud environments for distinct purposes are being set up and opened to be subscribed and used by many. Individuals, institutions, and innovators are extremely optimistic about the cloud formation. Especially businesses are destined to gain immense benefits. That is, cloud-inspired IT agility, adaptivity, and affordability result in businesses becoming inspiringly agile, adaptive, and affordable. There is a third factor oozing out. That is, energy efficiency is turning out to be crucial for future. The cloud movement is to be a game-changer for the environmental sustainability.

The Emergence of Cloud Environments

The key driver for the raging cloudification is that expensive IT resources are lying idle. The first and foremost thing for building cloud is to do an initial assessment of all the resources, workloads, databases, and platforms. There are other nuances to be sounded out for arriving at competent clouds. Clouds definitely play a very deep role in enterprise transformation. The following tasks need to be specifically focused in order to reach the following goals:

1. Infrastructure optimization
2. Process excellence

3. Architectural assimilation
4. Technology adoption
5. Insights-driven decision-making and execution through data analytics

The enterprise transformation becomes a neat and nice reality via a wide array of actions such as process excellence, infrastructure consolidation, and intrinsic assimilation of potential architectural styles and technologies. If there is a glut in IT infrastructure, then infrastructure rationalization, consolidation, and optimization procedures are widely and wisely being recommended. That is, a lean infrastructure is the most desired state of any growing and glowing business, and this significantly reduces the tightly aligned infrastructural complexity and cost (capital as well as operational) in due course of time. With the adoption of autonomic computing concepts, infrastructures are turning out to be the prime target for innately incorporating self-diagnosing, self-healing, self-configuring, self-defending, and self-managing capabilities in order to sharply decrement human intervention, instruction, and interpretation.

Process innovation is the next thing to be contemplated very seriously for enterprise automation, acceleration, and augmentation. Process reengineering, integration, orchestration, management, and governance techniques need to be leveraged in order to bring in lean processes that in turn would have a cascading effect on shifting enterprise operations, outputs, and offerings. Third newer architectural styles are showing a lot of promises and potentials in refining enterprise outlooks. The recently erupted enterprise-scale and business-critical SOA, event-driven architecture (EDA), model-driven architecture (MDA), web oriented architecture (WOA), resource-oriented architecture (ROA), and so on are becoming very popular in designing, developing, deploying, delivering, and sustaining on-demand, adaptive, real-time, dynamic, flexible, and modular applications.

Finally, disruptive, transformative, and inventive technologies are emerging and evolving fast in the IT landscape. Verifying and validating these technologies to be fit for the purpose are very vital for the delectable success. There are pathbreaking technologies that can be generically or specifically utilized for different IT functions. Miniaturization, connectivity, service orientation, virtualization, mobility, cloud, analytics (traditional as well as the most recent phenomenon of big data), and visualization are some of the shining and sustainable trends in the technology space.

Data capture, storage, processing, mining, and analysis for squeezing out actionable insights is turning out to be a game-changer for business behemoths to sustain their journey. Having data analytics infrastructure, applications, and platforms besides information visualization tools in place is essential for any size organization to surge ahead.

Energy Optimization

Energy security and environmental sustainability are the top two global concerns with immense societal impacts. Significant energy assets go toward electricity generation, and electricity is a pervasive service whose reliable supply is essential for modern civilization. Not only generation but also transmission and distribution need to be systematically done toward energy conservation. There is a strong view that clouds enable greenness. To assess the environmental impacts of cloud computing, Microsoft engaged with Accenture—a leading technology, consulting, and outsourcing company—and WSP Environment and Energy—a global consultancy dedicated to environmental and sustainability issues—to compare the energy use and carbon footprint of Microsoft cloud offerings for businesses with corresponding Microsoft on-premise deployments. The analysis focused on three of the Microsoft's mainstream business applications (Microsoft Exchange,

Microsoft SharePoint, and Microsoft Dynamics CRM). Each application is available both as an on-premise version and as cloud-based equivalent. The team compared the environmental impact of cloud-based versus on-premise IT delivery on a per-user basis and considered three different deployment sizes—small (100 users), medium (1,000 users), and large (10,000 users).

The study found that, for large deployments, Microsoft's cloud solutions can reduce energy use and carbon emissions by more than 30% when compared to their corresponding Microsoft business applications installed on-premise. The benefits are even more impressive for small deployments: energy use and emissions can be reduced by more than 90% with a shared cloud service. Though large organizations can lower energy use and emissions [3] by addressing some of these factors in their own data centers (private cloud), providers of public cloud infrastructure are best positioned to reduce the environmental impact of IT because of their scale. By moving applications to clouds, IT decision-makers can take advantage of highly efficient cloud infrastructure, effectively *outsourcing* their IT efficiency investments while helping their company achieve its sustainability goals.

IoT and Cloud-Inspired Smarter Environments

As indicated above, clouds emerge as the one-stop, all-encompassing, fast-growing, state-of-the-art, malleable, green, and lean IT environment for depositing, deploying, and delivering a host of enterprise, mobile, web, wearable, social, environment-specific (smart home, office, manufacturing, retail, hospital, etc.), and embedded applications in an affordable, articulative, and adaptive manner. Not only applications but also all kinds of IT platforms (design, development, execution, integration or middleware, management or governance or security, rule or policy or knowledge engines, orchestration, etc.) are finding these newly crafted, competitive, and elastic cloud infrastructures comfortable, convenient, and caring. In this section, we are to see some sample applications moving to be operated from cloud environments. We have on-premise home automation or networking or integration solutions fully installed in advanced homes. However, with the unprecedented maturity and stability of cloud environments, most of the common, shareable, and sustainable functionalities are tenderly separated and hosted in remote clouds, whereas home-specific features are with on-premise home gateways. This sagacious segregation goes a long way in eulogizing and employing the hybrid path.

Smarter Environments

Having understood the inherent need for context awareness in order to develop and sustain a variety of smarter environments, there are a number of viable and value-adding context-awareness frameworks by industry researchers as well as academic scholars. IT product vendors and academic institutions have been working together and bringing forth a number of nimbler computing paradigms in order to accomplish widely changing expectations of businesses and users. However as it turned out, the reality is that computing systems could do only preprogrammed things. That is, software applications on receiving specific inputs are capable of producing predetermined outputs. Inputs are typically fixed beforehand and the outputs are as per the expectations. However, with the penetration of IT into different industry sectors, the role and responsibility of IT are bound to grow substantially. All kinds of runtime changes need to be taken care of by software packages in order to be distinct in their actions and reactions. That is, as context changes naturally or forcefully, the processing software has to accurately absorb the changes in time to turn and tune the outputs. That is, the challenge lies in empowering software services to perform real-time capture of all kinds of changes (social, business, environmental, spatial, temporal, etc.) to come out with more situation-specific and aware results. Multimedia, multimodal, and multifaceted applications are the need of the hour. That is, next-generation software will be more aligned and applicable directly or indirectly to end users. Precisely talking, IT is tending from business to be people-centric.

That is, futuristic compute machines can take several types of internal as well as external input data from distributed and disparate sources to produce smarter results that are more relevant to humans' situational needs. That is, the user(s)' context is being flawlessly captured and profusely leveraged by compute clusters to produce right and relevant results for humans. Users' context is being primarily decided based on the implicit capability of establishing seamless and spontaneous connectivity and integration with a dynamic pool of software services and applications (social, enterprise, mobile, embedded, and cloud), multiple data sources, scores of devices, appliances, and sensors in the user(s)' environment. In a nutshell, the fast-emerging paradigm of context-aware computing is to produce context-sensitive outputs for human beings to act on that with all the clarity and confidence. Figure 6.1 vividly illustrates how different systems, sensors, and actuators are being quickly integrated to do a real-time capture of disparate and distribute data and leverage them cognitively to arrive at appropriate and actionable insights.

Smarter Homes

Home automation elements are being manufactured in plenty, linking of distributed and disparate devices are being smoothened out, conceiving newer and nimbler services are in full swing, enabling frameworks, infrastructures are virtualized and pooled, and proven processes are in place, clustered, brokered, federated, and cloud architectures are being worked out, and so on.

The present-day smart home involves home servers inside homes for integrating diverse household electronics and for their effective control and usage. However, the need to manage, even

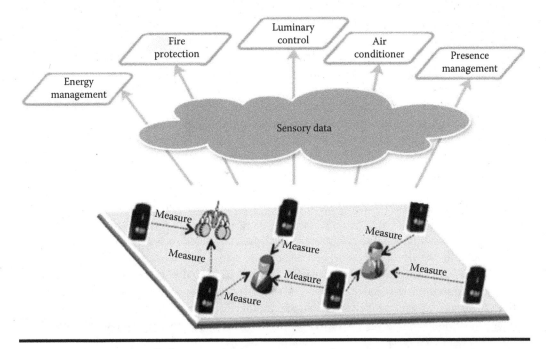

Figure 6.1   A sensor-stuffed smarter environment.

if done remotely, very complex IT devices in the home has prevented this approach from being widely adopted. A more effective approach is to connect the devices to services in the cloud. This enables the centralization of services. Putting the intelligence into services in the network cloud reduces the complexity of managing software in the home-bound devices and simplifies the interoperability of devices. This is accomplished by bridging the services throughout the network through services interfaces, translating the different device protocols to a common platform, and then connecting the devices through the network cloud. This is a far less expensive and more flexible way to aggregate services and compose new services out of existing devices. This takes out the complexity out of the connected devices in the home. The consumer moves from being the IT manager of their home to a consumer of services through their connected devices. A local services *clone* or services cache in the home can safeguard the availability of services against network problems and guarantee continuous availability all with a simple control by the consumer. With new cloud-hosted services, newer possibilities emerge for an appliance as simple as a pool pump or refrigerator when it has the ability to sense and respond to changing conditions, to communicate with other systems, and to inform decision-making.

In summary, a smarter home is a personal and personalized place atheistically designed to add life value, comfort, choice, care, and convenience, energy-efficiency, safety and security, and future expansion. Without an iota of doubt, home is the most lively and lovely place for people in their everyday lives. People spend more time in their homes and hence automating home operations acquires special significance. A growing array of edge and digital technologies is being retrofitted to be usable and useful for easily and quickly producing and sustaining smarter homes. A copious production of home automation elements, industry-strength and open standards, trendy electronics, application development platforms, dynamic, virtualized, and converged infrastructures and proven processes are being given a fresh coat of life and thrust in order to build digital and cognitive homes.

Wireless broadband communication, ambient, agile and adaptive sensors and actuators, smart heating, lighting, ventilation, and air control systems, sophisticated, energy-efficient and connectable edutainment, and infotainment electronics, home security appliances, kitchen utensils, and so on will be profusely and prominently utilized in futuristic home environments in order to sufficiently enhance the quality of life. Digital electronics, technology-enabled and gripped spaces, the information superhighway, analytics platforms, the Internet of services and things and energy, and the arrival of cognitive systems complying with cognitive computing all singlehandedly and collaboratively contribute to the greater goals of smarter homes. Sophistication and smartness are the trends that decisively hold the home ICT. The powerful arrival of cloud technology syncs up with the smart home technologies and methodologies to lead to smarter homes.

A cloud-based monitoring framework for Smart Home: In [4], Lingshan Xu and his team have proposed a cloud-based monitoring framework to implement the remote monitoring services of a smart home. The main technical issues considered include data-cloud storage, local-cache mechanism, media device control, and network address translation traversal. The implementation shows three scenarios: (a) operating and controlling video cameras for remote monitoring through mobile devices or sound sensors, (b) streaming live video from cameras and sending captured image to mobile devices, and (c) recording videos and images on a cloud computing platform for future playback. This system framework could be extended to other applications of smart home.

Smarter Grids

Due to vociferous demands, the modern power grid is transforming into a cyber-physical systems (CPS), where the physical infrastructure and cyberinfrastructure must coordinate to ensure an efficient and reliable power energy grid. However, there are some practical challenges. Existing grid operations require human decisions. Also, renewables such as wind and solar energy are inherently unreliable and cause the electricity supply to be susceptible to the vagaries of nature. On the demand side, intelligent appliances, electric vehicle adoption, and rooftop solar panels make the consumer load profile variable. Any demand-supply mismatch causes grid instability unless rapidly rectified. Here the importance of big data analytics (BDA) (see Chapter 7 for an explanation of BDA and its growing influence on establishing and sustaining smarter environments) plays a critical role toward empowering automated decisions as human grid operators are actually ill-equipped to analyze large amounts of data from millions of distributed smart electric meters and from other data and control points. BDA infrastructures and platforms are able to capture, store, process, analyze, and mine an unprecedented influx of sensing data from multiple sources toward the timely extraction of actionable insights to decisively empower control systems to proceed without any specific interpretation, instruction, and involvement of humans.

The typical requirements include energy usage events streaming from millions of smart meters, sampled every 15 minutes, and must be collected and correlated with a consumer's historical profile. Data mining and pattern matching are necessary for online detection of critical situations and their correction with low latency for grid stability. Analytical and computational models can help predict the power supply and demand to take preemptive actions for curtailing demand by notifying consumers of time. These efforts are incidentally multidisciplinary and require power engineers, data analysts, behavioral psychologists, and microgrid managers to share knowledge for optimal operations with the active participation of consumers. Having understood these specific requirements, the authors have built a cloud-based software platform for data-driven analytics that takes a giant and ground-breaking step toward the smart grid vision [5].

Their efforts have addressed dynamic demand response (D2R) optimization, a unique challenge-application, in which supply-demand mismatch must be detected and preemptively corrected by initiating demand-side management from consumers. This software platform supports D2R activities through a semantic information integration pipeline to ingest real-time data from sensors and dynamic data sources, a secure repository for researchers and engineers to collaborate and share data and results, scalable machine learning (ML) models that are trained over massive historical data sets to predict demand, and a web portal and mobile app to visualize current and historical energy consumption patterns. This software package got deployed in a cloud environment, and it has been found to be fruitful in many ways.

IoT and Cloud for Smarter Cities

Technological innovations such as extremely and deeply connected devices, distributed, disposable, and diminutive sensors and actuators, and the emergence of the Internet as the open, public and affordable WAN communication infrastructure, clouds as the core, centralized and cognitive one-stop platform for hosting software applications and services, and so on, are enabling cities to capture valuable data, develop and deploy new services, and enhance existing services substantially, ushering in the era of smarter cities. These services can bring definite improvement in the effectiveness of city management, generate new growth opportunities for businesses, empower innovations in all aspects, and raise the quality of citizens' lives.

An early example of a smart city, South Korea's Busan Green u-City [6], is using a cloud-based infrastructure delivered by a successful collaboration between the local government and a global technology supplier. The benefits of these new services to citizens are varied and numerous:

- Increase citizens' benefits by timely welfare services information distribution.
- Improve information accessibility by delivering information through various media channels and devices.
- Improve learning experiences by two-way video communication enabled mentoring.
- Increase free education contents and its quality for low-income community residents and students, and thus to deal with social divide issues.
- Reduce overall or regular health care cost, especially for low-income residents and solitude living aged people.
- Improve access to care services for chronic diseases, reducing the need for patients to visit remote hospitals.
- Create new markets for participatory urban regeneration projects applying u-City technologies.
- Provide wider revenue creation opportunities by open innovation-based urban regeneration framework.

Sensor-Cloud Integration for Smarter Cities

Sensors and actuators are the eyes and ears of future IT in order to effortlessly capture disparate data from an increasing array of distinct sources. Correspondingly there are cloud-based analytical solutions to incredibly capitalize the accumulated data to extract actionable knowledge toward achieving and sustaining the smarter world vision. With clouds emerging as the web-scale, enterprise-class, highly organized, and optimized IT infrastructures, there is a persistent and pressing need for sensors at the ground to be seamlessly and spontaneously integrated with online, on-demand, and on- or off-premise cloud environments. That is, sensors and actuators could be interfaced with remote clouds for exchanging data and control messages then and there.

It is going to be a two-way communication. That is, data gets transmitted to the cloud and on the other hand, cloud-based services, in turn, monitor, measure, manage, and maintain scores of physical sensors and devices. In a nutshell, by adding sensors and actuators into the mix, new opportunities and fresh possibilities for contextualization and geoawareness are exploding continuously. In future, we may read, feel, and even experience *Sensing and Actuation as a Service* (SAaaS). This advancement will lead to insights as a service (IaaS). Thus, every ordinary object [7] is connected with one another as well as service-enabled in order to interact with cloud-based applications so that they could exhibit exemplary behavior. Sensors [8] are thereby empowered to be smart in order to join in the mainstream computing to be a great enabler of people in the days ahead. Every small or big environment being stuffed and saturated with a number of different sensors are going to be a greater contributor toward smart cities.

Social and Sensor Data Fusion in Cloud

Mobile phones are not only enabled with communication capabilities but also blessed with more computing power these days. Further on, a variety of minuscule sensors are smartly embedded inside mobile phones to make them multifaceted in their offerings and outputs. That is, with the unprecedented advancements in the miniaturization technology domain, phones are becoming slim and sleek, trendy and handy, yet are multimedia, multisensor, multimodal, and multipurpose devices. Phones are also cloud-enabled, thereby all kinds of software applications and data being deposited in cloud repositories can be discovered, accessed, and used by phones at any time and any place. That is, mobile phones readily become smart through the internal integration of multiple electronics and the external integration with sophisticated services getting hosted in service registries and repositories installed on off-premise or on-premise or edge clouds.

Smartphones could capture or record, accumulate large volumes of data related to our daily lives, and upload them in social websites, and in remote powerful storage systems. Smartphones facilitate connected people just as sensors and actuators enable common, casual, and cheap items to become connected entities. That is, people are increasingly connected with one another all the time as well as with the outside world through smartphones. In a nutshell, phones are not only competent input or output devices but also a data capturing, aggregation, and transmission platform. A broader category of cloud-based people-centric applications is being delivered to humans through smartphones.

Without an iota of doubt, the two popular day types are social and sensor data, and they are passionately collected from different and distributed sources and fused to be right and relevant for people in their daily walks and works. Social-networking services facilitate users to share their ideas, opinions, pictures, videos, news, and other various forms of contents over the Internet, the most pulsating and pioneering communication infrastructure. On the other hand, sensors and actuators are primarily for gathering environmental data toward self, surrounding, and situation-aware information. In short, advanced context-aware applications exceptionally run in the cloud. Social and sensor data are gleaned, cleansed, and fed to cloud-based applications, and platforms to be crunched as any cloud in simplistic terms provides tremendous processing, memory, and storage capabilities. The resulting insights can be readily and rewardingly shared to people through smartphones in time and given to automated systems.

Surender Reddy Yerva and his team [9] have built a travel recommendation system that allows blending the heterogeneous social and sensor data for integrated analysis and then extracting weather-dependent people's mood information. This system offers the information of people's moods regarding the predicted weather on where and when users wish to travel. The architecture of the recommendation system comprises several components for accomplishing effective, large-scale social, and sensor data fusion. In concluding, such kinds of sensor and social data fusion feature and functionality leads to a sequence of activities toward the ultimate knowledge engineering and delivery: gathering and fusing of data from multiple sources, applications deployed in clouds receiving and leveraging them in real time to aggregate, process, transform, mine, and analyze to emit actionable insights, and smartphones emerging as the all-encompassing device for disseminating the emitted context knowledge to empower the concerned to ponder about the next course of actions with all confidence and clarity, and so on.

Smarter Health Care

As mentioned above, there are several types of smarter environments emerging and a litany of attractive use cases is being proposed. Ambient assisted living (AAL) is a very prominent use case for smarter homes. The need is to empower bed-ridden, debilitated, and diseased people to lead an independent and digitally assisted living. For example, if a person living alone wants to have a cup of filtered coffee, he or she can instruct the coffee maker in the kitchen through a smartphone command. Once the coffee is ready, a robot can be ordered to fetch the prepared coffee from the kitchen to his or her bedside. Similarly, medicine cabinets can have an alert or reminder facility to take tablets on time, the movement of the person can be monitored remotely, household items can be bought over through mobile commerce sites, food stuffs can be purchased online, all kinds of consumer electronics, energy managers, kitchen vessels and wares, instruments, micro ovens, infotainment and edutainment systems, dishwashers, toasters, refrigerators, and health care monitors, and so on can be instrumented and interconnected to have intelligent behaviours, thereby the everyday activities and requirements can be met with all choice and convenience.

There are universal remote devices to operate all kinds of connected devices within home environments. Home networking and automation technologies, topologies, tools, and techniques are being unearthed in order to have smarter homes resulting in hitherto unforeseen services for house owners, occupants, visitors, guests, and so on. New services getting developed and loaded in service repositories deployed on worldwide cloud-based platforms and infrastructures can be automatically subscribed by home-bound devices to be empowered accordingly. Events are captured and processed immediately to emit real-time insights. Both push and pull mechanisms are recommended to enable people all the time.

Cloud-Inspired Smarter Health Care Services

The unprecedented adoption of the cloud concepts by various business verticals has impacted the health care industry too. The health care industry's technology infrastructure has been highly fragmented, inflexible, closed, and expensive. Due to the widely expressed concerns of data security, IT platforms, and health care applications and data are overwhelmingly maintained in-house IT infrastructures. Now having understood the strategic benefits, the health care sector across the world is keen to systematically leverage the cost and agility benefits of the cloud paradigm without compromising on the aspect of data security. The key question here is whether the cloud scheme is a definite and decisive game changer for every aspect such as operating models, premium service offerings, collaborative capabilities, and end user services of the health care industry. As per the changing scenarios, the health care segment too is going through a variety of elegant transformations such as appropriating the digitization, connectivity, and collaboration technologies tirelessly. The health care data volume, velocity, and variety are consistently on the climb with the mass availability of high-end and connected machines, instruments, and devices for precisely and perfectly enabling health care services and process automation. Therefore, the appetite for latest cloud infrastructures and platforms for hosting health care applications and depositing patient data safely and securely is growing. Electronic health record (EHR) services are increasingly cloud-based. Telediagnosis and telemedicine tasks are being activated and accomplished through cloud-based software applications.

Health care data posted in cloud environments [10] are easily accessible and shared across the regions by doctors, practitioners, and so on. Governmental rules and regulations stringently mandate to store data for an extended period of time. Besides the mainstream applications, the data backup, archival, and recovery requirements force hospitals and clinics' IT manager to ponder about the cloud movement. Medical imaging is a very critical need for health care. Extracting reusable patterns and insights out of medical images in time goes a long way in empowering physicians, medical field experts, and caregivers in prescribing the correct medicine in perfect dosage. It is, therefore, clear that the cloud technology is going to be hugely critical for visualizing next-generation medical applications and delivering them with all the quality of service (QoS) attributes embedded. Clouds will emerge as the one-stop solution for taking patient care to the next level with all ease and elegance.

The Era of Hybrid Clouds

Due to a variety of reasons, private cloud options are being seriously considered by business houses. Especially for the sake of having deeper visibility of the total IT environment, the end-to-end controllability, the guaranteed performance and dependability with nil network latency, and above all, impenetrable, and fool-proof security, private cloud environments are being prescribed as a part of IT strategy enterprise. Public clouds are also important as they are web-scale, cost-effective, being manned by trained, experienced and skilled experts, being continuously standardized toward open, interoperable, connected, and federated clouds. Other noteworthy cases for public clouds include every kind of customer-facing workloads and are being modernized and migrated to public clouds, and there are a number of social networking sites running in public clouds. That is, everything is service and cloud-enabled to be found, bound, and composed toward better and bigger things. Thus, public clouds are turning out to be the core and central service-oriented platform for all kinds of applications (social, business, embedded, mobile, analytical, operational, transactional, and IoT) and data. The noteworthy point here is that there are certain deficiencies and drawbacks with public and private clouds. Thus for any growing enterprises, hybrid cloud, which is the seamless combination of private as well as public clouds, is being positioned as the best way forward.

Further on, there are cloud integrators, orchestrators, and brokers hitting the market enabling the interconnection of diverse and distributed cloud environments in deriving complicated and composite processes. Hybrid clouds are being studiously rolled out by establishing a linkage between traditional IT infrastructures, private and public clouds, and third-party services. The hybrid cloud ensures most of the IT infrastructures do not go waste as there are ways and means of capitalizing the already made investments.

There are several parameters such as data locality and security, workload performance and throughput, and network latency, being considered to choose clouds these days. The aspects of workload partitioning, factoring, and offloading are being systematically researched to arrive at compact methods for workload fitment and consolidation to achieve the intended success in this hybrid era. Hybrid clouds are gaining a lot of mind and market shares as they are capable of surmounting the various constrictions associated with public and private clouds. Again the scope for hybrid clouds is bound to widen and deepen further, considering the faster adoption of the cloud idea. Specific technical, scientific, and professional communities are keen in establishing community clouds. Thus, it is not an overstated statement that the cloud journey in transforming businesses as well as individuals is on the right track.

The widely circulated and castigated vendor lock-in issue is being attended through open and industry-strength standards so that the real spirit of hybrid clouds can be voluntarily accomplished. These standards enable the migration of workloads among multiple CSPs so that the hybrid cloud vision is to see the light sooner than later.

Envisioning Federated Clouds

With the overwhelming cloud adoption, multiple CSPs are putting their shops with different capacities and capabilities across the globe. Definitely, the multicloud environments are the new normal. Cloud federation refers to the runtime synchronization of software, platform, and infrastructure services from geographically distributed and disparate cloud toward fulfilling specific business demands. The Internet is the primary communication infrastructure for users to access the federated applications and resources anytime anywhere any device and any network. Brokers and network gateways are the most important gluing and fusing mechanisms for federating multiple clouds. Hybrid clouds are being meticulously extended to accommodate newer demands resulting in federated clouds. With the technological maturity and stability, there will be a further impetus toward the vision of the Intercloud.

There are several key drivers and strategic advantages for cloud federation. The IT service delivery is bound to be greatly optimized and organized through the federation of cloud resources. Selecting a cloud service provider for a particular workload in terms of affordability, availability, and amenability gets realized through cloud federation. The enlarged utilization of cloud resources is guaranteed through cloud federation. The real value of distributed computing through an integrated and centralized dashboard can be attained through the federation of clouds. Composite and process-aware services can be obtained through federation. The disaster and data recovery tasks can be simplified through federation. Fault-tolerance toward business continuity, resource clusters and grids, scale-out or horizontal scalability, policy-based activation, and so on are some of the key benefits of cloud federation.

Cloud Federation Approaches

As inscribed above, brokers and gateways play a very vital role in shaping up the cloud federation idea further. There are at least three architectural styles for implementing cloud federation as articulated in Figures 6.2 through 6.4.

In the centralized scheme (Figure 6.2), cloud brokers find to bind and create a cloud federation out of multiple clouds to fulfill the requirement.

In the decentralized scheme (Figure 6.3), clouds, in a peer-to-peer manner, negotiate themselves to establish the required partnership to have a cloud federation. They typically do the tasks of a cloud broker such as cloud discovery, communication, verification, and selection of appropriate clouds to achieve the job in hand.

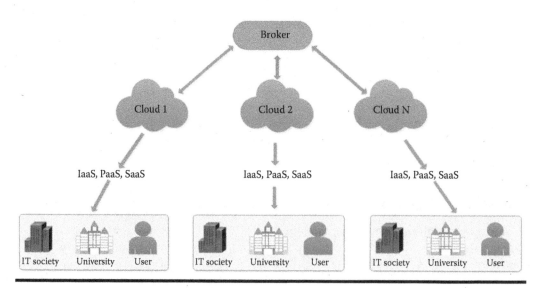

Figure 6.2 The centralized approach.

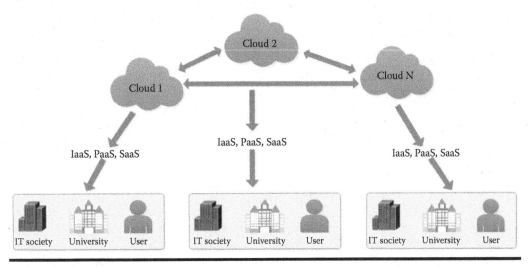

Figure 6.3 The decentralized approach.

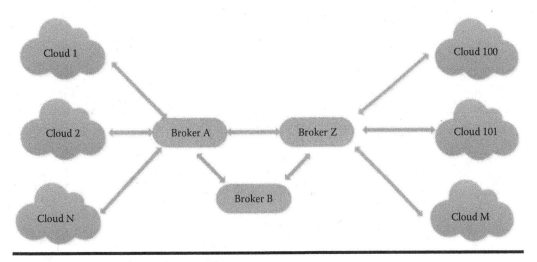

Figure 6.4 The hierarchical approach.

Clouds are connected to a broker and each broker can also interact with other brokers in order to look for fitting clouds for realizing the cloud federation. Federated clouds are typically multicloud environments for efficiently accomplishing mission-critical business requirements. The slow yet steady realization of federated clouds has laid a stimulating foundation for the era of the Intercloud. With standard organizations and other agencies painstakingly endeavoring for arriving at simplified and streamlined standards, the days of the Intercloud are not too far away.

Special-Purpose Clouds

Apart from the generic public, private, community, and hybrid clouds, there are several purpose-specific clouds being built and sustained by various organizations. For example, there are mobile backup clouds for stocking up all kinds of mobile messages, videos, audio clips, photos, e-mails, and so on.

iCloud is the Apple's cloud environment (http://www.apple.com/in/icloud/) that connects you and your Apple devices in amazing ways. iCloud photo library and iCloud drive keep all your photos, videos, and documents stored securely and updated everywhere. Family sharing lets you easily share music, films, photos, and more with everyone in your family. Find my iPhone even helps you find your device if you lose it. With iCloud, you always have what is most important to you on whatever device you have at hand. And it is all done automatically.

Similarly, there are other backup clouds such as Dropbox for storing all kinds of files of Android phones. Object storage solutions are very prevalent in public clouds. There are science, knowledge, sensor, storage, and data clouds. In the ensuing section, we are to talk about device clouds.

Device Clouds

As we all know, read, and experience, the device ecosystem is on the fast track these days. Every human being is all set to be assisted by tens of devices (wearable, portable, pocketable, implantable, etc.) in his daily walks and works. Every home is getting stuffed with hundreds of hi-fi electronics, appliances, media players, Wi-Fi routers, and so on, every car is being empowered with hundreds of edge devices such as in-vehicle infotainment system, network gateway, controllers, sensors, chips, and actuators, every manufacturing floor is saturated with a number of connected machines, equipment, instruments, and so on, every library is filled up with hundreds of tagged books, and so on. Every center of interest is being adorned with a number of sensing, monitoring, measuring, managing, and actuation devices. Devices will follow us wherever we go. Devices being deployed in and around us are going to be multifaceted and hence capable of producing a lot of data every second.

All kinds of devices in our every environment are getting hooked to faraway clouds to be accordingly empowered by cloud-based services and data. On the other hand, device and environment data are shared with cloud-based analytics databases and platforms. Cloud-based analytics is gaining a lot of momentum because of clouds' cost-effectiveness and elasticity. Device clouds are being formed in public clouds wherein all kinds of device data gets accumulated and subjected to a variety of investigations to emit out actionable insights that can be fed back to devices on the ground or to cloud-based applications to be distinctively superior in their deals, deeds, and deliveries.

The other use cases of device clouds include the following:

■ A device cloud can be a mobile testing environment that enables developers to remotely evaluate the performance of applications on a wide range of smart devices.
■ The device cloud gives organizations access to modern and legacy devices so that they need not expend on buying, installing, configuring, and operating a variety of devices in their own backyards.

Wind River Helix Device Cloud [http://www.windriver.com/] is a ready-made, cloud-based platform for IoT that greatly reduces the complexities of building and rolling out large-scale embedded

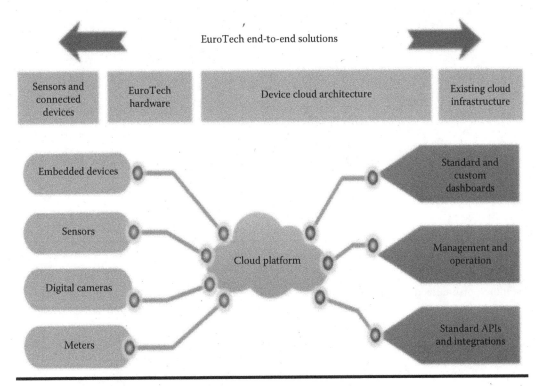

Figure 6.5 Cloud-based device management platform.

device networks. The device cloud securely manages the movement of data from devices, through gateways, and into the enterprise. It helps integrate that data with other systems and data sources, which it then uses to automate control of IoT devices and machines. And with device cloud, organizations can easily update hundreds or thousands of devices through remote software updates.

The Eurotech Everyware Device Cloud (EDC) [http://www.eurotech.com/en/] is an end-to-end solution (Figure 6.5) that includes purpose-built hardware, connectivity, and embedded device management through the Eurotech Software Framework, the Everyware Device Cloud Client, and machine-to-machine (M2M) cloud-based services to deliver actionable insights from the field to downstream applications and business processes, dashboards, and reports.

The cloud platform [http://www.whiznets.com/] allows dynamically controlled, configured, and evolved application that runs on the field device through a fully integrated feature-rich device management layer. Cloud automatically stores device data into a database, which is fault-tolerant and elastically scalable. This database stores any data in any format and enables access to real-time data, for use by the application. The platform (Figure 6.5) enables business decisions to be instantly triggered based on real-time rules applied to collected data. These unique capabilities, including data filtering, continuous queries, aggregation and correlation between devices, and event pattern recognition to ensure rapid reaction to business-critical situation scenarios (Figure 6.6).

The HealthSuite digital platform [http://www.usa.philips.com/healthcare] represents a new era in connected health care for both patients and providers, as health care continues to move outside the hospital walls, and into our homes and everyday lives. HealthSuite, supported by salesforce.com, is an open, cloud-based platform, which collects, compiles, and analyzes clinical and other data from multiple devices and sources. Health systems, care providers, and individuals can access data on personal health, specific patient conditions and entire populations—so care can

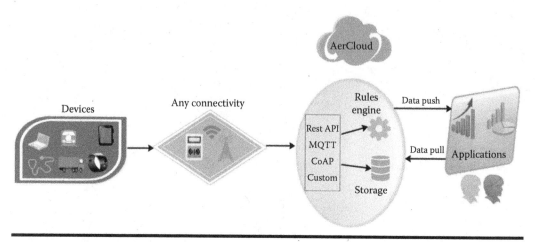

Figure 6.6 Empowering device applications.

be more personalized and people more empowered in their own health, well-being, and lifestyle. Connecting solutions from the hospital to the home, we can enable a path to healthier living and well-being throughout the health continuum.

However, the recent focus is not only about the extreme connectivity but also on smartly leveraging the compute, storage, and network capabilities of devices among us. The idea is to create a kind of personal or local or edge or fog clouds for accomplishing an emerging array of real-time and personalized applications with all security and sagacity. The next section is allocated for explaining the specifics about edge clouds.

The Emergence of Edge/Fog Clouds

Edge computing pushes applications, data, and computing power (services) away from centralized points to the logical extremes of a network. The industrialization and commoditization aspects that considerably elevated the power of cloud computing are now penetrating into everyday devices in our midst. That is, devices are becoming steadily miniaturized yet computationally powerful, fitted with more storage capability, increasingly interconnected, and service-enabled. It is expected that these new-generation devices are to substantially embolden and extent the traditional cloud model to form and firm up even bigger, cheaper, high-performing, resource-aware, extensible, versatile, and resilient clouds that are more right and relevant for end users. Now with the copious arrival and overwhelming acceptance of generic as well as purpose-specific devices, the prevailing concept of cloud is bound to change forever. That is, time and mission-critical and real-time data processing happen locally using the computing, networking, and storage capabilities of one or more networked devices. That is, some of the computational resources could reasonably be drawn from the ensemble of personal devices that commonly surround us such as our own smartphones, tablets or phablets, home automation gateways, Wi-Fi routers, set-top boxes, connected cars, home and portable storage devices, wearables, and special-purpose computing hardware.

That is, everyday devices join in the mainstream computing arena with most of the high-end data storage, processing, mining, and analytics largely delegated to the remote high-end clouds. Coarsely defined, real-time IoT, and streaming data analytics get accomplished through a host of devices at the ground level, whereas BDA is being readied for large-scale cloud infrastructures at the cyber level. In summary, computing tasks are to be distributed to nearby devices and the cloud. The storage on a mobile device expands seamlessly by including local and cloud storage under a common namespace. Finally, media distribution occurs over home and public Wi-Fi networks with even media precaching on Wi-Fi routers.

Emiliano Miluzzo [11] writes that this well-intended and mixed approach would help mitigate some of the perpetual shortcomings of a pure cloud-centric model. Local processing can reduce network latency and ensure the QoS attributes such as performance. Edge device participation in personal data storage can increase data privacy, allow faster data storage and retrieval, and reduce the monetary cost of storing data in the cloud by reducing traffic in the backbone network. At the same time, less traffic in the network promotes bandwidth savings and could reduce congestion in a scenario where a growing number of devices and sensors are increasingly network-enabled. Local device interaction for computing and storage requirements occurs over short-range radio technology such as Wi-Fi and Bluetooth using single-hop connections, whereas communication with the cloud is enabled via high-speed wireless data connections (such as LTE), wired broadband (WAN) and the open, public, and cheap Internet communication infrastructure.

The Compelling Use Cases for Next-Gen Edge Clouds

Our personal gadgets and gizmos such as smartphones, tablets, and laptops are becoming exceedingly powerful and varying in their offerings, operations, and outputs. For example, cell phones are fast transitioning to be smartphones. There are multiple smartphone operating systems and even microvisors (the device version of hypervisors). Further on, smartphones, besides slim and sleek, are inherently empowered through a seamless and spontaneous integration with remote cloud-based services. That is, the integration of a myriad of modules inside and on the outside, the much-demanded cloud-connectivity together stands out for the spellbinding success of today's smartphones.

Due to the microscopic embedding of several smart sensors that could learn our activities or assignments and monitor our physical health parameters ceaselessly, smartphones are turning out to be not only our faithful digital assistants but also participate decisively in our physical well-being. This accumulation trend is bound to continue with the delectable advancements in miniaturization and automation technologies. That is, heart monitor (electrocardiogram), brain monitor (electroencephalography), blood sugar and BP monitor, hi-fi 3D or stereo cameras, projectors, biometrics, radar or sonar sensors, and so on are to be attached to future smartphones to be sufficiently self-, surrounding-, and situation-aware. Smartphones are also tending toward the universal remote operator for all kinds of devices.

Use Cases—The Computation and Actionable Insights

Emiliano Miluzzo further writes that with air quality sensing, municipalities could rely on 24/7 crowd-sourced pollution-level measurements without setting up and sustenance of specialized and costly measurement stations across town. Cameras with 3D or stereo capabilities will enable advanced and touch-free gesture recognition on mobile devices. Radar and sonar sensing will make people more aware of their surroundings, for example, incoming cars, walking, and cycling can issue preemptive alerts to any incoming perils. People with visual impairments could rely on radar or sonar sensing on their mobile devices to navigate in any environment. Smart glasses, with their onboard cameras and microphones, are expected to become the mainstream mechanism along with other wearables to monitor vital signs ahead on the move. Connected cars are emerging and evolving with the unprecedented success and stability of connectivity technologies.

Vehicles can talk to other vehicles on the road, vehicles will be connected with road-side diverse infrastructures, and also off-premise clouds for acquiring a variety of new capabilities and competencies while on the move.

By applying intelligence and ML reasoning to the growing volumes, variety, and velocity of sensor data, we can interpret and infer hidden and prospective patterns to activate multiple components, realize higher-level applications, and offer new forms of interactions such as context-awareness, activity recognition, augmented reality (AR), or voice commands. In a nutshell, the next-generation hybrid cloud leverages local computation to a major extent to tackle a number of specific use cases. Besides the local computation and proximate processing, real world, and real-time intelligence can come from a single device or through a federation of multiple and colocated devices (edge clouds).

Speech recognition engines and image-processing algorithms for, respectively, voice commands and AR applications on smartphones and smart glasses could complete their compute jobs on their own or through interactions with each other. Because of these devices' powerful processing power, less engagement of the remote cloud might be necessary, resulting in less bandwidth usage, and possibly a smooth user experience owing to faster application responsiveness. If sensor data are needed in the cloud to improve an MR algorithm, the local device could send these data to the cloud opportunistically at a later time, for example, during off-peak hours. If the device generating the data is a mobile platform, it can send data when it is in the Wi-Fi range, or during battery charging sessions. The real-time analytics through edge clouds is therefore recommended for certain scenarios. The security of device and user data is safe and secure as the analysis happens inside the environment.

The Storage Use Cases

Although big data is maturing as an important business paradigm, there is another paradigm steadily attracting the attention of professionals. Researchers refer to this new paradigm as small data, which lets users draw interesting inferences, extract hidden patterns related to a person's own well-being, and enable applications to mine lifelogging data. Small data storage requirements, along with users' growing digital footprint including the still and dynamic pictures from mobile devices that account for most personal storage needs, are driving the demand for more capable personal storage solutions.

With the average household digital footprint skyrocketing and the high costs of cloud storage services, the new-generation hybrid cloud (employing traditional clouds as well as the recent phenomenon of edge clouds) can be a viable solution to expand cloud storage capabilities and meet users' storage requirements at a lesser cost. To achieve this goal, hybrid clouds can intelligently combine traditional cloud storage with available storage from personal edge devices. This free space on the order of tens of gigabytes today is likely to increase to terabytes in the near future. This could be well suited for transparently expanding the storage available to users beyond the boundaries of centralized cloud offerings.

The empowered hybrid cloud storage services can provide a flexible and scalable platform for personal data storage, including backup, intelligent file placement and retrieval, and data sharing. By applying smart data replication techniques across different personal devices, this solution provides not only flexibility but also resiliency to failure. In addition, this new storage model offers enhanced scalability properties: a user can add more storage as needed by provisioning a new device to their existing personal storage system, which transparently reconfigures with no need for manual data migration or painful data synchronization.

Data Dissemination

Smartphones and tablets are fuelling the rapid growth of mobile video streaming traffic, surpassing media consumption on PCs. Connected cars will soon accelerate this phenomenon, with thousands of vehicles simultaneously fetching media on the go. Content delivery networks (CDNs) are a solution introduced to meet increasing traffic demand and deliver high-quality customer experience by decentralizing media storage and caching infrastructures. The new cloud model can enable new generations of CDNs by pushing the ability to store and cache content further out to edge nodes to enhance the user experience and reduce the backbone traffic load.

By storing media content on the road-side infrastructure, a data download session from moving cars could complete faster because of the high-speed, short-range radio connection. When, in a few years, autonomously driving cars to make their appearance and passengers are busier consuming data than driving. Similarly, smart caching on a set-top box based on television users' watching patterns could promote an enhanced user experience by making content readily available and reduce backbone data traffic during peak hours. For example, if Bob watches the first episode of a 20-episode TV show, the next time, he would most likely select the second episode. This prediction can allow intelligent prefetching of the episode on Bob's set-top box at a prior time during off-peak hours.

In summary, the new edge cloud model looks very promising and potentially fabulous. That is, processing and storage are distributed across all kinds of devices including traditional computers and storage appliances, thereby the network bandwidth usage and costs are bound to come down sharply. By optimally using local computing and storage capabilities, the remote clouds and the network infrastructures are being spared from heavy bombardment.

Mobile-Edge Computing (MEC)

Mobile devices have traditionally been viewed as *thin clients* or *edge devices* that serve primarily as user-input devices. That is why all the compute-intensive processing are offloaded to (nonedge and backend) servers. Now with technology advances, there is a realization that mobile devices can be *thick clients* and going even to be *thin servers*. Mobile-Edge Computing (MEC) offers application developers and content providers the cloud-capabilities and an IT service environment at the edge of the mobile network. This environment is characterized by ultra-low latency and high bandwidth as well as real-time access to radio network information that can be leveraged by applications. MEC provides a new ecosystem and value chain. Operators can open their radio access network (RAN) edge to authorized third parties, allowing them to flexibly and rapidly deploy innovative applications and services toward mobile subscribers, enterprises, and vertical segments. MEC will enable new vertical business segments and services for consumers and enterprise customers. With the 5G communication facility all set to see the light, the value and vitality of MEC will grow up considerably.

The Hyrax project [http://hyrax.dcc.fc.up.pt/] proposes a novel vision of a hyperlocal edge-cloud, that is, a computational or storage cloud comprised solely a collection of nearby wireless edge devices, with the purpose of pooling these devices' data and processing power to support a new class of proximity-aware applications that benefit the owners of these devices. The premise behind these edge clouds is that all of the constituent nodes are edge (and not server-caliber) computers, and that any and all computation is performed completely within the edge cloud, that is, there is no offloading or tethering of the computation or data to a nonedge, back end, and traditional cloud infrastructure.

Edge Analytics-Enabled Smarter Traffic Systems

Traffic lights are becoming very prominent and pervasive in urban areas for enabling pedestrians as well as vehicle drivers. There are high-fidelity video cameras in plenty along the roads, expressways, tunnels, and so on in order to activate and accelerate a variety of real-time tasks for pedestrians, traffic police, and vehicle drivers. Wireless access points like Wi-Fi, 3G, 4G, road-side units, and smart traffic lights are deployed along the roads. Vehicle-to-vehicle, vehicle-to-access points, and access-point-to-access-point interactions enrich the application of this scenario. All kinds of connected vehicles and transport systems need actionable insights in time to derive and deliver a rich set of context-aware services. Safety is an important factor for car and road users, and there are additional temporal as well as spatial services being worked out. With driverless cars under intense development and testing, insights-driven decisions, and knowledge-centric actions are very vital for next-generation transports.

The impending need is to have smarter traffic systems in order to fulfill the unique goals behind the smarter traffic. This system has to be deployed at each intersection within the city areas, and they can be networked with one another to have hooked up with centralized control and analytics systems. It also has to be equipped with a variety of sensors to measure the distance and the speed of approaching vehicles from every direction. The other requirements include detecting the presence of pedestrians and cyclists crossing the street or road in order to proactively issue *slow down* warnings to incoming vehicles and instantaneously modifying its own cycle to prevent collisions. Besides ensuring utmost safety and the free flow of traffic, all kinds of traffic data need to be captured and stocked, in order to do specific analytics to accurately predict and prescribe the ways and means of substantially improving the traffic system. Ambulances need to get a way out through traffic-free open lanes in the midst of chaotic and cruel traffic.

The noteworthy factor here is that the smarter traffic system has to learn, decide, and act instantaneously in order to avert any kind of accidents. That is, the real-time reaction is the crucial need and hence, the concept of edge clouds out of edge devices for collaboratively collecting different data and processing them instantaneously to spit out insights is gaining widespread and overwhelming momentum. Another point here is that data flows in streams. Thus, all kinds of discreet or simple, as well as complex events, need to be precisely and perfectly captured and combined to be subjected into a bevy of investigations to complete appropriate actions. The whole process has to be initiated at the earliest through a powerful and pioneering knowledge discovery and dissemination platform to avoid any kind of losses to people and properties. Here collecting and sending data to remote cloud servers to arrive at competent decisions are found inappropriate for real-time and low-latency applications. However, the edge data can be aggregated and transmitted to powerful cloud servers casually in batches to have a historical diagnostic and deterministic analytics at the later point of time.

The Architectural Components of the Smarter Traffic System

1. As articulated above, as far as physical components are concerned, a smarter traffic system has to include traffic lights, sensors, and actuators within its jurisdictional region so that the reaction time is on the order of <10 milliseconds.
2. A miniaturized orchestration platform is an overseeing software solution, which has to be a part and parcel of the system. This module is greatly obligated to orchestrate and manage all the other software modules of the system effectively. It has to be policy-aware. That is, well-intended policies can be established easily and enforced accordingly toward effective governance.

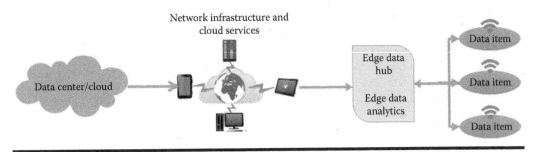

Figure 6.7   A hybrid version of local and remote clouds.

3. A centralized decision-enabling module is another noteworthy one for garnering data from all the deployed traffic lights and pushing the decisions to individual traffic lights through a messaging bus, which is another mandatory software solution for enabling data transmission on both directions.

There can be multiple smarter traffic systems from different providers tied up with different networking and communication service providers. All these deviations and deficiencies need to be addressed systematically in order to accomplish edge analytics. Thus, any edge analytics software solution has to take multiple scenarios and factors into consideration in order to be right and relevant for realizing real-time applications such as smarter traffic. Such systems are capable of taking lightning-fast yet correct decisions, which are turning out to be essential for the projected smarter world. A hybrid version of traditional and edge analytics is vividly illustrated in Figure 6.7.

Tending toward Software-Defined Clouds

The arrival of cloud concepts has brought in tremendous changes in the IT landscape that in turn lead in realizing big transitions in the delivery of business applications and services, in the solid enhancement of business flexibility, productivity, and sustainability. Formally cloud infrastructures are centralized, virtualized, automated, and shared IT infrastructures. The utilization rate of cloud infrastructures has gone up significantly. Still there are dependencies curtailing the full usage of expensive IT resources. Employing the decoupling technique among various modules to decimate all kinds of constricting dependencies, more intensive and insightful process automation through orchestration and policy-based configuration, operation, management, delivery, and maintenance, attaching external knowledge bases are widely prescribed to achieve still more IT utilization to cut costs remarkably.

Bringing in the much-discoursed modularity in order to enable programmable IT infrastructures, extracting, and centralizing all the embedded intelligence via robust and resilient software, distributed deployment, centralized management, and federation are being touted as the viable and venerable course of actions for attaining the originally envisaged success. That is, creating a dynamic pool of virtualized resources, allocating them on demand to accomplish their fullest utilization, charging them for the exact usage, putting unutilized resources back to the pool, monitoring, measuring, and managing resource performance, and so on are the hallmarks of next-generation IT infrastructures. Precisely speaking, IT infrastructures are being software-defined to bring in much-needed accessibility, consumability, malleability, elasticity, and extensibility.

On-demand IT has been the perpetual goal. All kinds of IT resources need to have the inherent capability of preemptively knowing of users' as well as applications' IT resource requirements and accordingly fulfill them without any instruction, interpretation, and involvement of human resources. IT resources need to be scaled up and down based on the changing needs so that the cost can be under control. That is, perfect provisioning of resources is the mandate. Overprovisioning raises up the pricing, whereas underprovisioning is a cause for performance degradation worries. The cloud paradigm transparently leverages a number of software solutions and specialized tools in order to provide scalability of applications through resource elasticity. The expected dynamism in resource provisioning and deprovisioning has to become a core and concrete capability of clouds.

That is, providing right-sized IT resources (compute, storage, and networking) for all kinds of business software solutions is the need of the hour. Users increasingly expect their service providers' infrastructures to deliver these resources elastically in response to their changing needs. There is no cloud services infrastructure available today capable of simultaneously delivering scalability, flexibility, and high operational efficiency. Deeper automation and software-based configuration, controlling, and operation of hardware resources are the main enablers behind the vision of SDI.

An SDI is an enabler of private, public, and hybrid clouds. That is, software-defined computing, networking, and storage are the principal components in a futuristic SDI. With the ultimate flexibility and full-fledged automation capabilities, a software defined environment (SDE) is a vital component of cloud that enables data center administrators to use a single graphical user interface to do everything from deploying virtual machines to assigning storage to configuring networks, hence allowing clouds to become more streamlined, simplified, and adaptively responsive. There are a few connotations such as software-defined clouds, software-defined data centers (SDDCs), and cloud-enabled data centers (CeDCs) for SDEs. Originally it was just data centers (DCs) for every decent enterprise across the globe.

The next milestone is the much-published and pampered server consolidation through virtualization. This server consolidation results in a dynamic pool of virtual as well as bare metal servers. That is, data centers have been continuously subjected to a series of noteworthy technology-inspired transformations, optimizations, and so on. The next in line is the availability and adoption of powerful tools in order to automate many manual activities. Automated capacity planning, job scheduling, billing and charging, resource provisioning and deprovisioning, resource monitoring, performance measurement and governance, self-servicing, and so on are being activated through highly competent configuration and management tools. These enhancements have led to the flourishing of cloud centers in prime locations across the world.

Having tasted the expected successes on server machines, the focus has been directed toward storage and network virtualizations (NVs). As enunciated above, the tried and tested abstraction and decoupling have been the hallmarks for virtualization. Further on, all the hardware-bound intelligence is smoothly extricated and developed as centralized and clustered controllers that are extensively stuffed with software for attaining the capabilities of extensibility, modifiability, and sustainability. Controllers facilitate policy and configuration changes, remote access, policy-based operations, and so on. The Gartner Group [12] breaks the software-defined system down into four processes:

- *Abstraction*: The decoupling of a resource from the consumer of the resource.
- *Instrumentation*: The process of opening up the decoupled infrastructure elements with programmatic interfaces (typically XML-based RESTful APIs).

- *Automation*: The use of APIs to wire up the exposed elements using scripts and other automation tools to remove *human middleware*.
- *Orchestration*: The automation of provisioning through linkages to policy-driven orchestration systems.

These four processes are the keys to the data center of the future—a data center defined and controlled by software. This new paradigm removes existing barriers related to the management of server, storage, and network resources. Any changes to infrastructure that used to require days and weeks to implement can now be made in minutes. In this new software-intensive era for IT, application workloads are not tied to dedicated servers, storage, and network resources. Instead, they move dynamically to have balanced workloads in order to optimize infrastructure utilization.

The Building Blocks of Software-Defined Clouds

The software-defined clouds (SDCs) encompasses software-defined compute, storage, and networking components. The substantially matured server virtualization leads to the realization of software-defined compute machines. Highly intelligent hypervisors [alternatively recognized as virtual machine monitors (VMMs) act as the perfect software solution to take care of the creation, provisioning, deprovisioning, live-in migration, and decommissioning of computing machines (virtual machines, bare metal servers, etc.], and so on. In the following sections, we would focus on SDN and storage.

Software-Defined Networking (SDN)

The emerging technology trends indicate that networks and network management are bound to change once for all. Today's data centers (DCs) extensively use physical switches and appliances that have not yet been virtualized and are statically provisioned. Further on, the current environment mandate, significant and certified expertise in each vendor's equipment lack an API ecosystem toward the envisioned programmable network solutions. It is quite difficult to bring in the expected automation (resource provisioning, scaling, etc.) on the currently running inflexible, monolithic, and closed network modules. The result is the underutilization of expensive network equipment. Also, the cost of employing highly educated and experienced network administrators is on the higher side. Thus besides bringing in a bevy of pragmatic yet frugal innovations in the networking arena, the mandate for substantially reducing the capital as well as the operational expenses incurred by the traditional network architecture is clearly playing in the minds of technical professionals and business executives.

As virtualization has been contributing immensely to server consolidation and optimization, the idea of NV has picked up in the recent past. The virtualization aspect on the networking side takes a different route compared to the matured server virtualization. The extraction and centralization of network intelligence embedded inside all kinds of network appliances such as routers and switches bring in a number of strategic advantages for data centers. The policy-setting, configuration, and maneuvering activities are being activated through software libraries that are modular, service-oriented, and centralized in a controller module and hence the new terminology *software-defined networking* has blossomed and is hugely popular. That is, instead of managing network assets separately using separate interfaces, they are controlled collectively through a comprehensive, easy-to-use, and fine-grained interface. The API approach has the intrinsic capability of putting a stimulating and sustainable foundation for all kinds of IT resources and assets to be easily discoverable, accessible, usable, and composable. Hardware infrastructure programming and thereby their remote manipulations and machinations are gaining momentum.

The control plane manages switch and routing tables, whereas the forwarding plane actually performs the layer 2 and 3 filtering, forwarding, and routing. SDN decouples the system that makes decisions about where traffic is sent (the control plane) from the underlying system that forwards traffic to the selected destination (the data plane). Therefore, standards-compliant SDN controllers provide a widely adopted API ecosystem, which can be used to centrally control multiple devices in different layers. Such an abstracted and centralized approach offers many strategically significant improvements over traditional networking approaches. For instance, it becomes possible to completely decouple the network's control plane and its data plane. The control plane runs in a cluster setup and can configure all kinds of data plane switches and routers to support business expectations as demanded. That means data flow is regulated at the network level in an efficient manner. Data can be sent where it is needed or blocked if it is deemed a security threat.

A detached and deft software implementation of the configuration and controlling aspects of network elements also means that the existing policies can be refurbished, whereas newer policies can be created and inserted on demand to enable all the associated network devices to behave in a situation-aware manner. As we all know, policy establishment and enforcement are the proven mechanisms to bring in the required versatility and vitality in network operations. If a particular application's flow unexpectedly needs more bandwidth, SDN controller proactively recognizes the brewing requirement in real time and accordingly reroute the data flow in the correct network path. Precisely speaking, the physical constraints are getting decimated through the software-defined networking. If a security appliance needs to be inserted between two tiers, it is easily accomplished without altering anything at the infrastructure level. Another interesting factor is the most recent phenomenon of *bring your own device* (*BYOD*). All kinds of employees' own devices can be automatically configured, accordingly authorized, and made ready to access the enterprise's network anywhere anytime.

The Key Motivations for SDN

In the IT world, there are several trends mandating the immediate recognition and sagacious adoption of SDN. CeDCs are being established in different cool locations across the globe to provide scores of orchestrated cloud services to worldwide businesses and individuals over the Internet on a subscription basis. Application and database servers besides integration middleware solutions are increasingly distributed, whereas the governance and the management of distributed resources are being accomplished in a centralized manner to avail the much-needed single point of view. Due to the hugeness of data centers, the data traffic therefore internally as well as externally is exploding these days. Flexible traffic management and ensuring *bandwidth on demand* are the principal requirements.

The consumerization of IT is another gripping trend. Enterprise users and executives are being increasingly assisted by a bevy of gadgets and gizmos such as smartphones, laptops, tablets, and wearables in their daily chores. As enunciated elsewhere, the *BYOD* movement requires enterprise networks to inherently support policy-based adjustment, amenability, and amelioration to support users' devices dynamically. BDA has a telling effect on IT networks especially on data storage and transmission. The proprietary nature of network solutions from worldwide product vendors also plays a sickening role in traditional networks, and hence there is a clarion call for bringing in necessary advancements in the network architecture. Programmable networks are therefore the viable and venerable answer to bring in the desired flexibility and optimization in highly complicated and cumbersome corporate networks. The structural limitations of conventional networks are being overcome with network programming. The growing complexity of traditional networks leads to stasis. That is, adding or releasing devices and incorporating network-related policies are really turning out to be a tough affair in the current setup.

As per the leading market watchers, researchers, and analysts, SDN marks the largest business opportunity in the networking industry since its inception. Recent reports estimate the business impact tied to SDN could be as high as $35 billion by 2018, which represents nearly 40% of the overall networking industry. The future of networking will rely more and more on software, which will accelerate the pace of innovation incredibly for networks as it has in the computing and storage domains (explained below). SDN has all within to transform today's static and sick networks into calculative, competent, and cognitive platforms with the intrinsic intelligence to anticipate and allocate resources dynamically. SDN brings up the scale to support enormous data centers and the virtualization needed to support workloads-optimized, converged, orchestrated, and highly automated cloud environments. With its many identified advantages and astonishing industry momentum, SDN is on the way to becoming the new norm and normal not only for cloud but also corporate networks. With the next-generation hybrid and federated clouds, the role of SDN for fulfilling network functions virtualization (NFV) is bound to shoot up.

In short, SDN is an emerging architecture that is agile, adaptive, cheaper, and ideal for network-intensive and dynamic applications. This architecture decouples the network control and forwarding functions (routing) enabling the network control to become directly programmable and the underlying infrastructure to be abstracted for applications and network services, which can treat the network as a logical or virtual entity.

The Need of SDN for the Cloud

Due to a number of enterprise-wide benefits, the adoption rates of cloud paradigm have been growing. However, the networking aspect of cloud environments has typically not kept pace with the rest of the architecture. There came a number of enhancements such as NV, NFV, and SDN. SDN is definitely the comprehensive and futuristic paradigm. With the explosion of computing machines (both virtual machines as well as bare metal servers) in any cloud centers, the need for SDN is sharply felt across. Networks today are statically provisioned, with devices that are managed at a box-level scale and are underutilized. SDN enables end-to-end based network equipment provisioning, reducing the network provisioning time from days to minutes, and distributing flows more evenly across the fabric allowing for better utilization.

On summarizing, SDN is the definite game-changer for next-generation IT environments. SDN considerably eliminates network complexity in the midst of multiple and heterogeneous network elements. All kinds of network solutions are centrally configured and controlled to eliminate all kinds of dependencies-induced constrictions and to realize their full potential. Network capabilities are provisioned on demand at the optimal level to suit application requirements. In synchronization with other infrastructural models appropriately, the on-demand, instant-on, autonomic, and smart computing goals are easily delivered.

Software-Defined Storage (SDS)

We are slowly yet steadily getting into the virtual world with the faster realization of the goals allied with the concept of virtual IT. The ensuing world is leaning toward the vision of anytime anywhere access to information and services. This projected transformation needs a lot of perceivable and paradigm shifts. Traditional data centers were designed to support specific workloads and users. This has resulted in siloed and heterogeneous storage solutions that are difficult to manage, provision of newer resources to serve dynamic needs, and finally to scale out. The existing setup acts as a barrier for business innovations and value. Untangling this goes a long way in facilitating instant access to information and services.

Undoubtedly storage has been a prominent infrastructural module in data centers. There are different storage types and solutions in the market. In the recent past, the unprecedented growth of data generation, collection, processing, and storage clearly indicates the importance of producing and provisioning of better and bigger storage systems and services. Storage management is another important topic not to be sidestepped. We often read about big, fast, and even extreme data. Due to an array of technology-inspired processes and systems, the data size, scope, structure, and speed are on the climb. For example, digitization is an overwhelming worldwide trend and trick gripping every facet of human life, thereby the digital data is everywhere and continues to grow at a stunning pace. Statisticians say that every day, approximately 15 petabytes of new data are being generated worldwide, and the total amount of digital data doubles approximately every 2 years. The indisputable fact is that machine-generated data are larger compared to man-generated data. The expectation is that correspondingly there have to be copious innovations in order to cost-effectively accommodate and manage big data.

SDS is a relatively new concept and its popularity is surging due to the abundant success attained in software-defined compute and networking areas. As explained above, SDS is a part and parcel of the vision behind the establishment and sustenance of SDDCs. With the virtualization concept penetrating and piercing through every tangible resource, the storage industry also gets inundated by that powerful trend. Software-defined storage is a kind of enterprise-class storage that uses a variety of commoditized and, therefore, cheap hardware with all the important storage and management functions being extricated and performed using an intelligent software controller. With such a clean separation, SDS delivers automated, policy-driven, and application-aware storage services through an orchestration of the underlining storage infrastructure. That is, we get a dynamic pool of virtual storage resources to be picked up dynamically and orchestrate them accordingly to be presented as an appropriate storage solution. Unutilized storage resources could then be incorporated into the pool for serving other requests. All kinds of constricting dependencies on storage solutions simply vanish with such storage virtualization. All storage modules are commoditized and hence the cost of storage is to go down with higher utilization. In a nutshell, storage virtualization enables storage scalability, replaceability, substitutability, and manageability.

An SDS solution [13] remarkably increases the flexibility by enabling organizations to use nonproprietary standard hardware and, in many cases, leverage existing storage infrastructures as a part of their enterprise storage solution. Additionally, organizations can achieve massive scale with an SDS by adding heterogeneous hardware components as needed to increase capacity and improve performance in the solution. Automated, policy-driven management of SDS solutions helps drive cost and operational efficiencies. As an example, SDS manages important storage functions including information lifecycle management (ILM), disk caching, snapshots, replication, striping, and clustering. In a nutshell, these SDS capabilities enable you to put the right data in the right place, at the right time, with the right performance, and at the right cost automatically.

Unlike traditional storage systems such as storage area network and network attached storage, SDS simplifies scale out with relatively inexpensive standard hardware, while continuing to manage storage as a single enterprise-class storage system. SDS typically refers to software that manages the capture, placement, protection, and retrieval of data. SDS is characterized by a separation of the storage hardware from the software that manages it. SDS is a key enabler modernizing traditional, monolithic, inflexible, costly, and closed data centers toward software-defined data centers that are highly extensible, open, and cost-effective. The promise of SDS is that separating the software from the hardware enables enterprises to make storage hardware purchase, deployment, and operation independent from concerns about over or underutilization or interoperability of storage resources.

Cloud-Based Big Data Storage

Object storage is the recent phenomenon. Object-based storage systems use containers or buckets to store data known as objects in a flat address space instead of the hierarchical, directory-based file systems that are common in the block and file-based storage systems. Nonstructured and semistructure data are encoded as objects and stored in containers. Typical data includes e-mails, pdf files, still, and dynamic images, and so on. Containers stores the associated metadata (date of creation, size, camera type, etc.) and the unique object ID. The object ID is stored in a database or application and is used to reference objects in one or more containers. The data in an object-based storage system is typically accessed using HTTP using a web browser or directly through an API like REST (representational state transfer). The flat address space in an object-based storage system enables simplicity and massive scalability. But the data in these systems cannot be modified and every refresh gets stored as a new object. Object-based storage is predominantly used by cloud services providers (CSPs) to archive and backup their customers' data.

Analysts estimate that more than 2 million terabytes (or 2 exabytes) of data are created every day. The range of applications that IT has to support today spans everything from social computing, BDA, mobile, enterprise and embedded applications, and so on. All the data for all those applications has got to be made available to mobile and wearable devices and hence data storage acquires an indispensable status. As per the main findings of Cisco's global IP traffic forecast, in 2016, global IP traffic will reach 1.1 zettabytes per year or 91.3 exabytes (one billion gigabytes) per month, and by 2018, global IP traffic will reach 1.6 zettabytes per year or 131.9 exabytes per month. International Data Corporation (IDC) has predicted that cloud storage capacity will exceed 7 exabytes in 2014, driven by strong demand for agile and capex-friendly deployment models. Furthermore, IDC had estimated that by 2015, big data workloads will be one of the fastest-growing contributors to storage in the cloud. In conjunction with these trends, meeting service-level agreements (SLAs) for the agreed performance is a top IT concern. As a result, enterprises will increasingly turn to flash-based SDS solutions to accelerate the performance significantly to meet up emerging storage needs.

The Key Characteristics of Software-Defined Storage

SDS is characterized by several key architectural elements and capabilities that differentiate it from the traditional infrastructure [14]:

Commodity hardware: With the extraction and centralization of all the intelligence embedded in storage and its associated systems in a specially crafted software layer, all kinds of storage solutions are bound to become cheap, dumb, off-the-shelf, and hence commoditized hardware elements. Not only the physical storage appliances but also all the interconnecting and intermediate fabric is to become commoditized. Such segregation goes a long way in centrally automating, activating, and adapting the full storage landscape.

Scale-out architecture: Any SDS setup ought to have the capability of ensuring fluid, flexible, and elastic configuration of storage resources through software. SDS facilitates the realization of storage as a dynamic pool of heterogeneous resources, thereby the much-needed scale-out requirement can be easily met. The traditional architecture hinders the dynamic addition and release of storage resources due to the extreme dependency. For the software-defined cloud environments, storage scalability is essential to have a dynamic, highly optimized, and virtual environment.

Resource pooling: The available storage resources are pooled into a unified logical entity that can be managed centrally. The control plane provides the fine-grained visibility and the control to all available resources in the system.

Abstraction: Physical storage resources are increasingly virtualized and presented to the control plane, which can then configure and deliver them as tiered storage services.

Automation: The storage layer brings in extensive automation that enables it to deliver one-click and policy-based provisioning of storage resources. Administrators and users request storage resources in terms of application need (capacity, performance, and reliability) rather than storage configurations such as redundant array of independent disk levels or physical location of drives. The system automatically configures and delivers storage as needed on the fly. It also monitors and reconfigures storage as required to continue to meet SLAs.

Programmability: In addition to the inbuilt automation, the storage system offers fine-grained visibility and control of underlying resources via rich APIs that allows administrators and third-party applications to integrate the control plane across storage, network, and compute layers to deliver workflow automation. The real power of SDS lies in the ability to integrate it with other layers of the infrastructure to build end-to-end application-focused automation.

The maturity of SDS is to quicken the process of setting up and sustaining SDEs for the tactic as well as the strategic benefits of CSPs as well as the consumers at large.

The Onset of Cognitive Clouds

Cognitive clouds are the next evolution of cloud computing and a new class of data interpretation and learning systems that accelerate the development of cognitive applications. Cognitive clouds weave insights and advice in the fabric of business and daily life while learning continuously from user engagement and multistructured data interactions.

Conclusion

The aspect of IT optimization is continuously getting rapt and apt attention from technology leaders and luminaries across the globe. A number of generic, as well as specific improvisations, are being brought in to make IT aware and adaptive. The cloud paradigm is being touted as the game-changer in empowering and elevating IT to the desired heights. There have been notable achievements in making IT being the core and cost-effective enabler of both personal as well as professional activities. There are definite improvements in business automation, acceleration, and augmentation. Still there are opportunities and possibilities waiting for IT to move up further.

The pioneering virtualization technology is being taken to every kind of infrastructure such as networking and storage to complete the IT ecosystem. The abstraction and decoupling techniques are lavishly utilized here in order to bring in the necessary malleability, extensibility, and serviceability. That is, all the configuration and operational functionalities hitherto embedded inside hardware components are now neatly identified, extracted, and centralized, and implemented as a separate software controller. That is, the embedded intelligence is being developed now as a self-contained entity so that hardware components could be commoditized. Thus, the software-defined compute, networking, and storage disciplines have become the hot topic for discussion and dissertation. The journey of data centers SDEs is being pursued with vigor and rigor.

References

1. IBM Smarter City Solutions on Cloud, a White Paper published by IBM Global Services, 2011.
2. R. Arpagaus and A. Auner, *A Presentation on Smarter Cities on Cloud,* IBM, 2012.
3. *Cloud Computing and Sustainability: The Environmental Benefits of Moving to the Cloud,* Accenture, Dublin, 2010.
4. L. Xu et al., Cloud-based monitoring framework for Smart Home. IEEE 4th International Conference on Cloud Computing Technology and Science, 2012.
5. Y. Simmhan et al., *Cloud-Based Software Platform for Big Data Analytics in Smart Grids,* University of Southern California, Copublished by the IEEE CS and the AIP, 2013.
6. South Korea: Busan Green u-City Smart City Builds on Cloud Services Delivered by Public-Private-Partnership, a Report by GSMA Connected Living Programme, 2012.
7. W. Wang et al., Integrating Sensors with the Cloud using Dynamic Proxies, IEEE 23rd International Symposium on Personal Indoor and Mobile Radio Communications (PIMRC),Sydney, Australia, 2012.
8. N. Mitton et al., Combining Cloud and Sensors in a Smart City Environment, *EURASIP Journal on Wireless Communications and Networking,* 2012.
9. S. R. Yerva et al., Cloud-Based Social and Sensor Data Fusion, The International Conference on Information Fusion, Singapore, 2012.
10. M. Grindle, J. Kavathekar, and D. Wan, A New Era for the Healthcare Industry - Cloud Computing Changes the Game, A white paper by Accenture, 2013.
11. Emiliano Miluzzo, AT&T Labs Research, I'm Cloud 2.0, and I'm Not Just a Data Center, Published by the IEEE Computer Society, May/June 2014 (18, 03), pp. 73–77.
12. Managing Performance in Dynamic IT Environments, a Technical White paper by HP, 2013.
13. Software Defined Storage Networks™: An Introduction, A Jeda Networks White Paper, 2013.
14. The Fundamentals of Software-defined Storage – Simplicity at Scale for Cloud Architectures, a white paper by Coraid, 2013.

Chapter 7

Describing the Emerging Field of IoT Data Analytics

Abstract: As explained in the beginning of this book, the overwhelming leverage of miniaturization, digitization, distribution, consumerization (mobility), consolidation, centralization and industrialization (cloud), compartmentalization (virtualization and containerization), and deeper connectivity technologies has a number of trendsetting and transformational implications on information technology (IT) organizations and business houses/behemoths across the globe. Edge or fog computing through cloudlets and microclouds is another potential phenomenon for next-generation IT. There will be a cool convergence in forming and firming up hyperconverged cloud environments to host and deliver smarter and sophisticated applications for the total humanity.

All these advancements are bound to bring forth a number of distinct outputs and opportunities. The principal one among them is the enormous growth in data size and the greater variability and variety in data scope, structure, and speed. That is, with the continuous growth of newer data sources and resources, the amount of data getting generated, captured, transmitted, and stored is tremendously huge. As data are turning out to be a strategic asset for any organization to be decisive, distinctive, and disciplined in its operations, offerings, and outputs, a host of competent technologies, tips, and tools are being unearthed to smartly stock and subject all incoming and stored data to a variety of deeper investigations to gain actionable insights in time.

Especially extracting and extrapolating knowledge out of data heaps in time go a long way in empowering every kind of enterprises and endeavors to be exceptionally efficient and effective in their deals, deeds, and deliveries. In this chapter, we would like to dig deeper and dwell at length on the various analytical approaches, frameworks, algorithms, platforms, engines, and methods for squeezing out value-adding and venerable insights out of Internet of Things (IoT) data.

Introduction

Leading market watchers, analysts, and researchers have clearly indicated that the data getting generated are doubling every two years. There are several noteworthy developments being given as the principal reason for such a monumental and massive growth of decision-enabling data. Deeper and extreme connectivity technologies and topologies supplemented by service-enablement standards are the most crucial advancements and articulations creating a cascading and chiller effect on our enterprises. Business strategies and enterprise architectures of various business behemoths across the globe are being adequately reconsidered and remedied to be synched up varying peoples' expectations.

Newer data sources and resources are emerging and evolving; edge/fog technologies are empowering every concrete and casually found object to be computational, communicative, sensitive, perceptive, decisive, and responsive; all kinds of physical, mechanical, electrical, and electronics systems are being functionally enabled through a seamless integration with cyber applications and services to be smartly participative and contributive; every sort of digital assistants (personal as well as professional) are equipped with smart software to be context-aware and people-centric; every commonly found, cheap, and casual article in our working, wandering, and walking environments are becoming digitized artifacts signaling their valiant and salient entry into the mainstream computing arena; and clouds are being positioned as the core and central IT infrastructure for hosting IT and business workloads, databases, and warehouses, data marts and cubes, integrated platforms, millions of web, and social sites.

Further on, every noticeable event, transaction, interaction, collaboration, corroboration, correlation, request and reply, and so on are being expectantly captured and persisted in storage appliances and arrays for real-time as well as posterior investigations. Ordinary objects are being readily digitized to be extraordinary in their actions and reactions. These then are capable of getting interconnected with one another in the vicinity and with remote ones laying out a stimulating and sparkling foundation for sophisticated networks that are simply going to be creatively autonomic, event-driven, mission-critical, software-defined, and service-oriented. In a nutshell, the realization of extremely connected and service-enabled digital objects and machines in our midst is the grand foundation for big, fast, streaming, and IoT data, which is typically multistructured, massive in volume, and mesmerizing in variety, velocity, and value. Precisely speaking, the IoT data are going to be big but the challenge is to capture, clean up, ingest, and process them immediately to bring forth real-time insights. In the following sections, we are to throw more light on big data platforms and infrastructures.

As widely experienced, data are the fountainhead of information and knowledge that can be wisely used to bigger and better things. For the dreamt knowledge era, data are being carefully collected, cleansed, classified, clustered, and conformed. This end-to-end process is being portrayed as a simplifying and streamlining one toward its final destination (actionable insights). Big data storage solutions are feverishly prevalent and paramount these days. The most respectable activity on big data is to do synchronized and systematic analytics to rightly and readily emit big insights. Big data analytics (BDA) frameworks primarily comprising data processing and storage modules, toolsets, distributed and centralized publish-subscribe engines, drivers, and adaptors are made available by open source as well as commercial-grade solution vendors. Due to the extreme complicity and complexity induced by multiplicity and heterogeneity of big data, enabling BDA products and procedures are being derived and released by IT professionals to do BDA easily and quickly.

The Principal Steps toward Knowledge Discovery and Dissemination

Next-generation systems are expected to be elegantly and extremely sensitive and responsive to be highly relevant for people in their daily decisions, deals, and deeds. Apart from embedding a variety of real-world features inside, modern IT systems need to be adequately enabled through external systems and data-driven insights in order to be proactively and perceptively reactive. The renowned examples include smart energy grids, automatic financial trading, homeland security, logistics, and production control. For example, in a smart grid scenario, the timely detection of a deviation between the energy consumption and the energy production can lead to the instantaneous deployment of an intelligent demand response system. For such kinds of real-time applications, incoming data streams of low-level information arriving from different and distributed sources at high rates need to be programmatically subjected to purpose-specific processing, mining, and analysis in real time in order to identify more complex situations. Thus, knowledge discovery for cognitive businesses relies upon competent data and event stream processing engines.

With the faster maturity and stability of the IoT paradigm, there are fresh challenges as well as opportunities for both business executives and IT teams (enterprise and cloud). The first and foremost is the capture, storage, and analysis of massive collections of data. Because of large volumes of polystructured data, the following IT requirements are being insisted for enabling data analytics:

- Highly optimized and organized IT infrastructures (compute, storage, and network) for transmitting, storing, and processing large volumes of data published at a high speed.
- Data security while in transit, rest, and usage.
- Robust and resilient mining, processing and analysis algorithms, processes, and patterns.
- Highly synchronized platforms for faster data virtualization and ingestion, pioneering data analytics, and knowledge visualization.
- With the projected trillions of digitized objects and billions of connected devices, the data, user, and analytics loads on IT infrastructures are hugely variable, and hence load-aware infrastructures are insisted.
- Data and application integration standards and middleware with diverse sensors, devices, networks, and systems.
- Data archival, backup, and recovery plus access control are very important for the big, fast, streaming, and IoT data world.

The following are the key phases for extracting and exposing insights from data heaps gleaned from multiple sources:

1. *Aggregate* from multiple data sources through data integration and virtualization tools.
2. *Preprocess* and transform captured data to be compatible with the target environments.
3. *Ingest and store* the cleansed and polished data in memory as well as in disk-based databases. There are in-memory data grids (IMDGs), in-memory databases, clustered, parallel, analytical, and distributed SQL databases, NoSQL, and NewSQL databases, and so on in order to efficiently stock IoT data.
4. *Investigate* for extracting actionable insights leveraging competent statistical, machine-learning, mathematical, and data-mining algorithms, complex queries, and renowned

methods such as searching, scanning, filtering, slicing, and dicing. There are programming and script languages in plenty to code specific analytics requirements and run.

5. *Visualize* the knowledge generated via portals, dashboards, consoles, report-generation tools, maps, charts, graphs, and so on in different devices (smartphones, wearables, tablets, etc.).

6. *Actuate the knowledge extracted*: Decision-makers can go ahead with appropriate plan and smart execution with all the clarity and confidence.

It is indisputably clear that data lead to insights which in turn productively and pragmatically participate and pamper individuals, innovators, and institutions in their enterprising journey.

The Rewarding Repercussions of the Data Explosion

The exponential growth of disparate data has brought in several challenges as well as advantages for business establishments and enterprise IT teams. The following is a list of strategically significant implications of multistructured, multisourced, and massive volumes of data:

1. *Novel analytical capabilities and competencies* (prognostic, predictive, prescriptive, and personalized analytics)
2. *To have and sustain repositories comprising insights-driven business and IT services*
3. *To dynamically craft and compose smarter applications* out of those containerized, composable, configurable, and portable services by purpose-specific service integration and orchestration tools

In short, it is all about fulfilling the smarter planet vision skillfully by realizing context-aware, connected, and cognitive applications through the leverage of versatile and resilient technologies and tools. The growing number of software services (business and IT) getting stored and continuously refined in private as well as public repositories is another booster for the increasingly software-driven world. Thus, new analytical thinking and types are constantly emerging to enable every kind of industry domains to be inspiringly insightful in their operations and offerings. These are bound to expeditiously mature and stabilize to become common among us.

Describing Big Data Analytics

Big data represents huge volumes of data in petabytes, exabytes, and zettabytes in near future. As we move around the globe, we leave a trail of data behind us. Business to consumer (B2C) and consumer to consumer (C2C) e-commerce systems, and business to business (B2B) e-business transactions, online ticketing, and payments, web 1.0 (simple web), web 2.0 (social web), web 3.0 (semantic web), web 4.0 (smart web), still and dynamic images, and so on are the prominent and dominant sources for data. Sensors and actuators are deployed in plenty in specific environments for context awareness and for enabling the occupants and owners of the environments with a new set of hitherto unforeseen services. In short, every kind of integration, interaction, orchestration, automation, acceleration, augmentation, and operation produces streams of decision enabling data to be plucked and put into transactional and analytical data stores for initiating analytics and mining activities. As the whole world and every tangible entity in it are interconnected purposefully and programmatically, the data generation sources and resources are bound to grow ceaselessly resulting in heaps and hordes of data.

We have discussed the fundamental and fulsome changes happening in the IT and business domains. The growing aspect of service-enablement of applications, platforms, infrastructures (servers, storages, and network solutions), and even everyday devices besides the varying yet versatile connectivity methods has laid down a strong and stimulating foundation for big interactions, transactions, automation, and insights. The tremendous rise in the data collection along with all the complications has instinctively captivated both business and IT leaders and luminaries to act accordingly and adeptly to make sense out of this huge impending and data-driven opportunity for national governments, corporates, cities, and organizations. This is the beginning of the much-discussed and discoursed big data computing discipline.

This paradigm is getting formalized with the collaboration among product vendors, service organizations, independent software producers, system integrators, cloud service providers (CSPs), academics, and research labs. Having understood the strategic significance, all the different stakeholders have come together in complete unison in building and sustaining easy-to-grasp and use techniques, synchronized platforms elastic infrastructures, integrated processes, best practices, design patterns, and key metrics to make this new discipline pervasive and persuasive. Today, the acceptance and activation levels of big data computing are consistently on the climb. However, it is bound to raise a number of critical challenges, but at the same time, it is to be highly impactful and insightful for business organizations to confidently traverse in the right route if it is taken seriously. The continuous unearthing of prickling issues, data science methods, and incredible solutions are the good indicators for the shining and strategic big data phenomenon.

The implications of big data are vast and varied. The principal activity is to do a variety of tool-based and mathematically sound analyses of big data for instantaneously gaining bigger insights. It is a well-known fact that any organization having the innate ability to swiftly and succinctly leverage the accumulating data assets is bound to be successful in what they are operating, providing, and aspiring. That is, besides instinctive decisions, informed decisions go a long way in shaping up and confidently steering organizations. Thus, just gathering data is no more useful, but IT-enabled extraction and squeezing of actionable insights in time out of those data assets serve well for the betterment of world businesses. Analytics is the formal discipline in IT for methodically doing data collection, filtering, cleaning, translation, storage, representation, processing, mining, and analysis with the aim of extracting useful and usable intelligence. BDA is the newly coined word for accomplishing various sorts of analytical operations on big data. With this renewed focus, BDA is getting more market and mind shares across the world. With a string of new capabilities and competencies being accrued out of this recent and riveting innovation, worldwide corporates are keenly jumping into the BDA bandwagon with all the optimism. This chapter is designed for demystifying the hidden niceties and ingenuities of the raging BDA.

The Strategic Importance of Big Data Analytics

Big data is the general term used to represent massive amounts of data that are not stored in the relational form in traditional enterprise-scale databases. New-generation database systems are based on symmetric multiprocessing (SMP) and massively parallel processing (MPP) techniques. These are being framed in order to store, aggregate, filter, mine, and analyze big data efficiently. The following are the general characteristics of big data:

- Data storage is defined in the order of petabytes, exabytes, and so on in volume to the current storage limits (gigabytes and terabytes).
- There can be multiple structures (structured, semistructured, and less-structured) for big data.

- Multiple types of data sources (sensors, machines, mobiles, social sites, etc.) and resources for big data.
- Data are time-sensitive (near real-time as well as real-time). That means big data consists of data collected with relevance to the time zones so that time-sensitive insights can be extracted.

Thus, big data has created a number of rightful repercussions for businesses to give a prominent place for big data in their evolving IT strategy in order to be competitive in their dealings and decisions.

The future of business definitely belongs to those enterprises that swiftly embrace the BDA movement and use it strategically to their own advantages. It is pointed out that business leaders and other decision-makers, who are smart enough to adopt a flexible and futuristic big data strategy, can take their businesses toward greater heights. Successful companies are already extending the value of classic and conventional analytics by integrating cutting-edge big data technologies and outsmarting their competitors. There are several forecasts, exhortations, expositions, and trends on the discipline of BDA. Market research and analyst groups have come out with positive reports and briefings detailing its key drivers and differentiators, the future of this brewing idea, its market value, the revenue potentials, and application domains, the fresh avenues, and areas for renewed focus, the needs for its sustainability, and so on.

This recent entrant of BDA into the continuously expanding technology landscape has generated a lot of interest among industry professionals as well as academicians. Big data has become an unavoidable trend, and it has to be solidly and succinctly handled in order to derive time-sensitive and actionable insights. There is a dazzling array of tools, techniques, and tips evolving in order to quickly capture data from diverse distributed resources and process, analyze, and mine the data to extract actionable business insights to bring in technology-sponsored business transformation and sustenance. In short, analytics is the thriving phenomenon in every sphere and segment today. Especially with the automated capture, persistence, and processing of the tremendous amount of multistructured data getting generated by men as well as machines, the analytical value, scope, and power of data are bound to blossom further in the days to unfold.

Precisely speaking, data are a strategic asset for organizations to insightfully plan everything in advance and to embark on the appropriate activities that decisively and drastically power up their short as well as long-term offerings and outlooks. Business innovations can happen in plenty and be sustained too, when business processes are being constantly evaluated and enhanced through business insights. In the recent past, real-time analytics has gained much prominence and several product vendors have been flooding the market with a number of elastic and state-of-the-art solutions (software as well as hardware) for facilitating on-demand, ad hoc, real-time, and runtime analysis of batch, online transaction, social, machine, operational, and streaming data. There are a number of advancements in this field due to its huge potential for worldwide companies in considerably reducing operational expenditures while gaining operational insights. Hadoop-based analytical products are capable of processing and analyzing any data type and quantity across hundreds of commodity server clusters. Stream computing drives continuous and cognitive analysis of massive volumes of streaming data with submillisecond response times.

There are enterprise data warehouses, analytical platforms, in-memory appliances, and so on. Data warehousing (DW) delivers deep operational insights with advanced in-database analytics. The EMC Greenplum data computing appliance (DCA) is an integrated analytics platform that accelerates analysis of big data assets within a single integrated appliance. IBM PureData System for Analytics architecturally integrates database, server, and storage into a single, purpose-built, and easy-to-manage system. Then SAP HANA is an exemplary platform for efficient BDA. Platform vendors are conveniently tied up with infrastructure vendors especially CSPs to take analytics to the cloud so that the goal of analytics as a service (AaaS) sees a neat and nice reality sooner than later. There are multiple start-ups with innovative product offerings to speed up and simplify the complex part of big data analysis.

Big Data Analytics: The Prominent Use Cases

Enterprises can understand and gain the value of BDA based on the number of value-added use cases, and how some of the hitherto hard-to-solve problems can be easily tackled with the help of BDA technologies and tools. Every enterprise is mandated to grow with the help of analytics. As elucidated before, with big data, big analytics is the norm for businesses to take informed decisions. Several domains are eagerly enhancing their IT capability to have embedded analytics, and there are several reports eulogizing the elegance of BDA. The following are some of the prominent use cases:

Customer Satisfaction Analysis

This is the prime problem for most of the product organizations across the globe. There is no fool-proof mechanism in place to understand the customers' feelings and feedbacks about their products. Gauging the feeling of people correctly and quickly goes a long way for enterprises to ring in proper rectifications and recommendations in product design, development, servicing, and support, and this has been a vital task for any product manufacturer to be relevant for their customers and product consumers. Thus, customers' reviews regarding the product quality need to be carefully collected through various internal as well as external sources such as channel partners, distributors, sales and service professionals, retailers, and in the recent past through social sites, microblogs, and surveys. However, the issue is that the data being gleaned are extremely unstructured, repetitive, unfiltered, and unprocessed. Extraction of actionable insights becomes a difficult affair here, and hence leveraging BDA for a single view of customers (SVoC) will help enterprises to gain sufficient insights into the much-needed customer mindset, and to solve their problems effectively, and to avoid them in their new product lines.

Market Sentiment Analysis

In today's competitive and knowledge-driven market economy, business executives and decision-makers need to gauge the market environment deeply to be successful in their dreams, decisions, and deeds. What are the products shining in the market, where the market is heading, who are the real competitors, what are their top-selling products, how they are doing in the market, what are the bright spots and prospects, and what are customers' preferences in the short as well as long-term perspective through a deeper analysis legally and ethically? The above-mentioned pieces of information are available in a variety of websites, social media sites, and other public domains. BDA on this data can provide an organization with the much-needed information about strength, weakness, opportunities, and threats (SWOT) for their product lines.

Epidemic Analysis

Epidemics and seasonal diseases like flu start and spread with certain noticeable patterns among the people, and so it is pertinent to extract the hidden information to put a timely arrest on the outbreak of the infection. It is all about capturing all types of data originating from different sources, subjecting them to a series of investigations to extract actionable insights quickly, and contemplating the appropriate countermeasures. There is a news item that says how spying on people data can actually help medical professionals to save lives. Data can be gathered from many different sources, but few are as superior as Twitter; and tools such as TwitterHose facilitate this data collection allowing anyone to download 1% of tweets made during a specified hour at random and giving researchers a nice cross section of the Twitterverse. Researchers at Johns Hopkins University have been taking advantage of this tool, downloading tweets at random, and sifting through this data to flag any and all mentions of flu or cold-like symptoms. Because the tweets are geotagged, the researchers can then figure out where the sickness reports are coming from, cross-referencing this with flu data from the Centers for Disease Control to build up a picture of how the virus spreads, and, more importantly, predict where it might spread to the next.

In a similar line, with the leverage of the innumerable advancements being accomplished and articulated in the multifaceted discipline of BDA, myriad industry segments are jumping into the Big data bandwagon in order to make themselves ready to acquire superior competencies and capabilities especially in anticipation, ideation, implementation, and improvisation of premium and path-breaking services and solutions for the world market. BDA brings forth fresh ways for businesses and governments to analyze a vast amount of unstructured data (streaming as well as stored) to be highly relevant to their customers and constituencies.

Using Big Data Analytics in Health Care

The health care industry has been a late adopter of technology when compared to other industries such as banking, retail, and insurance. As per the trendsetting McKinsey report on Big data from June 2011, if US health care organizations could use big data creatively and effectively to drive efficiency and quality, the potential saving could be more than $300 billion every year.

■ *Patient monitoring—inpatient, outpatient, emergency visits, and ICU*: Everything is becoming digitized. With rapid progress in technology, sensors are embedded in weighing scales, blood glucose devices, wheelchairs, patient beds, X-ray machines, and so on. Digitized devices generate large streams of data in real time that can provide insights into patient's health and behavior. If these data are captured, it can be put to use to improve the accuracy of information and enable practitioners to better utilize limited provider resources. It will also significantly enhance patient experience at a health care facility by providing proactive risk monitoring, improved quality of care, and personalized attention. Big data can enable complex event processing (CEP) by providing real-time insights to doctors and nurses in the control room.

■ *Preventive care for ACO*: One of the key accountable care (ACO) goals is to provide preventive care. Disease identification and risk stratification will be very crucial to business function. Managing real-time feeds coming in from health information exchange (HIE), pharmacists, providers, and payers will deliver key information to apply risk stratification and predictive modeling techniques. In the past, companies were limited to historical claims and health risk assessment/survey data, but with HIE, the whole dynamic to data availability for health analytics has changed. Big data tools can significantly enhance the speed of processing and data mining.

- *Epidemiology*: Through HIE, most of the providers, payers, and pharmacists will be connected through networks in the near future. These networks will facilitate the sharing of data to better enable hospitals and health agencies to track disease outbreaks, patterns, and trends in health issues across a geographic region or across the world allowing determination of source and containment plans.
- *Patient care quality and program analysis*: With the exponential growth of data and the need to gain insight from information comes the challenge to process the voluminous variety of information to produce metrics and key performance indicators (KPIs) that can improve patient care quality and Medicaid programs. Big data provides the architecture, tools, and techniques that will allow processing terabytes and petabytes of data to provide deep analytic capabilities to its stakeholders.

Machine Data Analytics by Splunk

All our IT applications, platforms, and infrastructures generate a host of data every millisecond of every day. The machine data are one of the fastest growing and most complex areas of big data. It is also one of the most valuable insights containing a definitive record of users' transactions, customer behavior, sensor activity, machine behavior, security threats, fraudulent activity, and more. Machine data hold critical insights useful across the enterprise as follows:

- Monitor end-to-end transactions for online businesses providing 24 × 7 operations
- Understand customer experience, behavior, and usage of services in real time
- Fulfill internal service level agreements and monitor service provider agreements
- Identify spot trends and sentiment analysis on social platforms
- Map and visualize threat scenario behavior patterns to improve security posture

Making use of machine data is beset with challenges. It is a difficult proposition to process and analyze machine data by simply following traditional data management and analytics methods. Another challenge is to do the analytics in an interactive fashion in order to bring forth real-time insights. Machine data are generated by a multitude of disparate sources, and hence correlating meaningful events across these is definitely complex. The data are unstructured and difficult to fit into a predefined schema. Machine data are of high volume and are majorly time-series data. Hence, there is a valid insistence for novelty-filled approaches for their effective management and analysis. The most valuable insights from machine data are often needed in real time. Traditional business intelligence (BI), data warehouse, or IT analytics solutions are simply not designed and engineered for this class of high-volume, dynamic, and poly-structured data.

As indicated in the beginning, machine-generated data are more voluminous than man-generated data. Thus without an iota of doubt, machine data analytics is occupying a more significant portion in BDA. Machine data are being produced 24 × 7 × 365 by nearly every kind of software application and an electronic device. The software applications, server farms, network devices, storage and security appliances, sensors attached to machines, browsers, cameras, and various other systems deployed to support various business operations are continuously generating data relating to their status, situations, any noteworthy events, and activities. Machine data can be found in a variety of formats such as application log files, call detail records (CDRs), user profiles, KPIs, and clickstream data associated with user web interactions, data files, system configuration files, alerts, and tickets. Machine data are generated by both machine-to-machine (M2M) as well as human-to-machine (H2M) interactions. Nowadays, machines are being empowered by remotely held cloud-based services. So the strengths, sizes, scopes, and speeds of machine interactions and collaborations are on the growth trajectory.

Outside of the traditional IT infrastructure, every controller and processor-based system including HVAC controllers, smart meters, global positioning system (GPS) devices, actuators and robots, manufacturing systems, and radio frequency identification (RFID) reader tags, and consumer-oriented systems such as medical instruments, personal gadgets and gizmos, aircraft, scientific experiments, and automobiles that contain embedded devices are continuously generating machine data. As the device ecosystem is growing, the list of participating and contributing is constantly growing. With the solid growth of mobiles, wearables, portables, implantables, nomadic and fixed devices, and so on, the amount of machine data has grown up exponentially. Accordingly, the IT infrastructure complexity has gone up remarkably in order to host, manage, and deliver machine-centric applications, services, and data. As organizations open up for the brewing trend of "bring your own devices (BYODs)," the enterprise IT team is tasked with several complicated activities.

The goal here is to aggregate, parse, and to visualize machine data to spot trends and act accordingly. By monitoring and analyzing data emitted by a deluge of diverse, distributed, and decentralized data, there are opportunities galore. Someone wrote that sensors are the eyes and ears of future applications. Environmental monitoring sensors in remote and rough places bring forth the right and relevant knowledge about their operating environments in real time. The arrival of advanced algorithms for enabling sensor data fusion leads to develop context and situation-aware applications. With machine data analytics in place, any kind of performance degradation of machines can be identified in real time and corrective actions can be initiated with full knowledge and confidence. Security and surveillance cameras pump in still images and video data that in turn help analysts and security experts to preemptively stop any kind of undesirable intrusions. Firefighting can become smart with the utilization of machine data analytics. Log analytics is all that is expected to realize preventive maintenance for mission-critical machines.

The much-needed end-to-end visibility, analytics, and real-time intelligence across all of their applications, platforms, and IT infrastructures enable business enterprises to achieve required service levels, manage costs, mitigate security risks, demonstrate, and maintain compliance, and gain new insights to drive better business decisions and actions. Machine data provide a definitive and time-stamped record of current and historical activity and events within and outside an organization, including application and system performance, user activity, system configuration changes, electronic transaction records, security alerts, error messages, and device locations. Machine data in a typical enterprise are generated in a multitude of formats and structures, as each software application or hardware device records and creates machine data associated with their specific use. Machine data also vary among vendors and even within the same vendor across product types, families, and models.

There are a number of newer use cases being formulated with the pioneering improvements in smart sensors, their ad hoc and purpose-specific network formation capability, data collection, consolidation, correlation, corroboration and dissemination, knowledge discovery, information visualization, and so on. Splunk is a low-profile big data company specializing in extracting actionable insights out of diverse, distributed, and decentralized data. Some real-world customer examples include the following:

- *E-Commerce*: A typical e-commerce site serving thousands of users a day will generate gigabytes of machine data which can be used to provide significant insights into IT infrastructure and business operations. Expedia uses Splunk to avoid website outages by monitoring server and application health and performance. Today, around 3000 users at Expedia use Splunk to gain real-time visibility on tens of terabytes of unstructured, time-sensitive machine data (from not only their IT infrastructure but also from online bookings, deal analysis, and coupon use).
- *Software as a Service (SaaS)*: Salesforce.com uses Splunk to mine the large quantities of data generated from its entire technology stack. It has >500 users of Splunk dashboards from IT users monitoring customer experience to product managers performing analytics on services like "Chatter." With Splunk, Salesforce.com claims to have taken application troubleshooting for 100,000 customers to the next level.
- *Digital publishing*: National Public Radio uses Splunk to gain insights of their digital asset infrastructure, to monitor and troubleshoot their end-to-end asset delivery infrastructure, to measure program popularity and views by the device, to reconcile royalty payments for digital rights, and to measure abandonment rates and more.

Figure 7.1 vividly illustrates how Splunk captures data from numerous sources and does the processing, filtering, mining, and analysis to generate actionable insights out of multistructured machine data.

Splunk Enterprise is the leading platform for collecting, analyzing, and visualizing machine data. It provides a unified way to organize and extract real-time insights from massive amounts of machine data from virtually any source. This includes data from websites, business applications, social media platforms, application servers, hypervisors, sensors, and traditional databases. Once our data are in Splunk, we can search, monitor, report, and analyze it, no matter how unstructured, large, or diverse it may be. Splunk software gives us a real-time understanding of what is

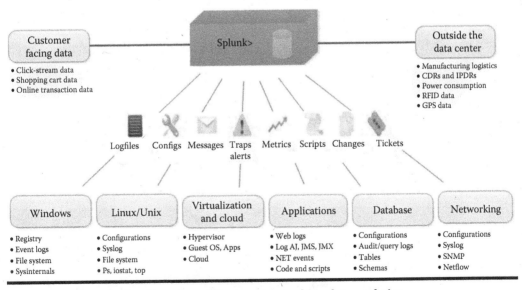

Figure 7.1 The Splunk reference architecture for machine data analytics.

happening and a deep analysis of what has happened, driving new levels of visibility and insight. This is called operational intelligence.

Most organizations maintain a diverse set of data stores—machine data, relational data, and other unstructured data. Splunk DB Connect delivers real-time connectivity to one or many relational databases and Splunk. Hadoop Connect delivers bidirectional connectivity to Hadoop. Both Splunk apps enable us to drive more meaningful insights from all of our data. The Splunk App for HadoopOps provides real-time monitoring and analysis of the health and performance of the end-to-end Hadoop environment, encompassing all layers of the supporting infrastructure.

Real-Time and Streaming Analytics

We have discussed extensively BDA. When the data size is massive, generally it is being subjected to batch and historical processing techniques to extract all kinds of hidden intelligence. However, on the other hand, there are fast and streaming data which are relatively small in size but widely vary in structure and speed. There are open source and commercial-grade platforms emerging and evolving for undertaking real-time and streaming analytics on fast and streaming data. Recently, there is a cry for doing immediate and interactive analytics not only on fast data but also on big data to emit out insights in time. With the grand availability of exemplary solutions, systems, and services, the days of accomplishing real-time analytics on big data are not too far away.

All these advancements do not imply that the fully matured and stabilized BI and DW solutions are going away. But there is a telling need to complement them with newer technologies for big, fast, streaming, and IoT data storage, management, and analytics. The era of real-time and streaming analytics is steadily arriving, and there are a number of use cases being unearthed mandating real-time and streaming analytics capabilities and competencies for any organization to grow fast. There are well-known use cases such as full-text indexing, recommendation systems (e.g., Netflix movie recommendations), log analysis, computing web indexes, and data mining. These are the well-known processes that can be allowed to run for extended periods of time.

The high-level architecture for real-time processing is shown in Figure 7.2.

Operational analytics (OA) is a kind of real-time analytics that provides enhanced visibility into business processes, events, and operations as they are happening. The practice of OA is succulently

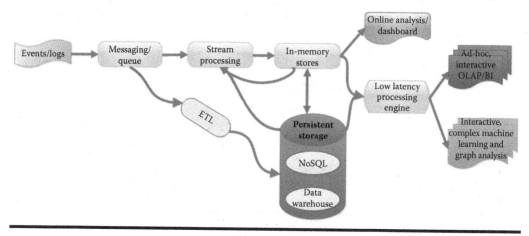

Figure 7.2   The real-time and streaming analytics architecture.

enabled by special technologies that can handle machine data, sensor data, event streams, and other forms of streaming data and big data. OA solutions can also correlate and analyze data collected from multiple sources in various latencies (from batch to real time) to realize and reveal actionable information. Organizations can act on extracted knowledge by sending an appropriate alert notification to the correct manager in time, updating a management dashboard, offering an incentive to a churning customer, adjusting machinery, or preventing fraud.

Majorly, Apache Hadoop and MapReduce (MR) technologies have been in the forefront of BDA. However, this parallelization framework was primarily designed for big data storage, data management, statistical analysis, and statistical association between various data sources using distributed computing and batch processing. However, today's environment demands all of the above plus real-time analytics. Very recently, Apache Spark and Storm frameworks are drawing an extensive attention and attraction for real-time analytics. Spark use cases include stream processing (e.g., credit card fraud detection), sensor data processing, and real-time querying of data for analytics.

The MR frameworks such as Hadoop have inefficient performance when conducting iterative computations because it requires extensive disk I/O for reloading the data from disk storages at each iteration. To avoid such extensive disk I/O, distributed in-memory computing platforms become popular. Apache Spark is a general-purpose in memory cluster-computing platform. Apache Spark is one of the most widely used open source processing engines for big data, with rich language-integrated application program interfaces (APIs) and a wide range of libraries. This platform allows users to develop Spark applications by high-level APIs. Spark enables the machines to cache data and intermediate results in memory instead of reloading them from disk at each iteration. In order to support parallel programming, Spark provides resilient distributed datasets (RDDs) and parallel operations. Spark offers a general engine based on task directed acyclic graphs and data sharing on which workloads such as batch jobs, streaming, SQL, and graph analytics can run.

Organizations can now store large data sets in Hadoop distributed file systems (HDFS), which is a distributed file system designed for storing and manipulating large-scale data. HDFS is highly fault-tolerant because it ensures data replication to avoid any kind of data loss. The master or name node is in charge of all the underlying data nodes. The name node manages the namespace of HDFS, and the data nodes store data as blocks. HDFS heartbeats are periodically sent from data nodes to the name node. When the name node does not receive the heartbeat from a specific data node, it marks that data node as dead one and assigns its work to another node.

In Spark, a partition is a distributed segment of data. When a driver program loads data into memory, a partition is a basic loading unit for the cache manager of Spark. If there is enough memory in the slave nodes, partitions will be cached in memory or otherwise in the disk. In Spark, a training data set is represented by a resilient distributed dataset (RDD), which consists of partitions. An RDD is created from HDFS files or by transforming other RDDs. The usage of RDDs is an important technique to realize parallel computing not only outside but also inside a slave node. A slave node only needs to maintain some partitions of the training data set. Instead of handling the original whole data set, every slave node can focus on its partitions simultaneously. This mechanism achieves parallelism if the number of partitions is enough.

Spark provides two types of parallel operations on RDDs: transformations and actions. Transformations, including operations like map and filter, create a new RDD from the existing one. Actions, such as reduce and collect, conduct computations on an RDD and return the result to the driver program. The Spark architecture is given in Figure 7.3.

The Spark platform is implemented in Scala and is hence run within the JVM. It can be deployed as a stand-alone application on a cluster as a client application of either Apache Hadoop

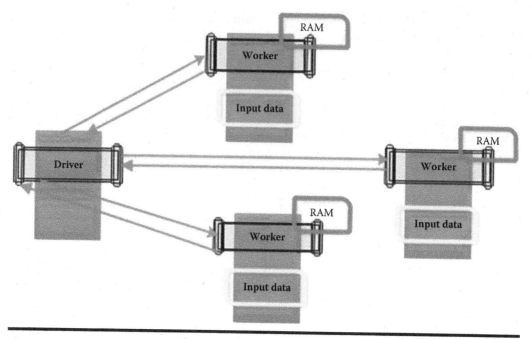

Figure 7.3 **The Apache Spark architecture for real-time processing through in-memory data storage.**

2+ (YARN) or Apache Mesos or to a simulated cluster on a single machine. It has APIs for Java, Scala, Python, and R.

- Spark provides a more flexible, concise, and easy-to-learn programming model for developers with significantly better performance in most production scenarios.
- Spark supports traditional batch-mode applications, but it also provides a streaming model for reactive applications.
- The functional programming foundation of Spark and its support for iterative algorithms provide the foundation for a wide range of libraries, including SparkSQL, for integrated SQL-based queries over data with defined schemas, Spark streaming, for handling incoming events in near real time, GraphX for computations over graphs, and MLlib for machine-learning.
- Spark scales down to a single machine and up to large-scale clusters. Spark jobs can run in Hadoop using the YARN resource manager, on Mesos clusters, or in small, "standalone" clusters.

There are research works on automating and advancing several tasks through the Spark paradigm. For example, there is a master thesis depicting and describing a valid use case "Real-Time Anomaly Detection in Water Distribution Networks using Spark Streaming." Andrew Psaltis has worked on and presented his findings through a PPT file with the title "Exploring Clickstream Analytics with Kafka, Spark Streaming, and WebSockets." VoltDB people have focused on the scalability and performance aspects of the Spark framework. Reactive applications are a special kind of next-generation applications getting readily developed, deployed, and delivered via the Spark programming model. Performing fast and interactive analytics over Hadoop data with

Spark is getting accelerated. OA is increasingly accomplished through the smart leverage of Spark. The widely discoursed use case of insider threat detection is quickly realized through the deftness of Spark. Another research paper explains how Spark comes handy in soft and real-time GPRS traffic analysis for commercial M2M communications. Thus, there is a grandiose concentration by worldwide industry researchers and academic professors in taking the notion of data analytics to the next level with the impressive and influential contributions from Spark.

Similarly, doing real-time analytics on streaming data gains an immense momentum. Spark also can do streaming analytics. On the commercial side, IBM InfoSphere Streams is a highly synchronized and syndicated engine for streaming analytics. There are other vendors bringing forth competent and compatible solutions for easing up real-time and streaming analytics. There are so many other ways and means of speeding up the process of real-time analytics. In-memory and in-database analytics are being touted as the most sensible and logical way forward for real-time and streaming analytics. There are supercomputers, purpose-specific appliances, clusters, grids, and other parallel computers to achieve real-time analytics.

Expounding the IoT Data Analytics Domain

The traditional BI capability for structured business data for extracting tactical as well as strategic business-centric insights is no more efficient and sufficient. There is, therefore, an insistence for comprehensive yet cognitive analytics to be performed on all kinds of value-adding, insights-generating, and decision-enabling data emanating from different and geographically distributed sources, which are incidentally on the rise, to spit out rewarding insights in time. There are increasingly big, fast, streaming, and IoT data, whereas the prominent data processing formats include batch/ad hoc, interactive, iterative, and real-time processing. The widely available Hadoop implementations have accentuated the realization of big insights via batch data processing. However in the recent past, there is a clarion call for interactive processing on multistructured data to craft and carve out real-time insights. Especially with the massive volumes of fast IoT data, the extraction of real-time insights is going to be a game-changing affair.

On the other hand, the cloud-enabled IT optimization has been a new revelation and revolution for the impending era of cloud-based analytics. Forming edge clouds are the latest buzzword in the fast-expanding cloud landscape, and hence, the aspect of edge analytics is gaining a surging popularity for real-time analytics. That is, analytics happens not at the faraway cloud servers instead at the proximate edge devices so that the security of data is ensured and the scarce network bandwidth gets saved.

The Key Drivers for IoT Data Analytics

Recently, there are a number of interesting things happening simultaneously. The emergence of smart sensors and actuators in large numbers with generic as well as specific capabilities, the grand revelation of cutting-edge technologies, the ICT infrastructure optimization and organization through cloud technologies and tools, the process excellence through rationalization and synchronization, the commendable improvements in the connectivity technologies and topologies, the pace at which smarter environments (smarter homes, hospitals, hotels, etc.) being realized and accepted across, and so on are the widely discussed and discoursed transitions in business and IT landscapes. There are market analysis and research reports proclaiming that there will be millions of software applications, billions of connected devices, and trillions of digitized entities by the year 2020. These revolutionary and evolutionary advancements clearly are bound to lead to the accumulation of massive amount of multistructured and sourced IoT data. The reality is that data are simply pouring in from different sources at varying speeds, structures, sizes, and scopes. The ultimate value out of data-driven insights and insights-driven decisions seems to be tantalizingly transformational for any small, medium, and large enterprises across the globe.

On the infrastructure front, technologically advanced server, storage, and network infrastructures are being put in place for next-generation data analytics. Data collection, cleansing, and ingestion are speeded up through a variety of data connectors, drivers, adapters, and other middleware solutions. The conventional extract, transform and load (ETL) tools are also being leveraged to establish an adaptive linkage with an array of home-grown, packaged, and enterprise-class business applications. Specialized storage appliances and networks are being readied to duly persist and protect incoming and even processed data. Further on, there are standards-compliant data virtualization and visualization tools coming up fast for contributing immensely toward the requirement of knowledge engineering and exposition. Having considered the short as well as long-term significance of systematic and sagacious data analytics for strategically enhancing the business efficiency and value, the open-source community as well as commercial-grade product vendors across the globe have come out with a few solid and succulent advancements in their analytical solutions and services to smartly streamline and speed up the process of knowledge discovery and dissemination.

The need now is to have an end-to-end and converged data analytics platform for performing purposeful and pioneering analytics on all kinds of IoT data at different layers and levels in order to conceptualize and concretize scores of state-of-the-art and sophisticated systems for the envisioned smarter planet. In other words, highly modular IoT data analytics platforms and infrastructures collectively lay a stimulating and sustainable foundation for deriving and deploying a growing collection of people-centric and situation-aware applications to be delivered as publicly discoverable, network accessible, composable, and unobtrusively deliverable services. That is, for the ensuing smarter world, the rewarding and resplendent roles and responsibilities of highly competent and cognitive IoT data analytics solutions and services cannot be taken lightly. In the following sections, we would like to insist on the urgent necessity for hyperconverged and hybrid IoT data analytics platforms (can run on edge clouds as well as on traditional clouds) for building and sustaining pathbreaking applications and services that are more tuned and tipped for people empowerment.

The Key Movements and Motivations of IoT Data

There are pioneering technologies and tools being unearthed with a passion for sustainably empowering the IT contributions toward business automation and acceleration. This continuous stream of technological advancements is resulting in fresh possibilities and opportunities for businesses that in turn vouch for enhanced care, choice, comfort, and convenience for customers and consumers. The noteworthy implications out of all these transformations are that the number of data sources goes up considerably, and the amount of data being generated and garnered is also exponentially growing. The principal contributors to the heightened data collection are listed below:

- Sentient materials/smart objects/digitized entities through the deeper digitization enabled by technologies (nano and microscale sensors, actuators, codes, chips, controllers, specks, smart dust, tags, stickers, LED, etc.)
- Connected, resource-constrained, and embedded devices and machines

- Ambient sensing, vision, and perception technologies
- Social media and knowledge-sharing sites
- Consumerization (mobiles and wearables)
- Centralization, commoditization, containerization, and industrialization (cloud computing)
- Communication (ambient, autonomic, and unified)
- Integration (D2D, D2E, D2C, C2C, etc.)
- Technical and scientific experimentation data
- Operational, transactional, and interactions data

The Emergence of Edge Clouds for Real-Time Insights

With the runaway success of the pioneering digitization and edge computing technologies and tools, every tangible thing in our daily environments is becoming digitized/smart/sentient object. It is foreseen that everyone in this world will have a smartphone. Every unique asset and artifact (physical, mechanical, electrical, and electronics) in our daily lives are systematically enabled through edge/fog technologies. Ultimately, our everyday environments are to be decked with a variety of smart sensors and actuators to fulfill the prime goals of precision-centric context-awareness and activity recognition. There will be deeper and decisive interactions among enabled objects, devices, and humans in the days ahead. Further on, the cloud-based cyber applications will have a salivating role in empowering physical items on the ground.

In today's digitally connected society, the large volumes of multistructured data getting generated through the interactions and collaborations of different and distributed digital elements, smartphones, social media, satellite telemetry, and imagery lead to various new analytical competencies, such as social media analytics, and sentiment analytics for people empowerment. The prickling challenge is how efficiently and effectively subject captured and cleansed data to various specific investigations to extract real-time intelligence.

There is a new paradigm of fog or edge computing vigorously and rigorously capturing the imagination of IoT professionals these days. That is, the real-time and relatively small-scale processing are shifted to edge devices instead of aggregating and transmitting device data to far-away cloud servers to squeeze out insights. Localized and personalized decisions are essential in certain scenarios, and hence the fast-evolving concept of fog computing is being gleefully received. The edge devices are dynamically discovered and linked through body, personal, and local-area networks (LANs) to form ad hoc edge clouds to accelerate and accentuate edge analytics. With the exponential explosion of connected things, devices, and services, it is understandable that the decentralized networking is the best way forward as it has the inherent potential to reduce infrastructure and maintenance costs. Decentralization guarantees increased robustness by removing single points of failure. By shifting from centralized to decentralized processing, devices at the edges gain greater autonomy to become the core and central point of transactions toward enhanced productivity and value for owners and users.

The public cloud idea typically represents the online, off-premise, and on-demand computing whereas the fog computing is for proximity computing. Of course, there are private and hybrid clouds that use dynamically changing clusters of commodity server machines for data processing and logic execution. But the fog computing paradigm extends the computing to the network of edge devices. The fog vision was conceived and aptly concretized in order to comprehensively attend some specific use cases for the smarter computing era. There are specific applications such as gaming and video conferencing mandating very low and predictable latency.

Then there are geodistributed applications (smarter traffic, grid, etc., pipeline monitoring, environmental monitoring, and management through the sensor and actuator networks, etc.). Further on, mobility applications such as connect cars and transports are pitching for the fog paradigm. The next logical step is to have hybrid environments by seamlessly and spontaneously integrating edge and traditional cloud environments for availing advanced and aggregated analytics.

Deep Diving and Digging into Edge Analytics

Devices are increasingly instrumented and interconnected to be expressly adaptive, assistive, articulative, and capable of accomplishing smarter actuation. In other words, edge devices are gradually and glowingly joining in the mainstream computing. That is, they are capable of data capture and processing toward knowledge discovery. Precisely speaking, devices are inherently empowered to perform the transition of data to information and to intelligence. Typically, there are three prominent levels in which usable intelligence can be generated.

The first level is that every participating and contributing device is capable of processing the data it gathers. For example, in a smarter home environment, every type of articles and artifacts such as refrigerators, electrical switches, consumer electronics, media players, machines, instruments, utensils, wares, and equipment could process their data and take decisions as per the situation warrants.

The second level covers the so-called gateways and data-aggregation devices. The other probable nomenclature includes hubs, brokers, middleware, adapters, and so on. As we all know, there are bountiful resource-constrained and networked embedded systems in our everyday environments to take care of everyday needs of people. Further on, the maturity and stability of digitization, distribution, and decentralization technologies lead to a massive number of digitized/sentient/smart objects (these are originally ordinary stuff and are enabled to be computational, communicative, sensitive, responsive, perceptive, etc., by various edge and fog technologies such as sensors, actuators, tags, motes, speckles, chips, controllers, stickers, codes, LEDs, etc.). The relevance of gateways and other intermediaries is being felt here as these individual entities need to be clubbed together to get consolidated and composite data to enable the gateways to indulge in analyzing to arrive at insights.

The final level is the cloud-based analytics. That is, edge devices individually and/or through the above-mentioned gateways can connect and integrate with cloud-based analytical platforms and applications to reap compact and specialized analytics. The innovations in edge and gateway devices are bringing forth sophisticated algorithms, and it is cost-effective to store and analyze granular data at edge devices. With the pervasiveness of network infrastructures, the edge-to-cloud movement is laying a stimulating and sparkling foundation for higher end analytics at cloud servers. Let us discuss a couple of use cases in the subsequent sections.

The emerging trend of in-memory computing can be a game-changing phenomenon for carving out real-time insights. Cloud-based MQTT, XMPP, and other RESTful servers are being used to capture and store data from different and distributed sensors and instruments. And from there, analytics engine or any other specific systems such as context aggregator and decider can comfortably proceed for producing insights. The idea is for performing historical and comprehensive analytics at the cloud, which is affordable, all-encompassing, and elastic. That is, all the gleaned data have to be sent across to powerful cloud environments for embarking on predictive, prescriptive, and posterior analytics.

The Renowned Edge Analytics Use Cases

Smart Water System

This is a specialized system wherein smart sensors for measuring water and flow levels and water quality are the prominent entities deployed on water tanks, reservoirs, and water pipes. This local IoT system comprising multifaceted sensors is connected to the faraway cloud applications and data sources via the public Internet through a local IoT gateway device. These sensors emit events periodically and report observations such as the water level in the tank, quality parameters such as total dissolved solids, chlorine content, temperature, and the volume of water flow. The sensor data can be processed by the gateway device, and the results can be immediately communicated to actuators at the ground level in order to go ahead with the clean-up operations. The sensor data also can be transmitted to cloud systems in order to have comprehensive analytics. But for real-time systems, edge analytics is the best course of action.

Smarter Grid

This has been one of the widely quoted use cases as the energy optimization has been the universal goal for the nations across the globe. The smart grid application may run on network edge devices such as smart meters and microgrids. Based on the brewing energy demand, the power availability, and the lowest price, these devices automatically switch to alternative energies like solar and the wind. Gateways at the edge capture, store, and process the data generated by grid sensors and devices, and accordingly issue control commands to the actuators to proceed with the decisions made. Edge analytics devices also filter the data to be consumed locally and send the rest to faraway powerful systems for coordinated and compact analysis to generate tactical as well as strategic insights, reports, maps, charts, graphs, and so on to be disseminated into and displayed by knowledge visualization tools and dashboards.

Smarter Homes and Buildings

Edge analytics enables localized monitoring and decision-enablement in time. One or more edge devices in the neighborhood are purposefully forming ad hoc clouds in order to accomplish coordinated processing. The trend is clearly tending toward decentralized decision-making with all the household consumer electronics, utensils, and monitoring systems such as air conditioning, elevators, security and surveillance cameras that are getting instrumented and interconnected to share their capabilities with one another seamlessly and spontaneously. There is a spurt in deploying a growing array of sensors and actuators for monitoring, measuring, management, and maintenance purposes within homes and buildings. Temperature, humidity, gas, fire, presence, and pressure levels are being minutely monitored by these sensors, and the data captured are systematically combined to form reliable and holistic measurements. The local gateway devices are then leveraged to process and take decisions in time. That is, insights-driven actuators can plunge into appropriate actions with all the intrinsic clarity and confidence. Automated energy management through continuous observations and actions is a well-known edge analytics application.

Similarly, other important junctions, eating joints, auditoriums, battlefields, airports, railway stations, entertainment plazas, educational institutions, manufacturing plants and floors, warehouses, theaters, and so on are going to be technologically stuffed, saturated, and sandwiched to be smarter in their operations and offerings. The security, safety, emergency, and concierge services are going to be very common, casual, and cheap through edge clouds and analytics.

Smarter Retailing

The shopping experience for shoppers at hypermarkets and malls is going to be unique with recently attained edge processing and knowledge delivery capabilities. For example, designing and delivering location and context-based services to users, implementing augmenting reality, improving the overall shopping experience, or dealing with secured online payment are going to be the technology-sponsored features and facilities.

Self-Maintaining Trains

Sensor monitoring on a train's ball-bearing can detect heat levels, allowing applications to send an automatic alert to the train operator to stop the train at next station for emergency maintenance and avoid potential derailment.

Smarter Mines

In lifesaving air vents scenario, sensors on vents monitor air conditions flowing in and out of mines and automatically change airflow if conditions become dangerous to miners.

Device Integration

It is going to be the connected era. Devices are getting integrated with one another in the vicinity as well as with remote ones. The device connectivity enables interactions and coordination resulting in a lot of data to be meticulously captured and methodically investigated to derive actionable insights. Today, every industry segment is blessed with a number of differently enabled devices. The faster maturity and stability of edge/fog computing along with innumerable connected devices have laid down a stimulating and scintillating foundation for venturing into hitherto unexplored avenues for aggregating fresh revenues for investors, entrepreneurs, start-up companies, and established business houses and behemoths.

Smarter Traffic Systems

Traffic lights are becoming very prominent and pervasive in urban areas for enabling pedestrians as well as vehicle drivers. There are high-fidelity video cameras in plenty along the roads, expressways, tunnels, and so on in order to activate and accelerate a variety of real-time tasks for pedestrians, traffic police, and vehicle drivers. Wireless access points like WiFi, 3G, 4G, road-side units, and smart traffic lights are deployed along the roads. Vehicles-to-vehicle, vehicle-to-access points, and access points-to-access points' interactions enrich the application of this scenario.

All kinds of connected vehicles and transport systems need actionable insights in time to derive and deliver a rich set of context-aware services. Safety is an important factor for car and road users, and there are additional temporal as well as spatial services being worked out. With driverless cars under intense development and testing, insights-driven decisions and knowledge-centric actions are very vital for next-generation transports.

The impending need is to have smarter traffic systems in order to fulfill the unique goals behind the smarter traffic. This system has to be deployed at each intersection within the city areas, and they can be networked with one another to have hooked up with centralized control and analytics systems. It also has to be equipped with a variety of sensors to measure the distance and the speed of approaching vehicles from every direction. The other requirements include detecting the presence of pedestrians and cyclists crossing the street or road in order to proactively issue "slow down" warnings to incoming vehicles and instantaneously modifying its own cycle to prevent collisions. Besides ensuring utmost safety and the free flow of traffic, all kinds of traffic data need to be captured and stocked in order to do specific analytics to accurately predict and prescribe the ways and means of substantially improving the traffic system. Ambulances need to get a way out through traffic-free open lanes in the midst of chaotic and cruel traffic.

The noteworthy factor here is that the smarter traffic system has to learn, decide, and act instantaneously in order to avert any kind of accidents. That is, the real-time reaction is the crucial need, and hence the concept of edge clouds out of edge devices for collaboratively collecting different data and processing them instantaneously to spit out insights is gaining widespread and overwhelming momentum. Another point here is that data flow in streams. Thus, all kinds of discreet/simple as well as complex events need to be precisely and perfectly captured and combined to be subjected into a bevy of investigations to complete appropriate actions. The whole process has to be initiated at the earliest through a powerful and pioneering knowledge discovery and dissemination platform to avoid any kind of losses for people and properties. Here, collecting and sending data to remote cloud servers to arrive at competent decisions are found inappropriate for real-time and low-latency applications. However, the edge data can be aggregated and transmitted to powerful cloud servers casually in batches to have a historical diagnostic and deterministic analytics at the later point in time.

The Architectural Components of the Smarter Traffic System

1. As articulated above, as far as physical components are concerned, a smarter traffic system has to include traffic lights, sensors, and actuators within its jurisdictional region so that the reaction time is on the order of <10 milliseconds.
2. A miniaturized orchestration platform is an overseeing software solution, which has to be a part and parcel of the system. This module is greatly obligated to orchestrate and manage all the other software modules of the system effectively. It has to be policy-aware. That is, well-intended policies can be established easily and enforced accordingly toward effective governance.
3. A centralized decision-enabling module is another noteworthy one for garnering data from all the deployed traffic lights and pushing the decisions to individual traffic lights through a messaging bus, which is another mandatory software solution for enabling data transmission on both directions.

There can be multiple smarter traffic systems from different providers tied up with different networking and communication service providers. All these deviations and deficiencies need to be addressed systematically in order to accomplish edge analytics. Thus, any edge analytics software solution has to take multiple scenarios and factors into consideration in order to be right and relevant for realizing real-time applications such as smarter traffic. Such systems are capable of taking lightning-fast yet correct decisions, which are turning out to be essential for the projected smarter world. A hybrid version of traditional and edge analytics is vividly illustrated in Figure 7.4.

Most edge devices exchange data and send the information to centralized control, storage, and analytical systems at private or public cloud. But the businesses expect more deft and decisive services quickly, and hence edge devices individually as well as collectively are more often empowered

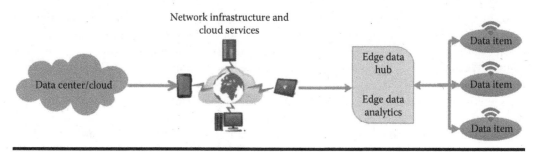

Figure 7.4 The technological components of the hybrid IoT analytics platform.

to arrive at actionable insights instantaneously through local and proximate processing. At the edge, there can be a litany of sensors and actuators (cyber-physical systems, connected devices, robots, consumer electronics, autonomous agents, intelligent machines, etc.). It is going to be a grand cluster of resource-constrained as well as computationally powerful entities. To have pragmatic edge analytics, it is prudent and paramount to smartly leverage a combination of promising and proven technological solutions.

Open Service Gateway Initiative (*OSGi*) is a sound framework for the realization of highly modular Java applications. Modular applications are being built as a collection of bundles that are typically dynamic components that can be installed, started, or updated without the need to restart the application or service. OSGi also enables the remote management of bundles. Purpose-specific as well as generic bundles crafted and curated by worldwide bundle developers can be found in publicly available and accessible repositories. Not only bigger systems but also for resource-constrained embedded systems, the OSGi framework is found to be extremely fit. OSGi provides better resource management, since it allows multiple Java applications to run using a single JVM. With enabled machines, instruments, and appliances joining in the mainstream computing, the role and responsibility of OSGi have grown exceedingly in bringing forth device-centric modular applications.

With machines communicating one another in the vicinity as well with remote ones through personal, local-, and wide area networks (WANs), there came a number of newer applications such as home, building, and industry automation systems. The domains of telematics and telemetry have grown significantly since then. There are a few popular messaging protocols enabling the capture and communication of device data and event messages to their respective destinations. All these tectonic technological advancements gel well in building and deploying sophisticated situation-aware applications. In short, the usage of OSGi framework has advantages over standard OS-specific applications, since it ensures high modularity, portability, and resource effectiveness.

Extensible Messaging and Presence Protocol (*XMPP*) is one of the popular communication protocols providing additional security features such as secure communication and authentication of end users. XMPP can be used for the unified communication of messaging, presence information, and file transfer. XMPP brings up a number of applications such as sensor-enabled monitoring and management of systems and even environments.

Complex Event Processing (*CEP*): Relational databases (DBs) are mainly designed to collect and store data. As far as the analysis aspect is concerned, DB is extensively used for aggregating and filtering data, searching for unique patterns, and arriving at high-level summary information. However, the analysis happens offline. But any standards-compliant CEP engine is capable of receiving incoming streams of messages and runs them through a set of predefined and continuous queries to produce hidden patterns, usable associations, and tips in time.

CEP is the key technology for processing volumes of low-level events and transforming them into higher level and composite events for visualization and automated response. For example, CEP is being used to detect any suspicious credit card usage by monitoring credit card activity as it occurs. It can perform time-series analysis and trending over streams of events, and it can correlate a stream of real-time information with stored and historical data, such as new credit card activity with customer information from a customer relationship management system.

With the focus turning toward edge analytics, the CEP technology is being tweaked to be used in edge devices apart from being taken to high-end cloud servers. As indicated previously, with our everyday environments being stuffed with innumerable sensors, the scale of messages emanating is going to be tremendously large. The brewing need here is how to smartly partition the CEP query execution across the edge devices and even the cloud. Transmitting data to the off-premise cloud is beset with data privacy, locality, and security issues besides wasting the precious network bandwidth. However, considering the limited capacities and capabilities of edge devices for proper analytics, a kind of lighter version of CEP engine is being implemented to speed up the process of knowledge discovery out of large-scale event messages. The control flow is as follows: Sensor and actuator data being generated are gleaned to be routed through an edge/fog data aggregator.

The Key Capabilities of Next-Generation IoT Data Analytics Platforms

IoT data analytics are not only for making sense out of IoT data to empower everyday devices (physical, mechanical, electrical, and electronics) to be intelligent in their operations and outputs but also enable end-users and knowledge workers to benefit immensely in their everyday occupations and obligations. There are IoT application enablement platforms (AEPs) and gateways in plenty, but there are a lot of recently expressed needs to build and sustain highly competent IoT data analytics platforms in order to exploit IoT data efficiently and effectively. These end-to-end analytical platforms are slated to connect, extract, preprocess, analyze, and mine data from a large number of sensors, actuators, transactional and operational systems, engineered systems, and so on. Typically, operational and information technologies' (OT and IT) systems are transitioning from the systems of records to the systems of engagements due to the incredible fact that new-generation systems are intrinsically empowered to have purposeful collaboration, correlation, and corroboration with one another and with faraway services too. Data virtualization, integration, capture, cleansing, and ingestion into data storage and file systems are the other tasks accomplished through a host of publish-subscribe servers, the tweaked ETL tools, and a litany of connectors, adaptors, and so on. Finally, the proposed platforms have to have a seamless integration with different report-generation tools, dashboards, consoles, and other visualization platforms to disseminate and display what is extracted in multiple preferred forms and formats.

Figure 7.5 clearly articulates the trends and transitions happening in the data analytics space. Originally it was batch processing on big data, but the direction and destination are to do real-time processing of big data to generate real-time insights. The IoT data volume is tremendously huge, and there is an insistence for instantaneous extraction of intelligence to enable timely decision-making. To benefit out of IoT data, interactive processing is being recommended. This is the reason for the emergence of competent solutions for real-time IoT analytics.

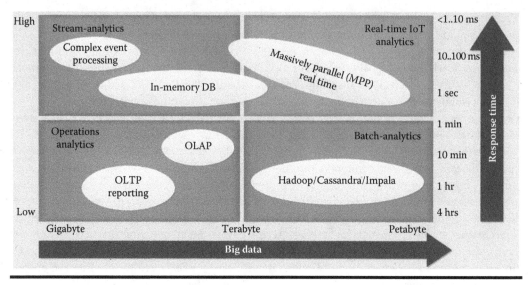

Figure 7.5 The real-time processing of big data.

The Key Capabilities

An IoT data analytics platform in smart synchronization with IoT AEPs and IoT gateways is capable of doing the following:

- Enables interoperable, portable, scalable, and reusable application building
- Uncovers timely and actionable insights
- Works on personal, campus, local, metro, and wide area networks
- Enables the realization of smart objects, devices, networks, and environments
- Leads to the production of pioneering and people-centric applications and services
- Helps to come out with precise predictions and prescriptions
- Facilitates process excellence
- Embraces IoT protocols such as AMQP, MQTT, XMPP, CoAP, and REST
- Guarantees preventive maintenance of infrastructures
- Ensures the optimized utilization of distributed assets through monitoring, measurement, and management
- Safeguards the safety and security of people and properties
- Monitors complex environments to guarantee business performance, productivity, and resilience

There are viable frameworks and management platforms for integrating sensors and devices to remote cloud centers. These enable cloud connectivity to facilitate capabilities such as data capture, rules/policy engine, configuration, and file transfer.

Precisely speaking, with the ready availability of versatile technologies and enabling tools, the long and arduous process of data to information and knowledge gets accelerated and augmented to fulfill the long-drawn vision of the smarter planet. Actionable insights produced in time go a long way in elevating machines becoming smarter and men the smartest.

The Prime Modules of IoT Data Analytics Platforms

Considering the rising complexity of next-generation analytics requirements and hence the enabling platforms, the sophistication of contributing modules for IoT data analytics platforms should be consistently on the climb. In this section, the key modules and their unique features and functionalities are being expounded.

1. *Data virtualization, integration, and ingestion modules*: Millions of connected devices and sensors are pumping out a complicated set of data of their own as well as about their environments, and they need to be captured, transformed, and ingested into the underlying IoT database with higher write performance. There are proven ETL and ELT tools in order to speed up data movement.

2. *Data analytics platforms*: There are big, fast, and streaming data analytics platforms in plenty from both open-source software community as well as commercial-grade product vendors. However, IoT data analytics are gaining the mind as well as market shares considering their uniqueness in setting up and sustaining next-generation smarter systems, networks, and environments. Data storage and management systems are very important. There are parallelized, clustered, and distributed relational database management system (SQL) systems, NoSQL, and NewSQL systems. For accelerated analytics, there are in-memory databases, in-database analytics, specially made appliances, and so on.

3. *Data visualization platforms*: Dashboards, portals, consoles, reports, maps, graphs, charts, and so on are the main components for vividly and vivaciously visualizing the knowledge obtained. The seamless integration with visualization tools for displaying the knowledge obtained in a user-preferred fashion and format is a must for any standard IoT data analytics platform.

4. *IoT application enablement platforms* (*AEPs*): This platform is enabling the aspect of service design, development, deployment, and delivery quickly with a little coding. Typically, these platforms come with a variety of libraries, connectors, drivers, adapters, services, and so on, and through composing and configuring rather than coding, pioneering applications for all kinds of industry verticals can be accomplished quickly.

On the nonfunctional aspects, the platforms need to be high-performing, highly scalable, available, and secure, easily configurable and customizable, and so on.

The Reference Architecture for IoT Data Analytics Platform

The architecture diagram in Figure 7.6 illustrates the principal components of the platform in accelerating the IoT data analytics toward squeezing out hidden patterns, beneficial associations, fresh possibilities and opportunities, actionable tips and techniques for enhanced business efficiency and value, lower total cost of ownership, higher return on investment, and faster time to market, real-time alerts, and so on.

A typical IoT analytics platform has to have the capability to rapidly build and refine extensible models of empowered objects of the physical world and their interrelationships with the artifacts of the cyber world. All kinds of advanced algorithms need to be carefully identified and incorporated to enable deeper and decisive analysis of incoming data, pinpoint possible opportunities and spots of botherations, and deliver insights through visualization tools, dashboards, portals, reports, graphs, maps, charts, and so on.

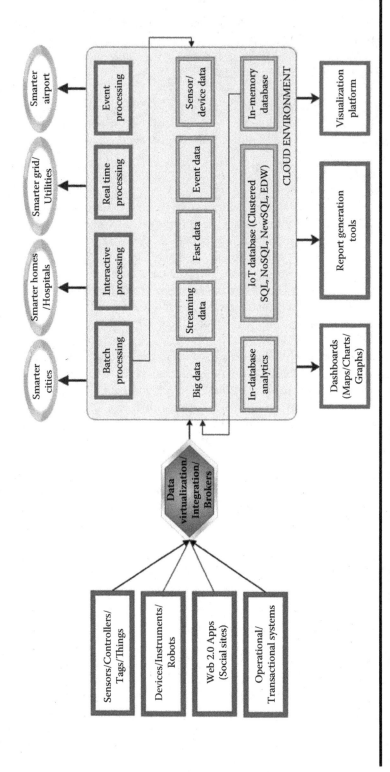

Figure 7.6 The reference architecture (RA) for IoT data analytics platform.

The Renowned Use Cases for IoT Data Analytics

As exemplified above, the insights drawn out of IoT data are going to be game-changing for many industry verticals. There are deeper studies and exhortations eulogizing the contributions of IoT data analytics for steadying and steering all kinds of businesses in a safe and smart manner.

1. *Smarter manufacturing*: Asset tracking, optimal utilization, and management of machines and processes for next-generation manufacturing.
2. *Smarter vehicles*: GPS receivers can communicate with sensors and actuators installed in each vehicle to allow enterprises to monitor the location, movements, status, and behavior of a vehicle or fleet of vehicles remotely.
3. *Smart health care* through connected instruments, smart beds, medical electronics, surgery-assisting robots, hospital management, and patient-monitoring systems, remote diagnostics, medical expert systems, and so on.
4. *Predictive maintenance using sensors-attached assets*: Asset tracking and management are gaining attraction across industry verticals. Due to the mission-critical nature of industry machinery, defense equipment, health care instruments, robots, connected electronics, cyber-physical systems (CPS), and digitized entities in peoples' lives, identifying their fragile nature, and predicting maintenance duration are very vital for ensuring the longevity of assets and the business continuity. Devices are bound to deteriorate over time until they eventually break. By closely monitoring their functioning and contributions, it is possible to spot the pain and problem areas proactively and preemptively. The OA of device data is the way forward for prolonging the device life.
5. *Smarter grids*: The voluminous production of smart electricity meters, the arrival of advanced metering infrastructure (AMI), and the real-time analytics of IoT data have led to the realization of smarter grids. Energy conservation and preservation are seeing the light, energy management is getting fully automated, energy utilization is highly optimized, and so on. It is all about monitoring and controlling network devices, managing service outages, and dispatching crews in time with all the relevant resources. The energy data get processed in real-time in order to give consumers, distributors, and generators all the timely intelligence to plan the best course of actions with all clarity and confidence.

Almost all the industry segments are getting readied to be relevant for their constituents by centralizing the analytics capabilities. Figure 7.7 tells how the IoT data analytics takes the manufacturing domain to greater heights.

Connected Cars

This is another celebrated example for IoT analytics. A specialized IoT data analytics platform is capable of bringing the much-needed transformations for the automotive enterprise with a number of new-generation capabilities such as real-time data about vehicles and their parts and pragmatic insights in time for car users and producers through highly advanced diagnostic, predictive, prescriptive, and prognostics analytics. Automobile service providers are increasingly collaborating with analytical services providers to bring forth a bevy of insights-driven capabilities to help automotive manufacturers to gain valuable insights by systematically analyzing real-time data being streamed from connected cars. There are big and real-time data analytics platforms for processing sensor data from connected cars for knowledge discovery. The insights include real-time alerts on

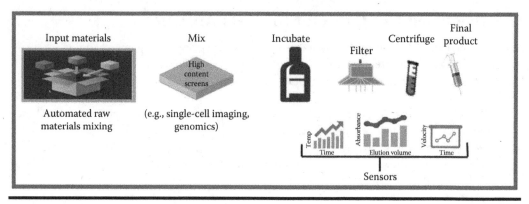

Figure 7.7   The IoT data analytics process.

driver behavior, traffic level, road safety, or the need for maintenance and repairs. Any end-to-end platform ensures a single yet comprehensive view of cars' data and the associated insights to inform automotive engineers about the various aspects of the car such as their safety records, predictive maintenance, and performance. Actionable insights are being insisted on realizing smarter parking assistance and traffic management systems, self-driving cars, and so on. Precisely not only car drivers, owners, mechanics, and manufacturers but also all kinds of car occupants gain immense benefits out of the IoT data analytics solutions and services.

In summary, with the amount of IoT data getting generated, collected, and subjected to a variety of deeper and decisive investigations that is going to be in the range of exabytes, the IT infrastructures and platforms need to be specially and smartly engineered and enhanced to comfortably crunch data heaps to derive actionable intelligence. Therefore, with software-defined clouds emerging as the one-stop IT infrastructure solution, cloud-hosted, end-to-end, and converged analytical solutions and services are turning out to be the mandatory ones for the ensuing knowledge era.

The Data Analytics Locations

With IoT data produced and pumped in big quantities, apart from the well-known infrastructural and platform challenges, there is a fresh set of analytical capabilities and competencies being accentuated these days by IoT luminaries and visionaries to speed up the process of accomplishing IoT data analytics. With the increased complexity, there will be insistence for advanced algorithms. As articulated above, first the analytics can be accomplished at the level and layer of edge/fog devices, and second the data can be captured and communicated to a cloud-based analytics platform to carry out historical, batch, ad hoc, and even real-time processing of device and sensor data.

There are a few options being experimented, expounded, and exposed. The edge devices can be clustered together in an ad hoc fashion and enabled to take crucial decisions in time to accordingly feed and activate actuators, controllers, robots, and other devices to embark on the correct journey. That is, forming edge clouds is highly recommended in order to facilitate proximate processing and decision-making as the processing power, storage capacity, and memory range of individual edge devices are typically on the lower side. Through a cloud formation, several devices in the

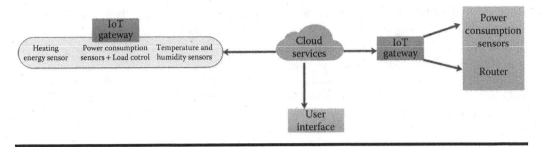

Figure 7.8   The role of IoT gateway for IoT data analytics.

vicinity can be clubbed together to enable the required processing. In other words, the processing and storage capabilities of all the participating devices are being subtly and smartly used to fulfill any analytical needs at the edges itself.

The second option is to leverage IoT and sensor gateways for performing analytical computations out of all the data emanating out of edge devices. Smartphones, Wi-Fi routers, Internet-connected media players, and other reasonably powerful devices in the environment can be tasked to do real-time processing to make right inferences. Further on, a standardized publish–subscribe server software can be deployed on a nearby machine to receive all coming event messages that can be in turn supplied to all the subscribers.

Specific and generic analytical services and applications are being developed, curated, and stored in cloud-based service repositories. A standardized OSGi gateway installed at any high-end edge device can download the appropriate services from different cloud registries over the Internet communication infrastructure, install, and activate them dynamically to fulfill varying analytical requirements. Device-specific as well as analytics-centric services can be discovered from various remote sources, downloaded, configured, and activated in runtime in order to empower edge devices as well as to arrive at people and situation-aware services. The OSGi platform brings in the much-needed dynamism and adaptivity. For distributed device analytics, this modularization platform is of immense help. Originally, the OSGi framework was developed for embedded devices. However, considering its key differentiators in providing highly modular applications, enterprise-scale applications too overwhelmingly use the OSGi concept to be dynamic and distinct. For edge analytics, the OSGi-sponsored modularity and the Java-induced portability come handy.

Another method is to use a lightweight CEP engine at the edge side in order to capture and crunch event messages and send all sorts of insights and inferences to respective systems to con-template countermeasures with all the clarity and confidence. Figure 7.8 vividly illustrates how IoT gateway empowered with different software components and capabilities facilitate real-time analytics.

Why Have Cloud-Based IoT Data Analytics?

The following are the major reasons for going ahead with cloud-based data analytics. The cloud landscape is consistently on the growth path. Exceedingly, public clouds are leveraged for analytical platforms and applications. The reasons for such a turnaround and transformation are given below. Not only public clouds, the other cloud arrangements such as private, hybrid, and community clouds are also being experimented in order to speed up the analytics process in an efficient and effective fashion. As insisted in this chapter, the idea of edge clouds is flourishing because most of the data are getting generated by edge devices.

That is, besides the astounding journey of conventional clouds, the days of edge clouds are really fascinating. Considering the undiminishing needs of data security and real-time intelligence, performing analytics at edge devices is the right approach and answer.

- *Agility and affordability*: No capital investment of large-size infrastructures for analytical workloads. Just use and pay. Quickly provisioned and decommissioned, once the need goes down.
- *Data analytics platforms in clouds*: Therefore, leveraging cloud-enabled and ready platforms (generic or specific, open or commercial-grade, etc.) are fast and easy.
- *NoSQL and NewSQL databases and data warehouses in clouds*: All kinds of database management systems and data warehouses in cloud speed up the process of next-generation data analytics. Database as a service (DaaS), data warehouse as a service (DWaaS), business process as a service (BPaaS), and other advancements lead to the rapid realization of analytics as a service (AaaS).
- *WAN optimization technologies*: There are WAN optimization products for quickly transmitting large quantities of data over the Internet infrastructure.
- *Social and professional networking sites* are running in public cloud environments.
- *Enterprise-class applications in clouds*: All kinds of customer-facing applications are cloud-enabled and deployed in highly optimized and organized cloud environments.
- *Anytime, anywhere, any network, and any device information and service access* are being activated through cloud-based deployment and delivery.
- *Cloud integrators, brokers, and orchestrators*: There are products and platforms for seamless interoperability among geographically distributed cloud environments. There are collaborative efforts toward federated clouds and the Intercloud.
- *Sensor/device-to-cloud integration frameworks* are available to transmit ground-level data to cloud storages and processing.

While public clouds are on the verge of reaching out the much-expected maturity in accomplishing well-intended analytics processes, other kinds of clouds are steadily tending toward the mainstream computing resources for ambient analytics.

The Distinct Capabilities of IoT Data Analytics Platforms

Several things occur simultaneously. That is the positive news indeed for the total humanity! We all know that all sorts of ground-level physical systems are systematically enabled to be smart in their operations and offerings through smooth and spontaneous integrations with faraway cyber/virtual systems and services. This fledgling yet fabulous domain of intense study and research is called cyber-physical systems (CPS). On the IoT side, there are conscious efforts to spontaneously integrate digitized/smart/sentient objects. And every kind of everyday devices from specific domains such as manufacturing, retail, utilities, energy, logistics, health care, buildings, and cities are linked up with other devices in the vicinity as well as with cloud-based software applications, services, and data sources. Now, there are supercharged platforms for collecting and crunching all

IoT and CPS data in time to extract value-adding information and insights in time. For getting the intended success and support, the platforms have to be intrinsically blessed with the following functionalities:

Scalability: This is an important factor for large-scale data processing. The envisioned platform has to have this feature to enable the underlying database systems as well as the cloud infrastructures.

Faster data ingestion: Typically, millions of sensors would transmit their data, and hence data loading has to be really quick in order to enable real-time processing and knowledge discovery. The database system has to be designed from the ground up in such a way to load a few millions of rows per second without affecting query performance. There are a number of standards-compliant protocols such as MQTT, CoAP, XMPP, and RESTful for handling massive amounts of messages.

Faster query processing: This is another vital requirement for the IoT era. The database system has to be capable of handling and executing all kinds of queries at high speed to bring forth timely insights.

Flexibility and portability: The platform has to have the innate capability of frictionless running on single as well as cluster servers in on-premise as well as cloud environments.

Distributed processing: The much-maligned distributed architecture is the way forward for efficiently tackling the challenges thrown by big and real-time data. The concept of fog or edge computing insists for initial processing at the end-user devices directly or on some powerful intermediaries locally in order to lessen the data transmission and processing loads on cloud servers. That is, there is a tectonic shift in the processing paradigm. The processing logic increasingly travels to locations wherein data get generated or reside. The centralized processing steadily paves the way for edge computing. A kind of hybrid processing model based on edge as well as cloud computing models is to emerge and evolve faster in order to enable ground-level devices to partake in the much-complicated processing.

Better data compression: Due to the large size of data, it is paramount to have a good compression mechanism in place so that the data getting persisted and transmitted over any network have to be of lower size.

Data analytics: Batch and real-time processing of big, fast, streaming, and IoT data are essential requirements for spitting out actionable insights. There are several ready-made platforms for capturing different kinds of data at different speeds. The CEP engine is another indispensable module for making sense out of event messages.

Interfaces: RESTful APIs are being touted as the simple and straightforward way of interfacing with a variety of remote systems. Because of its simplicity, even resource-constrained devices can easily get integrated with enterprise and cloud applications.

Deep learning: The requirement of machine learning capabilities on analytical platforms is being insisted considering the irrefutable fact that machine learning especially deep learning helps to go deeper in order to extract precise and powerful insights.

In summary, any IoT data analytics platform destined for success and stardom has to have the features and facilities for doing path-breaking analytics. The platform has to be modular enough for running on-premise as well as off-premise (cloud) environments. As explained above, edge clouds are the brewing concept for facilitating the much-discoursed edge analytics. As there are powerful devices joining in the network to function as IoT gateways and the age-old decentralized networking aspect is salivatingly resurrecting, analytics at source, intermediaries, and clouds are to see the light. Ultimately, it is all about ambient "Analytics as a Service" (AaaS) or analytics everywhere every time toward the world of ambient intelligence (AmI).

Conclusion

It is a well-known truth that the volume of machine-generated data is much heavier than man-generated data. With the projected trillions of digitized objects, billions of connected devices, and millions of software applications, the data size of polystructured data is going to grow exponentially. We need to explore and expedite the data analytics processes, platforms, patterns, and practices toward data-driven insights and insights-driven decisions.

The delectable advancements in the spectacular domain of analytics are leading to a variety of innovations for business automation and acceleration. There are platform solutions and services emerging for the batch as well as interactive processing of big data. In this chapter, we have described various analytical capabilities at different levels and layers needed for extracting pragmatic insights out of IoT data. At one end, cloud-based analytics is fast-maturing and stabilizing; and at the other end for certain scenarios, IoT data analytics is being recommended by forming edge clouds out of different and distributed edge devices. Real-time decision-enablement and actuation are made possible through the proximate processing, filtering, and analytics through the lighter versions of various analytical solutions.

Bibliography

A Simplified TOGAF Guide for Enterprise Architects, www.peterindia.net.

Cloud Infrastructures for Big Data Analytics, IGI Global, Hershey, PA (The chief editor and the author of four chapters), http://www.igi-global.com/book/cloud-infrastructures-big-data-analytics/95028, 2014.

High-Performance Big Data Analytics: The Solution Approaches and Systems, Springer-Verlag, London, http://www.springer.com/in/book/9783319207438, November 2015.

Intelligent Cities: The Enabling Technologies and Tools, CRC Press, Boca Raton, FL, http://www.crcpress.com/product/isbn/9781482299977, June 2015.

Learning Docker, Packtpub, Birmingham, https://www.packtpub.com/, July 2015.

Next-Generation SOA, Prentice Hall, Upper Saddle River, NJ, http://www.amazon.com/Next-Generation-SOA-Introduction-Service-Orientation/dp/0133859045, 2014.

Chapter 8

Expounding the Edge/Fog Computing Paradigm

Abstract: As we all know, smart sensors and actuators are being randomly deployed in many significant environments such as homes, hospitals, and hotels in order to minutely monitor, precisely measure, and insightfully manage the various parameters of the environments. Further on, powerful sensors are embedded and etched on different physical, mechanical, electrical, and electronics systems in our everyday environments in order to empower them to join in the mainstream computing. Thus, not only environments but also all tangible things in those environments are also smartly sensor-enabled with a tactic as well as the strategic goal of making them distinctly sensitive and responsive in their operations, offerings, and outputs. Sensors are sweetly turning out to be the inseparable eyes and ears of any important thing in the near future. This systematic sensor-enablement of ordinary things not only makes them extraordinary but also lays out a stimulating and sparkling foundation for generating a lot of usable and time-critical data. Typically, sensors and sensors-attached assets capture or generate and transmit all kinds of data to the faraway cloud environments (public, private, and hybrid) through a host of standards-compliant sensor gateway devices. Precisely speaking, clouds represent the dynamic combination of several powerful server machines, storage appliances, and network solutions and are capable of processing tremendous amounts of multi-structured data to spit out actionable insights.

However, there is another side of this remote integration and data processing. For certain requirements, the local or proximate processing of data is mandated. That is, capturing sensor and device data and transmitting them to the faraway cloud environments is not going to be beneficial for some time-critical applications. Thereby, the concept of edge or fog computing has emerged and is evolving fast these days with the concerted efforts of academic as well as corporates.

The reasonably powerful devices such as smartphones, sensor and IoT gateways, consumer electronics, set-top boxes, smart TVs, web-enabled refrigerators, and Wi-Fi routers are classified as fog or edge devices to form edge or fog clouds to do the much-needed local processing quickly and easily to arrive and articulate any hidden knowledge. Thus, fog or edge computing is termed and tuned as the serious subject of study and research for producing people-centric and real-time applications and services. In this chapter, we are to discuss fog/edge computing and analytics through fog/edge clouds.

Introduction

The faster maturity and stability of edge technologies have blossomed into a big factor in realizing scores of digitized elements/smart objects/sentient materials out of common, cheap, and casual items in our midst. These empowered entities are data-generating and capturing, buffering, transmitting, and so on. That is, tangible things are peppered with and prepared for the future. These are mostly resource-constrained, and this phenomenon is called the Internet of Things (IoT). Further on, a wider variety of gadgets and gizmos in our working, walking, and wandering locations are futuristically instrumented to be spontaneously interconnected and exceptionally intelligent in their behaviors. Thus, we hear, read, and even feel connected and cognitive devices and machines in our everyday life. Once upon a time, all our personal computers were connected via networks (LAN and WAN), and nowadays our personal and professional devices (fixed, portables, mobiles, wearables, implantables, handhelds, phablets, etc.) are increasingly interconnected (BAN, PAN, CAN, LAN, MAN, and WAN) to exhibit a kind of intelligent behavior. This extreme connectivity and service-enablement of our everyday devices go to the level of getting seamlessly integrated with off-premise, online, and on-demand cloud-based applications, services, data sources, and content. This cloud-enablement is capable of making ordinary devices into extraordinary ones. However, most of the well-known and widely used embedded devices individually do not have sufficient computation power, battery, storage, and I/O bandwidth to host and manage IoT applications and services. Hence, performing data analytics on individual devices is a bit difficult.

Clouds have been the prominent and dominant infrastructures to develop, debug, deploy, and deliver pioneering business and IT applications. However, cloud computing cannot solve all problems due to its own drawbacks. Applications, such as real-time gaming, augmented reality (AR), and data streaming, are too latency-sensitive to be deployed on the cloud. The networks are clogged due to the growth in data transmission. Sharing sensor and device data over any network is beset with security and privacy challenges and concerns. Real-time analytics is being positioned as the most important requirement for generating real-time insights and making timely decision-making. Since cloud centers are geographically distributed, those applications and services will suffer unacceptable round-trip latency, when data are transmitted from/to end devices to/from the cloud data center through multiple gateways. Cloud-based data analytics sometimes misses the real-time mandate, and hence there are efforts in order to craft ad hoc clouds out of devices in the local environment. Multiple and heterogeneous devices in the vicinity are readily identified and connected with one another to form edge or fog clouds to tackle the rising volume of device and sensor data to make sense out of it.

The Introduction of Fog/Edge Computing

Traditional networks, which feed data from devices or transactions to a central storage hub (data warehouses and data marts), cannot keep up with the data volume and velocity created by IoT devices. Nor can the data warehouse model meet the low latency response times that users demand. The Hadoop platform in the cloud was supposed to be an answer. But sending the data to the cloud for analysis also poses a risk of data bottlenecks as well as security concerns. New business models, however, need data analytics in a minute or less. The problem of data congestion will only get worse as IoT applications and devices continue to proliferate.

There are certain interesting use cases such as rich connectivity and interactions among vehicles (V2V) and infrastructures (V2I). This emerging domain of IoT requires services like entertainment, education and information, public safety, real-time traffic analysis and information, support for high mobility, context awareness, and so forth. Such things see the light only if the infotainment systems within vehicles have to identify and interact with one another dynamically and also with wireless communication infrastructures made available on the road, with remote traffic servers, FM stations, and so on. The infotainment system is emerging as the highly synchronized gateway for vehicles on the road. Local devices need to interact themselves to collect data from vehicles and roads/expressways/tunnels/bridges to process them instantaneously to spit out useful intelligence. This is the salivating and sparkling foundation for fog/edge computing.

The latest trend of computing paradigm is to push the storage, networking, and computation to edge/fog devices for availing certain critical services. As devices are interconnected and integrated with the Internet, their computational capabilities and competencies are uniquely being leveraged in order to lessen the increasing load on cloud infrastructures. Edge devices are adequately instrumented at the design stage itself to interconnect with nearby devices automatically so that multiple devices dynamically can be found, bound, and composed for creating powerful and special-purpose edge clouds. Thus, the concept of fog or edge computing is blooming and booming these days.

The essence and gist of fog computing are to keep data and computation close to end-users at the edge of the network, and this arrangement has the added tendency of producing a new class of applications and services to end-users with low latency, high bandwidth, and context awareness. Fog is invariably closer to humans rather than clouds, and hence the name "fog computing" is overwhelmingly accepted across. As indicated and illustrated above, fog devices are typically resource-intensive edge devices. Fog computing is usually touted as the supplement and complement to the popular cloud computing. Students, scholars, and scientists are keen toward unearthing a number of convincing and sellable business and technical cases for fog computing. Being closer to people, the revitalized fog or edge computing is to be extremely fruitful and fabulous in conceptualizing and concretizing a litany of people-centric software applications. Finally, in the era of big, fast, streaming, and IoT data, fog/edge computing can facilitate edge analytics. Edge devices can filter out redundant, repetitive, and routine data to reduce the precious network bandwidth and the data loads on clouds. Figure 8.1 vividly illustrates the fast-emerging three-tier architecture for futuristic computing.

The digitized objects (sensors, beacons, etc.) at the lowest level are generating and capturing polystructured data in big quantities. The fog devices (gateways, controllers, etc.) at the second level are reasonably blessed with computational, communication, and storage power in order to mix, mingle, and merge with other fog devices in the environment to ingest and accomplish the

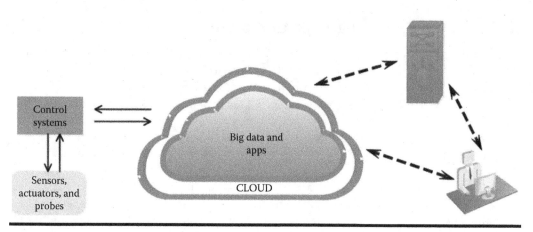

Figure 8.1   The end-to-end fog—cloud integration architecture.

local or proximate data processing to emit viable and value-adding insights in time. The third and final levels are the faraway cloud centers. This introduction of fog devices in between clouds and digitized elements is the new twist brought in toward the ensuing era of knowledge-filled services. Fog devices act as intelligent intermediaries between cloud-based cyber/virtual applications and sensor/actuator data at the ground level.

Fog versus Edge Computing

This is the opportune time to clarify the perceptible differences between fog and edge computing models. With the faster penetration of the IoT devices, instruments, monitors, controllers, sensors, actuators, robots, machines, and so on in our daily environments, there is a leaning toward performing a portion of computing at IoT devices. However due to the constrained resources of these IoT devices, the overwhelming usage of microcontrollers as the IoT device gateway for remote connectivity (IoT device-to-enterprise/cloud integration) has dawned upon us. That is, microcontrollers contribute immensely for data communication. Now for doing computation and data analytics on IoT devices, a suite of workable methods and mechanisms such as microcontrollers, cloudlet architecture, microclouds, and mobile base stations are being proposed, prototyped, and proclaimed. These solutions facilitate computation and data processing near the IoT devices rather than in faraway data or cloud centers. Having understood the evolving trends, Cisco has come out with the fog computing concept.

The raging IoT paradigm is to be sustained and supported by "fog computing," in which computing, storage, control, and networking power may exist anywhere along the architecture either in traditional data centers, cloud centers, edge devices such as gateways or routers, and edge equipment itself such as a machine or in sensors.

In contrast to the cloud, fog platforms have been described as dense computational architectures at the network's edge. The paramount characteristics of such platforms reportedly include low latency, faster response, context awareness, and wireless communication. The real benefits include real-time analytics and improved security.

While edge computing or edge analytics may exclusively refer to performing analytics at devices that are on, or close to, the network's edge, a fog computing architecture would perform analytics on anything from the network center to the edge.

In Figure 8.2, Cisco shows what kinds of analytics could be performed along a fog network. Figure 8.3 describes the class of data that needs fog analytics and cloud analytics.

Precisely speaking, there are no major differences between edge and fog computing styles. Leveraging reasonably powerful IoT devices such as IoT gateways and smartphones in order to do proximate processing is all about edge computing for real-time analytics (milliseconds-level latency). For near real-time analytics, nearby microclouds or cloudlets can be leveraged. The fog concept covers not only the computing using edge devices but also powerful yet nearby cloud servers and appliances.

Illustrating the Game-Changing IoT Journey

The mesmerizing number of smart sensors and actuators being deployed in specific environments ultimately produces massive volumes of data, and currently the collected data are faithfully transmitted over the Internet or any private network to faraway cloud infrastructures in order to be concertedly and calculatedly crunched to extract exceptional insights. As we all know, clouds are the best bet for doing the batch or historical processing through the renowned Hadoop framework. That is, cloud-based analytics is the overwhelming practice. However, the emerging trend is to come with microscale clouds in between the ground-level sensors and the cyber-level cloud applications toward edge analytics. This specialized cloud, which is being formed out of networked and resource-intensive devices in that environment, takes out the constricting stress on the traditional clouds. The proximate processing gets accomplished through these microclouds, whereas the device data security and privacy are maintained. This kind of cloud-in-the-middle approach is capable of unearthing fresh IoT use cases. As any microcloud is very near the data-emitting sensors and sensors-attached assets, the faster processing and response are being achieved in an affordable fashion.

It Is All About the Extreme and Deeper Connectivity

As the inventive paradigm of networked embedded devices expands into multiple business domains and industry verticals such as manufacturing facilities and floors, health care centers, retail stores, luxury hotels, spacious homes, energy grids, and transportation systems, there is a greater scope for deriving sophisticated applications not only for businesses but also for commoners. The world is tending toward the connected world. Recent devices come with the connectivity feature, and there are a vast number of hitherto unconnected legacy devices. Further on, there are resource-constrained devices such as heart rate monitors to temperature and humidity sensors in plenty, and enabling them to be integrated with other devices and web applications is definitely a big challenge. Thus, connectivity solutions and platforms are being brought in to enable every tangible device to be connected. The connectivity is not only with adjacent devices in the vicinity but also with the remotely held applications and data sources on the web/cloud.

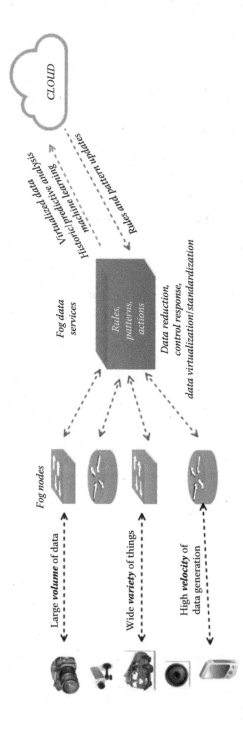

Figure 8.2 Depicting the control flow for the fog device data analytics.

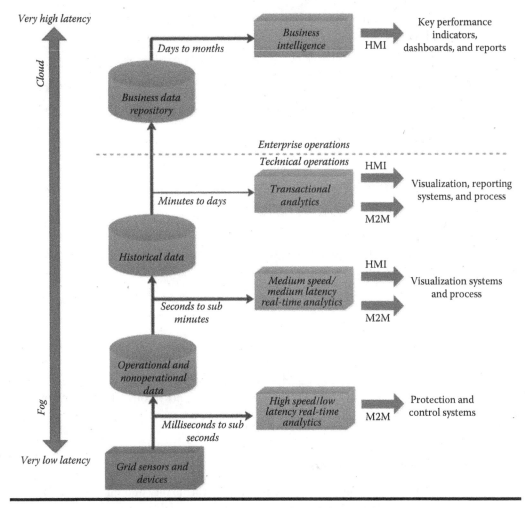

Figure 8.3   Describing fog device-based and cloud-based data analytics.

The Humongous Volumes of IoT Data

We have been fiddling with transaction systems extensively. The IT infrastructures, platforms, and applications are designed to be appropriate for streamlining and speeding up transactions. However with the faster penetration of devices and digitized entities, there is a relook. That is, operational systems are becoming more prevalent and prominent. In the impending IoT era, a sensor or smart device that is monitoring temperature, humidity, vibration, acceleration, or numerous other variables could potentially generate data that need to be handled by back-end systems in some way every millisecond. For example, a typical Formula One car already carries 150–300 sensors; and more controllers, sensors, and actuators are being continuously incorporated to bring in more automation. Today, these hundred sensors already capture data in milliseconds. Race cars generate 100–200 KBs of data per second, amounting to several terabytes in a racing season. There are twin challenges for back-end systems. Not only the storage concern but also the real-time processing of data is also equally important.

That is, missing a few seconds of sensor data or being unable to analyze it efficiently and rapidly can lead to risks and, in some cases, disasters.

Major IoT Data Types

There are three major data types that will be common to most IoT projects. They are as follows:

Measurement Data

Sensors monitor and measure the various parameters of the environment as well as the states of sensors-attached physical, mechanical, electrical, and electronics systems. Heterogeneous and multiple sensors read and transmit data very frequently; and hence with a larger number of sensors and frequent readings, the total data size is bound to grow exponentially. This is the crux of the IoT era. A particular company in the oil and gas space is already dealing with more than 100 TB of such data per day.

Event Data

Any status change, any break-in of the threshold value, any noteworthy incident or untoward accident, and any decision-enabling data are simply categorized event data. With devices assisting people in their daily assignments and engagements, the number of events is likely to shoot up. We have powerful simple and complex event processing (CEP) engines in order to discover and disseminate knowledge out of event data.

Interaction and Transaction Data

With the extreme and deeper connectivity among devices, the quality and quantity of purpose-specific interactions between devices are going to be greater. Several devices with unique functionality can connect and collaborate for achieving composite functions. The transaction operations are also enabled in devices. Not only inter-device communication but also human-device communication is fairly happening.

Diagnostics Data

The delectable advancements in the IoT domain has led to millions of networked embedded devices and smart objects, information, transactional, analytical, and operational systems. There are online, off-premise, and on-demand applications, data sources, and services in plenty. The application portfolio is consistently on the rise for worldwide enterprises. There are software infrastructure solutions, middleware, databases, data virtualization, and knowledge visualization platforms, and scores of automation tool. The health of each of these systems is very important for the intended success of any business transaction. Diagnostics is the type of data that gives an insight into the overall health of a machine, system, or process. Diagnostic data might not only show the overall health of a system but also show whether the monitoring of that system is also working effectively.

Precisely speaking, the IoT data are going to be big, and we have techniques and platforms for big data processing. However, the intriguing challenge is to do real-time processing of IoT big data. Researchers are on the job to unearth path-breaking algorithms to extract timely insights out of big data. Fog computing is one such concept prescribed as a viable and venerable answer for the impending data-driven challenges.

Describing the Fog Computing-Like Concepts

There are multiple trends emanating and evolving in the information and communication technologies (ICT) spaces. The number of smartphones across the globe is already more than 3 billion empowering people to do both communication and computation seamlessly on a single device. Similarly, every specific environment such as homes, luxury cars, and heavy vehicles, manufacturing floors, shopping malls, eating joints and junctions, entertainment and edutainment centers, nuclear installations, research labs, and business parks are being stuffed and sandwiched by a number of purpose-specific as well as generic sensors and actuators. Thus, the prediction that there will be trillions of digitized objects, billions of connected devices, and millions of software services in the near future is all set to become true sooner than later. There are different approaches and articulations in order to pointedly focus on this fog/edge computing concept. There are myriads of nomenclatures and buzzwords.

Local/Proximate Clouds

We have public, private, and hybrid clouds in order to cater different requirements. There are specific clouds such as mobile, storage, knowledge, science, data, device, and sensor clouds. Specific communities even have their own clouds. Now with the accumulation of sensors and sensor-attached physical assets, there is a demand for localized and nearby cloud environments for performing proximate processing. Local clouds, a kind of dedicated IT environments, can interoperate with other traditional clouds (private, public, hybrid, and community) for doing comprehensive and historical data processing.

There are literature eulogizing and expressing local clouds as micro or nanoclouds considering their slim and sleek nature. As it turns out, there will be thousands of local clouds in the near future. That is, every noteworthy environment has its own local cloud. The various computation and communication devices apart from consumer electronics in the neighborhood come together to collaboratively form local clouds.

Cloudlet Facilities

There are highly reliable and resilient cloud appliances and hyperconverged clouds in the form of bars and boxes these days. Instead of using commodity servers, powerful, integrated, and turnkey appliances are also being used in specific contexts. Cloudlet is "a cloud in a box," which follows the same cloud paradigm but relies on high-end server machines. Cloudlets are very easy and quick to set up and activate and are being recommended to provide delay-sensitive and bandwidth-limited applications. A cloudlet is a new architectural element that arises from the convergence of mobile computing and cloud computing. It represents the middle of a three-tier hierarchy such as mobile device, cloudlet, and cloud.

The following use cases for crowd-sourced videos insist the need for cloudlet facilities.

The aspect of crowdsourcing has seen a phenomenal growth these days with the widespread deployment of security and surveillance cameras in important junctions. There are sellable and workable use cases being unearthed for sustaining its surging popularity. A few of them are as follows:

MARKETING AND ADVERTISING

Crowd-sourced videos can provide a lot of real-time and decision-enabling insights based on observational data. For example, which billboards attract the most user attention? How successful is a new store window display in attracting interest? Which clothing colors and patterns attract the most interest? and so on.

CAPTURING THEME PARKS' VISIT

Visitors to places like Disneyworld can capture and share their delectable experiences, including rides, throughout the entire day. With video, audio, and accelerometer capture, the recreation of rides can be quite realistic and mesmerizing.

LOCATING PEOPLE, PETS, AND THINGS

A missing child was last seen walking home from school. A search of crowd-sourced videos from the area shows that the child was near a particular spot an hour ago. The parent remembers that the child has a friend close to that location. She calls the friend's home and locates the child. When a dog owner reports that his dog is missing, a search of crowd-sourced videos captured in the last few hours may help to locate the dog before it strays too far.

FRAUD DETECTION

A driver reports that his car was hit, while it was parked at a restaurant. However, his insurance claims adjuster finds a crowd-sourced video in which the car is intact when leaving the restaurant.

Why Cloudlet-Like Arrangement Is Mandated?

Video footages from a mobile device only travel up to its currently associated cloudlet. Computer vision analytics are run on the cloudlet platform in near real time. Only the results (recognized objects, recognized faces, and so on), along with metadata (such as the owner, capture location, and timestamp), are then sent to the remote cloud. The tags and metadata can guide deeper and more customized searches of the content of a video segment during its (finite) retention period on a cloudlet. Automated modification of video streams to preserve its privacy is done at cloudlet level.

Mobile Edge Computing (MEC)

We have mobile base stations in many locations in order to fail-safe relay mobile communication. These facilities are being recommended for doing the edge data processing and analytics.

The utilization rates of those base stations go up significantly with this extra favor and flavor. Base stations act as an intelligent intermediary between smartphones and the faraway cloud environments.

Mobile Cloud Computing (MCC)

As we all know, smartphones do not have sufficient processing, memory, and storage capabilities as a typical and traditional cloud does (of course, as per newspaper reports, there are smartphones empowered with 6-GB memory). Therefore, there are research works initiated in order to bring in an appropriate partition of software applications into a set of easily manageable modules. The specific and smaller modules are kept within smartphones, whereas the common and reusable service modules are being taken to cloud environments. The data sources are being kept in cloud environments, and smartphones can access the data on a need basis. Now with cloudlets and mobile edge computing (MEC) models maturing quickly, there will be a consolidation, and mobile cloud computing (MCC) will slowly disappear from the scene altogether.

Thus having understood the need for pioneering intermediaries between devices, machines, equipment, instruments, sensors, robots, actuators, and so on at the ground level and a bevy of software applications and data sources at the cyber level, researchers have proposed several propositions as described above. With the overwhelming acceptance of fog computing, all these diverging concepts are bound to converge to fulfill all the originally envisaged benefits of fog or edge computing.

The Use Cases of Fog/Edge Computing

The rapid growth of personal, social, and professional devices at our daily environments has seeded this inimitable computing style. The communication becomes wireless, sensors and devices are heterogeneous and large in number, geodistribution becomes the new normal, the interconnectivity and interactions among various participants emit a lot of data, and so on. The amount of data getting generated and gathered at the edge of the network is really massive in volumes.

Usually, these data are transported back to the cloud for storage and processing which incidentally requires high bandwidth connectivity. In order to save network bandwidth, there is a valid proposition of using a moderately sized platform in between to do a kind of preprocessing in order to filter out the flabs. Differently enabled cameras, for example, generate images and videos that would aggregate easily in the range of terabytes. Instead of clogging expensive and scarce network bandwidths, a kind of fog/edge processing can be initiated to ease networks. That is, reasonably powerful devices in the environment under monitoring can be individually or collectively leveraged to process cameras-emitted files in real time. That is, the data gleaned can be subsequently segmented and shared to different devices in the vicinity in order to do the distributed processing quickly. As we all know, with more devices joining in the mainstream computing and the amount of data getting stocked growing exponentially, the distributed computing concept has soared in the recent past and is being touted as the mandated way forward for the data-centric world.

There are a number of convincing use cases for fog/edge computing. Fog devices locally collect, cleanse, store, process, and even analyze data in order to facilitate real-time analytics toward informed decisions. There are research papers describing how connected vehicles, smart grids, wireless sensor, and actuator networks, and so on are more right and relevant for people with the fast-moving fog computing paradigm. Smart building, manufacturing floors, smart traffic and retail, and smart cities are some of the often-cited domains wherein the raging fog idea chips in with real benefits. AR, content delivery, and mobile data analytics are also very well documented as the direct beneficiaries of fog computing. One use case for fog computing is a smart traffic light system, which can change its signals based on surveillance of incoming traffic to prevent accidents or reduce congestion. Data could also be sent to the cloud for long-term analytics. Other use cases include rail safety, power restoration from a smart grid network, and cyber security. There are connected cars leveraging the vehicle-to-vehicle (V2V) and vehicle-to-cloud (V2C) communication capabilities. Smart city applications such as intelligent lighting and car parking systems are also gaining a lot of attraction.

Smart Homes

There is a home security application profoundly discussed in a research paper. As we all know, there are a myriad of home security products (smart lock, video/audio recorder, and security sensors) and monitors (alarm, presence, occupancy, motion sensors, etc.). These are stand-alone solutions; and due to disparate data transport protocols and data formats, these products do not interoperate with one another. However, the emergence and emancipation of fog computing have simplified the process of dynamically integrating these diverse security products in order to enhance the timeliness and trustworthiness of any security information. The uniqueness of fog computing platform is that it can be flexibly deployed on a virtual machine or in a Docker container. Existing and new sensors and actuators register and get connected with the fog platform which ensures a seamless and spontaneous interoperation between different and distributed devices and machines toward the goal. This ad hoc collaboration capability senses any kind of security threats and immediately stimulates the necessary countermeasures through connected actuators. Energy management, device clustering and coordination, ambient assisted living (AAL), activity recognition/context awareness for formulating and firming up people-centric services, and so on are getting streamlined with the fog computing nuances.

Smart Grids

Smart electric grid is an electricity distribution network with smart meters deployed at various locations to measure the real-time power consumption level. A centrally hosted supervisory control and data acquisition (SCADA) server frequently gathers and analyzes status data to send out appropriate information to power grids to adapt accordingly. If there is any palpable increment in power usage or any kind of emergency, it will be instantaneously conveyed to the power grid to act upon. Now with the fog idea, the centralized SCADA server can be supplemented by one or more decentralized microgrids. This salient setup improves scalability, cost-efficiency, security, and rapid response of the power system. This also helps to integrate distributed and different power generators (solar panels, wind farms, etc.) with the main power grid. Energy load balancing applications may run on edge devices such as smart meters and microgrids. Based on energy demand, availability, and the lowest price, these devices automatically switch to alternative energies like solar and wind.

Wireless Sensor and Actuator Networks

Traditional wireless sensor networks fall short in applications that go beyond just sensing and tracking. That is, actuators need to plunge into physical actions like the opening, closing, or even carrying sensors. In this scenario, actuators serving as fog devices can control the measurement process itself, the stability and the oscillatory behaviors by creating a closed-loop system. For example, in the scenario of self-maintaining trains, sensor monitoring on a train's ball-bearing can detect heat levels, allowing applications to send an automatic alert to the train operator to stop the train at next station for emergency maintenance and avoid potential derailment. In lifesaving air vents scenario, sensors on vents monitor air conditions flowing in and out of mines and automatically change air-flow, if conditions become dangerous to miners.

Smart Vehicles

The fog concept can be extended to vehicular networks also. The fog nodes can be deployed along the roadside. The fog nodes can send and receive information from vehicles. Vehicles through their in-vehicle infotainment systems can interact with the roadside fog systems as well as with other vehicles on the road. Thus, this kind of ad hoc networks lead to a variety of applications such as traffic light scheduling, congestion mitigation, precaution sharing, parking facility management, and traffic information sharing. A video camera that senses an ambulance flashing lights can automatically change street lights to open lanes for the vehicle to pass through traffic. Smart street lights interact locally with sensors, detect the presence of pedestrian and bikers, and measure the distance and speed of approaching vehicles.

Smarter Security

Security and surveillance cameras are being fitted in different important junctions such as airports, nuclear installations, government offices, and retail stores. Further on, nowadays, smartphones are embedded with powerful cameras to click selfies as well as produce photos of others. Running images can be captured and communicated to nearby fog nodes as well as to faraway cloud nodes in order to readily process the photos and compare them with the face images of radicals, extremists, fundamentalists, terrorists, arsonists, trouble-makers, and so on in the already stored databases. Further on, through image processing and analytics, it is possible to extract useful information in the form of unusual gestures, movements, and so on. All these empower security and police officials to proceed in their investigations with clarity and confidence.

Smart Buildings

Like homes, office and corporate buildings are stuffed with a number of sensors for minute monitoring, precise measurement, and management. There is a school of thought that multiple sensor values, when blended, throw more accurate value. There are advanced sensor data fusion algorithms, and hence smart sensors and actuators work in tandem toward automating and accelerating several manual tasks. For providing a seamless and smart experience to employees and visitors, the building automation domain is on the fast trajectory with a series of innovations and improvisations in the IT space. That is, computing becomes pervasive, communication is ambient, sensing is ubiquitous, actuation is intelligently accomplished, and so on. The computer vision and perception topics gather momentum, knowledge engineering and enhancement are becoming common and cheap, and decision-enablement becomes perfect. The edge devices participating in and contributing for the edge cloud facilitate multiple things intelligently, so that the strategic goal of building automation through networking and integration is getting accomplished.

Today, a medium-sized office building could have hundreds of sensors on its equipment. A great example is chillers, a product needed to cool a building. The product manufacturer (http://www.johnsoncontrols.com/) monitors chillers remotely using predictive diagnostics to identify and solve issues before they become problems. The company uses internal operational data and historical records to better plan machine maintenance, leading to better operational efficiency and decreasing energy usage, in addition to increasing reliability and equipment lifespan. Even better, the company has external data resources like weather patterns and grid demand costs to drive greater operational savings.

IoT and Cyber-Physical Systems

Increasingly, the physical world is integrated with the cyber world through a host of adaptors, connectors, drivers, brokers, orchestrators, integrators, and other middleware software. There are technology-centric expositions and exhortations about the significance of the IoT and cyber-physical systems (CPS) for the bright future of this planet. Hitherto unforeseen applications and services are being formulated with the emergence and convergence of these two game-changing concepts. The IoT and CPSs promise to transform our world with new relationships between computer-based control and communication systems, engineered systems, and physical reality. The concept of fog or edge computing is to facilitate a lot toward the smarter planet vision by facilitating the seamless and spontaneous integration between all kinds of participants. The common, cheap, and casual articles in our daily environments will become digitized objects/sentient materials/smart artifacts, reasonably powerful devices in and around us will become connected and cognitive, and software applications getting hosted in different cloud infrastructures are empowered to be context-aware and adaptive. Thus, the fog computing is to bring forth the much-needed revolutions and revelations in the form of the intelligent intermediary.

Software-Defined Networking

Software-defined networking (SDN), a fast-emerging networking phenomenon, is a grandiose component of software-defined clouds (SDCs). It separates control and data communication layers. The control is taken care of at a centralized server, and data nodes just follow the communication path decided by the control server. This is a kind of client-server architecture. The centralized SDN server may have to go the distributed way in order to cater new-generation needs. The SDN concept does not facilitate the interactions among the data nodes. However for smarter vehicles, there is a need for inter-vehicle communication. Further on, vehicles need to interact with the roadside infrastructures. Thus, the SDN concept has to be seamlessly integrated with fog computing in order to facilitate fruitful associations between vehicles as well as between vehicles and infrastructures.

There are several other industry verticals and business domains yearning to get immensely benefited out of all the decisive and delectable advancements in the field of fog computing.

Why Is Fog Computing Crucial for the Envisaged IoT Success?

There are strategic advantages of fog computing for the projected success of the IoT paradigm. The introduction of a middle layer between heterogeneous devices at the ground level and software applications at the cloud level brings forth a number of innovations, disruptions, and transformations as enumerated below:

Weeding Out Irrelevant Data at the Source

The IoT represents trillions of digitized objects, billions of connected devices, and millions of software applications. The direct offshoot is that the amount of data getting generated, captured, and transmitted is really voluminous. However, most of the data are repetitive, redundant, and routine. The edge computing facilitates filtering out the inconsequential data at the edge of the network, so that useful and usable data can be communicated to cloud environments in order to have speedy and sagacious analytics. There is very minimal wastage of network bandwidth with this preprocessing at the edges.

Real-Time IoT Data Analytics

For certain scenarios such as historical, comprehensive, and posterior processing, the traditional clouds are insisted. Faraway clouds are typically for batch processing or at the most near real-time processing. But the faster maturity and stability of edge computing readily enable real-time processing of device data. That is, there are scenarios craving for real-time data capture and analysis in order to emit out real-time insights. We have discussed the fog/edge analytics in the below sections.

Instantaneous Response

There are many use cases wherein faster responses are not needed. Turning on the lights, closing the garage door, or checking the vending machine status, and so on come under this category. However, there are use cases expecting a faster response. For example, vehicles on the road or any moving object has to respond immediately to surrounding situations. Thus, it is indispensable to have fog compute infrastructure in place in order to accomplish actions with very low latency.

Resource-Constrained Sensors Behind Fog Devices

Many sensors do not have enough compute, memory, and storage power in order to have their own IPv6 address. Hence, they can hide behind an edge device which has the power to have its own IPv6 address. It is, therefore, pertinent to configure ground-level and resource-constrained sensors and actuators behind the edge device. The arrival of edge computing has henceforth solidified the sensors to be slimmer, purpose-specific, and cheaper.

IoT Data Security

Any external attack on sensors can be stopped at the edge device, which acts as a shelter, strength, stronghold, and savior for feeble sensors. The idea is to prolong the livelihood of sensors. Also, the sensor data are transmitted to edge devices to be stocked and subjected to specific investigations over any local network only. That is, the sensor data are kept away from the public and porous Internet. Sharing sensor data to public cloud environments is beset with challenges. There can be further advancements on the security front in the days to unfurl.

The Formation of Edge Clouds

All kinds of powerful edge devices can be clubbed together dynamically to form device clusters. Having such edge clouds is an important precursor for doing edge data analytics to emit out real-time intelligence to act upon with all the confidence and clarity. Thus, fog devices with the capability of realizing ad hoc clouds are the real trendsetter for doing local or proximate processing of device and sensor data.

Building Composite Applications

Devices and equipment being deployed in a specific environment (say, a restaurant) communicate to their vendors directly in order to push a variety of data. Specifically, the lighting data would go to the lighting vendor, the kitchen equipment data to the kitchen equipment vendor, and so forth. However, there is very little for the environment occupants and owners. Now with the surging popularity of fog computing, all kinds of sensor and equipment data get aggregated at the restaurant fog device. Edge device messages are getting accentuated, enriched, secured, and directed to their proper destination through a fog middleware. The message-centric device orchestration is being facilitated by intelligent fog devices. The messages also can be combined with other relevant messages from other internal as well as external sources to supply viable and venerable insights to decision-making, recommender, and expert systems. That is, street traffic data, weather report, demographic information, and so on can be cleansed and enriched to be a stimulant for a range of path-breaking applications including corporate, in-restaurant operational optimization, supply chain, and perhaps a variety of applications for third-party constituents, such as government regulators and suppliers.

Policy-Based Fog Devices

With fog devices being positioned as the most crucial component for the proclaimed success of the IoT idea, it becomes paramount for fog devices to be enabled policy-aware. The brewing idea is to establish and enforce security, governance, role-based access, activation, and configuration policies. Different policies can be inserted in fog devices to have a firm grip and control on all the sensors and actuators attached.

Precisely speaking, the unprecedented and phenomenal acceptance and adoption of the edge computing are breakthroughs for sustaining the strategic journey of the IoT concept. There is this new paradigm of fog or edge computing vigorously and rigorously capturing the imagination of IoT professionals these days. That is, the real-time and relatively small-scale processing is shifted to edge devices instead of aggregating and transmitting device data to faraway cloud servers to squeeze out insights. Localized and personalized decisions are essential in certain scenarios, and hence the fast-evolving concept of fog computing is being gleefully received. The edge devices are dynamically discovered and linked through body, personal, and local-area networks to form ad hoc edge clouds to accelerate and accentuate edge analytics. With the rapid explosion of connected things, devices, and services, it is understandable that the decentralized networking is the best way forward, as it has the inherent potential to reduce infrastructure and maintenance costs. Decentralization guarantees increased robustness by removing single points of failure. By shifting from centralized to decentralized processing, devices at the edges gain greater autonomy to become the core and central point of transactions toward enhanced productivity and value for owners and users.

Delving into Fog/Edge Analytics

With the unprecedented success of the pioneering digitization and edge computing technologies and tools, every tangible thing in our daily environments is becoming a digitized/smart/sentient object. It is foreseen that everyone in this world will have one or more smartphones/personal digital assistants/wearables soon. Every unique asset and artifact (physical, mechanical, electrical, and electronics) participating in our daily deals and deeds are systematically and sagaciously enabled through edge/fog technologies and cloud applications to be computational, communicative, sensitive, perceptive, responsive, and cognitive. Ultimately, our everyday environments are to be bedecked with a variety of smart sensors and actuators to fulfill the prime goals of precision-centric context awareness and activity recognition. Further on, cloud-based cyber applications will have a salivating and scintillating role in empowering physical items on the ground. In short, the ensuing era is all about producing and providing knowledge-filled services that are people-centric, situation-aware, and event-driven.

In today's digitally connected society, there will be deeper and decisive affinity among enabled objects, connected devices, and humans in the days ahead. The result is that large volumes of multistructured data are getting generated at different speeds, sizes, scopes, and schemas through the interactions and collaborations of heterogeneous digital elements, smartphones, technical experiments, social media, health care instruments, machines, satellite telemetry, and imagery. These data lead to formulating and firming up various new analytical competencies such as social media analytics, sentiment analytics, predictive, prognostic, prescriptive, and personalized analytics for people empowerment. The prickling challenge is how efficiently and effectively the captured and cleansed data subject to various specific investigations can readily extract real-time intelligence to make right inferences. In this section, we will dig deep and describe at length about the uniqueness of edge analytics.

The Greatness of Edge Data

It is a known fact that the unprecedented rise in data sources has led to the emergence of the strategically sound big data discipline and its allied technologies. The big data landscape is therefore relentlessly and rightly growing. Besides the enormity of the data being produced by knowledge workers and social animals, the growing size of machine-generated data is to get prime importance in the impending big data era. Machine data especially of edge devices are progressively playing a very pivotal role in shaping up the crucial aspect of data-driven insights and insights-driven decisions. The story thus far is that first, there are a voluminous production and extensive deployment of smart sensors and actuators in a variety of environments (home, industrial, social, entertainment, education, etc.) for different purposes. The much-discussed connectivity, which is constantly becoming deeper and extreme, connects them via different modes such as wireless, wireline, and the mix of them. That is, there are millions of devices at the edges of networks, and it is projected that the number of devices will turn out to be in the range of billions in the years to unfurl.

All these are being intensively deciphered and deliberated these days because of the unparalleled advancements in the embedded and connectivity domains. Both resource-rich and constrained devices are systematically hooked together in an ad hoc fashion to interchange their data and share their unique capabilities. Further on, edge devices are grandly integrated with cyber applications and services hosted at distant cloud environments. These direct as well as indirect integrations and interactions have laid a strong and stimulating foundation for a sharp hike in edge data generation. Data are being collected by an enormous variety of equipment, such as smart utility meters, surveillance and security cameras, actuators, robots, radio frequency identification (RFID) readers, biometrics, factory-line sensors, mobile phones, fitness machines, defence equipment and weapons, launchers and satellites, avionics and automobiles, information appliances, household utensils and wares, electronic gadgets and gizmos, lab-experimentation devices, and medical instruments.

The ubiquitous connectivity and the mass production of modern sensors and actuators have opened up a whole new powerhouse for valuable information. It is clear that edge data can bring forth significant value and a rich set of sophisticated services to all stakeholders including end-users. The careful and cognitive capture, processing, and analysis of edge data in time can go a long way in empowering organizations to respond to both positive as well as negative events pre-emptively and solve many problems that were previously out of reach.

The point here is that this untapped resource of edge data has the inherent potential to deliver dependable insights that can transform the operations and strategic initiatives of public and private sector organizations. Incidentally, the edge data are becoming larger, speedier, and trickier, but the hidden value is definitely greater. And hence, distinct research endeavors on making sense out of edge data are drawing phenomenal attention. On the other hand, there are standards-compliant big data analytics platforms (open source as well as commercial-grade), data ingestion and crunching toolsets, data virtualization and visualization tools, knowledge engineering techniques, high-performance multicore processors, gigabits Ethernet solutions, and inexpensive storage options including object storage to extract and extrapolate knowledge.

On summary, as the size of edge data is growing significantly, there is a bigger challenge to information management professionals to evolve a pragmatic strategy for effectively leveraging all sorts of edge data for the well-being of their organizations. With the faster maturity and stability of data analytics platforms, knowledge systems and services are bound to grow and glow.

Edge Analytics: The Prominent Use Cases

Edge data are carefully captured and crunched using fog devices for generating intelligent data immediately. Here are a few interesting use cases for edge analytics.

IoT Sensor Data Monitoring and Analysis

It is clear that the massive deployment of heterogeneous sensors leads to the tremendous amount of sensor data. Moving sensor data analytics to the edge with a platform that can analyze batch, fast, and streaming data simultaneously enables organizations to speed and simplify analytics to get the insights they need, right where they need them.

Remote Monitoring and Analysis of Oil and Gas Operations

Edge analytics is a boon for companies in oil and gas exploration, refinement, storage, and distribution. Any kind of delay in sensing and responding to such kinds of rough and risky environments paves for disaster. Cloud-based analytics is time-consuming, and it is not possible to expect real-time responses from faraway cloud environments. Having near-instant analysis at the site as the data are being created can help these organizations see the signs of a disaster and take measures to prevent a catastrophe before it starts.

Smarter Cities

Intel defines that the smart city concept mandates the use of smart-grid infrastructures to improve environmental sustainability, manage energy consumption, better coordinate public resources, and protect the quality of life for urban and metropolitan citizens, and plan for sustainable growth. The edge data here play a very incredible role. For example, utility companies and governments are using data from the smart grid to understand the complex relationships between generation, transmission, distribution, and consumption with the goal of delivering reliable energy and reducing operating costs. Consumers are also empowered with insights from the smart grid to better manage their personal energy requirements. For example, a "not-home" state might turn off lights, shut down unused equipment, and adjust the home temperature. Utility meter readings and grid data are brought into centralized analytical systems to bring forth timely insights.

Thus, edge devices collaboratively contribute immensely for arriving at better decisions than only at a centralized control center. Communication between devices helps to determine when, where, and how much energy should be produced, and consumers can use home management tools to monitor and adjust energy consumption accordingly.

Smart Retailers

It is a well-known thing that supermarkets and hypermarkets across the globe duly collect a lot of data every day. If they are properly collected, cleansed, and categorized, worldwide retailers can substantially enhance their grip on their customers and their buying patterns. This incredible knowledge on customers prepares retail stores to think big and to bring forth scores of premium services in time to retain and delight their loyal customers as well as to attract new customers. The enduring challenges thrown by the hugeness in the data being captured and processed are being tackled through highly versatile Hadoop framework/Spark that can totally change the retail economics by radically lowering the cost of data storage and processing, bringing in new flexibilities to gain new insights, automated replenishment, and more accurate market to individuals rather than a demographic.

Retailers are using a variety of intelligent systems that gather data and provide immediate feedback to help them to engage shoppers fruitfully. The well-known data-generation systems include digital signage, point of sale systems, vending machines, transaction, in-store cameras, dispensing kiosks, and so on. The ability to gain reliable insights from the data shared by these systems makes it possible to provide customer-centric "connected stores." Context awareness is the main theme of these connected machines to precisely and perfectly understand the customer situation. The context information then greatly differentiates in showering customers with a host of unique services. In short, the insights-driven shopping experience is enabling customers immensely in getting items for the best price. Based on the edge data, retailers can integrate their supply chain activities intelligently. Further on, retailers can provide their customers with opportunities to engage with their preferred brands in more meaningful ways to cement customer loyalty.

Smart Automobiles

The number of digital electronics and other automation elements in a vehicle is steadily on the climb for providing different kinds of services to drivers and the occupants. The convenience, care, choice, and comfort induced through these connected devices are definitely awesome.

Sensors are being attached in every critical component in a car to preemptively get to know the component's status, and this reading provides some leeway for drivers to ponder about the next course of action. Another interesting and involving module is the in-vehicle infotainment system, which is emerging as the core and central gateway for securing and strengthening the connectivity outside for a range of use cases. All kinds of communication, computing, and entertainment systems inside vehicles will have a seamless connection with the outside world through the well-defined in-vehicle system so that the occupants can enjoy their travel in a fruitful manner. Global positioning system (GPS) devices and smart meters of cars throw a lot of data to be captured and analyzed.

Sensors provide information to automated parking systems to substantially lessen the driver's workload. There are sensors-enabled driver assistance systems for automobiles. Location data could be combined with road work and other traffic information to help commuters avoid congestion or take a faster route. Digital signage, cameras, and other infrastructures on the roadsides in synchronization with the in-vehicle infotainment module (V2I) aid drivers to give a pleasant travel experience to all. Vehicles today talk to other vehicles (V2V) on the road and interact with remote cloud services and applications (V2C). Vehicles share their data to the remotely held databases in order to facilitate the different aspects of vehicle analytics. Maps are the other salivating tool for reaching out the destination in a cool and controlled manner. Detecting real-time traffic flow from each direction and automatically changing traffic signals are to improve flow. Edge data further enable automated, intelligent, and real-time decisions to optimize travel across the transportation infrastructure as cars become capable of connecting to the roadway, safety systems, and one another.

Smart Manufacturing

Every tangible machine and tool in manufacturing floors and production facilities are being stuffed with a manifold of smart sensors, communication modules, and so on. That is, today's devices are instrumented to interoperate and be intelligent in their operations and obligations. Machines are not only networked with others in the neighborhood but also with remote cloud environments. Today, all the production-related data are being shared to the centralized systems in the form of excel sheets at the end of the day through emails. But new-generation machines are capable of integrating with cloud-enabled software applications and cloud storages instantly and insightfully. That is, machines transfer all the ground-level information to the cyber-level transaction and analytical systems then and there. This technology-inspired real-time connectivity facilitates a number of fresh possibilities and opportunities for corporates in visualizing hitherto unforeseen competencies. In addition, chief executives and other decision-makers, who are on the move in a far away land, can be provided with decision-enabling productivity details through a real-time notification capability in order to ensure any course correction if necessary, commit something solid to their customers with all the confidence and clarity, ponder about new offerings, bring operational efficiencies, explore newer avenues for fresh revenues, and so on.

That is, smart factories connect the boardroom, the factory floor, and the supply chain for higher levels of manufacturing control and efficiency. Sensors and actuators in devices such as cameras, robotic machines, and motion-control equipment generate and use data to provide real-time diagnosis and predictive maintenance, increased process visibility, and improved factory uptime and flexibility. Thus, edge data lay a sparkling foundation for smart manufacturing.

Facilities and Asset Management

The big data generated by increasingly instrumented, interconnected, and intelligent facilities and assets are useful only if transactional systems could extract applicable information and act upon it as needed. The appropriate and real-time usage of this big data is to help improve decisions or generate corrective actions that can create measurable benefits for an organization. Big data analytics can help to generate revenue by providing a contextual understanding of information that the business can then employ to its fullest advantage. For example, geographic information systems (GIS) can help location-sensitive organizations such as retailers, telecommunications, and energy companies to determine the most advantageous geographies for their business operations. A world's largest wind energy producer has achieved success using a big data modeling solution to harvest insights from an expanded set of location-dependent factors including historical and actual weather to help optimizing wind turbine placement and performance. Exact pinpointing the optimal locations for wind turbines enables energy producers to maximize power generation and reduce energy costs as well as to provide its customers with greater business case certainty, quicker results, and increased predictability and reliability in wind power generation.

An effective facility and asset management solution has to leverage big data analytics to enable organizations to proactively maintain facilities equipment, identify emerging problems to prevent breakdowns, lower maintenance and operations' costs, and extend asset life through condition-based maintenance and automated issue-notification. To help mitigate risks to facilities and assets, predictive analytics can detect even minor anomalies and failure patterns to determine the assets that are at the greatest risk of failure. Predictive maintenance analytics can access multiple data sources in real time to predict equipment failure which helps organizations to avoid costly downtime and reduce maintenance costs. Sensors could capture the operating conditions of critical equipment such as vibrations from ship engines and communicate the captured data in real time to company's command center for proceeding with failure analysis and predictive maintenance. Similarly, the careful analysis of environmental and weather-pattern data in real time is another way of mitigating any kind of visible or invisible risks. Organizations can receive alerts of potential weather impacts in time to shut down facilities' operations or prelocate emergency response teams to minimize business disruption in case of any advancing storms.

Big data is admirably advantageous when applied to the management of facilities and assets (everything from office buildings to oil-drilling platforms to fleets of the ship). This is due to the increased instrumentation of facilities and assets, where the digital and physical worlds have synchronized to generate massive volumes of data. Therefore, considering the mammoth volume of data, tools-supported analysis of big data can lead to bountiful benefits such as increased revenue, lowered operating expenses, enhanced service availability, and reduced risk. In a nutshell, edge data are a ground-breaking phenomenon for all kinds of industrial sectors to zoom ahead with all the required conviction.

Carving Out Edge Clouds for Edge Analytics

The ultimate aim of edge clouds is to deliver low-latency, bandwidth-efficient, and resilient applications. Edge clouds are being formed out of connected and resource-intensive fog devices in order to do certain functionalities locally. Edge clouds stand in between faraway clouds in the cyber world and scores of sensors/actuators at the physical world. Edge clouds store every machine and sensor data, subject them to specific investigations, and spit out actionable insights that can be given directly to fog devices and to resource-constrained actuators at the ground level. This level of extreme and deeper connectivity and process integration leads to the consistent eruption of path-breaking and people-centric applications. Similarly, the insights emitted out by edge clouds can be readily integrated with cloud-based applications in order to build sophisticated applications.

The edge cloud facilitates a kind of new-generation architecture for seamlessly integrating local edge networks and cloud networks. This is to keep latency-sensitive computation and user interaction components close to end-users at the edge nodes while hosting additional heavy-duty processing and database components in cloud center nodes. Another perceptible benefit is that the bandwidth gets conserved by doing the initial activities at the edge so that only highly compressed and compact data get transmitted to cloud environments over the Internet communication infrastructure. The edge cloud is able to access various physical assets, mechanical and electrical devices, consumer electronics, and so on and receives their data. Edge clouds contribute to the application and system resilience. If edge cloud or one of its components fails for any reason, then the traditional cloud environment takes care of the processing. On the reverse side, when something happens to the cloud center due to network failure, natural calamities, or power outage, and so on, then the edge cloud takes care of the processing. Thus, edge cloud comes as a complementary cloud environment for faster sensing and responding.

Edge computing is pushing computing applications, data, and services away from centralized cloud data centers to the edges of the underlying network. The objective is to perform data analytics near the source of data to quickly raise right alerts and indulge inappropriate actions immediately. Finally, edge clouds enable end-users getting empowered with knowledge-filled services. In short, edge clouds are for local data processing. Traditional clouds are being realized through a set of homogeneous server machines, storage appliances, and network solutions. Edge clouds are, on the other hand, being formed through clubbing together of decentralized and heterogeneous devices. Edge clouds are generally ad hoc.

The public cloud idea typically represents the online, off-premise, and on-demand computing, whereas the fog computing is for proximity computing. Of course, there are private and hybrid clouds that use dynamically changing clusters of commodity server machines for data processing and logic execution. But the fog computing paradigm extends the computing to the network of edge devices. The fog vision was conceived and aptly concretized in order to comprehensively attend some specific use cases for the smarter computing era. There are specific applications such as gaming and video conferencing mandating very low and predictable latency. Then there are geodistributed applications (smarter traffic, grid, etc., pipeline monitoring, environmental monitoring, and management through the sensor and actuator networks, etc.). Further on, mobility applications such as connect cars and transports are pitching for the fog paradigm. The next logical step is to have hybrid environments by seamlessly and spontaneously integrating edge and traditional cloud environments for availing advanced and aggregated analytics.

Deep Diving and Digging into the Aspect of Edge Analytics

Devices are increasingly instrumented and interconnected to be expressly adaptive, assistive, articulative, and capable of accomplishing smarter actuation. In other words, edge devices are gradually and glowingly joining in the mainstream computing. That is, they are capable of data capture and processing toward knowledge discovery. Precisely speaking, devices are inherently empowered to perform the transition of data to information and to intelligence. The edge devices can form an edge cloud in order to accomplish highly complicated analytics. Typically, there are three prominent levels in which usable intelligence can be generated.

The first level is that every participating and contributing device is capable of processing the data it gathers. For example, in a smarter home environment, every type of articles and artifacts such as refrigerators, electrical switches, consumer electronics, media players, machines, instruments, utensils, wares, and equipment could process their data and take decisions as per the situation warrants. Instrumented devices and digitized entities cooperate on need basis on processing and analyzing data.

The second level covers the so-called gateways and data-aggregation devices. The other probable nomenclature includes hubs, brokers, middleware, adapters, and so on. As we all know, there are bountiful resource-constrained and networked embedded systems in our everyday environments to take care of everyday needs of people. Further on, the maturity and stability of digitization, distribution, and decentralization technologies lead to a massive number of digitized/sentient/smart objects (these are originally ordinary stuff and are enabled to be computational, communicative, sensitive, responsive, perceptive, etc., by various edge and fog technologies such as sensors, actuators, tags, motes, speckles, chips, controllers, stickers, codes, LEDs, etc.). The relevance of gateways and other intermediaries is being felt here as these individual entities need to be clubbed together to get consolidated and composite data to enable the gateways to indulge in analyzing to arrive at insights.

The final level is the cloud-based analytics. That is, edge devices individually and/or through the above-mentioned gateways can connect and integrate with cloud-based analytical platforms and applications to avail compact and specialized analytics. The innovations in edge and gateway devices are bringing forth sophisticated algorithms, and it is cost-effective to store and analyze granular data at edge devices. With the pervasiveness of network infrastructures, the edge-to-cloud movement is laying a stimulating and sparkling foundation for higher-end analytics at cloud servers. Let us discuss a couple of use cases in the subsequent sections.

The emerging trends of in-memory computing and in-database processing can be a game-changing phenomenon for carving out real-time insights. Forming edge clouds to quickly setting up a local, purpose-specific, and ad hoc computing environment for doing edge analytics toward real-time intelligence is another interesting domain getting a lot of attention these days. Cloud-based MQTT, XMPP, and other RESTful servers are being used to capture and store data from different and distributed sensors and instruments. CEP engines are the other popular mechanisms for IoT data analytics. There are end-to-end analytics platforms, analytics engines, and other specific systems such as context aggregator and decider for producing insights out of those MQTT and other publish-subscribe servers. Supercomputing, parallelization frameworks, and analytics appliances are also smartly combining and significantly contributing to having high-performance analytics.

Introducing Integrated Fog Computing Platforms

Fog devices individually cannot do much. They need to be integrated and empowered through a pioneering platform. In other words, we need highly efficient and elegant platform for accomplishing and acquiring the originally envisaged benefits of fog computing and analytics. The traditional enterprise, cloud, and web-based platforms are not suitable for fog computing as fog devices are not resource-intensive. We need highly modular and extremely adaptive platforms to activate and accentuate the fog computing ideals and ideas. Any fog computing platforms need to be fully synchronized for performing IoT data ingestion, processing, analytics, decision-making, and actuation. The platform has to have the device management and gateway capabilities. This is due to the fact that devices are typically dynamic and nomadic and can come, join, and even go out of the network. In this section, we are to discuss the breakthrough techniques in building competitive fog platforms that in turn lead to highly competitive IoT gateways.

The typical fog or edge devices include reasonably powerful controllers, communication gateways, Wi-Fi routers, smartphones, consumer electronics, robots, and so on. On the other side, these fog devices interact with a variety of resource-constrained sensors, actuators, digitized objects, sensors-attached physical assets, and so on with the intention of getting, cleansing, curating, translating, and transforming the IoT data. Further on, fog devices crunch the data to discover actionable insights to perform many things intelligently. Fog devices, based on the inputs and insights obtained through the stringent analytics process, activate IoT devices to do many things. Fog devices contribute as a well-intended broker and bus to enable fruitful interactions between IoT entities at the ground with cloud-based applications.

As technology continuously advances, the product vendors are steadily incorporating advanced operational as well as management capabilities into IoT elements, especially in fog devices. These capabilities vary ranging from the simple ability to turn a device on and off to more complex actions such as updating software, managing Wi-Fi connections, configuring security policies, or changing data parameters. Now, the next major requirement is to have an intelligent and policy-aware platform to emphatically empower and manage fog/edge devices and the ground-level IoT devices. Raspberry Pi controllers and Arduino boards are the well-known and widely used intermediaries and gateways at this point of time for gathering data from sensors and passing them to centralized control systems. The issue here is that these microcontroller-based solutions do not exhibit any kind of sophisticated management capabilities.

The OSGi Standard for Building Device Management Frameworks

Many times, we have experienced the power of the Open Service Gateway initiative (OSGi) solutions toward having modular applications. OSGi provides a vendor-independent, standards-based approach to modularizing Java software applications, and its proven services model allows software components to communicate locally and across a distributed network. The OSGi specification defines modular-based software management and its execution. OSGi makes software management and its execution simpler by making large application into a small bunch of pieces (called as modules). These modules are working in an independent way so that when we need them, we can start and stop modules. As for OSGi, a module is termed as Bundle or Plugin-in. OSGi provides execution environment enabling module management (we can install, start, and stop modules). The OSGi stack is depicted in Figure 8.4.

Java-based applications or components come as an OSGi deployment bundle and can be remotely installed, started, discovered, stopped, updated, and uninstalled. OSGi inherently offers advanced remote management capabilities of embedded devices. An OSGi-based device application framework brings forth a layer between the OS and the business application on the OSGi platform. This growing collection of cohesive software components lets customers modify,

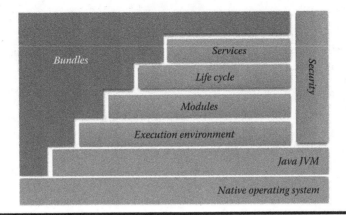

Figure 8.4   The OSGi stack.

reconfigure, and maintain their application over time as per the changes mandated. That is, application evolves with the changes happening around. Furthermore, the adaptability and flexibility of the OSGi application architecture provide competitive advantages. The ability to easily modify functionality is a must-have for device application frameworks today. A device application framework built on open standards enables communication with multiple management systems, and any platform based on the Java/OSGi deployment model can manage various parts of the device from an application standpoint. The OSGi model can be ingeniously extended to develop an IoT device management framework to build powerful IoT gateways and scores of next-generation IoT applications that are generally dynamic.

The Eclipse Kura—An IoT Device Management and Analytics Platform

The Eclipse Kura framework is being developed on the proven and potential OSGi idea to build next-generation IoT gateways/fog devices with device management capabilities. This Kura framework has been fitted with innovative device management features. For example, the Kura solution is exceptional here. Consider a vending machine company with machines distributed worldwide. Parameters change frequently to reflect inventory, price, and preference, and operators can benefit from remote management in order to fix the broken machine, update software, add new product lines or services, and more. That is, the Kura-empowered fog device monitors and manages different and distributed vending machines at the ground. There can be one or multiple fog devices interacting with one another. That is, fog devices are locally distributed and clubbed together on need basis to tackle compute and data-intensive needs. In other words, fog or edge devices form an ad hoc compute and data cluster, which is touted as the fog or edge cloud. The Kura framework facilitates the formation and deployment of edge clouds.

Eclipse Kura is an open-source project that provides a platform for building IoT gateways through the use of a smart application container that enables remote management and provides a wide range of developer application program interfaces (APIs). The goals of the Eclipse Kura project can be summarized as follows:

Provide an OSGi-based container for IoT applications running in service gateways: Kura complements the Java and OSGi platforms with APIs and services covering the most common requirements of IoT applications. These extensions include I/O access, data services, watchdog, network configuration, and remote management.

Kura adopts existing javax.* APIs when available: When possible, Kura will select an open-source implementation of APIs that are compatible with the Eclipse license and package it in an OSGi bundle to be included in the Kura default build (e.g., javax. comm, javax.usb, and javax.bluetooth).

Design a build environment: The Kura build environment isolates native code components and makes it simple to add ports of these components for new platforms in the Kura build and distribution.

Provide an emulation environment for IoT applications within the Eclipse IDE: From the Eclipse IDE, applications can then be deployed on a target gateway and remotely provisioned to Kura-enabled devices in the field.

Eclipse Kura provides a foundation on top of which other contributions for field bus protocols and sensor integration can reside, allowing Java developers to control behavior at the edge. The built-in functionalities include turning the serial port on or off, Wi-Fi management, remote data processing, and more. These remote management services also allow IoT applications installed in Kura to be continuously configured, upgraded, and deployed.

Everyware Software Framework

The everyware software framework (ESF) is a commercial and enterprise-ready edition of Eclipse Kura, the open source Java/OSGi middleware for IoT gateways. Distributed and supported by Eurotech, ESF adds advanced security, diagnostics, provisioning, remote access, and full integration with Everyware Cloud, Eurotech's IoT integration platform. ESF is a smart application container that enables remote management of IoT gateways and provides a wide range of APIs allowing you to write and deploy your own IoT application. ESF runs on top of the Java virtual machine (JVM) and leverages OSGi, a dynamic component system for Java, to simplify the process of writing reusable software building blocks. ESF APIs offer easy access to the underlying hardware including serial ports, GPS, watchdog, USB, GPIOs, and I2C. They also offer OSGi bundles to simplify the management of network configurations, the communication with IoT servers, and the remote management of the gateway.

ESF components are designed as configurable OSGi declarative services exposing the service API and raising events. While several ESF components are pure Java, others are invoked through Java native interface (JNI) and depend on the Linux operating system. The stack is depicted below.

The Eurotech ESF provides extensions in the areas of security, field protocol support, and native integration with the Everyware Cloud IoT service and application-enablement platform. Through ESF, Eurotech provides a set of the common device, network, and service abstraction tools for Java developers building IoT applications, including I/O access, data services, network configuration, and remote management.

Apache Quarks

As indicated elsewhere, our everyday environments are being stuffed and sandwiched by hundreds of connected and purpose-specific devices and diminutive sensors. All these are empowered to interact and collaborate for providing specific functionality. The result is a lot of data. There has to be a way forward to collect and analyze all of the data locally. That is, we need analytics engine in edge devices.

Quarks is an open-source programming model and runtime for edge devices that enable to analyze data and events at the device. A Quarks application uses analytics to determine when data need to be sent to a back-end system for further analysis, action, or storage. For example, we can use Quarks to determine whether a system is running outside of normal parameters, such as an engine that is running too hot. If the system is running normally, then there is no need to send this data to the back-end system. However, if Quarks detects an issue, we can transmit that data to the back-end system to determine why the issue is occurring and recurring, and how to resolve the issue.

Apache Quarks is a programming model and microkernel style runtime that can be embedded in gateways and small footprint edge devices enabling local, real-time analytics on the continuous streams of data coming from equipment, vehicles, systems, appliances, devices, and sensors of all kinds (e.g., Raspberry PIs or smartphones). Working in conjunction with centralized analytic systems, Apache Quarks provides efficient and timely analytics across the whole IoT ecosystem: from the center to the edge. Apache Quarks is API-driven and modular and can be used in conjunction with the vendor and open-source data and analytics solutions such as Apache Kafka, Apache Spark, and Apache Storm. The macrolevel architecture is illustrated in Figure 8.5.

The Quarks analytics engine performs real-time analytics on the edge device, separating the interest from the mundane; so you do not have to send every sensor reading over a network. If 99% of readings are normal, Quarks detects the 1% anomaly and just transmits those for further processing. The Quarks platform makes devices more intelligent, enabling them to take immediate action. For example, a connected vehicle running Quarks can adjust traction control based on the weight of the cargo/passengers. The Quarks runtime enables connected devices to learn from related devices. For example, a truck maneuvering roads in Oregon can adjust based on the data received from trucks operating under similar loads and conditions in Colorado, data such as altitude, cargo, weather, and traffic conditions.

Predixion Software

According to ABI Research, 90% of machine data never make it to the cloud. Predixion Software helps to capture and use this data and analyze and act on it at the edge. Predixion Software is the only advanced analytics technology that enables real-time analytics on the device, on the gateway, and in the cloud. Predixion Software has solved big problems in health care, fleet, telecommunications, energy, and manufacturing. With Predixion Software, various analytic

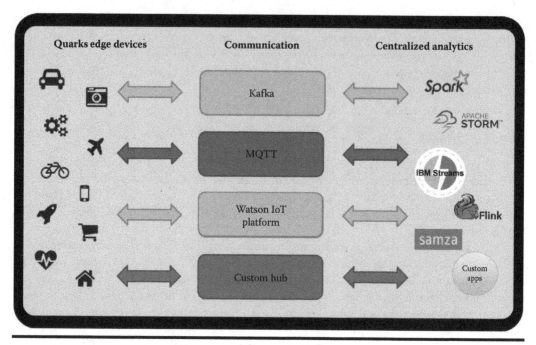

Figure 8.5 The reference architecture of Apache Quarks.

models can be embedded on the device, can gather real-time data from devices, and push it to the gateway, and can aggregate all this information in the cloud. This flexibility, combined with an advanced predictive model, leads to predict when a failure will occur and prescribes what action to be taken when.

With predictive maintenance, real-time predictive insights are delivered to the point of action—whether that is into the hands of a front-line operator, the dashboard of a project manager, or back onto the device for emergency protocols. All the empowered assets will send alert signals when they are likely to fail. The prediction capability at the edge removes the delays and expenses that result from unplanned downtime. Businesses today collect and crunch historical data to gain workable intelligence. That is not sufficient anymore. All kinds of IoT device data need to be combined with historical data in order to activate comprehensive analysis to extract both tactical as well as strategic insights in time to initiate appropriate actions at different levels with all the clarity and confidence. Predixion Software's unique Predixion IQ™ technology allows analytic models to be deployed on the device, on the gateway, and in the cloud, so actionable insights are delivered at the point of decision. With Predixion, hospitalists know which interventions to apply to high-risk patients, technicians know where to focus their resources, productivity goes up, and costs plummet.

The Solair Smart Gateway

The Solair smart gateway is an industrial-grade smart device that provides communications, computation power, and a lightweight, flexible application framework for the IoT platform integration. It is designed to streamline safe and secure bidirectional communication as follows:

- *Collect*, *store*, and *process* sensor data at the edge of the network.
- *Streamline* safe bidirectional communication between the field and the cloud.
- *Ensure* that only meaningful data are sent into the cloud.
- *Enable* local intelligence and performance optimization. The Solair gateway technology is based on Kura.

The Solair Platform—IoT Devices: The Integration Options

Direct Collection

A common industrial scenario is when data are transmitted directly from the machine to the Solair platform using its own internal connectivity, for example, Wi-Fi, Ethernet, or 3G/4G.

Mobile Bridge

The data exchange between objects and the Solair cloud is typically managed through mobile phones, via Wi-Fi or Bluetooth.

Smart Gateway

The gateway collects data from machines or equipment through a series of possible protocols—most frequently field protocols such as Modbus—and submits them to the platform while optimizing a number of processes at the edge. Figure 8.6 clearly articulates how different entities get connected with Solair platform through a bevy of protocols.

The Solair smart gateway supports communications through multiple interfaces and multiple protocols, enabling various types of devices and sensors to interact and exchange encrypted data and commands seamlessly.

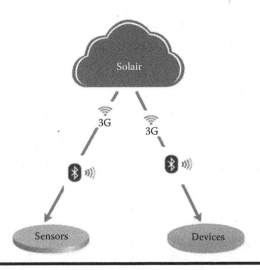

Figure 8.6   The Solair platform.

Altiux Innovations

GWStax, a part of Altiux's IoTStax product portfolio, is a comprehensive framework of modular components that enables seamless connectivity, interoperability, security, remote management, edge analytics, and application enablement in IoT gateways. It enables original equipment manufacturers (OEMs) to quickly develop and deploy gateway products for IoT that essentially connect end nodes to the cloud. This is built on industry standards and technologies such as 6LoWPAN, IPv6, Thread, CoAP, and LWM2M and scalable to support application layer protocols such as OIC and AllJoyn. GWStax is suitable for applications such as smart home gateways, building automation, smart parking and lighting, and industrial automation.

NodeStax is a comprehensive framework of modular components that enables seamless connectivity, security, remote management, and application-enablement in constrained IoT devices. End node devices in IoT deployments are typically constrained in terms of processing power, memory availability, power availability, communication bandwidth supported, cost considerations, and so on. By addressing the needs of such devices, NodeStax enables OEMs to quickly develop and deploy constrained end node products for IoT. This is built on industry standards and technologies such as 6LoWPAN, IPv6, Thread, CoAP, and LWM2M and is scalable to support proprietary protocols; NodeStax is suitable for constrained devices in smart homes, building automation, smart appliances, industrial automation, and smart cities' use cases.

ParStream Edge Analytics Appliance

ParStream, the IoT analytics company, has come out with its own IoT analytics platform. It is purpose-built to handle the volumes and velocity of IoT data. The new version includes the capability to perform edge analytics with ParStream's geodistributed analytics (GDA) feature. GDA delivers a faster, more economical, and secure way to analyze large volumes of data streaming from geographically disperse sources, such as cell phone towers, manufacturing operations, wind parks, oil rigs, and supply chains. ParStream's GDA software can be installed at or close to the source of data, eliminating the need for a massive and expensive central database, which enables faster queries and real-time answers. Queries are executed centrally after which ParStream's GDA transparently breaks up the query, sends them to the relevant remote servers, collects, and delivers the results back to the application. This substantially lowers operational costs of data transfer and preserves network bandwidth for other purposes.

ParStream also has announced EdgeAnalyticsBox, the industry's first ruggedized appliance designed for edge analytics. EdgeAnalyticsBox comes preloaded with ParStream's GDA software and allows data to be captured and analyzed at the source. In addition to ParStream's EdgeAnalyticsBox, customers can also use their own hardware to implement ParStream's edge analytics solution. ParStream's light footprint allows ParStream GDA to be installed on small, standard-based servers or embedded in existing appliances already installed locally.

Dell Edge Gateway 5000 Series

It is all about collecting, analyzing, relaying, and acting on IoT data at the edge of the network with this IoT gateway purposely built for building and industrial automation. The Dell Edge Gateway 5000 Series is designed to aggregate, secure, and relay data from diverse sensors and equipment. The Intel® Atom processor provides the capacity to perform local analytics, so only meaningful information is sent to the next tier which could be another gateway, the data center, or the cloud. This minimizes consumption of expensive network bandwidth and reduces overall solution latency. The Dell Edge Gateway 5000 Series is designed to attach to a wall or DIN rail in commercial and industrial environments. This is engineered with an industrial-grade form factor and fanless, solid-state design. The Dell gateway can reliably run 24 × 7 with long life at extended temperatures, in addition to withstanding the higher levels of humidity and dust typical of industrial environments.

On summary, remote management saves time and money by enabling updates, configuration, and troubleshooting without physically reaching out the device. In the medical field, the remote management capability impacts a network of thousands of devices. That is, end-user devices can be updated remotely at once, so patients can access the most up-to-date care available. In the industrial market, managing devices remotely saves money by eliminating the need for technicians to service devices in the field. Advanced Java-based device application frameworks that abstract the complexity of hardware and networking subsystems simplify the development, reuse, and remote management of cross-platform IoT applications. The emergence of an IoT service gateway model, running modern software stacks, and operating on the edge of an IoT deployment as an aggregator and controller has opened up the possibility of enabling enterprise-level technologies to IoT gateways.

Conclusion

The IoT is undoubtedly the game-changing technology that is set to transform the world forever. With applications in areas ranging from manufacturing to health care and smart cities, the leverage of all kinds of delectable and decisive advancements in the IoT field is set to take off as never before. With devices and sensors joining in the mainstream computing, we need highly synchronized and smarter platforms for enabling them to form device clusters to accomplish local computing. For building real-time and real-world applications, real-time analytics is the mandatory thing. Fog computing is the best bet for supplying the real-time needs with all simplicity and sagacity. This chapter has covered up a lot of useful information on the fast-emerging and evolving fog/edge computing.

Bibliography

www.cisco.com.
http://www.fogcomputingworld.com/.
http://www.openfogconsortium.org/.

Chapter 9

Envisioning Futuristic Smart Airports Using IoT Integration

Abstract: Present day airports are at the forefront of technological innovation. This is mainly due to the fact that the number of air travel passengers is exponentially increasing every year, and the present day airports do not have the infrastructure to support this ever-increasing number of passengers and offer them a pleasurable travel experience. Travel experience of the passengers plays a vital role in determining the revenue which is generated by the aviation sector. In order to boost the revenue by apt adoption of processes and technological interventions, present day airport authorities have become frontrunners in the adoption of all cutting edge technologies like cloud computing, big data analytics, and Internet of Things (IoT). The focus of this chapter will be on the usage of IoT concept to build futuristic intelligent airports.

To get started, we have classified the airports into three categories; they are as follows:

- *Airport 1.0*: This depicts the first generation airports where basic airport operations were done in silos with no interaction between the various components of the airport ecosystem.
- *Airport 2.0*: Many airports of today fall under this category. However, some of the technologies which are described for this class of airports will continue to be used for Airport 3.0.
- *Airport 3.0*: This depicts the futuristic concept of airports which are in the various stages of evolution at present.

The main focus of this chapter is on Airport 3.0 as they form the true bed for the adoption and implementation of IoT concepts. Various components of IoT ecosystem which form the core pillars of this airport are as follows:

- Mobile devices
- Mobile technology
- Wearables
- RFID/sensors
- Beacons

The integration of each of these components into the airport ecosystem is examined in detail in this chapter. Ample use cases and real-life examples are provided in this chapter in order to provide an interesting reading experience for the readers.

Introduction

The airports are in a continuous phase of evolution in order to cater to the ever-increasing and ever-changing demands of air travel passengers. It is predicted that by 2020, the number of travelers who use the airports worldwide for travel would be roughly around 10 million. But the present day airports do not have the capacity to accommodate and serve this huge number of passengers. This calls for devising intelligent processes, technologies, and revenue strategies in order to use existing airport infrastructure to accommodate the passengers and also warrant them a pleasurable travel experience.

Airports of today are facing critical efficiency issues due to the fact that the technology and processes which are present in them are not enough to manage the ever-increasing passenger flows which in turn leads to dip in passenger experience.

From Figure 9.1, it is evident that soon the number of passengers will surpass the revenue growth in the aviation sector [1].

Some of the burning issues faced by passengers are as follows:

- *Baggage issues*: Missing, lost or mishandled baggage, delay in baggage claiming and tracking
- *Check-in delays*: Delays for check-in at airport entrance and check-in counters especially in peak travel and holiday season
- *Disruption management*: Passenger inconvenience caused due to delayed and cancelled flights

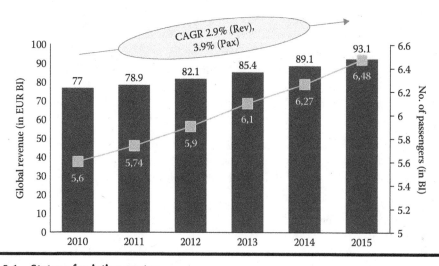

Figure 9.1 Status of aviation sector.

Table 9.1   Challenges Faced by Air Travel Passengers

Challenge	Solution Theme	Key Technologies
Capacity shortfalls	• Improve productivity and reduce operational costs through data capture, predictive analysis, and optimization of real-time operations • Informing the mobile workforce of potential changes and disruptions for effective responses	• Global collaboration facilities/airport operations command center/ notifications • Optimization through real-time operational and business performance analytics • Self-service kiosks, mobile • Automation, Wi-Fi, barcode, sensors, and devices
Dissatisfied passengers	• Touchless service processes with no wait time • Timely event notifications • On demand contextual info-delivery	• E-service and mobile service • Personalized location-based information delivery • Automation bar code/RFID/ sensors
Declining share of aeronautical revenue	Improve passenger spend at airport through commercial promotions	• Target promotional offerings on end-user devices • Analytics and CCTV video • Bluetooth and Wi-Fi access points in order to locate passenger concentration points
Increasing competition	Continuous innovation and brand building	Technology innovation models and portals for brand building

Apart from these critical issues, the other challenges faced by the air travel passengers are summarized in the Table 9.1.

The focus of this chapter will be on how to address the challenges which are summarized in the table using the IoT technology which in turn comes under the broad umbrella of information and communication technology.

Airport Infrastructure

Airport infrastructure has continuously been in an evolutionary phase. The first phase of airport infrastructure had the necessary amenities to ensure safety and security of passengers and also provided the features required for basic airport operations. For these airports, the land was typically provided by some real estate owner or agency, and all other components of the airport ecosystem were set up by the respective business environments. The various components of the airport ecosystem operated in silos with limited or no interaction with one another. The technologies which were used for the operation of airport infrastructure worked in a stovepipe fashion with no provisions for centralized monitoring and management. The operational model of manual airport is summarized in Figure 9.2.

Figure 9.2 Operational model of manual airport.

Airport 1.0	– All about manual and analog processes – Long lag time between resource solicitation and airport answer
Airport 2.0	– Implementation of self-service options to some key flow processing tasks like bag-drop, passport check, etc.
Airport 3.0	– Several focused initiatives to leverage digitalization so as to optimize flow monitoring and processing

Figure 9.3 Classification of airports.

Based on the type of infrastructure and processes present in airports, the airports can be classified into three levels of maturity which is summarized in Figure 9.3.

Airport 1.0

Airport 1.0 or convention airports refer to the conventional airport, and this is the type of airports which existed in the initial stages of evolution of airports in the early 1980s when airline travel was becoming prominent. These airports had the necessary infrastructure to ensure safety and security of the passengers and the aircrafts. But the focus was only on the safety aspects, and no specific attention was given to facilities which was given to the passengers to improve their travel experience. The characteristics of the airports are classified based on two major components which form the pillars of airport ecosystem; they are as follows:

- *People and processes*: Minimal automation and lot of manual work were involved. IT was used only for critical processes like passenger details entry and tracking. There were lot of forms which had to be filled manually by the passengers and by the airport staff. This introduced significant delays in the system and also introduced a lot of errors due to manual data entry. Lot of staff was required as there was limited automation.

- *Technology integration*: Operations to ensure safety of passengers and aircrafts were in place though it was limited, and there was not much of technology integration to ensure safety and security of passengers. There was no system in place for energy consumption monitoring and tracking. This led to the wastage of lot of utilities like power and water. There was absolutely no focus on the travel experience of the passengers. They had to wait in long queues to check in their baggage and also wait for extended hours to board their flights only to be intimated in the last moment that their aircrafts are further delayed. There was no concept of malls or other shopping outlets to improve the travel experience. Some limited stores/retail outlets for essential commodities were only present in the airport.

Airport 2.0

In Airport 2.0, lot of IT-enabled infrastructure is already in place, and they have realized the need for collaboration among the various components and the business units of the airport ecosystem. Passenger travel experience has also been given a lot of focus by these airport models. These airports use a converged network architecture which will help them to offer a set of common shared services to the passengers. This is in contrast to the stovepipe model which is used by Airport 1.0. Some of the key technologies which have found their way to Airport 2.0 are wireless broadband, video surveillance, and various types of mobile applications, and other social media applications which are capable of providing improved travel experience to the passengers. We will categorize these technologies and process improvements into four as follows:

- *Personal technology/processes for passengers*: In this category we will discuss mainly about the mobile applications which are designed for airports or air travel passengers.
- *Technology/processes to streamline passenger journey*: In this category, we will discuss mainly about biometric applications which are used to streamline passenger journey.
- *Technology/processes to enhance passenger experience*: In this category, we will discuss some processes/technology which are used in airports to increase leisure experience of air travel passengers.

One important point to be noted is that many technology integrations which are planned for Airport 2.0 will be fully implemented only in Airport 3.0.

Personal Technology/Processes for Passengers

Mobile Applications for Air Travel Passengers

- *iFly Pro*: This mobile app provides in-depth information of about more than 700 airports from across the world. The information covers details like flight statuses, in-terminal navigation, vehicle parking rates, and details of various types of services and basic amenities which are present near passengers. This app is also equipped with flight tracking and Global Positioning System (GPS). This is a paid app and has been rated as Travel & Leisure magazine's "most comprehensive airport guide."
- *GateGuru*: This free mobile app provides information about the location of shops, hotels, and other amenities in both domestic and international airports across the world, though it is prominently used for airports in the United States. This app has partnership agreements

with airport management companies which helps to ensure that the information provided by the app is always up-to-date. There are several other interesting features which are offered by the app; they are as follows:

- Options to check a passenger's mileage
- Options to check the number of airports visited by a passenger and other related statistics
- Options to compare travel-related statistics with other app users

■ *FlySmart*: This free mobile app is very similar to GateGuru, and it provides reviews and other details about hotels and other retail outlets in a specific airport. An additional feature offered by this app is the capability to offer notification on delayed flights so that passengers can plan accordingly.

■ *MiFlight*: This free mobile app collects information about the wait times in security check-point lines from over 50 airports around the world and provides it to passengers.

■ *Entrain (free)*: This interesting mobile app was developed by researchers at the University of Michigan and helps the passengers to manage their sleep schedules and get over jet lag-related issues quickly. This app maps out a passenger's sleep schedule according to their body's circadian rhythms. This mobile app relies on reported light data by the passenger to recommend best sleeping and waking hours in the new time zone of the passenger. For this app to provide proper guidance to a passenger, the passenger needs to enter the following data correctly:

- Current time zone
- Destination time zone
- Brightest amount of light that can be tolerated during a trip

Technology/Processes to Streamline Passenger Journey

Interactive Displays and Bill Boards in Airports

Interactive touch displays are useful in any real-life situation. More so when it comes to airports, many airports across the world have interactive maps. These maps can be used by the passengers to view the route information about their favorite spot within the airport like a restaurant or the gate to which a passenger needs to go in order to board a specific flight.

Nowadays, many leading players in the IT industry are trying out new innovative approaches for the use of interactive displays in airports. One such interesting approach is an interactive billboard in airports which is designed by Google. These interactive billboards from Google use Red Crystal software to stream the required content onto users' smartphones. The users can select the type of content that they want to be displayed on the advertising displays. Apart from this, the users can also download movies, games, or anything of their interest from the Google Play Store to their smartphones.

Technology/Processes to Enhance Passenger Experience

Interactive Surfaces

Interactive screens/displays which respond to gestures of people by providing different types of multimedia content are used in many airports across the world. The main objective of using such components in airports is to provide an enhanced traveling experience to passengers.

The underlying technology used is the gesture recognition technology where the system is equipped with technology, which can examine the surrounding area and respond to the movement of the people around by displaying various types of content which are preloaded and preconfigured into the system.

These interactive surfaces can also be used to display logos and brand messages of various organizations. The interactive screen content can be designed in such a way so as to offer a simple transition from one brand image to another along with 3D and other visual effects, audio and video.

Apart from interactive screens, it is also possible to have interactive floors which respond to gesture recognition technology and provide a fully immersive traveling experience for the passengers. In the context of airports, apart from using these interactive surfaces as advertising media, it is also possible to use these interactive surfaces to provide valuable insights to passengers about their destination locations and the various points of interest which are located in a specific destination location.

Processes for Increased Leisure Experience

Air travel passengers have expressed a strong opinion that they would like to have some leisure activities as a part of their travel experience. This is more prominent when there is additional time available between connecting flights. The limited support available in various airports for virtual reality, multimedia, and other entertainment technologies is also a reason for the rise in passenger demand for leisure facilities in airports. Some of the leisure facilities available in various airports are explained below.

Finnish Sauna at Helsinki Airport

The national airlines of Finland (Fin air) which operates flights between Helsinki and Singapore airport has introduced a spa and sauna offer for transit passengers at Helsinki. The facility is being offered at the Finnair lounge in the single terminal building. The lounge is available to passengers on production of a business class ticket, oneworld Emerald/Sapphire card, or €45. The spa alone costs €45 for access to various spa pools, saunas, and baths, while treatments range from €51 to €141. Combined lounge–spa access costs €70. With the direct Finnair flight from Helsinki to Singapore, business travelers will find Helsinki a geographically convenient connection to many European cities that are not directly served by a one-stop flight from Australia. Singapore's Changi airport is renowned as a thoroughly enjoyable place to transit, so adding Helsinki to the mix will make a thoroughly enjoyable experience [2].

Free Sightseeing Tour at Changi Airport, Singapore

If there is any chance to spend more than a couple of hours in transit at Changi airport, there is a free guided tour service for the passengers. The passengers are provided a bus and then a ride through the Singapore river to get a view of the entire Singapore city. This feature has come with such a great success that many passengers traveling via Changi airport opt for a forced delay in their transit in order to enjoy the free city tour.

Free Cooking Classes at Paris Orly Airport

Passengers in transit through the Paris airports get a chance to attend free cooking classes during their transit at Paris Orly Airport. In these cooking classes, French chefs teach French specialty delicacies to the passengers. The passengers also have an option to try the recipes and carry them back to their destinations if they opt for it.

Traditional Culture Workshops at Incheon International Airport, South Korea

Traditional culture workshops are organized at Incheon International Airport for the passengers who are in transit and also for those who are flying to various destinations across the world. In these culture workshops, activities which have a deep linkage to the culture of Korea are exhibited in the workshops. As of now, the workshops cover over 70 art and craft themes which span various aspects of Korean culture like Korean ceramic ware, clothing, and accessories.

Apart from the leisure activities which are listed above, many present day airports also have facilities like fish spa, art zone, Christmas markets, watch movies, and so on.

Airport 3.0

Airport 3.0 is still in the evolutionary phase, and many of the technological features which are laid down for Airport 2.0 will be fully functional only in Airport 3.0. One of the core technologies which will form the core of Airport 3.0 is IoT. Several enabling technologies for IoT like big data analytics, cloud computing, and cognitive computing will also play a pivotal role in the design of Airport 3.0. Intelligent airports of future will be data rich in nature with thousands of devices which are communicating with one another. These huge network of communicating devices will form the core of the IoT concept. In the context of airports, this huge network of communicating objects will help us to communicate with each passenger within the airport vicinity.

With the integration of IoT into the airport ecosystem, there will be a significant automation in the processes of the airport ecosystem as shown in Figure 9.4.

The results of recent studies of IoT integration in airports are summarized in Figure 9.5 [3].

The following are the key components of IoT ecosystem in airports (Figure 9.6).

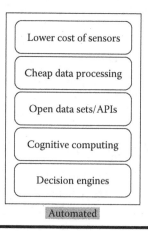

Figure 9.4 Features of automated airports.

Airlines getting ready for IoT

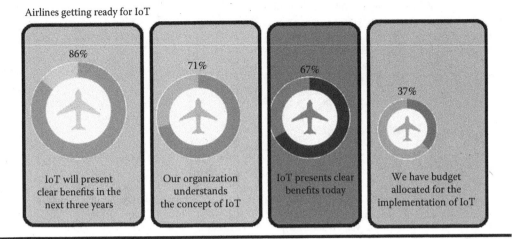

Figure 9.5   Recent studies of IoT integration in airports.

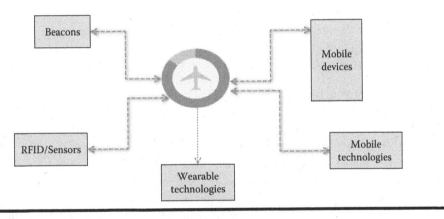

Figure 9.6   Components of IoT ecosystem in airports.

Mobile Devices in Airports

The key aspect of improving passenger experience is to provide personalized travel experience to each of them. This can be achieved to a great extent using mobile devices like smartphones and tablets. It is estimated that over 75% of airports plan to provide personalized passenger services through smartphones in the next three years. The results of the survey are summarized in Figure 9.7 [2].

For the majority of the airports, the future is mobile devices. Smartphones with access to 4G and Wi-Fi technologies which are available in airport will provide permanent Internet connectivity options to air travel passengers. Using mobile devices, passengers will derive benefits of a personalized journey with continuous suggestions throughout the airport based on passenger-specific personal details.

Smartphones will facilitate passenger tracking services and technologies to be introduced in majority of airports. These technologies will allow flow monitoring which in turn will help in

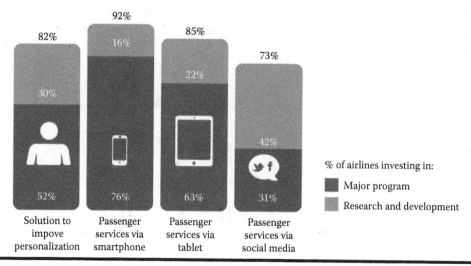

Figure 9.7 Role of mobile devices in airports.

allotting various resources to the passengers in a preemptive manner, thus avoiding congestion and reducing queues. The use of geolocalization technology in smartphones will allow the airport authorities to predict and estimate the amount of time spent by passengers in different zones of an airport.

In addition to all this, Internet technologies available in airports will allow the passengers to make their travel experience a pleasurable one by providing access to a wide range of mobile apps and gaming options. Another prospective opportunity which smartphones can provide for air travel passengers is the possibility of m-commerce.

Research has shown that smartphones will be a major motivating factor for the adoption of context-aware applications. This will pave way for intelligent networks which will facilitate context-aware computing. Airports which are equipped with geolocation software will allow their existing networks to become more intelligent and will provide them the capability to pinpoint the location of thousands of Wi-Fi-enabled devices such as smartphones and wireless tagged assets which may include trolleys and baggage.

MOBILE-AUGMENTED REALITY APPLICATION FOR AIRPORTS

Mobile-augmented reality applications are available in some airports like Malaysian Airport and Copenhagen Airport. Some of the features provided by these applications is to provide a list of the fares offered by different airlines to different destinations, provide the locations of restaurants, retail outlets, check in baggage counters, and so on.

One of the key pain points of the passengers is the absence of self-service check-in options in airport counters. International Air Transport Authority estimates that within the next couple of years, more than 70% of the passengers will use one of the self-service check-in options like mobile, kiosk, or web.

MOBILE BAGGAGE TRACING AND MANAGEMENT APPLICATION

Mobile baggage tracing and management application called World Tracer is used by 450 airlines, and it can continuously trace baggage up to 100 days. This application also maintains a repository of baggage claims that are pending, settled, or closed as a result of a passenger's bag being delayed or damaged. The extension of World Tracer to mobile devices enables airline staff to assist passengers upon arrival either at the baggage carousel or in the customs hall.

Another important application of mobile devices in airports is for the use of social media applications. The various uses of social media for airports are summarized in Figure 9.8.

Social Media Applications in Airports

The results of the most recent social media usage are as follows [1]:

- 72% of Internet users now actively use social media networks.
- 18–29-year olds have an 89% usage of social media networks.
- The 30–49-year olds have a social media usage of 72%.
- 60% of people between the age group of 50–60 years are active on social media.
- In the 65 plus age group bracket, 43% are using social media.
- Time spent on Facebook per hour spent online by country. Here are the top three. U.S. citizens get the top gong at 16% followed by the Aussies at 14 minutes and the Brits at 13 minutes.
- 71% of users access social media networks from a mobile device.

This statistics clearly illustrates the potential for social media usage in airports to foster improved communication between the passengers and various components of airport ecosystem. The results of the survey is shown in Figure 9.9.

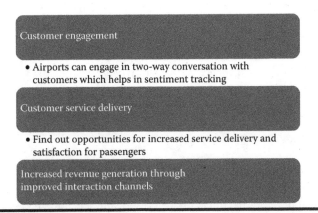

Figure 9.8 Uses of social media for airports.

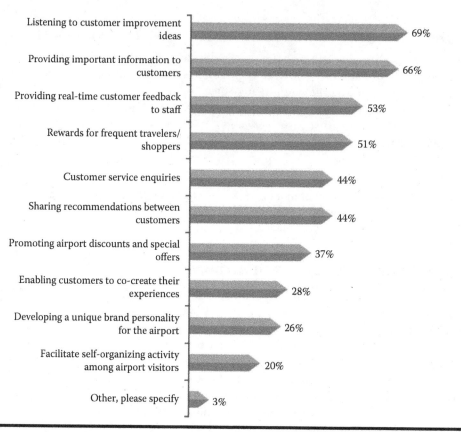

Figure 9.9 Social media applications in airports. Source: Amadeus survey.

Source: Amadeus Survey

Results regarding the use of social media in airports are summarized in the graph which is given in Figure 9.9.

Many airports and airlines have realized the tremendous potential which lies in the usage of social media networks, and they are using social media networks extensively to sell travel tickets and also interact with passengers to understand their feedback and the various pain points which are experienced by them. Some of the key aspects in which social media are used by some of the present day airports and airline services are as follows:

- Selection of copassengers based on their social media profiles
- Providing key flight details like timings, delayed flights, and so on through social media networks
- Comparison of the services offered by various airports/airline service providers using surveys which are conducted using social media networks
- Advertise special promotional offers for air travel using social media networks
- Use social media to provide communication between passenger and crew

USE OF SOCIAL MEDIA PROFILES FOR CHOICE OF PASSENGERS—KLM

KLM provides a feature which is called KLM meet and seat. Using this feature, it is possible for the passengers to know various types of information about the other passengers in the same flight by accessing their social media profiles. Using these profiles, the passengers also have the option to reserve their seats so that they can travel with like-minded people or people who are traveling to attend the similar event and so on.

Social media networks are also used by various airports and airlines as a means to enhance their brand value in the market by advertising the various value-added features offered by them in the social media networks, so that it will reach huge masses of people. The most recent statistics regarding the use of social media networks by airports is given in Figure 9.10.

Mobile Applications for Airports

With the ever-increasing use of mobile applications by human beings, mobile devices and applications have found their way into every stream of our life and activities. When it comes to airports, this is never an exception with a host of mobile applications which are devised exclusively to provide various kinds of applications. We will discuss some of those applications in this section.

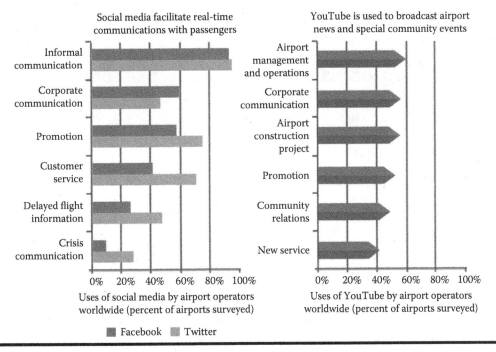

Figure 9.10 Social media applications in airports.

1. *Skyscanner*: This mobile application proves to be very useful if a scheduled flight gets can-celled, and it becomes necessary to look out for alternate flights which operate in the same routes. This mobile application works on Android, iPhone, and windows mobile phones. It provides the alternate flights which are available based on the required search criteria. The cost of the flight ticket is also displayed in this mobile application.

2. *Flight predictor*: This mobile application is very useful to predict whether a specific flight will arrive on time. The flight's time is predicted based on various factors like the statistics of the flight over a period of time, delays at other airports, and so on. This application works on WebOS devices, Windows phone, and Android. This application also has the location map of many other airports. These location maps provide a layout of the entire airport and the various aspects of the airport like restaurants and other retail outlets.

3. *Flight status*: This mobile application provides the various types of status information per-taining to your flight-like arrival and departure times, the specific gate-related information through which the boarding needs to be done. This application works only on Windows phone 7 devices.

4. *Car locator*: All the airports provide car parking facilities which will be used to park cars of the flight passengers. Many times, it so happens that after the return journey, the passengers tend to forget the location of their parked cars. This is the exact situation in which the Car locator application comes into the picture. It helps you mark your car's parking location using GPS, and this will guide you back to the correct parking location. This works on Windows 7 devices.

5. *Airport codes*: This application provides codes of all the airports in the world and is very helpful for airline travelers. Airport codes are added by the airport authorities to the check-in baggage tags of the airline passengers. If the passengers know the airport codes, they can double check to ensure that their baggage is being sent to the correct destination locations. Airport code application is available for mobile Windows 7 version at present.

MOBILE-AUGMENTED REALITY APPLICATION FOR AIRPORTS

Mobile-augmented reality applications are available in some airports like Malaysian Airport and Copenhagen Airport. Some of the features provided by these applications are to provide a list of the fares offered by different airlines to different destinations, provide the locations of restaurants, retail outlets, check-in baggage counters, and so on.

Mobile Technologies

Quick Response Codes in Airports for Mobile Check-In

Quick response (QR) code is a two-dimensional bar code which is machine readable and can be used to gather more information about the item to which it is attached. One recent trend which had emerged is the use of QR code for mobile check-in to the airports. This is done in the following manner:

■ The airline authorities will send a boarding pass to the passenger with a link to the QR code which is assigned to the passenger. This information is typically sent in an e-mail which can be accessed using a smart mobile phone.

- The passenger will click the link and obtain the QR code which is assigned to them and store the code in the mobile device as well.
- Anytime the passenger needs to present the boarding pass, the passenger instead presents the QR code stored in the mobile phone to the scanner which reads the information.
- The QR code also acts as an unique link to all of the flight-related information of the passenger like the seat details and so on. In case of any changes to any of these details, the QR codes can be refreshed to display the updated or new information.

The use of QR codes for mobile check-in saves a lot of time and goes a long way in improving the travel experience of the passengers. This is already used in many prominent airports across the world. However in some other airports, it is yet to be introduced and used.

Near Field Communication

Near field communication (NFC) is revolutionizing the airport industry by trying to alleviate some of the key pain points faced by air travel passengers. One key concern of the passengers is carrying hard copies of boarding passes and standing in long queues in order to get them verified by airport officials before boarding the flight. NFC comes with a right set of solutions in order to solve this pain point by providing possibility to carry bar-coded boarding passes as NFC tokens in the mobile devices. These NFC tokens can be validated by means of sensors which are located at various touch points in the airport.

Another use case of NFC for air travel convenience is the concept of mobile wallets. It will help people to abandon their credit cards and other physical cards like loyalty cards and replace them with NFC-enabled mobile wallets. This will help passengers to make payments from the account by tapping the phone on NFC payment terminal at checkout counters.

Following are the strengths of NFC technology which make it very promising for the years to come:

- It is backed up and supported by many prominent players in the telecom space.
- It has high levels of security.
- Using it by tapping is very easy and convenient for customers.
- It can work even if the mobile phone is turned off or has a flat battery.
- Lot of related applications are gaining prominence like advertising, data collection, and so on.

Another method which is gaining prominence in the market is cloud-based mobile payments. This approach uses a mobile app which provides links to payment details which are stored online. After this, payment can be made by tapping the payment button or displaying a 2D barcode which can be used for scanning by the retailer.

The main advantage of cloud-based payments over NFC is that they can work with any device which has a 3G or Wi-Fi connectivity option. Downside of this approach is that they are not considered very secure, and they do not meet many security standards which are laid down for credit card issuers in different parts of the world.

Telepresence

Telepresence refers to a group of technologies which provides a person with a feeling as if he/she is actually present in a location which is other than their actual or true location. The major application of telepresence is video conferencing. Most of the present day organizations follow a borderless concept. Borderless concept means organizations which are split across different parts of the world function as a single entity despite time zone and all other types of differences. The support for telepresence is present in many present day airports. This technology helps the employees to attend important official meetings via video conferencing and allows employees to be productive even during transit at airports.

Wireless Broadband

Wireless broadband access is provided in most of the present day airports. Some airports have imposed a restriction on the duration for which wireless broadband could be used free of cost. After the specific duration, the wireless broadband becomes a paid service. Apart from wireless broadband service, many airports offer personal computers with pay as you go Internet service for the benefit of air travel passengers. These facilities are widely used and appreciated by the air travel passengers for official work and entertainment purposes.

RFID/Sensors

Biometric Passports

Traditional document-based methods for verification of passengers which are used in airports are error prone and time consuming. They rely on the photographs of the passengers for their identity verifications, and many times the photograph can be forged or duplicated. Also the information about the criminals resides in multiple databases and systems without any integration or communication. Identity verification of passengers is a crucial task when it comes to the security of airports, flights, and countries on the whole.

In order to ensure accurate and apt verification of passengers, nowadays the concept of biometric passports is very prominent in many countries across the world. These biometric passports, also called as e-passports, contain a smart card with biometric information of the passenger, and they are provided along with the traditional paper-based passports. The biometric information of the passenger is validated against the biometric information which is present in the smart cards of the passports, and this provides an efficient and reliable mechanism to verify the identity of the passengers.

SINGAPORE—THE FIRST TO IMPLEMENT BIOMETRIC PASSPORTS

The Immigration and Checkpoints Authority of Singapore (ICA) was one of the first organizations in the world to adopt and implement the concept of e-passports. They adopted this technique in order to ensure secure immigration at their various borders and checkpoints. The ICA uses a combination of smartcard and fingerprint matching to help them validate the identity of passengers who are traveling through automated lanes. This biometric-based authentication process gets completed in less than 12 seconds.

Other Biometric Applications in Airports

Early detection of suspicious people/passengers is a key to the safety and security of airports. This task becomes very much difficult and challenging in a huge and high-traffic airport until and unless appropriate tracking and verification mechanisms for passengers are present at each and every point within the airport. Typically, the passenger flow begins at airport check-in counters where passengers check in their baggage and receive their boarding pass. At this stage, security can be integrated into the system using the concept of e-boarding. E-boarding provides self-service kiosks, which have fingerprint readers and cameras for facial authentication of the passengers. In some cases, this can also be done with the help of smart cards which are attached to the biometric passports. This process ensures that the passenger's identity is verified at the starting point of entry into the airport itself.

Apart from this, facial recognition and fingerprint reading systems can be deployed near the airport gates to ensure that only authorized people are walking around the gates of the airports. Such systems can also be used in aerobridge and other security areas around the airport to detect any suspicious individuals or vehicles. These biometric-based authentication systems are a reliable and trustworthy way to ensure safety of airports. The various ways in which biometric systems can be integrated with the airport infrastructure are summarized in Figure 9.11.

RFID-Based Tracking of Baggage in Airports

Radio frequency identification (RFID) technology is used extensively across the world for tracking in the supply chain industry. It uses radio waves for tracking, and hence does not require line-of-sight. Hence it is very beneficial when compared to the bar code technology, which was traditionally used in airports for baggage tracking.

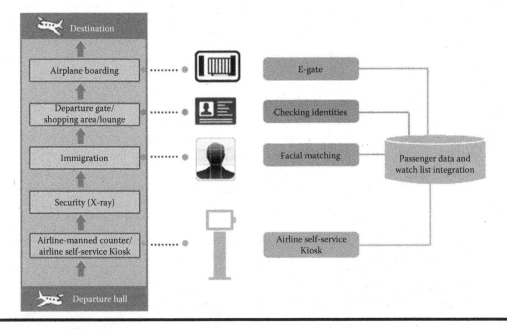

Figure 9.11 Biometric applications in airports.

RFID-based tracking of baggage offers the following benefits to the airport when compared to the conventional bar code-based tracking of baggage:

- They reduce instances of baggage loss and baggage theft as RFID tags can be tracked from a distance also using RFID readers. This in turn reduces the amount paid by the airport authorities for lost and stolen baggage.
- RFID-based tracking of baggage also increases the customer satisfaction due to reduction in the number of instances of lost or stolen baggage. This is because the baggage can be tracked continuously from the entry point until they are loaded into appropriate aircrafts.
- RFID also reduces the staffing cost for baggage handling in airports because of the nature of technology and the benefit it offers.

NFC/RFID-BASED PRECISION PARKING TECHNOLOGY FOR AIRPORTS

This technology helps passenger to locate empty parking slots and also guide vehicles in parking spaces which are available in airports. This reduces the time which is spent in searching for an appropriate parking space. RFID technology-based smart cards like E-Z pass can be used to make payment for airport parking as well.

Beacons for Airports

Beacon technology is used to provide proximity and context-related information to mobile devices. Beacons can be of various sizes, and they are available in various shapes too. They work using Bluetooth low energy (BLE). When any BLE-enabled device moves in the proximity of a beacon, the beacon can trigger an action on the device. For example, providing some alerts about specific offers on certain products when a user enters that area of the shop, providing guidance to some shops, restaurants when the user in a location close to that, and so on are some of the use cases of Beacons. Beacons hold lot of promises for airport also.

Beacons work using BLE 4.0 version. Hence, beacons are supported by all smartphones starting from Android phone 4.0 and Android phone 4.3.

Following are the key benefits of beacons:

- *Low cost*: Beacons are available at low cost. They have the capability to send signals to BLE-enabled devices which are up to 70 meters away. This feature provides a cheaper option when compared to other available options such as Wi-Fi.
- *Energy efficient*: Beacons require very less energy for their working. They do not need to be plugged in, and they just require a coin battery to function for long periods of time. This makes maintenance of beacons hassle free.
- *Distance sensitive*: As and when a smartphone detects a beacon, it can detect the beacon's distance to the nearest meter accurately. This feature makes beacons more useful for location sensing on mobile devices when compared to other location sensing technologies like Wi-Fi and cellular triangulation. This capability makes beacons very useful for navigation and other contextual-aware possibilities inside buildings.

DIFFERENCE BETWEEN NFC AND BEACON

NFC and Beacons are two technologies which address separate use cases. NFC works very well when two devices are placed close to each other, but it is useless for larger area coverage. Beacons provide a proximity-based alerting system that can trigger an app on a smartphone at a much greater distance. Beacons require many additional components for their operation. For example, the PayPal beacon system is not very straightforward. It requires a number of components like PayPal app on the phone, a customized beacon (with dedicated payment security), a user with a PayPal account, and a merchant accepting PayPal. While it is a secure payment system, it is not a solution that will easily scale.

Applications of Beacons for Airports

Tracking Passenger Location

Airlines can develop the capability to combine passenger details stored in an app in a passenger's phone with the accurate knowledge of their location in the airport which can be derived from the beacon nearest to a passenger. This will be helpful to send relevant information to passengers and also for locating them precisely if they are late for boarding.

Triggering Mobile Boarding Passes

Beacons placed at various points in an airport like check-in, baggage drop, and so on can be used to pull out and display mobile boarding passes on passenger's smartphone as and when they arrive.

Navigating the Airport

Beacons will make it easier for airport apps to guide passengers to locate the correct gate. Beacons have been found to be far more accurate for indoor mapping when compared to other existing techniques like Wi-Fi and cellular signals. For example, a passenger who has a BLE-enabled smartphone can get the GPS location from any beacon which is in the range and then use the data for a mapping app to help navigation through an airport.

Promotions at Retail Outlets in Airports

Beacons can trigger contextually relevant information and messages to passenger's smartphone. These can give information to passengers about special promotional offers in retail stores, coupon redemption, and so on. This will go a long way in improving the shopping experience of the passengers.

Baggage Reclaim

A beacon can help passengers by giving them information about the carousel in which their baggage will arrive and the approximate time at which the baggage would arrive.

SOME INTERESTING FACTS ABOUT BEACONS

- Deployment of beacons is very simple and straightforward. Beacon ID values can be configured using a companion app.
- Range values can be configured in beacons, and it can advertised up to 70 meters. If the airport is crowded, the range will be reduced to half the original value.
- A smartphone app can detect the presence of a beacon in approximately one second.

Wearable Technology

Wearable technology market is expected to grow to US$50 billion over the next 3–5 years. The different types of components which come in this category are as follows:

- Smart glasses
- Smart watches
- Smart wrist bands and so on

At present, there are around eleven different types of smart watches available which can be roughly split into the following three categories:

- *Notification smart watches*: These watches offer notification messages for incoming calls, text messages, and other notifications.
- *Voice operational smart watches*: These watches enable users to take virtual calls and give some commands via the smart device or smart watch.
- *Smart watches with impendent operating system*: These watches offer lot of robust features and can connect to other types of consumer devices in order to set up IoT ecosystem of communicating devices.

SMART WATCH—APPLE iWATCH

Apple iWatch is a smart watch which operates like a smartphone and is worn on the user's wrist like any other normal watch. Following are some of the key features of iWatch:

- Capability to connect with other Apple iOS devices like iPhone and iPad
- Capability to make calls and check caller id
- Features to access stock market rate and weather updates
- Provide fitness capabilities with the help of pedometer and health monitoring sensors
- Provides map coordinates and directions

SMART GLASS—GOOGLE GLASS

Google glass augments world with contextual information. This glass has the ability to capture pictures and record video and sound. It also provides capabilities to view calendars, check messages, obtain weather updates, and also provides a display which has the capability to respond to voice commands. The glass frames are also equipped with Wi-Fi and Bluetooth.

INTEGRATING WEARABLE TECHNOLOGY AND BIOMETRICS

This enterprise angle is exactly the approach being taken by Allegiant Systems, which has developed a concept based on smart glasses from another manufacturer—Vuzix [4].

Brian Mooney—CEO of Allegiant Systems—explained that the smart glasses could be worn by an airline's staff and could be used either at the airport or onboard the aircraft to help create a more personalized passenger experience. For instance, the Vuzix smart glasses could be worn by staff at the entrance to security, at the gate, or at the aircraft door to identify passengers using facial recognition technology, or it could be used in a First Class cabin to identify a specific passenger's preferences based on their previous travel behavior.

The biometric-related functions mentioned by Mooney—integrating facial recognition technology into wearable devices, for instance—could be a key future development (Figure 9.12).

Benefits of Wearable Devices

Following are the benefits offered by wearable devices:

- Ability to perform hands-free computing.
- Ability to perform multitasking.
- They provide context-specific information of users.

Use Cases of Wearables for Airports

Some of the important use cases of wearables for airports are the following:

Major players in the wearable computing market

Product	Maker	Type	Capabilities
Google Glass	Google	Smart glasses	Phone calls, view messages, built-in camera for video and photos, run Android apps, Wi-Fi and Bluetooth connectivity
Galaxy gear	Samsung	Smart watch	Phone calls, email and social media alerts, photos, videos
Smart watch 2	Sony	Smart watch	Phone calls, read email and social media messages, photos, videos
Pebble	Pebble technology	Smart watch	Runs apps if connected to iPhone or Android device and has fitness tracker
Space glasses	META	Smart glasses	Similar to Google Glass but also includes 3D imaging, infrared camera, and virtual reality capabilities
Recon Jet	Recon instruments	Smart glasses	Real-time fitness tracker for athletes, can be connected to a smartphone for viewing text messages and answering calls
M100	Vuzix	Smart glasses	Phone calls, view messages, built-in camera for video and photos, run Android apps, Wi-Fi and Bluetooth connectivity

Figure 9.12   Classification of wearable technology.

Passenger Baggage Tracking

Smart watches and smart glasses can be used to scan baggage tags to find out mislaid bag information from WorldTracer, which is the airline industry database for finding lost or missing baggage.

Operational Efficiencies of Airports

The hands-free computing capability of wearable means they offer diverse benefits in several areas such as aircraft maintenance. The aircraft mechanic will have the option to communicate directly with aircraft database systems and sensors to perform step-by-step replacement or other operations on parts, while using both hands for doing work. This could speed up repair and maintenance turnaround times.

Aircraft turnaround time will also derive benefits from the strong notification capabilities of wearable technologies. Aircraft turnaround is a key activity which comprises numerous time-sensitive and event-driven tasks. The dispatch officer can receive timely information and updates on progress of repair activities without being tied to a desk.

Customer service is another potential use case. When a passenger interacts with airline staff, the staff member is typically behind a desk doing some other activity. About 90% of their attention is focused on some other activity and not at the customer. Smart glasses will help to change this and will facilitate customer service agents to focus more on the passenger.

Another use case is foreign language translation. This could be made easier by real-time language translations where smart glasses use voice recognition software to translate the customer's language into text which can be viewed on glasses' display.

Other Supporting Technologies for Smart Airports

In this section, we will discuss some other technologies which complement IoT for the design and creation of smart airports of future.

Cloud Computing

Present day airports across the world are embracing cloud computing because of the immense cost benefits offered by it. The main crux of cloud computing is anytime, anywhere access to all types of resources which are included as part of IT ecosystem as and when the user requires it. The cost benefit part of it stems from the fact that the user needs to pay only as per the usage.

Following are the main benefits offered by cloud computing to airports:

■ The infrastructural components which are required for maintaining the entire IT infrastructure of the airports is provided and maintained by the cloud service provider. This removes the capital expenditure component from the airport infrastructure management which in turn provides huge cost benefits for the airport authorities.

■ From an environmental perspective, as cloud-based solutions typically use only pooled hardware resources, there is less energy consumption which helps to reduce carbon emissions. Additionally, through the use of shared resources, e-waste can be reduced by a substantial margin.

Apart from the airport authorities, facility to use cloud computing services at airports becomes a very handy option for many air travel passengers to store and access data created by them while in transit at airports and access high-end applications, which are hosted in cloud infrastructure without any infrastructure limitations.

Big Data and Predictive Analytics

Big data analytics is emerging as a hot technology. Its usage in the context of airports to serve air travel passengers is a topic which had gained a lot of traction recently. In the context of airline industry, big data refers to the huge amount of customer and transactional data which are generated daily by airports across the world. These data could serve as storehouses of valuable information which could predict and unravel various patterns of customer behavior. Many tools to manipulate and handle these large data sets are available in the market now, but there are no specific tools which are custom-made for the airline industry. However, efforts are being made to develop big data analytics tools which are specific to domains so that the patterns which are derived could be directly used by the respective authorities without any further customization.

In future, there are plans to create data warehouses in airports to capture all types of information regarding a customer which may involve travel preferences, shopping preferences, and food preferences. This will enable creation of value-added service packages which are specific to the choices of each customer. This will go a long way in enhancing the travel experiences of air travel passengers.

Conclusion

A near "perfect storm" of influencing factors is dramatically driving the need for a radical rethinking in the concept of the airport ecosystem. The entire chapter revolved around this concept. The various challenges faced by the airport ecosystem were examined in detail, and this was used as a starting point for the infrastructure evolution models of the airports which are proposed by the authors.

The airports were grouped into three different classes based on various factors which contribute to Airport 2.0 and Airport 3.0, as they are more relevant to the context of our discussion.

The chapter focuses more on the description of various aspects of Airport 3.0. The IoT technology which is expected to revolutionize the airport ecosystem was discussed in length in this chapter.

The various dimensions of IoT which were discussed in this chapter are the following:

■ Mobile devices
■ Mobile technology
■ Wearables
■ RFID/sensors
■ Beacons

The chapter concluded with the discussion of some technologies which support IoT-like cloud computing and big data analytics. Ample real-life examples were provided throughout the chapter in order to emphasize the concepts which were laid down.

References

1. J.D. Power, 2010, Global Airline Traveler Survey.
2. 2015: AIR TRANSPORT INDUSTRY INSIGHTS by SITA.
3. 2015: A report on Airline IT Trends Survey, SITA.
4. http://www.futuretravelexperience.com/2014/05/can-airlines-airports-get-value-wearable-technology/.

Chapter 10

Envisioning Smart Health Care Systems in a Connected World

Abstract: The health care sector is amidst an era of technological revolution in an attempt to overcome the various issues which are faced by them due to various aspects like aging infrastructure and lack of adoption of appropriate technologies at correct points in time in the past. Another critical problem which is faced by the health care sector is the huge amounts of large-sized data sets which are generated by them. Traditional storage infrastructure and technologies are not efficient to handle these huge amounts of data. To add on to this array of problems is the change in the attitude and mindset of present day patients. Patients nowadays are not willing to compromise in terms of the quality of their health care experience with their health care service providers. Extended waiting times due to unavailability of various infrastructure components are no longer accepted by the patients. Internet of Things (IoT) offers lot of promises for the health care industry by ensuring that correct treatment reaches patients at the right point in time. The first half of the chapter focuses extensively on the IoT use cases for health care industry. The foundation technologies which are required for using IoT in the health care sector, challenges posed by the use of IoT for health care sector, and the future promises of IoT for the health care sector are also discussed in detail in this chapter.

The second half of the chapter focuses on how the IoT supporting technologies that is cloud computing and big data analytics are used in the health care industry. Cloud computing service providers can offer promising benefits to the health care organizations. Some of the key benefits which are offered by them are the following:

- Drastic reduction in the infrastructure cost of health care organizations
- Scalable infrastructure which can store the huge piles of data which are generated by the health care sector
- 24/7 availability of the infrastructure components which can offer enhanced experience for the patients

The various health care use cases of cloud computing are discussed in detail in this chapter. Big data analytics can revolutionize health care industry by offering diverse range of benefits to patients like early detection of disease symptoms and timely advice to the patients using real-time parameters, which are gathered from them using various mobile applications. The various use cases of big data analytics in health care sector are also discussed in detail in the second section of this chapter.

Introduction

Dependency of health care sector on the concept of IoT and other technologies which support IoT-like big data analytics and cloud are increasing everyday. The main drivers for this increased dependency are the following:

- Provide quick access to health care
- Increase the quality of health care facility
- Reduce the time required to get good-quality health care

In short, IoT and supporting technologies are making quality health care available to each individual at the right time. Another use of IoT in health care is to provide personalized health care. The concept of providing health care and patient support to an individual based on his/her unique biological, behavioral, cultural, and social characteristics is called personalized health care. A sustainable health care system should have the capability to ensure prevention, early pathology detection, and homecare instead of the expensive clinical one, thereby ensuring better outcomes and improved patient satisfaction. The IoT and the other supporting technology ecosystem hold lot of promises for personalized health care services. The focus of this chapter will be to highlight how IoT and other IoT supporting technologies can be used to offer personalized smart health care services to huge masses of population at affordable rates. This chapter will throw light on the usage of IoT, cloud, and big data analytics technologies for the design and development of smart health care systems with an increased impetus on IoT (Figure 10.1).

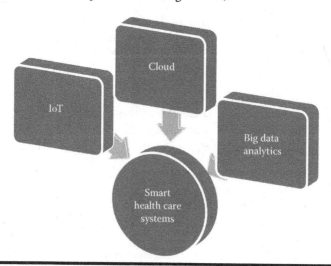

Figure 10.1   Role of IoT, cloud, and big data analytics in smart health care.

The two dimensions for the usage of IoT in health care are the following:

■ Clinical care
■ Remote monitoring

Clinical Care

Certain types of chronically ill patients require constant monitoring of vital body parameters. In normal scenarios, such patients are kept at intensive care units (ICU) in hospitals. IoT-driven noninvasive monitoring technology allows this type of monitoring to be done using sensors which collect comprehensive physiological information pertaining to the various vital body parameters of patients. The data collected using these sensors are sent using gateways and wireless networks to close relatives and caretakers who can take appropriate course of action to handle the patient. This IoT technique replaces the traditional in-person continuous monitoring at hospitals by health care professionals and doctors. This method provides improved automated health care at home at affordable cost to chronically ill patients (Figure 10.2).

Remote Monitoring

People who stay in remote areas typically do not have access to continuous health monitoring. Wireless solutions/sensors which are interconnected using IoT will make health monitoring available for these patients. These wireless solutions collect body parameters using sensors, apply complex algorithms for data analysis, and then share the analyzed data with doctors or health care professionals who can provide relevant health recommendations to patients. The different types of scenarios which demand monitoring are summarized in Figure 10.3.

Providing special care for pediatric and aged: IoT-based health care systems can be used for providing specialized care which is required for pediatric and aged population. This mainly facilitates administration of treatment at home. Pediatric patients require special care and attention. Aged

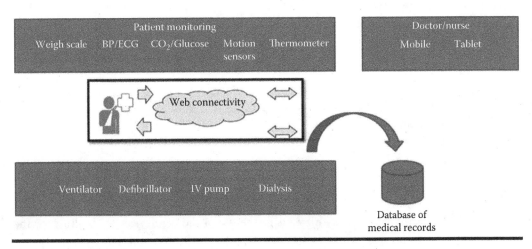

Figure 10.2   Clinical care system.

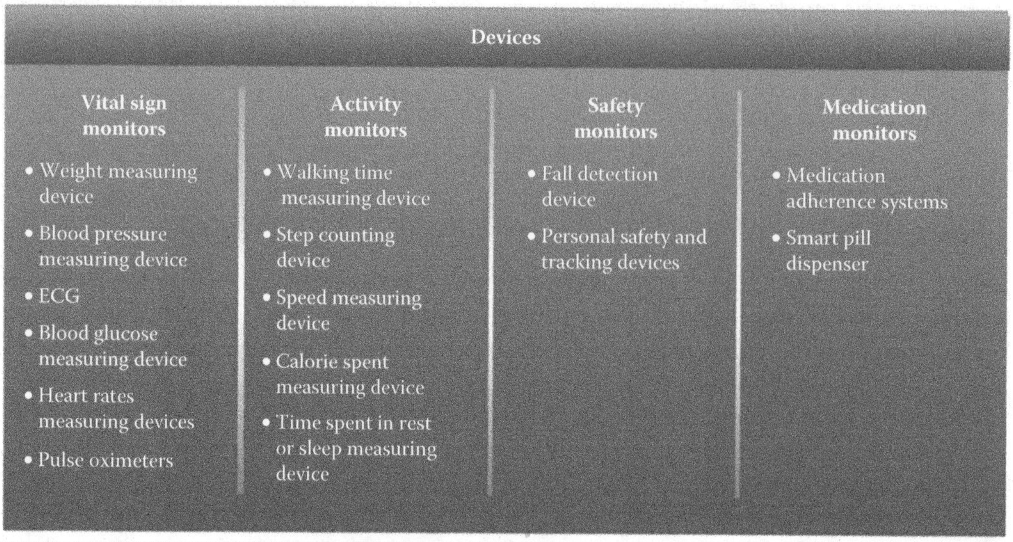

Figure 10.3 Different types of monitoring devices.

people have many chronic diseases. Monitoring such patients require careful tracking of their several physiological parameters, movements, and activities. In some cases, it is very important to track even the psychological state of patients with the help of IoT devices which have the capability to detect and track their mood and emotion.

Providing care for chronic disease management: Several chronic diseases like diabetes, high cholesterol, obesity, and cardiovascular diseases affect huge masses of population across the world. Management of these chronic diseases involves monitoring and managing the lifestyle of patients using continuous engagement methods. Such continuous engagement methods will help the patients to follow a personalized care plan which involves specific treatment, medication, and diet routines. One important category of applications which come under this group is termed as personal health and fitness management applications. These applications help people to follow a regime in order to stay fit and healthy. These applications typically provide facilities to the user to monitor and track their daily exercise and fitness regimes and will also have provisions to store these data and track the progress of such activities. Some of these applications will have the provision to provide a fitness schedule and help the users to track and monitor their activities against those captured in the schedule. The different types of sensors and devices which could be used in these applications are the following:

- Weight sensors
- Activity monitors
- Heart rate and pressure monitors
- Connected treadmill

Other Interesting Use Cases of IoT

mHealth: Mobile health care (mHealth) refers to the use of mobile devices for health care and communication services. There has been an increasing interest in this field from countries across the world. The proliferation of mobile devices, availability of high-speed wireless networks, and their impact on the day-to-day life of large masses of population have been the key factors which drive the adoption of mobile devices in the health care sector. To add on these aspects, in many parts of the world, there is still an acute shortage of health care workers, and this has been a matter of concern for government officials. Studies in the health care sector have also revealed the fact that health care services offered through mobile devices have better reach and impact even in very remote and resource-poor environments.

mHealth has emerged as an aftermath of eHealth which refers to the use of information and communication technology for health care-related services. Both mHealth and eHealth are interlinked, and they work hand in hand. For example, eHealth may involve digitization of patient records, thereby creating an electronic infrastructure for storing patient data; and mHealth could be used to gather and enter patient-related data into city health information systems and also answer various health-related queries for health care workers on their mobile devices.

The key applications of mHealth are the following:

Education and awareness: SMS using mobile devices has evolved as a simple and effective technique for addressing a wide range of health issues. SMS messages can be sent to mobile devices on various aspects of health care like disease management, disease symptoms, and about the availability of various health care services at various locations, and so on. SMS campaigns for health care services can be configured as one-way alerts or as two-way communication. In case of two-way communication, the citizen may be asked to take a health care survey which may go as inputs to the health care information system of that city. These SMS campaigns have proved to be having a powerful impact when compared to other modes of communication like radio and television.

Remote data collection: It is very important for health care departments to collect information about the various health care policies and their impact on citizens, so that they can create better policies which are more aligned to the requirements of the citizens. The data collection process is very efficient if done with the help of a mobile device as it helps in automated entry of data directly into the health care information systems rather than paper-based surveys which require a manual entry into the health care information systems. Lastly, the manual entry may also introduce errors at the time of data entry.

Remote monitoring: Remote monitoring using mobile devices ensures one-way or two-way communication to monitor various health parameters, provide doctor appointments, and also send reminders about medication regime or upcoming doctor visits.

Communication and training for health care workers: Training new health care workers and empowering the existing health care workers are the key requirements which exist in the health care sector. Mobile devices can be used to empower the health care workers by providing them access to health care databases. It is also a need of the day to provide effective communication among various health care centers, so that they can all work together efficiently and effectively to cater to the health care requirements of a specific area. This can also be achieved with the help of mobile devices.

Disease and epidemic outbreak tracking: Diseases often start in small pockets and later develop into widespread epidemics. Mobile devices play a very important role in making the people aware of the disease symptoms as well as the preventive measures. This will help in the containment of diseases at a very early stage.

Diagnostics and treatment support: mHealth applications are capable of providing expert advice and tips to the health care workers by providing them access to the medical databases with the help of their mobile devices. With the advancement of mHealth, people are able to receive timely treatment at remote places without the need for hospital visits, which might have proved to be a difficult or impossible task for them otherwise.

The mobile devices of the health care workers are typically equipped with built-in software. Through this software, the health care worker can enter the various symptoms of the disease in a step-by-step manner and use those steps to get expert advice from senior doctors or from the knowledge bases present in the hospital.

Virtual consultation (*telemedicine*): The idea is to use a combination of remote connectivity, video conferencing, and other multimedia systems to provide:

- Virtual medical care and consultation
- Medicine delivery
- Therapeutic procedures

Remote screening of patients has become very common in several countries across the world. The main objective is to provide high-quality health care to patients who do not have access to it, otherwise due to various reasons like stay in remote locations, lack of time to visit doctors in person due to their hectic work schedules, and so on. Another interesting trend is the emergence of telesurgery for performing procedures using robots and nurse assistants.

Architecture for telemedicine is given below. The whole idea is to connect patients to doctors in specialty hospitals with the help of semitrained health care professionals. These professionals have knowledge about standard diagnostics and defined clinical pathways with the help of clinical decision support system. These clinical pathways provide help to the health care professionals to identify diseases using guided and step-by-step clinical decision-making. This decision-making process uses a combination of standard health care practice and experience of doctor. These clinical pathways can be customized and authorized by the respective doctor and deployed with the help of a trained professional. Hence in this case, the whole purpose is not to replace the doctor but to enhance the efficiency and health care reach to all types of populations who do not have access to it (Figure 10.4).

Aging in place: The main purpose of this application is to provide continuous monitoring of body parameters of aging population. Devices which are mainly used for this include a wearable which is used for tracking the body parameters of patients without the need for manual intervention.

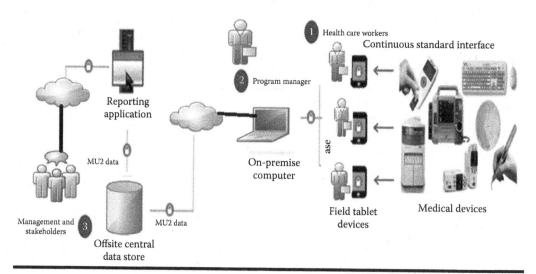

Figure 10.4 Architecture for telemedicine.

These body parameters which are captured from the elderly people are sent to a standard mobile device which acts as a network node for sending these data in real time to a doctor. This information can be used to provide correct medical assistance at the right point in time for the patients in case of some abnormality detection. There are also provisions in this application to send alert messages to nearby hospitals and relatives of patients in order to ensure intervention and correct mode of treatment at correct time.

Enabling Technologies which Make IoT in Health Care Possible

In order to facilitate efficient use of IoT in the health care sector, some technologies play an inevitable role. These technologies offer the usability, connectivity, and other essential capabilities which are required for using IoT in the health care sector. Some of these technologies are the following:

- *Smart sensors*: Smart sensors have a combination of a sensor and a microcontroller in order to utilize the power of IoT in health care sector by accurately measuring, monitoring, and analyzing the data in order to derive a variety of health status indicators. The data could include parameters like heart rate and blood pressure, glucose and oxygen saturation parameters in the blood. Smart sensors can also be embedded into pill bottles in order to track if a patient has consumed a specific dose of medications. For smart sensors to work efficiently, it is essential that it contains the following components:
- *Low power consumption/power conservation using energy harvesting devices/technologies*: For smaller device footprint and in order to ensure long battery life for IoT devices, it is essential to have some form of energy conservation mechanism in place. More has been discussed about this in an earlier chapter.
- *Integrated precision analog devices*: These devices allow sensors to have high level of precision at a low cost. This can be achieved using high-resolution analog-to-digital converters (ADCs).
- ADCs and low-power op-amps.
- *Low-power wireless networking technology options*: For the efficient functioning of IoT devices, it is necessary to have low-power wireless networking options like bluetooth low energy, ZigBee, Z-Wave, 6LowPAN, and so on.
- Gateways which are used to transfer data from IoT devices to a hub for detailed analysis.
- Graphical user interfaces (GUI) which are customized according to the nature and type of IoT device in order to enable ease of use.

Challenges in the IoT Health Care Sector

The integration of IoT into the health care sector presents a lot of challenges. Some of them are discussed and summarized in this section.

Managing diversity and interoperability of devices: When IoT is used in the health care domain, data are collected from a variety of devices and instruments and are sent to the databases which are present in the backend using gateways. Certain defined standards of communication are required in the network interface which is present in between the devices and the gateways. Similarly, the interface between the gateways and the backend databases also will be governed by certain regulations which enforce the use of certain approved standards and certification. The key problem today is the fact that products of several vendors do not conform to these standards and certification, which leads to interoperability issues and increased cost of system integration.

Data integration: In order to build an intelligent, context-aware health, and wellness applications that generate relevant patient alerts, it is required to integrate data from several sources. These sources include a plethora of devices like weighing scales, blood pressure monitors, electrocardiography (ECG) monitors, glucose meters, fitness equipments, social networks, imaging systems, and several other web resources. Data collection from these diverse sources will not yield correct and meaningful results until the syntax and structure and meaning of data are properly understood. Only correct understanding of semantics will help us to build intelligent applications or mash-ups. For this to happen, it is very important to ensure that semantics of data must be present as a part of data itself and not a part of application logic which could get buried in application silos.

Scale, data volume, and performance of data: As more and more devices are getting integrated into the IoT system, more will be the amount of data which will get ingested, stored, and analyzed in order to derive meaningful inferences. The type of data which is getting ingested will also vary, for example, some medical devices will generate image data whereas some others will generate video data, and so on. This will present a classic big data problem which will render standard architectures and platforms insufficient for handling them. The performance requirements of these applications/devices will also vary which will further add on to the complexity of data-handling mechanisms in the IoT health care ecosystem.

Rapid evolution of applications: As new use cases and business models emerge, medical devices with advanced capabilities will start getting created. This amounts to the fact that new applications and other software components require constant upgrade by specialists with specific technology and medical domain features. Many applications will be developed using a crowd-sourced model, and these applications in turn will be used by the end-users from an app market place like a play store, for example. Hence, there is a need to develop platforms and technologies which have the capability to sustain such a crowd-sourced model of application development and consumption.

Data privacy: Data which are collected from health care devices should be protected from unauthorized access. These data should be used only for those purposes for which the patient has given permission. Policies and processes to ensure that only authorized persons and applications will have access to data should be strictly followed.

Need for medical expertise: It is very critical to ensure that data which are captured from health care devices are interpreted correctly, and patients should not be given an opportunity for self-diagnosis. Diagnosis using data should be done with the help of automated decision support systems, where rules are made available by qualified doctors for each patient condition.

Future Trends for IoT in Health Care

In this section, some of the futuristic and interesting use cases of IoT in health care are discussed.

Ingestible Sensor

Ingestible sensor is the sensor technology which is made available in the form of a pill. The pill is made of ingredients which are present in normal food, and the sensor gets activated only on ingestion. This sensor-based pill is consumed along with other prescribed medications by tracking the exact time of ingestion of the pill in order to track compliance to medication. The sensor in the pill gets powered on by the fluids which are present in the human body. There is no battery or antenna present in the pill.

Once the pill is swallowed, fluid chemical reaction in the stomach activates the sensor and provides power which is required for the operation of sensor. This sensor which stays in the patient's stomach provides real-time updates on how the patient responds to medicine. No other types of diagnostic tests are required for these patients. Hence, these types of pills would be very useful for patients who take medicines for chronic diseases.

After activation, sensor also generates and transmits a unique number. Along with the unique number, the ingestible sensor also transmits various body parameters, activity, and rest patterns to the user's mobile device. These parameters from the mobile device are passed on to a central gateway from where it is sent to a secured data server. All the authenticated agents get necessary information from this data server.

The high-level architecture of ingestible sensor is summarized in Figure 10.5.

Digital Medicine

In case of digital medicine, the medicine itself goes digital. Digital medicines will resemble the medicines of present day with only an additional component: a tiny sensor which can provide vital information about medication-consuming behaviors and responsiveness of body to the medicine along with several other body parameters which may need to be tracked. These sensors are only activated when they come in contact with the acid present in the stomach.

Digital medicines will revolutionize the health care industry because of the capability to track and report a patient's vital body parameters on a 24/7 basis. Digital medicines are in various stages of development, and they have not yet received FDA clearance.

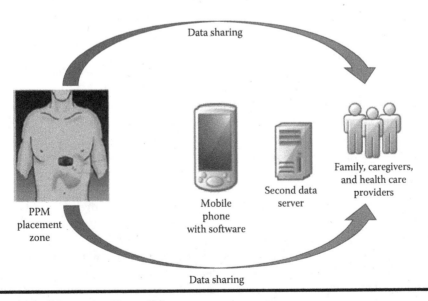

Figure 10.5   Architecture of ingestible sensor.

Mobile Apps in Health Care Sector

Some interesting mobile apps in the health care sector are discussed in this section.

Medscape: It is a very interesting mobile app which acts as a medical resource for over 3 million medical professionals in the United States. It provides extensive coverage of medical news and research in 30 different specialties. It caters to a wide range of audience starting from a practising doctor to a medical student. If you are looking for an app that offers comprehensive clinical reference content, reference information of drugs on 8000 brands, herbals, and supplements, a drug interaction checker, 129 medical calculators, formulary information on 1800 insurance plans, a disease and conditions reference of 30,000 clinical references, a procedural reference, medical news, continuing medical education courses, and a robust medical directory of physicians, pharmacies, and hospitals than this is the right app for you [1].

Ambulatory: It is a robust app which provides a workflow to doctors in order to track from the beginning to the end of a patient's visit to their practise. This app works on both iPhone and iPad. It is very ideal for use in iPad in order to gather information from patient, review past patient records, and write prescription for medicines.

3D4 medical: This app uses 3D technology to explore virtual human body and provides great learning experience for medical professionals. This app is very useful for health care professionals who are either learning about human anatomy for the first time or for those experts who want to review certain areas of a human body for detailed study/examination.

Neuromind: This app is very useful for neurosurgeons, and it is available free of cost for Android and iPhone users. The app provides high-resolution diagrams of different areas of brain that can be used as a powerful reference tool for surgeons. The diagrams can also be zoomed in to provide clear and comprehensive insights for its users.

iRadiology: This app offers a free catalog of over 500 radiology cases and is a very good tool for medical students who want to increase or improve their knowledge of radiology.

Cloud and Big Data Analytics in the Health Care Sector

Huge mountains of digital information are being created on a daily basis. These include diverse forms of data-like text, audio, video, and images. The proliferation of mobile devices into the daily lives has in fact created a data deluge. It is very surprising to note that majority of digital data has been created only in the last two years. This is the information landscape in general. Now if we look at the health care specifically, in 2012, the worldwide health care data were 500 petabytes. By 2020, the health care data are expected to multiply by 50 times and will be approximately 25,000 petabytes. The graph given in Figure 10.6 shows the amount of data which is generated by various industry sectors. It is very evident that health care sector is in the forefront of data generation.

The legacy storage systems and conventional technologies are not equipped to store and manipulate this massive amount of data. Hence, it is the need of the day to devise specialized mechanisms to store and handle these huge piles of data cost effectively. In addition to this, health care sector is under lot of pressure to lower the infrastructure costs by embracing new systems which provide good and secure data-sharing features for storing electronic medical records. Traditionally, health care sector has been very slow in adopting new technologies, and many hospitals retain their IT infrastructure longer than the defined time span of these equipments. The need to adopt electronic medical records and the pressure to adopt cutting edge technologies have led to an increase in interest in the adoption of cloud-based service options for the health care

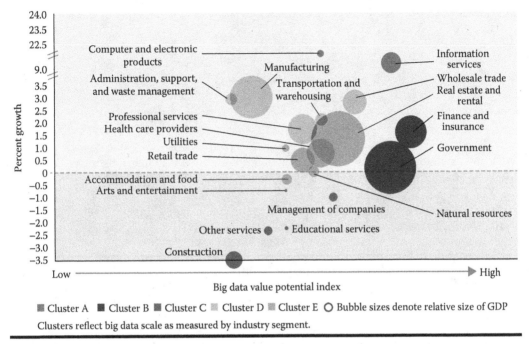

Figure 10.6   Amount of data generated by various industry sectors.

sector. Hence, cloud-based services are increasingly beginning to be adopted and used by health care organizations across the world. Big data analytics is of immense value in the health care sector because of the huge amount of large-sized data sets which are generated by the health care sector.

Cloud Services in Health Care Sector

Present day health care organizations are in tremendous pressure to cut down infrastructure cost and replace their existing aging infrastructure. In addition to this, heathcare sector generates huge amounts of data on a continuous basis like electronic medical record (EMR) and other patient-related data like scanning reports which have huge sizes. For storing and managing such huge amounts of data, significant investment is required by the health care organizations.

Cloud computing provides lucrative options for the health care organizations to implement new technologies for diverse aspects like electronic management of health care records which otherwise requires significant infrastructure investments. Health care organizations can utilize the services offered by cloud service providers to replace their aging infrastructure with new applications and solutions which offer more flexibility.

The main use cases of cloud computing in the health care sector are summarized in Figure 10.7.

Electronic Storage of Medical Records

Diverse types of health records are maintained by health care organizations, and most of them require huge storage space. In addition to the huge storage space requirements, there are many health care-related compliance controls which are imposed by the legislatures of various countries

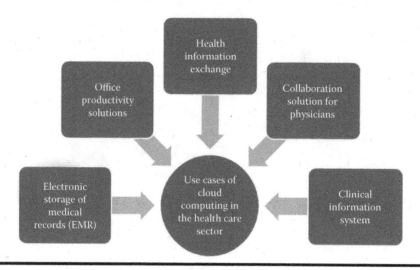

Figure 10.7   Use cases of cloud computing in health care.

across the globe. These aspects also need to be followed by health care organizations while maintaining the health care records. Electronic storage of medical records service offerings by cloud service providers comes as a boon to many health care organizations, and it provides the following benefits to them:

- No capital expenditure and only operating expenditure.
- Compliance-related aspects are taken care of by the cloud service provider as a part of service level agreement.
- Offers high levels of scalability to store huge amounts of health care data.

Office Productivity Solutions

Most of the organizations invest heavily on the infrastructure that is required for storing email and other office-related documents. In many cases, because of the legal restrictions, emails of employees need to be maintained for extended durations even after they leave the organization. This would further add to the infrastructure cost incurred by organizations. A cost-effective solution which is adopted by organizations to solve this problem is to store old emails in low-cost storage options, and this process of moving old emails and documents to the low-cost storage devices is called archiving. Many cloud service providers offer archive as a service to help organizations to maintain their archives without any additional investment. In the context of health care organizations, patient records of patients who have not visited them for a long time can be archived and stored as a service with the cloud service providers.

Health Information Exchange

Many cloud service providers are in the process of building heath information exchanges. These are portals for exchange of health care-related useful information by various health care organizations for the benefit of the public and other players in the health care sector. This is an arduous task as it requires bringing together many organizations in a common forum to share and collaborate with one another for their mutual benefit on a nonprofit basis.

Collaboration Solution for Physicians

There is a shortage of expert physicians across the world. In order to overcome this, telemedicine is used widely by the health care providers. Using telemedicine, expert doctors share their expertise using video conferencing in order to perform complex surgeries and help in the diagnostics of rare diseases. Many cloud service providers have started providing services which could be used to host video conferences which are required for telemedicine. This service comes as a boon to make telemedicine available in remote and disaster-prone areas.

Clinical Information System

Clinical information systems are required by the health care providers to maintain the notes of doctors, keep track of laboratory test which are prescribed to the patients, and ensure that the appointment slots of various patients are maintained accurately so as to ensure that the patients have a seamless health care experience. Many times, clinical information systems which are maintained locally by the health care providers run into problems making them unavailable for use for extended durations. This will incur significant delays in the treatment of patients. Nowadays, many cloud service providers offer clinical information system as a service, and this ensures that the systems are available for use 24 × 7, and this ensures zero waiting time for the patients and enhances their experience with the health care providers.

Big Data Analytics in the Health Care Sector

Different types of data get into health care systems from wide range of devices like fitness devices, genomics research, social media networks, and a variety of other sources. Most of this data have huge sizes, and they are of different formats which include both structured and unstructured types of data. Hence, big data analytics has also found a lot of traction into the health care sector off late. If big data analytics is used effectively in the health care sector, it can provide lot of benefits like:

■ Detection and prevention of infections at an early stage
■ Providing right kind of treatment based on the correct identification of disease symptoms
■ Early identification of new types of pathogens
■ Devising new drug discovery mechanisms against the new type of pathogens

There are different stakeholders for the application of big data analytics in health care sector. Each of them has a different expectation about the outcome of big data analytics in the health care sector. The different stakeholders are summarized in Figure 10.8.

Patients: They want an application which would provide them a dashboard to compare the services and the associated costs of the various health care providers. This would help the patients to choose the most cost effective health care provider for them.

Researchers: They want to use big data analytical tools to perform predictive modeling and other types of sophisticated statistical analyses in order to derive valuable insights and find out ways to solve unsolved problems which exist in the health care sector.

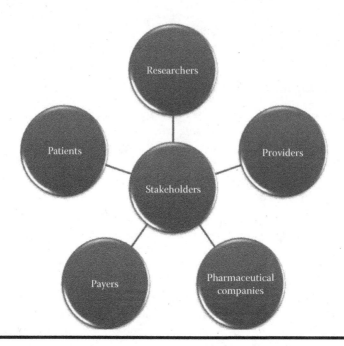

Figure 10.8   Stakeholders of big data analytics in health care sector.

Pharmaceutical companies: They want to use big data analytics to identify the causes of diseases quickly, identify candidates for specific types of drugs, and design efficient clinical trials in order to prevent failures. Pharmaceutical companies are also interested to use big data analytics to predict future disease trends so that they channelize their drug discovery attempts in those directions.

Providers: They want to use big data tools and technologies in order to get quick and real-time access to patient information. This will help them in their decision-making process and will in turn go a long way in providing timely and quick medical care to the patients.

Payers: They want to use big data to help them stratify population risk and guide them to adopt more sustainable business models that would promote their growth and development.

The different use cases for big data analytics in health care are shown in Figure 10.9.

Support Research in Genomics and Other Health Care Projects

Genomics is the branch of genetics which uses a combination of deoxyribonucleic acid (DNA) sequencing methods and bioinformatics in order to analyze the structure and function of genomes. Genomics has been the starting point of the big data revolution in the health care sector and holds lot of promises to facilitate personalized medicine. There are many health care organizations which are using big data analytics for genomics, but each of them is using a different approach. Some of the approaches which are adopted by some leading health care organizations are discussed below.

Genome Health Solutions (GHS) uses its expertise in the area of genomics to create a network of doctors and technology providers who can use genomics to devise a new standard of health care in order to treat patients who are suffering from cancer and other diseases. Following are the approaches used by GHS in order to facilitate this:

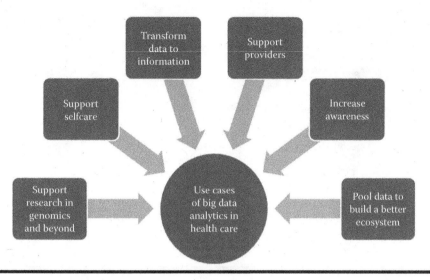

Figure 10.9   Use cases of big data analytics in health care.

- Designs and uses genomics oncology workflows that have the capability to guide patients to the right type of doctors at the correct time. The workflows are also designed in such a way that they will also provide right kind of diagnosis and treatment options for the patient.
- Develops education resources and decision support systems which can be used by patients and health care professional on diverse genomics topics.
- Provides consulting on genomic medicine and also develops diverse types of solutions for health care organizations.

GNS Health care uses REFS™ (reverse engineering forward simulation) in order to build mathematical cause-and-effect models. REFS is a scalable framework which uses super computers to construct causal models. These models are built from observational data, and they form the basis for the creation of visual interactive simulations. This framework also helps researchers to find out outcomes for different types of interventions. The different steps of the process used by GNS health care are summarized in Figure 10.10.

NextBio combines large public with private data sets to enable new-omics discoveries [1].

- Assembles vast amounts of curated and annotated clinical and molecular data enabling clients to make unique discoveries that would not be possible with their own private data sets alone.
- Uses big data technology to make correlations between the billions of data points from the public domain with private genomic and clinical data sets.
- Delivered as software as a service (SaaS).
- A rich set of application program interfaces (APIs) enable clients to integrate NextBio within their workflows.
- Current clients include pharmaceutical R&D and academic medical centers.
- Initial focus on oncology, now expanding into metabolic and autoimmune diseases.

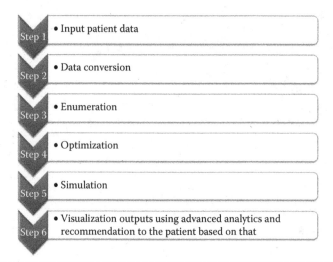

Figure 10.10   Process steps in GNS Healthcare.

Transform Data from Information

The most important requirement in the health care industry or any other industry is to transform data into useful information. This task becomes all the more complicated if the data which comes in are unstructured data. Converting the unstructured data into machine understandable and manageable format is the key to enable data-driven decision management in the health care sector. Explanatory analytics is a variant of analytics which uses a collection of tools that are based on data mining, cluster analysis, statistics, machine learning, text analytics, and natural language processing (NLP) to mine data for patterns and meaning [2].

Use of Explanatory Analytics by Predixion Software

Predixion Software is a health care organization which uses predictive analytic software that is hosted in cloud in order to uncover patterns which are present in hospital data sets. These patterns are mainly used to prevent patient readmissions. The analytic software used by Predixion works in the following manner:

- Pulls data from a wide variety of sources. Uses a combination of data mining and machine learning algorithm-based analytical tools to generate predictions.
- Uses a predictive analytics algorithm to assign a risk score to the patients which helps them to identify patients who have a risk of readmission. The results are about 86% accurate.

Use of Big Data by Health Fidelity

Health Fidelity uses NLP to convert unstructured data into information which is later on used as inputs by analytical and compliance applications (Figure 10.11).

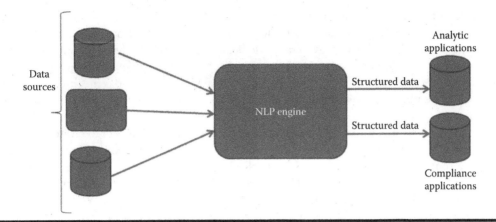

Figure 10.11   Architecture of NLP System.

Supporting Self Care

Another interesting use case of big data analytics in health care is helping patients to understand and keep track of their health parameters. This is done with the help of mobile applications which are equipped to track certain body parameters of an individual. Individual will also have options to enter additional health-related information. This information is transferred to an external health care service provider (with the individual's permission) who will use analytics to predict the onset of diseases and to advise appropriate corrective and preventive measures to the individual.

Numerous mobile applications are available for tracking health care parameters. Some of the applications are platform-specific, and they are available as free downloads from the application store. Some other applications require an amount to be remitted to the service provider before downloading and installing the application. Some examples of mobile health care applications were discussed in the previous chapter on mobile devices. Some other mobile application examples which are specific to cloud and big data are discussed below.

Supporting Self Care with Ginger.io

Ginger.io is a cloud platform which offers health care-based services by collecting real-time active and passive data from patients through their mobile phones. These collected data are used by doctors, family members, and caretakers to monitor and manage the health of patients. The novel approach used by this health care service provider uses a combination of machine learning and predictive modeling techniques to identify changes in normal behavior and lifestyle patterns which could predict the onset of some diseases or predict the possibilities of a disease getting worse.

Support for Providers

Providing support to the health care providers is one of the most interesting use cases of big data in health care sector. Providers always have less time, more money, and information, and they face immense competition in the health care sector. Many applications are being developed by the various service providers to help providers in the health care sector. The main challenge in dealing with the providers in the health care sector is their lack of flexibility to user interface changes and resistance to adopt new technology changes. However with the increasing pressure in the health care provider ecosystem, present-day health care service providers are embracing new technologies and applications to better support their customers (patients).

One Health Solutions is using a combination of social and hospital data to create and update health records in real time. This is done with the help of flexible APIs which can pull data from both the sources. This is one of the first health platforms which uses a combination of social media and hospital data for the benefit of patients. It also has necessary security measures to protect privacy of the data. This platform also supports the following addiction-related disorders such as smoking, alcohol, and drugs. It includes features for chronic disease management, overall wellness, and stress management, and patient care advice for specific diseases. This platform has several customers at present like health care providers (Figure 10.12).

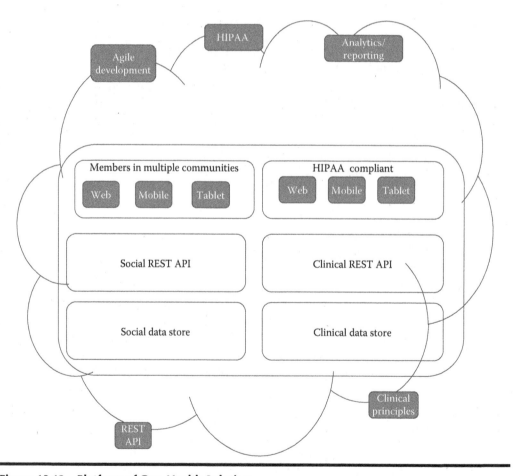

Figure 10.12   Platform of One Health Solutions.

Increase Awareness

Big data is providing increased awareness which helps to solve a wide arena of problems. Some of the common problems which are widely prevalent nowadays are as follows:

- Presence of counterfeit drugs in the market and lack of techniques to differentiate original and counterfeit drugs
- Lack of techniques to predict outbreak of epidemics or other diseases
- Lack of systems which provide proper preventive health care advice

Big data platforms and solutions for health care industry help to remediate all the above-mentioned problems because of their capability to assimilate data from large number of data sources and run predictive calculations on the data.

Sproxil Uses Big Data to Identify Counterfeit Drugs

Sproxil is a health care application which uses big data to identify counterfeit drugs. This is done by attaching pin codes to drug packages. These pin codes can be queried with the help of the service provided by the Sproxil to differentiate between real drugs and counterfeit drugs.

Sickweather LLC Uses Social Media to Track Disease Outbreaks

Sickweather LLC uses posts on social media networks to predict outbreaks of specific diseases in specific areas. It also offers disease forecast news to its users which is very similar to weather forecasts. Following are the key benefits of this service:

- Keeps citizens aware of disease outbreaks in their areas so that they can take appropriate precautions to safeguard them
- Provides features which will help citizens to add disease-related information pertaining to their areas
- Offers advice to the citizens about the various medication options which are available to handle diseases

Pool Data to Build a Better Ecosystem

Big data platforms help data from several sources to be combined to derive valuable insights about various aspects which are related to the health care sector which was never possible before because of the presence of disparate data sources. One typical example is IBM Watson which is known to be the most advanced processor for natural languages on earth, and this capability was demonstrated during its participation in Jeopardy competition.

IBM Watson comprises 21 supercomputer subsystems. Following capabilities of Watson facilitate very quick and accurate diagnostics and decision-making:

- Deep content analysis
- Evidence-based reasoning
- Natural language processing

IBM Watson has 16 TB of memory which will help it to store huge amounts of data. These data include patient-related information and all types of documents pertaining to different aspects of health care. IBM Watson has the capability to read 200 million pages of text in just three seconds, and it can also recall each and every word as and when required later on. Watson will pool in data from diverse sources like family history, patient history, disease symptoms, and so on in order to help doctors in their diagnostics and treatment.

Conclusion

Health care industry is facing a myriad of problems due to aging infrastructure which is incapable of handling the huge pile of data which is generated in the health care sector. Apart from that, health care organizations were not in the forefront for new technology adoption because of cost concerns. This has added on to the multitude of problems which are faced by them. Nowadays, patients are very demanding in terms of the quality of health care treatment they receive and also in terms of their experience with the health care providers. Patients are no longer ready to accept delay due to situations like unavailability of clinical information applications, incorrect appointment schedules with the physicians, and so on. This has further added on to the pressure which is experienced by the organizations in the health care sector. IoT technology holds lot of promises for health care sector. The main dimensions for the usage of IoT in the health care sector are the following:

- Clinical care
- Remote monitoring

These two aspects were discussed in detail in this chapter. Other interesting use cases of IoT in health care sector like virtual consultation, mHealth, and care for aging population were also discussed in this chapter. The foundation technologies which are required for using IoT in the health care sector were also discussed in this chapter. The challenges which are posed by IoT usage in the health care sector were discussed in this chapter. Some interesting health care mobile apps which are available in the market are also elaborated in this chapter.

Because of wide range of problems, present-day health care organizations have started embracing recent technologies like cloud computing and big data analytics. Cloud computing provides a lot of cost benefits for health care organizations. The use cases of cloud computing for health care organizations were discussed in detail in this chapter.

Majority of the data which is generated by the health care sector are good candidates to be treated as big data because of the huge size of the patient documents. If analytics is applied to this big data, very useful insights can be derived from them which can offer a wide range of health benefits to patients by detecting outbreak of diseases at an early stage, offering expert medical advice to patients based on the real-time monitoring of their body parameters, and so on. The use cases of big data analytics in the health care sector were discussed in detail in the second half of this chapter.

References

1. https://getreferralmd.com/2013/10/essential-health care-apps-2013/.
2. Big Data in Health care Hype and Hope, a white paper by Bonnie Feldman, Ellen M. Martin & Tobi Skotnes.

Chapter 11

Smart Use Cases of IoT

Abstract: By the year 2020, we are expected to have 7.6 billion people and approximately about 50–75 billion connected objects. What does this figure indicate? The number of connected devices will soon surpass the number of human beings who are present on earth. This figure itself throws light on the plethora of opportunities that IoT and its allied technologies offer to mankind. The key objective of using the IoT technology is for the transformation of objects into smart objects, which can make our lives easy. When we see around us, we have immense number of objects which belong to various diverse domains. So how do we categorize them into broad groups in order to quantify the benefits which are offered by them? That is what we have attempted to do in this chapter for the ease of highlighting the underlying technologies and the business benefits offered by them. The three broad categories, which we have considered in this chapter, are the following:

- Industrial use cases
- Consumer use cases
- Governance use cases

Under industrial use cases, we have mainly focused on two broad use cases:

- Smart energy
- Smart transportation systems

Under consumer use cases, we have mainly focused on the following:

- Smart homes
- Smart buildings
- Smart education systems

Under governance use cases, we have mainly considered smart cities. Some other use cases like smart airports and smart healthcare systems are dealt with as separate chapters.

Introduction

Smart use cases of IoT can be broadly classified into three main categories as depicted in Figure 11.1. We will be examining each of these classes of use cases in detail in this chapter.

Governance Use Cases

The most prominent use case that comes in this category is smart cities. The ultimate objective of smart cities is to improve the quality of life of its citizens. The key underlying technology that forms the foundation of smart city is IoT. Next question is how to design smart cities using IoT? The key features of smart cities, which are realized using IoT technology, are the following:

- Orchestration: It is vital to collect data pertaining to various domains of the city which will help us to understand the pain points faced by the citizens. This data is mainly collected with the help of sensors and other types of data gathering equipment, which form the foundation of the IoT ecosystem.
- Interconnection: One of the main problems that exist in cities is the lack of co-ordination between the various city domains, which in turn contributes to their working in individual siloes. It is very important to ensure proper co-ordination and data sharing among the various city domains. For this to happen, it is mandatory to devise techniques that enable one city domain to send, receive, and view data of other city domains. This can be done by collating the IoT data and providing a dashboard view of the entire city, which can be accessed by the various city agencies/domains for appropriate decision-making.
- Intuitiveness: It is the ability to use the data collected from sensors and other IoT devices in order to make intelligent decisions for the welfare of the citizens. For example, data collected from weather sensors may be used to predict the onset of a cyclone in a specific region. Intuitiveness lies in how quickly and efficiently this information is used in order to ensure safety and security of citizens by devising appropriate strategies.

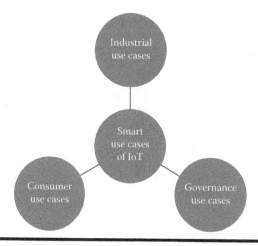

Figure 11.1 Smart use cases of IoT.

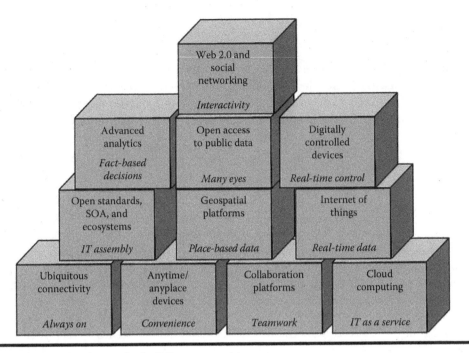

Figure 11.2 Technologies for building smart cities.

The other key technologies that are used for building smart cities (Figure 11.2) are discussed below.

Ubiquitous Connectivity

Ubiquitous connectivity is the essential infrastructure requirement of the twenty-first century. Access to high-bandwidth, low-cost Internet is the need of the day to meet the present-day ever-increasing demand of connectivity. The network infrastructure to support wireless networks is the vital component for the effective use of mobile broadband and all other city services, which are made available to the citizens via mobile devices. As per the most recent statistics, the number of mobile broadband users as of 2014 is about 2.3 billion. The mobile network and mobile device ecosystem with the fully equipped infrastructure in place is the ideal platform to support the sophisticated network of information sharing and communication required to operate a U-city as almost half the population of the earth now uses mobile devices as their main mode of communication.

NETWORK BROADBAND INFRASTRUCTURE DEVELOPMENT

One of the key epitome of national broadband investments is the Australian government's A$40bn network investment in a project called National Broadband Network (NBN). This project has a fiber-to-the-home open-access network, which will provide 93% of Australia's homes with 1 Gbps connectivity. The rest of the homes will have a network with 12 Mbps connectivity, which is provided with the help of satellite and other wireless technologies. The project started in the year 2010 and is expected to take eight years for its completion.

Omnipresent Devices

The present-day smartphones can be termed as any time any place devices (omnipresent) because of the large-scale penetration of mobile broadband networks. Smartphones help us to access any type of content from anywhere. The smartphones have also radically changed the way we interact with the Internet. Facebook recently announced a statistics that they have about 680 million active mobile users in addition to a billion active monthly users. The various smartphone platforms, the supported applications, and play stores have virtually changed the way people perceive about various applications and their availability.

Collaboration Platforms

Present-day unified communications and collaboration platforms have the capability to bring together many technologies like voice, SMS, calendars, online meetings, video conferencing, and other office automation tools, which were earlier available as standalone tools. These integrated communication and collaboration platforms can create borderless organizations, boost the productivity of the teams, and facilitate mobile or remote working concepts. Latest generation of online meetings and high-resolution video conference systems, such as Cisco's WebEx and IBM's Lotus Sametime meetings, serve as genuine alternatives for face-to-face team meetings.

Cloud Computing

Cloud computing refers to a model of computing in which IT-based services are made available to the end users on a pay-to-use basis over the Internet. The IT services include software applications, platforms for building applications and huge amounts of storage space, and other infrastructural components, which are needed by the various organizations. Cloud computing provides a cost-effective and viable alternative for deploying IT-based city strategies and IT-based society initiatives, as the usage of cloud models for deploying these services does not involve any capital expenditure. Cloud-based technologies are already creating a wave of IT innovation across the cities because of the cost effectiveness and simplicity of use, which is offered by this model.

CLOUD COMPUTING FOR SMART CITIES

The European Platform for Intelligent Cities (EPIC) is a pioneer project in the new "Smart Cities" and "Living Labs" initiatives and it is funded by the European Commission. This project experiences many technical stumbling blocks because of which the implementation could not be fully completed. But with the support of IBM's Cloud infrastructure, they were able to provision a web-service delivery platform successfully for the EPIC project.

Open Standards and Service-Oriented Architecture (SOA)

One of the most important trends in the IT industry is the evolution and development of open standards and published interfaces for development of applications in various domains. This had paved way for various vendors to produce diverse types of hardware and software systems using the concept of Service-Oriented Architecture. This approach facilitates a more dynamic approach where applications can be created or assembled by using the existing components and web services rather than having them built as monolithic projects. This is an intelligent approach using which various solutions that are required for the various aspects of city automation can be built and deployed rapidly avoiding huge amounts of waiting time, which would have been the case otherwise.

Geospatial Platforms

The availability of free or low-cost geographic information systems like Google Maps makes visualization of city-based information very easy. These maps when combined with Global Positioning System and other location-based services available in smartphones have made it very easy to manipulate and visualize various aspects of a city under different scenarios. For example, if there is an accident at a specific location in a city, maps and other location-based services available in a smartphone can be used to locate the nearest hospital and the type of facilities available in the hospital like the number of emergency units, ambulances, and so on. These maps provide a powerful mechanism to visualize and locate various assets, resources, and services, which are available in a city. These provide highly effective ways for engaging citizens in planning dialogs.

Neogeography in Smart Cities

Nowadays, there has been an increasing trend to create and distribute various types of geographic information publicly not by government or organizations but by individuals. The availability of low-cost geographic information systems and widespread use of Internet are the two factors that could be attributed to this stupendous development in the field of maps. These maps developed by individuals are many times personalized for their own use, and they provide useful information, which can be used by other organizations to create their own set of maps. For example, Wikimapia and OpenStreetMap are creating a huge footprint of geographic information that can be used by other individuals or organizations. Google Earth is encouraging individuals to develop their own geospatial applications using their own set of geospatial data. These trends could be taken as indicators for the democratization of the mapping and has paved way for the emergence of another stream called citizen science. Citizen science refers to an activity in which a group of citizens get engaged in some kind of scientific activity, for example, bird surveys, and then denote them on the maps accurately using the time and space co-ordinates. This field of geography where the maps are freely generated or used by the individuals for generation of different kinds of data is referred to as *neogeography*. This neogeographic data provides a lot of value proposition for the U-City government and city agencies as they provide lots of additional data, which would help the city officials in urban planning and mapping.

Internet of Things (IoT)

The Internet of Things (IoT) is the future of Internet technologies in which every object around us will be connected using some kind of network to every other object, and they will also have the capability to send and receive data from them. Our living, relaxing, and working environment is envisioned to be filled up with a variety of electronic devices including environment monitoring sensors, actuators, monitors, controllers, processors, tags, labels, stickers, dots, motes, stickers, projectors, displays, cameras, computers, communicators, appliances, gateways, high-definition IP TVs, and so on. Apart from these, all the physical and concrete items, articles, furniture, and packages will become empowered with computation- and communication-enabled components by attaching specially made electronics onto them. Whenever we walk into such kinds of empowered and augmented environments lightened up with a legion of digitized objects, the devices we carry and even our e-clothes will enter into calm yet logical collaboration mode and form wireless ad hoc networks with the inhabitants in that environment. For example, if someone wants to print a document in his smartphone or tablet, and if he enters into a room, where a printer is situated, then the Smartphone will begin a conversation with the printer automatically and sends the document to be printed. Thus, in that era, our everyday spots will be made informative, interactive, intuitive, and inspiring by embedding and imbedding intelligence and autonomy into their constituents (audio/video systems, cameras, information and web appliances, consumer and household electronics, and other electronic gadgets besides digitally augmented walls, floors, windows, doors, ceilings, and any other physical objects and artifacts, and so on). The disappearing computers, communicators, sensors, and robots will be instructing, instigating, alerting, and facilitating decision-making in a smart way, apart from accomplishing all kinds of everyday needs proactively for human beings. Humanized robots will be extensively used in order to fulfill our daily physical chores. That is, computers in different sizes, looks, capabilities, interfaces, and prizes will be fitted, glued, implanted, and inserted everywhere to be coordinative, calculative, and coherent yet invisible for discerning human minds. In short, the IoT world will make our environment a much smarter and intelligent environment. This in turn will be the main technological pillar of smart cities.

Advanced Analytics

The amount of data is exponentially increasing every year and according to the most recent IDC digital universe study, by 2020, about 33% of the data generated will contain information that will provide valuable insights if they are analyzed using appropriate analytical tools. These valuable insights could be derived from the data patterns, which appear in social media usage, correlations in scientific studies, which happen in diverse fields, trends in security footage, and so on. These insights can in turn fuel the fact-based decision-making process, which will help to monitor and control various events based on real-time statistics. The rise of cutting-edge analytical systems will be fueled by the fusion of the IoT concept (which generate more data) and cloud computing platforms (which provide scalable processing power and massive storage capacity).

Open Access to Public Data

Nowadays, most of the government agencies are moving toward a trend for making their data publicly available for their citizens. This is because they have realized the importance and the need for "many eyes to view data." This has fueled the creation of many applications, which help the citizens to derive valuable insights from these government generated data sets, which in turn will equip citizens to take diligent decisions.

Digitally Controlled Devices

With the IoT concept increasingly becoming prominent, there is an increasing tendency to develop equipments, which are capable of controlling all appliances and devices digitally using some kind of a centralized system. There is also an increased focus on integrating these centralized monitoring and controlling system capabilities to laptops and smartphones. This will help in the easy realization of concepts like computerized homes, buildings, vehicles, and other infrastructure systems. For example, it would be very easy to control all aspects of home automation like lighting, cooling, electrical appliances, and so on centrally and remotely with the help of a smartphone. These digitally controlled systems are the key building blocks for the conceptualization of intelligent construction systems, intelligent building systems, and intelligent transport systems. A key concept to be kept in mind during the design of these systems is that the different components of automation like sensors, actuators, and so on need to be finalized during the design phase itself, so that they can be integrated with the systems at the time of development. After development, it is very difficult to retrofit these components into the system.

Social Media Networking

The proliferation of Web 2.0 technologies have offered lot of capabilities for people to communicate and collaborate with one another. The Web 2.0 technologies have also fueled the growth and development of communities for diverse aspects like knowledge sharing, communication on topics of common interest, and so on. The soaring response of the people to social media sites like Facebook and Twitter have led to an offshoot of social media analytics called sentiment analytics, which is used extensively by the government agencies to understand the sentiments of the citizens on various decisions and policies of the government. These social media networking platforms are an inevitable component for building social networks in cities.

Strategic Governance Framework for the Implementation of Smart Cities

The strategic governance framework for the implementation of smart cities is shown in Figure 11.3.

The four layers mentioned in Figure 11.3 provide a logical framework, which can be used by the various city leaders to evaluate the various implementation options that are available in hand. For example, the first layer is about city objectives; if the prime objective of city leaders is to conserve water based on some metrics, which denoted poor water conservation (layer 2), then they have to examine the possibility of building an interconnected water network in the city, which has all the features to track real-time water consumption patterns of the citizens (layer 3). After making decisions about the design and the features, which are required in the water conservation system, the city leaders will have to examine similar water conservation measures and systems, which are implemented in other cities and derive the best practices so that they can be incorporated in the system under consideration. Each of the layers in the framework is detailed below for a better understanding.

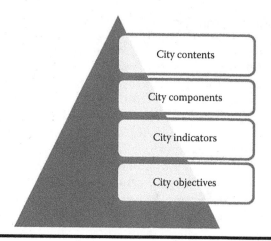

Figure 11.3   Strategic governance framework for smart city.

City Objectives

City objective is an important catalyst in the decision-making process. In order to arrive at the city objectives, the various domains that exist in the city like finance, energy and utilities, education, public safety, health care, and so on should be examined in detail to identify the sectors that need improvement. It is a vital aspect to include the citizen's views in the decision-making process in order to ensure that the entire cycle of evaluation and decision-making process is seamless. After analyzing the various domains, it is important to prioritize the sectors which need improvement and the amount of improvement which is required. This is a vital component which will finalize the city objectives and link them to the various projects, policies, and investments, which are planned for the city. While planning the city objectives, it is also very important for the city leaders to analyze the existing technological infrastructure and the present maturity level of a city that is whether it is a digital city, U-city, or so on.

City Indicators

Most of the times, city objectives are qualitative or empirical in nature. Hence, it is necessary to quantify them in order to arrive at various metrics. For this purpose, it is essential to link them to various existing and published city indicator indices. These indices benchmark the cities using well-defined and proved methodologies. Some of the standard city indicators which are available are Global City Indicators Facility (GCIF), Green City Index, and so on. Each of these indicators uses a different set of parameters for the evaluation of cities. Different cities may require different indicators based on their priorities and objectives. For example, if a city's objective is to improve the financial sector, then Green City Index might be appropriate.

City Components

At some point or the other, city objectives are linked to physical components, assets, resources, or locations. For example, if the city objective is to improve water conservation, then the following assets or resources are involved in that; some of them are as follows:

- Water network components like pipes, valves, and so on (asset)
- Water operators (resources)
- IT infrastructure (asset)
- Logistics for water operators (resources)

For the success of the laid out city objectives, it is essential to perform a detailed evaluation of the various components, which are a part of the system under consideration, and design a system to optimize the utilization of each system component.

City Content

Once all the other aspects of the city system under consideration are evaluated carefully, it becomes necessary to look at the multifarious implementations, which have been done in other cities across the world. It is necessary to do a careful examination of the various implementations in order to derive the pros and cons of the various implementations. It is very important to generate a framework comprising best practices from the various city implementations, which in turn could form the foundational component for the implementation of city objectives for the city under consideration.

FIRST SMART CITY IN THE WORLD

Songdo New city in South Korea is expected to be the first smart city in the world. Its construction began in 2008 and was completed in 2014. It is an outcome of the partnership alliance between South Korean Government and a private sector organization Cisco. This city is planned to have a unique urban environment where various computing devices like sensors and actuators are planned to be embedded across the entire city. This way it is planned to make these devices a part of everyday lives of citizens in an omnipresent and omnipotent manner. These technological components are integrated appropriately using wired and wireless networks in order to ensure that citizens anywhere in any part of the city will have access to them irrespective of infrastructure limitations. The computers used in different sectors will be interconnected through a series of networks, which includes wired and wireless, broadband systems, and sensor networks, which are ubiquitous in nature. This new way of engaging with the citizens is expected to instill new forms of participation in citizens, which would subsequently ensure increased transparency and democratization of services in the city.

Smart Industrial Use Cases of IoT

Industry use cases of IoT have the following common characteristics:

- Devices are machines operating in industrial, transportation, energy, or medical environment, which commonly form a part of this industry ecosystem.
- Data volumes and rates tend to be from sustained to relatively high.

- Applications that fall under this category are mission and or safety critical, for example, the failure of a smart grid has severe impact on our life and economy; the misbehaving of a smart traffic system can threaten drivers.
- Industrial IoT applications tend to be "system centric."

Intelligent energy conservation using smart grids: The following are some of the main challenges that exist in the energy and utilities sector:

Excessive growth in customer demands: By 2050, the demand for energy will almost be double when compared to the existing consumption. Finding new avenues for energy generation and satisfying the demands of the ever-increasing customer base is a real challenge.

Increase in infrastructure cost: In order to meet the growing needs of energy, it is necessary to invest in creation of new infrastructure and at the same time spend in maintaining the existing infrastructure. With the limited budgets, it becomes very difficult to accomplish these tasks. This task becomes all the more challenging because of the fact that most of the existing energy infrastructures and power generation systems have become worn out and obsolete because of aging.

Regulations imposed by government rules: Governments across the globe continuously bring out new laws with the aim of reducing carbon footprint and greenhouse gas. This in turn imposes lot of restrictions on the agencies that are involved in the energy and utilities sector.

The majority of these problems, which are faced by the energy and utilities sector, can be eliminated by the use of IoT technologies in this sector. It is estimated that by 2020, there will be around 1.5 billion IoT-enabled devices in the utility sector, majority being in smart meters.

Smart meters are a new type of energy meters. They have the capability to track the power consumption and send the readings to the energy supplier periodically. The duration at which the readings are sent back to the energy supplier is configurable. These smart meters help the consumers to keep track of their power consumption and will help the energy companies to create custom usage plans according to the consumption patterns. This will also provide a lot of customer satisfaction as the customers can track their usage on a regular basis. This in turn will help in the reduction of calls to the customer care centers.

Mobile devices and mobile network operators also have a vital role to play in this ecosystem. Their role can be summarized as follows:

1. They can provide connectivity among various devices and the utility operators by leveraging their existing wireless network infrastructure.
2. They can deliver energy consumption alerts to mobile devices, and in this way, it can provide a series of value-added services for the consumers.
3. They can leverage the existing capability to transfer data and bill end users in order to exchange huge amounts of real-time data and discrete transactions.

In addition to this, NFC technology can be leveraged to make payment of bills using mobile devices.

Mobile devices can also be used as a part of the smart energy grid as well. Smart energy grid helps to monitor consumption versus demand on a larger scale. Sensors and other components, which are part of the smart grid, monitor the energy usage patterns of homes and other industrial buildings and they come out with patterns which depict power usage. These patterns help us to predict the times of peak usage, which in turn would help in the creation of real-time adaptive pricing plans, which can be communicated to the various stakeholders as alerts to their mobiles.

These options to track and analyze usage patterns help to balance load at peak times by using distributed energy storage and also help to prevent energy wastage during nonpeak hours.

The smart grid also allows consumers to give back the excess power that they have self-generated back to the grid, without any technical or regulatory barriers. By analyzing and understanding the energy demands, you can conserve more energy and you are better placed in terms of the decision to utilize alternative power sources.

An architecture for intelligent energy conservation (Figure 11.4) using IoT is given below.

The lowest layer pertains to the actual physical devices and contains sensors and other smart meters which are used to obtain data about energy conservation and usage.

The data from this layer are collected and sent to the next layer that processes it. Following are the main types of processing which are likely to happen on the data:

- Store the data in various meter data management systems.
- Route the data to various asset tracking and management systems if applicable. This in turn will be used to perform further analysis like the power consumption of various assets in a building, predict maintenance schedules for various assets, and so on.
- Analyze the usage patterns and the various usage scenarios.
- Use intelligence embedded in the platform in order to find out energy optimization techniques by finding out peak and nonpeak hours and the difference in the usage levels.
- Send message alerts to the consumers about their energy consumption levels and customized energy tariffs or plans, which may be beneficial for them.
- Route the excess power if available to various devices or other infrastructural components, which may need them.

The last layer is the presentation layer through which the processed data can be viewed by the consumers. Some of the commonly used options are mobile devices, tablets, citizen portals where the citizens can log in to view their usage, dashboards for the energy suppliers to get a consolidated view of usage of their customer base, and reporting tools for generating various types of reports. The various options available in this layer could vary from one service provider to another.

In short, smart grids can form an important part of the energy and utilities ecosystem. This in turn will deliver a lot of value-added services to the citizens and will help to transform a city into smart city by enabling intelligent collection, analyses, and usage of data.

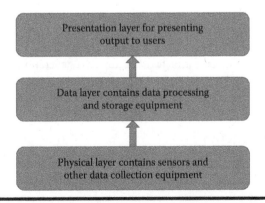

Figure 11.4   Architecture for intelligent energy conservation.

INTELLIGENT ENERGY IN PRACTICE

Ampla is an electric energy distributor, owned by Endesa Brazil, which provides electricity to 73% of the state of Rio de Janeiro and serves over two million customers. The rate of urbanization, the nature of the accommodation (slums), and the high crime rate led to an unsustainable level of energy theft and bad credit risk. A large number of customers did not have access to personal banking services and were limited in their ability to budget and manage their finances. Meters at residential and commercial sites were prone to tampering and to add on, bribes to employees encouraged fraud.

Ampla was averaging 23.6% energy losses on its network—reaching up to 52% in some areas. The result was a negative impact on the utility's profitability and a higher cost of energy passed through to its consumers. In 2003, Ampla began to roll out a pilot for a new mode of smart metering—located at the pole top—entitled Rede DAT. With Rede DAT, the consumption per household is recorded at the transformer and energy consumption data is communicated by the utility over a mobile network. Energy customers receive consumption data through their mobile phone. The pilot proved a great success with losses from theft reduced by more than 50%, the number of supply interruptions reduced by more than 40%, and lower operating costs. A wider roll out initiated providing hundreds of thousands of Ampla's residential and business customers with access to the Rede Ampla service.

Smart Lighting for Energy Conservation

Lighting is one aspect not to be taken lightly in the context of cities' energy needs. As we all know, buildings account for one-third of global greenhouse gas emissions and amounts to 40 percent of total energy consumption. Lights comfortably consume up to one-fifth of a building's total energy usage. Similarly, street lights, energy-guzzling billboards and advertisements at important junctions, electric signals at road joints, lightings for festivities and family confluences, and ornamental lightings at art galleries also gulp a lot of power at least for the night life. Therefore, technologies that make lights more energy efficient, customizable, and programmable for achieving more sustainable and vibrant cities are being given extra attention. Emerging lighting technologies are the next frontier in helping growing cities to reduce their energy consumption remarkably and to create more enjoyable landscapes for their residents. Undoubtedly, lighting is perceived as a low-hanging fruit toward substantial energy savings in buildings and urban infrastructures.

Lighting solution providers are brimming with confidence and bringing in a stream of innovation-packed and technology-driven smarter lighting solutions. Especially, sensors and actuators are extravagantly and intrinsically attached, thereby next-generation lights will be sensors intensive, interconnected, software defined, remotely monitored, and operated. Companies are working on an important theme to minimize ecological footprint through a host of energy-efficient systems.

Smart Lighting Approaches

As indicated above, at different levels and layers, energy preservation is being activated and accomplished. First of all, it is prudent to replace existing lights with energy-efficient lighting sources such as LED. Then, the automated management of lighting sources is another well sellable and workable option. That is, turning off lights when they are not needed and adjusting light levels to suit peoples' needs are the key ones. Having the automated control over lighting through proven technologies is the best way to go forward. Automation has been fast-penetrating into every tangible domain these days and the lighting field is not an exception to this overwhelming initiative across the globe. Thus, along with lights, lighting control solutions are gaining market and mind shares incrementally. New-generation lights are becoming software defined with the accumulation of wider variety of smart yet miniscule sensors and actuators. With the maturity and stability of wireless technologies, lighting is all set to be smart.

Lighting control systems could deliver the required amount of light according to the location and the time requirements. Lights can automatically turn on, off, or dim as per the changing needs. The control systems are the best bet for bringing the right and relevant changes to have optimal lighting everywhere at all times. Typically, lighting control systems have the following features:

- On/off and dimming controls
- Occupancy sensors to detect whether rooms are occupied
- Photo-sensors to detect the current illumination levels provided by natural and/or artificial light
- Scheduling that turns on, off, and dims luminaires at preset times
- A centralized control system interface (such as a wall panel or computer software) to manage all of the above
- A method of communication between the lighting equipment and control system
- A method of measuring, displaying, and responding to lighting energy usage
- Scheduling and timers

There are nimbler sensors coming up fast to empower control systems with enough firepower to speed up smart lighting.

- *Occupancy sensors*: Occupancy sensors are useful not only to address flexible working hours but also to control lights in areas with irregular usage patterns. When the sensors detect that someone has entered an area, the lights corresponding to the location in which the person is detected can be brightened to provide sufficient illumination. Occupancy sensors can also be used to create "corridors of light" to follow people like security guards and cleaners as they move through a building.
- *Photoelectric and daylight sensors*: One of the greatest areas of potential savings is to reduce lighting when illumination is already being provided through natural sources. When sunlight comes through windows or skylights, these specialized sensors can detect the level of natural illumination and dim or even turn off lights in the area. And as the natural light fades, the lights can automatically illuminate back up to the appropriate level. This helps not only to conserve lighting energy but also to reduce the amount of heat being emitted by the electric lights, which in turn can help save money on air conditioning costs.
- *Movement sensors*: In nonlinear activity areas (squares, car parks, residential streets, and places with a little nocturnal activity), the lighting can be dimmed to a minimum for most of the time. Using movement sensors, illumination levels can be raised as soon as a pedestrian or a slow vehicle is detected in the area. This light-on-demand capability enhances the safety and the well-being of the users while saving energy.
- *Speed and direction sensors*: Compared to movement sensors, a speed and direction sensor works with a wider detection area to classify the identified moving item following its speed

and its direction. This classification provides the right response according to predefined lighting scenarios. Solutions fitted with speed and direction sensors operate in large areas to ensure safety and well-being in the most sustainable way.

■ *Presence sensors*: Nowadays, it is becoming a common practice to leverage presence sensors inside buildings to switch on and off lights, thereby saving a lot of power and energy for a better future.

There are different situations and applications emerging wherein such kinds of lighting control system are of greater help:

■ *Task tuning*: Traditional lighting systems were often designed to maintain a consistent level of illumination across all areas all the time. This results in over-provisioning of lighting for many users and their tasks. Therefore, task tuning is an essential characteristic that allows facility managers, building owners, knowledge workers, and individuals to tune lighting levels in each area of a building via dimmable lights based on their requirements.

■ *Global as well as local control*: In the previous setup, every room in a building or house has separate switches for its lighting, and hence it requires someone to visit the place physically and operate those switches for switching them on and off. The recent lighting control systems can change this equation forever. That is, light control systems have decisive and delicate control over the entire building and are capable of controlling light settings collectively as well as individually. That is, a single light or multiple lights within a room, flat, floor, several floors, or the entire building can be simultaneously and remotely operated with just a click. This vastly improves the management cost and complexity. That is, the days of lighting flexibility, controllability, visibility, modifiability, maintainability, manageability, and sustainability are the hallmarks of next-generation control systems.

■ *Energy monitoring*: Monitoring and measurement lead to better management. With advanced lighting control systems, facility managers can access real-time and historical information about the usage of energy by light, room, zone, building, and more. This provides them with a set of tools for better decision-making, as well as the ability to test new strategies, verify results, and make changes over time to get the most energy savings out of their system. As real-time analytical systems are fast maturing, the extraction of real-time and actionable insights and the subsequent dissemination of comprehensive insights in time are laying a stimulating and sophisticated foundation for smart lighting environments.

■ *Demand management*: Increasingly, utilities are offering tremendous incentives for buildings to go beyond simple energy efficiency and reduce their demand for energy at peak times. Lighting control systems can tie into utility demand management and peak-day pricing parameters to temporarily reduce lighting usage.

Wireless Lighting Control Systems

This is the talk of the town. Although the current lighting control systems have been of tremendous help in energy saving, the capital, deployment, operational, and management complexities and costs are consistently on the rise. Therefore, by leveraging the noteworthy advancements in wireless communication technologies, next-generation wireless lighting control systems are being designed and deployed devoid of wires. The wireless nature completely decimates the need for wiring, eases the installation and use, enhances the extensibility, and so on.

Wireless lighting control systems utilize the powerful wireless technology to communicate commands between endpoints such as sensors, switches, and the stabilizers or LED drivers connected to lights. While traditional lighting control systems utilize a controller that is hard-wired to each device, a wireless system uses a controller with an antenna that communicates wirelessly between a set of devices. Each endpoint is wirelessly enabled, either directly by the device manufacturer or through an external wireless adapter. A software system provides managers or individuals with access to manage the system and change settings and policies, which are then routed through a controller to the individual endpoints. Wireless systems are often organized using the proven and potential "mesh" architecture. That is, the unshakable power of mesh network is that each device can talk to others in the network through a controller, and if there is a device failing or falling, then alternative paths can be chosen cognitively to route all incoming messages to the correct destination without any delay. The built-in redundancy of having multiple pathways available helps to make the mesh network robust and reliable.

In summary, the next-generation solutions for smart lighting have the following functionalities and features:

1. *Huge energy savings through a smart combination*: There are several praiseworthy smart lighting technologies forthcoming to make lighting robust, reliable, and rewarding. Lighting-specific software services are being conceptualized in plenty and deployed in remote clouds to be publicly discoverable, network-accessible, composable, and usable. On the other hand, the lighting hardware goes through a series of delectable transformations, miniaturizations, and so on. Instrumentation, integration, and intelligence have acquired special significance these days in designing personal as well as commercial devices, machines, and so on. Similarly, there are salivating improvisations in antenna, sensing, and actuation technologies. Communication has simply become wireless and hence vendors are highly optimistic about the grand success of wireless control systems in head-on meeting up all the existing and emerging challenges in the lighting segment. In short, technology-inspired solutions for smart energy are gaining momentum in the market. By smartly combining all the intrinsic innovations, the futuristic lighting solutions promise to offer huge energy savings of up to 85% and radically reduce the payback time of a new installation.

2. *Remote management and repair*: As lighting solutions are becoming more pervasive and attaining primacy, the management complexity is bound to go up remarkably. There are several cases and scenarios wherein remote operation of lighting arrangements is being insisted. For example, diversions and the closure of roads during maintenance bring in a whole series of inconveniences such as loss of money and time, increase in distances traveled, difficulties for residents, avoidable greenhouse gas emissions, and so on. Therefore, lighting solutions providers have expanded their solutions portfolio to monitor and access light installations independently and remotely to get the correct need and usage of lights and to proactively plan ahead in order to reduce all sorts of inconveniences to people as much as possible.

3. *Lighting on-demand*: The concept of on-demand lighting is fast on track as it has the wherewithal to considerably decrement energy expenditure. When the usage is at the low level, lighting at full illumination is a sheer waste of energy, which is incidentally becoming scarce, counterproductive, and expensive. There are occasions and opportunities wherein dimming of lights are expected. Any competent lighting solution with light-on-demand capability that can adapt the lighting to the real-time and real-world needs of the place, time, and users is definitely a boon for the betterment of societies. Each luminary level ought to be

configured individually with several parameters such as minimum and maximum light output, delay times from minimum to maximum, and the duration of on/off times.

4. *Reliability*: By monitoring every single lighting point, the advanced solutions proactively prevent failure by detecting operating issues (broken lamps, device temperature, power surges, and so on). Such pre-emptive nature goes a long way in positioning and prescribing control systems for massive adoption. If problems arise, the system switches to a default program ensuring that the lighting installation does not turn off.

Indisputably, lighting is one of the largest energy guzzlers on the planet. The most effective and easily attainable way to reduce the energy use is by turning off lights or making them dim at every opportune time. Lighting control systems can use multiple factors such as the occupancy level, available daylight and time of the day, and so on into account to decide the power needs. This sort of data-driven controlling provides significant energy and cost savings, a great level of flexibility and control for building owners and administrators, and above all, added comfort for occupants.

Finally, the traditional wired control systems have been limited by cost and complexity. Removing the cluttering wires delivers on the promise of lighting control by providing even greater benefits at a lower cost, and to a much broader set of potential customers. In short, wireless networking is bringing intelligence to a new generation of lighting control systems–helping companies take simple steps to save money and make our planet greener.

Smart Transportation Systems

Smart transport is another inclusive ingredient of smart cities. Travel for personal as well as professional purposes is very common, and is getting costly these days. All kinds of transportation vehicles are being prepared from the ground up or remedied for making driving simple and smooth while ensuring occupants' journey safe and useful by externally as well as internally incorporating all the right and relevant technology sophistications. Vehicles are increasingly becoming a tantalizing and trendsetting platform for ubiquitous infotainment, edutainment, and entertainment. Today's automobiles and their important components are being sensor attached facilitating them for remote monitoring, diagnosis, control, repairing, and maintenance. Sensors themselves are smart and are capable of forming ad hoc networking with one another on need basis (sensors are cooperative objects) in order to accomplish composite tasks that in turn automate one or more processes directly and fully. The underlying sensors-stuffed infrastructures, high-speed telecommunication networks, a bevy of enabling technologies, a growing range of sleek, handy gadgets, and a growing repository of cyber systems are being suitably readied to contribute individually as well as collaboratively to make all kinds of trips smooth, smart, safe, and secure. The persisting obligation is that the travel infrastructures and systems have to have very negligible impact on the environment.

Smart transports are gaining a lot of market and mind shares these days. Automobile companies, product vendors, and research labs across the globe are gearing up to bring in disruptive and transformative blueprints for next-generation smart vehicles that have less carbon footprint. Connected, sensor-laden, and insights-driven transports are the latest buzzes in the automobile sector. As automobiles are the main culprit in consuming a lot of precious energy (more than 70 percent of total oil getting produced) and in releasing a lot of carbon into our environment, vehicle manufacturers are seriously thinking of alternative fuels and vehicles. Electric vehicles are one important option described below in detail.

Electric Vehicles (EVs)

Economic and environmental pressures are continuously driving worldwide countries to electrify transportation. There are a plenty of electric cars on the roads these days and still there are some practical constrictions that come in the way of widespread usage. Technologies are forthcoming in order to overcome those barriers so that electric vehicles (EVs) will be more pervasive and persuasive for both commoners and governments in the years to come. EVs are more favorable for the environment and cheaper too. There will be more telling impacts as electric vehicles fundamentally change the way electric utilities function. There will be more intensive strains on electric utility infrastructures. Utilities need to have highly synchronized and competent solutions for facilitating the success of electric vehicles while minimizing any kind of risks and vulnerabilities. In short, the transportation getting electrified will have a series of influences as well as implications. The surging popularity of electric cars has already rekindled organizations to show more focused interest and investment in EVs. The main drawbacks and issues are being consciously identified and addressed through collaborative research initiatives and technology-inspired solutions.

There are some valid concerns on EVs. For example, on the part of customers, their main grouse is that electrical vehicles need frequent charging. Other important pain points are that certain limitations are imposed on car speed and size. Further on, it takes a considerable time to get fully charged. On the other hand, for electric utility service providers, infrastructure is the main stumbling block. Electricity charging stations and their associated infrastructures need to be in several places to facilitate the smooth passage of vehicles. Business models for utilities providing charging services need to be worked out to a win–win situation for both users and providers. The infrastructural considerations are very important. A single EV plugged into a fast charger can double a home's peak electricity demand, and hence it is very important to have a smart grid to effectively and efficiently manage EV charging.

A smart grid, the prime infrastructure for utilities, has the inherent capability of providing the much-needed visibility and power to protect the components, such as transformers, of distribution networks from being overloaded by EVs through continuous monitoring, measurement, and management. With a smart grid, utilities can fully adhere to customers' expectations while managing EV charging, collecting EV-specific metering data, applying customer and time-specific rates for EV charging, engaging consumers with information on EV charging, and finally collecting data for greenhouse gas abatement credits. Smart grids are therefore being positioned and prescribed as the silver bullet for all the ills of electricity management.

As the number of EVs is constantly growing, utilities can maximize the utilization of their infrastructure, create fruitful relationships with customers, and leverage EV communications investments for other energy initiatives. By bringing these transitions, there are better days for transportation electrification that can benefit all stakeholders including consumers, automakers, utilities, and the environment. Electronic transportation through smart grids and using electrical vehicles is to grow in the years to unfold due to its conduciveness to the human society.

Smarter Vehicles

As indicated in the beginning, transportation is a crucial cog in realizing smart cities. There is a cornucopia of novelties and ingenuities being investigated in the ever-growing transport sector. As discussed in the previous section, electrification of vehicles is one prominent aspect gaining a lot of market and mind shares. On the functional side, a variety of improvisations are being brought in as detailed below. Vehicles are increasingly connected, sensor laden, and extremely digitalized through the lavish and lustrous usage of IT. Hundreds of microcontrollers are being stuffed in advanced cars. All kinds of safety, security, simplicity, and smartness are being carefully embedded in modern-day vehicles to sharply enhance peoples' comfort, convenience, choice, and care.

New-generation in-vehicle infotainment system in sync up with an eye-catching and multipurpose dashboard has become the most indispensable module in any car. Automobiles are empowered through innumerable specialized sensors and actuators. A number of strategically sound advancements are happening silently to realize highly advanced and automated vehicles. Sensor-attached vehicle components send out their latest state and status update to the centralized infotainment systems for pre-emptive components' diagnosis and correction. Application developmental platforms, scores of enabling tools, and execution containers are very promising these days to orchestrate sophisticated applications for vehicles and their users. Cloud-based application stores are being formulated to store and maintain hundreds of vehicle-specific services and applications for worldwide vehicles.

People spend more time commuting to their offices, shopping malls with recreation facilities, and back to their homes. That is, people prefer much more in a vehicle than just pleasurable driving. That is, every moment of travel has become precise. The point here is to ensure occupants to be wirelessly connected with outside world at vehicular speed and to be entertained, educated, and informed. Vehicles emerge as the next-generation platform for ubiquitous learning, fruitful interactions, remote dictation, and purpose-specific collaborations. Vehicles are fast becoming software intensive, sensors, microcontrollers and actuators laden, connected (locally as well as remotely), highly digitalized, and continuously empowered by a growing array of cloud-based vehicle-specific services. The in-vehicle infotainment system is being positioned as the core and central gateway for realizing smarter vehicles.

Luminaries and visionaries foresee a bright future for creative thinkers and software engineers in flawlessly conceiving innumerable smart services exclusively for the transportation sector. There are many game-changing initiatives such as autonomous driving, vehicle-to-vehicle communication, vehicle-to-cloud integration, and so on. There are specialized software solutions for on-demand assistance to drivers while driving, parking, looking for landmarks, fuel stations, food joints, and so on. There are natural interfaces made available for drivers for hands-free interactions.

The Technological Implications on Vehicles

It is very clear that there are several technologies emerging to ensure and sustain a number of notable disruptions and transformations in our life journey. By carefully embracing these versatile technological developments, every business vertical is preparing for hitherto unheard and unforeseen acceleration, augmentation, and automation in their service deployment, delivery, and usage models in the days to unfold. Product vendors are envisaging a series of smarter environments and establishments as direct fallout of the undiminished stream of insightful and impactful technologies. That is, every organization is bound to be smarter in their cost optimization through resources rationalization, customer-centricity, fresh revenue generation, dynamic capacity addition, conceptualization of multifaceted services to retain their customers, and attract new clients and consumers. In this section, we are to discuss the possible and pragmatic derivatives in the fast-expanding transport sector.

Insights-Driven Connected Vehicles

The first and foremost outcome of these promising and potential technologies is connected vehicles. The second is vehicles empowered with timely, context-aware, and data-driven insights. There is a consistent increase in the number of diverse and distributed data sources pumping data from all directions that can be smartly captured and subjected to deeper and decisive analysis to extract all sorts of hidden patterns, tips, alerts, opportunities, associations, and so on for vehicle owners, operators, and so on to formulate both short-term and long-term plans. There are two prominent and dominant ways in which vehicles can be connected.

Vehicle-to-Vehicle Connectivity

This is the real-time exchange of decision-enabling data among vehicles. Such dynamic data exchange at a critical point offers ample opportunities for significant improvements especially on the vehicle safety aspect. By interchanging valuable vehicle data regarding its speed, direction, position, and location dynamically, the much-anticipated V2V communication capability enables vehicles to sense any impending threats and hazards with a 360 degree view and visualization of vehicles in synchronization with other vehicles' position. This vehicular interaction results in issuing appropriate advisories to drivers to proactively take counter-measures to avoid or to mitigate the intensity of crashes. There are specific sensors and GPS systems collaboratively working to arrive at accurate data (latitude, longitude, and so on) to make cars self-, surroundings-, and situation-aware.

The vision for V2V connectivity is that eventually all vehicles (sports cars, multiutility vehicles, buses, container trucks, goods wagons, and so on) on the road will be able to connect and communicate with one another beneficially. The data that is being generated and transmitted in time facilitates the production and delivery of next-generation applications for enhanced safety. The much-anticipated V2V communications will come handy in drastically reducing accidents on the road.

Vehicle-to-Cloud Connectivity

Clouds are being positioned as the best-in-class infrastructure (servers, storage arrays, and network modules) for effectively and efficiently hosting a variety of platforms. Integrated Development Environments (IDEs) and rapid application development (RAD) tools for application and service design, development, debugging, deployment, delivery, and decommissioning (end-to-end software lifecycle tasks) are increasingly finding their residence in clouds. Further on, advanced platforms comprising standards-based service integration, orchestration, management, governance, monitoring and billing, resource provisioning, capability planning and scaling, and enhancement capabilities are being migrated to cloud environments. Not only generic but also specific services implementation platforms are found to be efficient in clouds. That is, platforms for building, deploying, and delivering social, cloud, mobile, embedded, analytics, and even vehicle-specific applications are becoming very popular these days due to the unprecedented maturity and stability of respective technologies.

Not only platforms, but there is also an increasing number of service registries repositories in clouds. These multidevice services are opening up fresh opportunities for a bevy of everyday environments such as homes, hospitals, offices, vehicles, and so on. Thus, the raging cloud idea is bringing in real sophistications for humans. For example, the Ericsson's Multiservice Delivery Platform provides infotainment, applications, and communication services in Volvo's new cars. Drivers and passengers are bound to benefit from a growing array of cloud-enabled services and applications. This platform enables drivers, passengers, and the car to connect, access, and leverage all kinds of services (navigation, driving assistance, parking management, edutainment, and entertainment) being made available in the cloud. Content providers will have agreements with vehicle owners and other ecosystem partners such as Internet radio providers, road authorities, traffic patrols, ambulances, insurance providers, emergency services and cities' governments, toll-road operators, and so on in the near future.

Today's smartphones are loaded with many unique and universal applications which help accomplish a number of personal needs on-the-go at vehicular speed. Similarly, all kinds of in-vehicle infotainment systems and dashboards are being provided with a growing set of new-generation applications to significantly empower car drivers as well as occupants to be productive. With the increased push for more electric cars, car manufacturers will offer more digital and connected services like the ability to remotely warm up the car or to manage the charging time of the battery. In short, driving will be made more safe, secure, enjoyable, and educating. Whether it is a joy ride or goods transportation, future vehicles will be supplied and supplanted with converged, cognizant, and cognitive services. Insights-driven driving will become a common thing. The in-car infotainment system connects with Google Maps and Places in order to appropriately guide the car driver to reach the destination in a risk-free fashion on time. Car care can go to its next level with applications allowing users to check vehicle diagnostics, status, maintenance schedules, and driving behavior on a home computer or smartphone.

Vehicle Connectivity Platforms, Tools, and Applications

Developmental platforms are found in plenty in the IT world for producing a variety of applications (generic as well as purpose-specific). With connected vehicles being realized, integrated platforms play a very vital role in producing newer applications and enabling them to run efficiently.

Sprint Velocity Connect opens the way for automakers to explore innovative ways to serve their customers.

- *Fleet management*: Vehicle manufacturers could help fleet operators easily adopt value-added services provided by the manufacturer at any time after the vehicles are purchased. This includes applications that track and monitor vehicle locations, improve dispatch and routing, evaluate driving behaviors, and more efficiently manage vehicle maintenance.
- *Rental car features*: Automakers might offer rental car companies the opportunity to learn more about the status of their cars, such as distance traveled and vehicle maintenance needs.
- *Dealership sales*: Auto manufacturers could consider using Sprint Velocity Connect to add services for its dealership network, including new ways to differentiate previously owned vehicles with connected services.

Airbiquity's Choreo Service Delivery Platform is a global, open, and scalable cloud platform that is designed for automotive manufacturers, wireless carriers, tier one suppliers, and third-party app developers to deliver connected services to a better connected customer and driver. Choreo can be modularized for numerous applications including mobile integration, embedded connectivity in a vehicle's head unit, electric vehicle optimization, and fleet management. Airbiquity's smartphone application integration platform links vehicles to a range of mobile applications and cloud-based services delivered via Airbiquity's private cloud platform, delivering third-party applications like Yelp and Trip Advisor in addition to popular infotainment applications. Drivers will be able to download the applications to their smartphones and tether them to select vehicles via Bluetooth or USB using the Airbiquity platform, with in-built support for a range of popular music, social media, and navigation applications.

SiriusXM's in-vehicle telematics solution will provide vehicle owners 24/7 emergency support for accidents, stolen vehicle tracking, and roadside assistance, along with a host of additional services to be announced at a later date.

Use Cases of Technology-Inspired Vehicles

It is expected that there will be more internal as well as external systems voluntarily collaborating and contributing for the risk-free provision of enhanced care, choice, convenience, and comfort especially to car users. The prominent components in next-generation cars could be smartphones, in-vehicle infotainment systems, remote clouds and a repository of car-specific services, and all kinds of tangible car parts. There will be more number of elements in future cars for accurately providing precise and perfect automation. These modules can be interconnected among themselves as well as with the centralized car infotainment module inside the car and also with any remote cloud servers over the Internet. The infotainment system inside will be multifunctional and have multichannel communication capability with a comprehensive yet compact dashboard.

It is logical to expect every worthwhile part of vehicles to be self-, surroundings-, and situations-aware. Vehicle components can find other related entities within the car dynamically on need basis and network with them in ad hoc mode in order to enable seamless co-operation and co-ordination for producing specific and emergent functionality. In short, the extreme connectivity capability of service-enabled vehicle modules, infotainment system, car users' smartphones, and a growing collection of specific as well as generic applications on on-demand, online, and off-premise cloud platforms enables them to have fruitful interactions. Precisely speaking, futuristic cars emerge as the most elegant and evolving platform for ambient entertainment and remote monitoring besides facilitating business transactions with those empowered elements which find, bind, and leverage each other's unique capabilities and competencies in runtime.

An Assortment of Vehicle-Centric Applications

Due to the positive uptake in the eccentric connectivity and service-enablement aspects, there arise a series of nimbler services for vehicle users: information, knowledge, transaction, and physical services. These days a growing collection of travel-centric services (location maps, driving and parking assistance, fuel station identification, automated toll collection, road and traffic details, edutainment, entertainment, and context-aware services and applications) are being developed and hosted in geographically distributed clouds for ubiquitous access and leverage. Car maintenance and repair, postsale support, insurance, and so on are the leading services being facilitated with the spectacular advancements in the vehicle technology. Today, mobile users are bombarded with a number of mind-boggling mobile technologies (HTML 5) and services. Similarly, for vehicle users, owners, manufacturers, insurers, and service providers, there are specific platforms such as vehicle application development and service delivery platforms (SDPs) for simplifying service conceptualization, concretization, registration, discovery, accessibility, subscription, usage, billing, delivery, management, and enhancement.

Knowledge Services

Knowledge engineering through the fast-maturing discipline of big data analytics is on the rise. There are big data analytics platforms (on-premise as well as cloud-based) to efficiently perform data analysis. There are different visualization tools for the presentation of actionable insights.

All kinds of data originating from vehicles on the road and their body parts are getting collected and streamed to real-time data analytics platform wirelessly for generating real-time insights that enable drivers, manufacturers, insurance companies, and other stakeholders to confidently consider and perform pre-emptive measures. The vehicle infotainment system will evolve as the centralized data gathering, aggregation, and transmission engine. Any brewing problem in any part of the vehicle can be pre-emptively identified and users are accordingly notified to act on the identified needs instantly and insightfully. Car security, sanctity, and safety are fully guaranteed with the technological advancements.

There are newer in-vehicle systems and connectivity solutions for next-generation vehicles for activating and augmenting all the electronic devices and vehicle components within. The decision-enabling data includes the wheel air pressure, engine alerts, lubrication, temperature alert, and so on. The latest cars are being fitted with Automatic Emergency Braking Systems (AEBS), Air-Bag Systems (ABS), multifaceted sensors, and disposable as well as replaceable body parts (wheels, lights, brake shoes, wipers, windshield, tyre, bumpers, wheel alignment, and so on) to significantly enhance the production and delivery of smart and sophisticated telematics applications.

Finally, all kinds of fake components can be stopped from being incorporated in vehicles by scrupulous mechanics and repair persons in place of original components. All kinds of impending risks and existing problems can be immediately notified to the right owner at right time to attend them in time. The energy efficiency of vehicles can be measured and managed automatically so that cleaner and greener vehicles will see the reality sooner.

Big Data Analytics for Smarter Transports

As vehicles become networked devices, automakers and wireless telecommunication carriers are able to collect different kinds of data, especially driver-generated data such as automotive performance and driving patterns. Further on, hundreds of sensors embodied in every advanced vehicle produce a large amount of tactic as well as strategic data to be carefully collected and subjected to a stream of polished investigations that ultimately assist handsomely to finalize the viable means of bringing in more assuaging automations. In a nutshell, the amount of data generated by smart cars is expected to grow dramatically over the upcoming years. This emphasizes the need for high-performance data analytics solutions in order to conceptualize cognitive services for next-generation vehicles. The combination of significant rise in the production of connected car sales and a growing amount of information coming from the connected cars will result in the collection of some 11.1 petabytes of connected car data by 2020 according to a new IHS Automotive study. Today, auto manufacturers are systematically using the data they collect from connected cars for things like internal diagnostics, location, and vehicle status. Thus, the real-time analytics of vehicles' data is to seed a breed of innovations for car makers, owners, and occupants.

With the faster proliferation and penetration of promising connectivity technologies, vehicles are being empowered to have newer capabilities through seamless and spontaneous interactions with other vehicles on the road, vehicle manufacturers and mechanics, insurance providers, product vendors, and so on. With cloud connectivity, a bevy of nimbler services and applications can be made available to drivers and occupants. Besides making driving simpler, safer, and satisfying, those inside vehicles could be more productive through e-learning, e-commerce, entertainment, gaming, and infotainment. Application platforms are emerging and inspiring worldwide software developers to conceptualize and concretize sophisticated services for vehicles and their users. The platform features include data and application integration, data-driven knowledge discovery and dissemination, information visualization, and so on. Through these vehicle-specific and cloud-based application development platforms, a growing array of next-generation vehicle-enablement services and applications are being created and deposited in cloud application stores to be accessed and used by smartphones and in-vehicle infotainment systems and dashboards to substantially elevate the comfort, care, choice, and convenience levels of vehicle owners, drivers, and occupants.

The Approaches for Smarter Transportation

As discussed above, having a smart transportation is essential for all the cities across the nations to facilitate a smooth and safe movement of people and goods as it has been solidly proven that a well-developed and maintained traffic takes the city toward its economic prosperity and provides a better quality of life for city dwellers. Any badly managed traffic clogs the system and brings it into an unpalatable halt.

With the brimming population, the city transport system has to be well-oiled through the adoption of resilient technologies. In recent decades, significant increases in urbanization have placed an unbearable burden on most traffic systems around the world. Clogged traffic systems deter economic activity as well as drain resources. They also waste energy and release significant amounts of carbon dioxide (CO_2) into the atmosphere. The traditional approach to solving the perpetual traffic problems has been to increase the capacity of the underlying infrastructure by building more roads and bridges and to increase the number of vehicles providing transportation services such as more public buses and trains.

These initiatives have visibly reached their limits in existing cities. Cities need an altogether new approach to tackle these perennial challenges. There are smart city solutions and service providers, and IBM is prominent among them. The IBM's smarter traffic solution enables the following:

■ Predict demand and optimizing capacity, assets, and infrastructure
■ Improve the end-to-end experience for travelers
■ Increase operational efficiency while reducing environmental impact
■ Ensure safety and security

Predict Demand and Optimizing Capacity, Assets, and Infrastructure

A smarter traffic goal is to improve capacity utilization and make better use of existing investments in assets and infrastructure. This goal is accomplished by using the following methods:

■ Collecting data on real-time network conditions
■ Identifying mobility and usage patterns
■ Predicting demand
■ Encouraging a balanced use of available infrastructure and capacity

This goal is accomplished by using both near real-time analytics and historical data analysis on the data that is being captured from roadside sensors and on-board equipment. This is supplemented by data that is obtained from other agencies. Analysis helps traffic management centers and transit service providers make well-informed decisions about the use and optimization of transportation resources. The data collected can also be used to provide value-added services and propose new methods for funding road use and maintenance such as through congestion charges. These methods can be used to shape travelers' behavior to aid the environment.

Improve the End-to-End Experience for Travelers

Smarter traffic seeks to improve the traveler's experience. For example, the solution can provide driving directions, inform travelers of route changes because of an accident or traffic congestion, and suggest various public transit options. The solution can also offer incentives to travelers to balance the use of public versus private transportation systems. The data being collected from distributed and different sources are being smartly leveraged to give a newer experience to travelers. There will be close collaborations between traffic monitoring centers and ground-level traffic.

Increase Operational Efficiency While Reducing Environmental Impact

Smarter traffic is to enhance the operational efficiencies of individual transportation agencies, transit operators, and commercial fleet operators. Through tracking of assets, optimizing equipment availability, and ensuring maintenance effectiveness, smarter traffic techniques reduce waste, improve reliability, and remove operational costs for transportation operators.

Smarter traffic is bound to provide visibility of agency operations to other participants in the value chain. Included in this group are parts suppliers and maintenance crew contractors, enabling more effective collaboration. In addition, smarter traffic aids planning and decision-making, resulting in significantly enhanced operational efficiencies throughout the system.

Ensure Safety and Security

To ensure the safety of citizens, information from on-board vehicle-equipped sensors is integrated with information from sensors on-board other vehicles and from infrastructure sensors on roads, curbs, and rail tracks. This technique improves the range of warnings that the vehicle driver receives, such as wrong lane entry, slippery road, and proximity alarms. Moreover, sensors that monitor conditions on infrastructure such as roads or tracks help to detect hazardous conditions so that maintenance crews can respond effectively. Through smart surveillance systems, rail lines, airports, and roadways can be constantly scanned to detect suspicious activities.

Road safety has been a tricky issue for governments, city officials, and car manufacturers. There are promising vehicular technologies toward that. The latest wireless communication technologies facilitate the formation and firming up of vehicle ad hoc networks (VANETs) that ensure wireless intravehicular interactions and interactions between vehicles and infrastructures. VANETs are attracting a growing attention due to the promising important applications from road safety to traffic control, infotainment, and entertainment for passengers. Car accident prevention, safer roads, pollution, and congestion reduction are some goals of VANETs. The deployment of an efficient system to manage warning messages in VANETs has important benefits, from the perspective of both the road operators and the drivers. Efficient traffic alerts and updated information about traffic incidents will reduce traffic jams, increase road safety, and improve the driving in the city. Furthermore, from the sustainable and economic perspective, real-time traffic alerting will reduce the trip time and fuel consumption and therefore decrease the amount of CO_2 emissions. Traffic software systems are extensively deployed in order to make and manage traffic intelligently. Vehicles, traffic servers, and road infrastructures are interconnected on-demand to guarantee road safety. Smart traffic is an indispensable component of smart cities.

Intelligent Transport Systems (ITS)

Intelligent transport systems (ITS) have been around for a while now. But in the context of smart cities and with the availability of several competent technologies such as cloud, mobility, machine-to-machine (M2M) communication, and real-time analytics, new-generation intelligent transport systems are emerging with additional capabilities:

- Integrated fare management
- Enhanced transit/customer relationship management
- Traffic prediction
- Improved transport and traffic management
- Traveler information and advisory services
- Road user charging
- Variable parking pricing

In short, cloud-based software services for the transport sector, the power of doing real-time analytics out of heterogeneous data getting gleaned from different sources, the consistent growth of device ecosystem for drivers, vehicle users and operators, police officials, traffic monitoring personnel, and so on, the ad hoc nature of purpose-specific smart sensor/actuator networks, and so on are laying a sustainable platform for the next-generation smarter transports.

Connected Cars

Connected car is another prominent use case of IoT. The connected car enables the exchange of information between the car and its surroundings via the Internet to devices which are a part of the IoT ecosystem. The vehicle's connection to the Internet is provided either by a transmitter/receiver unit built into the vehicle itself or via third-party systems such as smartphones (Figure 11.5).

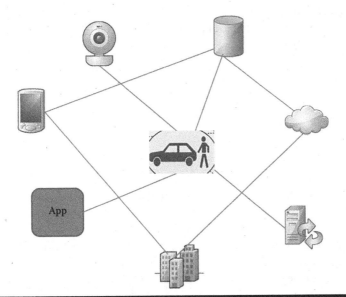

Figure 11.5   Connected Car.

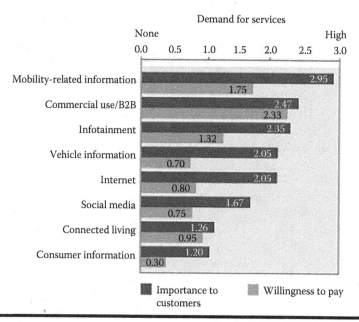

Figure 11.6 Drivers for connected cars.

Some of the main drivers for connected cars are summarized in Figure 11.6 [1]. Following are some of the key features of connected cars:

- Remote diagnostic service
- Infotainment
- Safety services
- Social media communication
- Customized speed-related advise/inputs for specific terrains
- Capability to communicate with other sensor-enabled cars in the vicinity and provide value-added inputs like traffic congestion in the approaching roads, road block due to accident, and so on

Consumer Use Cases of IoT

Following are some of the features of the consumer use cases of IoT:

- Devices are consumer devices, such as smart appliances, for example, refrigerator, washer, dryer, and personal gadgets such as fitness sensors, Google glasses, and so on.
- Data volumes and rates are relatively low.
- Applications are not mission or safety critical, for example, the failure of fitness gadget will make you, at worse, upset, but will not cause any harm.
- Consumer IoT applications tend to be "consumer centric."

Some of the smart IoT use cases which come under this category are discussed below.

Smart Homes/Buildings

The Key Drivers for Smarter Homes and Buildings

The first and foremost application of notable developments in ambient intelligence (AmI), Internet of things (IoT), cyber-physical systems (CPS), cloud computing, ubiquitous sensing, intuitive and natural interfaces, sentient materials, and autonomic communication disciplines is to insightfully establish and sustain smart homes. Besides handy and trendy devices, there are eye-catching multifaceted yet miniaturized devices hitting the market these days. In addition, device integration and collaboration standards are being schemed and specified for original equipment manufacturers (OEMs) and devices' components makers for enabling devices to coexist and cooperate purposefully. Machine interfaces are budding and boosting machine-to-machine (M2M) communications toward formulating and firming up innumerable facilities and functionalities that in turn make machines to be faithful and innovation-filled assistants for people in their daily chores. People-centric applications are being consistently unearthed with the maturity and stability of technologies. Self-, surroundings-, and situation-awareness are being realized with empowered devices and smart objects in capturing and conveying decision-enabling information. There are push- and pull-based approaches for information capture. Information visualization tools and techniques are other important factors in building smarter environments.

Context awareness is an important ingredient for conceptualizing and concretizing people-centric services. Smart sensor networks, sensor fusion algorithms, device-to-device (D2D) interactions, device-to-cloud (D2C) communication, devices subscribing cloud-based smart home services at runtime, the seamless collaborations between smartphones and smart home instruments, the increased usage of data analytics for usable knowledge, the spontaneous integration between physical things at homes with remotely hosted cyber applications through device middleware, and so on are some of the highly discussed and documented aspects for accelerating the realization of smarter homes.

There are standards-complying device integration appliances, gateways, proxies, and brokers toward smart homes. Smartphones are bound to play a very vital role in shaping up the idea behind futuristic smart homes. Embedded and embodied intelligence goes a long way in designing connected and cognitive devices for people empowerment. Internal as well as external connectivity are being insisted as devices and devices services are different places. Especially, with cloud emerging as the core and central place, scores of personal and professional applications are being hosted in multiple clouds (public, private, and hybrid) to be provided as services for worldwide users. Clouds are being positioned as the next-generation IT environment for deploying, subscribing, delivering, and enhancing several sorts of software platforms and applications as services. In a nutshell, the widespread acceptance of highly competent technologies and devices has laid a stimulating foundation for smarter environments.

The Prominent Use Cases of Smarter Homes and Buildings

The following use cases are the prominent ones eliciting greater attention from people. More and more compound applications can be realized by intelligently combining discrete use cases (Figure 11.7):

1. Elderly care/ambient-assisted living (AAL)
2. Home security (people and properties security and safety)
3. Remote monitoring, diagnostics, repair, management, maintenance, replacement, and even retirement of a growing array of home-bound devices and smart objects
4. Energy-efficient green homes through microgrids

5. Entertainment, infotainment, and edutainment
6. Enhanced comfort, convenience, choice, and control applications

Smarter Homes and Building Elements

A growing variety of smart sensors, software solutions, connected devices, cloud services, and so on is set to enable us in multiple forms and formats in our living and working environments. That is, apartment flats, office buildings, manufacturing floors, and other action-centric, lively and lovely places are to be extremely technology-empowered and splurged. Ordinary and everyday objects are being digitalized, connected with one another locally and cloud-enabled. That is, everything in our places is systematically empowered with relevant and right intelligence through the addition of functional modules internally as well as through the integration with remotely hosted software applications. Even communication networks are being stuffed with appropriate competencies and capabilities to simplify and streamline the task of making every common, casual, and cheap thing smart, every kind of electronics smarter, and ultimately people the smartest.

All kinds of deficiencies and dependencies are getting eliminated through a host of measures such as standardization, adaptors, bridges, middleware, common APIs, and so on. Plug and play capabilities are being guaranteed. Devices are manufactured accordingly and modernized to connect and collaborate with one another in realizing people-centric tasks. Information capture, aggregation, share and leverage for actionable insights, information dissemination, and visualization concepts are continuously strengthened toward the vision of smarter environments. Devices are being produced using the highly shining factory model/industrialization. All high-end IT servers, storages, and networking solutions are being commoditized. This is being achieved by identifying and abstracting all kinds of common functionalities, features, and facilities. Finally, all

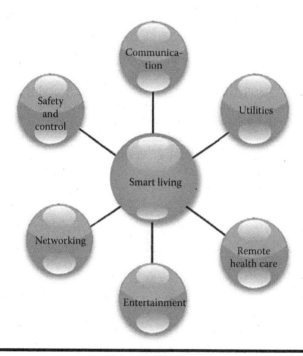

Figure 11.7   Use cases of smart homes.

are implemented through software. The important aspects such as modifiability, replacement, substitution, accessibility, consumability, and so on are easily incorporated in software. Policies and knowledge bases in synchronization with knowledge manager are emerging as the new-generation mechanism for establishing autonomic infrastructures. The software route is being recommended for policy establishment and enforcement. The growing list of prominent home networking and automation solutions includes the following:

- *Security and surveillance elements*: Security sensors for windows, doors, motion, glass break, and smoke can provide critical security information about our homes while at home or in office. IP-enabled security and surveillance cameras are very important for ensuring tight, unbreakable, and impenetrable security. Intrusion detection and prevention systems are other prominent security modules.
- *Heating, air condition, ventilation, lighting, and shade control systems*: Comfort is emerging as the decisive factor in next-generation homes. Novel machines are being instrumented to take care of different environmental conditions. Connectivity among various home-bound devices including light switches, wall-mounted touch panels, and so on is being ensured. Robots come in different varieties for doing physical works for people. Cloud-enabled robots will be a critical and crucial cog for humans in the days to unfold.
- *Computing and communications devices*: A wider variety of compute machines ranging from personal computers (PCs), notebooks/laptops/tablets, Wi-Fi routers and gateways, wearables, and smartphones are being extensively used in home environments these days. With the seamless convergence, computer and communicator are often interchanged.
- *Entertainment, edutainment, and infotainment media systems*: There are several notable innovations in media technologies and products. Today we boast about fixed, portable, mobile, and handheld devices for ubiquitous learning. IP-enabled television sets are being produced in mass quantities sharply increasing our choice, convenience, and comfort considerably. Web, information, and consumer appliances are plentiful and pioneering. Technologies for social sites (web 2.0) are on the climb facilitating higher productivity for humans and for forming digital communities for real-time knowledge sharing. Home theaters, hi-fi music systems, DVD devices, game consoles, and so on are for entertainment.
- *Home networking*: All passive, numb, and dumb items are getting transformed into digitalized objects. These are being wirelessly and wisely networked with all sorts of household electronics in order to connect and communicate (directly [peer-to-peer] or indirectly [through a middleware]) to derive competent people-centric, networked, and embedded e-services. Home networking infrastructures, connectivity solutions, bridging elements, and other brokering solutions are being found more in numbers these days. Home network also can connect with the outside world via the pervasive Internet. This enables remote monitoring, management, and maintenance of home devices. Car multimedia, navigation and infotainment systems, and parking management systems, and so on too gets connected to household systems directly or via a box-based middleware for real-time connectivity and interaction.
- *Home access control*: E-locks are emerging as a crucial security measure for home access control.
- *Kitchen appliances, wares, and utensils*: Modular kitchen comprising all kinds of electronics emerges as a key factor for smarter homes. Coffee makers, bread toasters, electronic ovens, refrigerators, dish washers, food processors, and so on are being enhanced to be smarter in home environments.
- *Relaxing and mood-creating objects*: Household items such as electric lamps, cots, chairs, beds, wardrobes, window panes, couches, treadmills, tables, and sofas besides the objects in

specific places such as gyms, spas, bathrooms, car garages, parking slots, and so on are being linked together in ad hoc manner in order to greatly enhance the experience of users.

■ *Health care systems*: Medicine cabinets, pills and tablets containers, humanoid robots, and so on are occupying prime slots in guaranteeing good health for home occupants.

There are statistical estimates and forecasts that there will be hundreds of microcontrollers in any advanced home/office environments in the days to emerge. The much-touted edge technologies such as cards, chips, labels, tags, pads, stickers, smart dust and motes, specks, and so on are enabling the onset of powerful environments. That is, our everyday places are going to be stuffed and saturated with a growing array of event producing and consuming entities, environmental monitoring and measurement solutions, controlling, actuation and notification systems, integration fabrics, hubs and buses, and visualization displays and dashboards, networking and automation elements, scores of handhelds, wearables, portables, implantables, and so on to make our lives and locations lovable and liveable.

Smarter Home/Buildings Capabilities

The outcomes of smarter homes are many including making consumers' lives more productive, healthier, and happier. The four service areas are as follows:

■ *Entertainment and convenience*: There is an increased convergence nowadays. Increasingly, the web contents are being made available via the television (TV), and, on the reverse side, TV programs are being viewed through web browsers. There are digital, smart, and the Internet-enabled TVs in plenty. There are product vendors, content creators, IT service providers, communication service providers, and end users working tougher in taking the entertainment industry to its next level. There are public displays, security and surveillance cameras, and flat panel TVs in public places as the threat quotient is on the rise. The convergence momentum is highly beneficial for people as well as building managers.

■ *Energy management*: Future demands on the electrical grid will encourage minute-by-minute home appliance management to prioritize energy services while delivering automatic savings to owners. Automatically synchronizing lighting, home appliances, climate and environmental sensors, and all household smart objects sharply minimizes energy consumption based on changing environment conditions and usage patterns in the home and buildings. Building automation systems (BAS) is a prominent module in streamlining occupants' needs. With the integration of smart grids, the role of BAS goes up significantly in conserving the scant power energy.

■ *Safety and security*: Many insurers now offer discounts for existing centralized alarm services using sensors and IP surveillance cameras. The ability to deploy home/building sensors that can instantly notify the homeowner, selected neighbors, or the police and fire departments can enhance home security. These services can also empower family members to remotely check on the safety of children and the well-being of elders.

■ *Health and wellness*: Healthcare providers could continuously monitor their patients with implanted devices or other at-home medical devices without hospitalization. Smarter home sensors monitor fitness, well-being, and advanced parameters consistently. These health electronic devices can collect evaluative information about current health condition for disease management and prevention and guarantee overall wellness.

Role of Building Automation Systems in Smarter Homes and Buildings

Apart from independent homes and luxurious houses, deluxe flats in high-rise apartments, condominiums, gated communities, spas, gardens, resorts and layouts, and so on, buildings coming in different sizes, scopes, and structures occupy more space in any typical city. There are corporate and government offices, manufacturing floors, star hotels, hospitals, auditoriums, food plazas, shopping complexes, and so on. There are different sets of stakeholders of these physical entities that are providing a wide gamut of newer and nimbler functionalities and facilities. Managing such a complex web of buildings is not a simple affair. IT solution and service providers are increasingly focusing on bringing in impactful automation through IT-enabled products. Especially, energy optimization is a vital parameter for energy-gulping and guzzling buildings. There are building management as well as energy management systems to take care of different automation needs of next-generation buildings.

These IT solutions are of help for building owners, keepers, users, and so on in linking together different building resources, assets, operational as well as controlling elements, people, and so on in visualizing and composing premium services and pragmatic applications. All kinds of noteworthy events are being captured instantaneously and leveraged through analytical platforms. The seamless and spontaneous connectivity among various automation modules within and outside goes a long way to unambiguously orchestrate through formally declared and described policies and preferences to produce sophisticated functionalities for building users. BAS has the inherent wherewithal to measure, manage, and maintain all the managed systems. Similarly, all the electrical systems and electronics stuff are optimized for lessening their energy consumption. Energy conservation is increasingly an important consideration. In short, buildings are becoming automated and intelligent. Building control and management systems in synchronization with various digitized objects, sensors, and actuators ensure enhanced users' comfort, choice, and care.

The appropriate design and installation of a BAS is the prime thing for achieving the expected success. All sorts of devices inside and applications outside have to be seamlessly integrated through a centralized/clustered or distributed BAS middleware to assure maximum impact on building users. Devices emit multistructured data, and hence the middleware has a big role in data translation. Another constraint is that there are manifold device protocols and they need to be transformed to ultimately have an integrated system. The proprietary nature of the traditional BAS is fast disappearing and a kind of freshness and openness is flourishing as there is a growing appetite for capturing batches and streams of data being emanated by hundreds of sensors and actuators in buildings and to pass on them to a common platform for further investigations. The BAS space is in adoption spree these days. That is, any BAS product is embedded with the unique capabilities of service orientation, cloud-enablement, IP protocols, Constrained Application Protocol (CoAP), and so on to be relevant for newer buildings. Emerging standards are enabling data sharing between building automation systems and other business applications to improve efficiency and enable real-time control over building systems. BAS plays a very vital role in decimating all kinds of differences and deficiencies so that all kinds of simple as well as sophisticated building systems dynamically cooperate to accomplish bigger and better things for building owners, facility managers, users, guests, and visitors.

Smarter Homes—Middleware Platforms

With the surging popularity of smart home applications, there are widespread initiatives and endeavors to creatively, convincingly, and comprehensively support for the cause of smarter homes. Due to that, there are international projects initiated, middleware solutions are being pumped out, development, execution, and change management platforms are being readied, enabling toolkits are being announced and articulated, and so on.

Name	Platform name	Description
http://www.pervasa.com/atlas.php	Atlas Middleware	By seamlessly connecting devices to the network, Atlas delivers embedded hardware as a software service to the developer. These services can then be combined to create a vast array of applications and solutions. Atlas follows a modular design offering maximum flexibility, adaptability, and return on investment. An Atlas node consists of several (typically three) layers connected using two board-to-board connectors. Wi-Fi, ZigBee, USB, and Ethernet communication layers are currently available. The processing layer is a low-power Atmel Atmega128L microcontroller supported by a 32K extended external memory. Several device connector layers offer physical connectivity to a large variety of sensors, actuators, and devices. Atlas is not only hardware; it is a middleware residing on the Atlas nodes and in the network. Based on the OSGi standard, Atlas offers the magic of plug and play to the widest array of sensors and devices. It does so by automating the sensor-to-service (hardware-to-software) conversion.
http://ws4d.org/	Web Services for Devices (WS4D)	WS4D is an initiative bringing SOA and Web services technology to the application domains of industrial automation, home entertainment, automotive systems, and telecommunication systems. WS4D is all about using Internet technologies like XML, HTTP, and Web Services to connect resource-constrained devices in ad hoc networks and still conserve interoperability with Web services as specified by the W3C. This enables the usage of high-level concepts for Web services also in low-level distributed embedded systems. So, WS4D provides technologies for easy setup and management of network-connected devices in distributed embedded systems. The WS4D toolkits comply to DPWS standard.

Name	Platform name	Description
https://forge.soa4d.org/	SODA Tools, Wikis, and Browsers	The SOA4D Forge is the support site for both developers and users of SOA4D technologies. SOA4D (Service-Oriented Architecture for Devices) is an open-source initiative aiming at fostering an ecosystem for the development of service-oriented software components (SOAP messaging, WS-* protocols, service orchestration...) adapted to the specific constraints of embedded devices.
www.linksmart.eu	The LinkSmart Middleware for networked devices	The LinkSmart middleware allows developers to incorporate heterogeneous physical devices into their applications by offering easy-to-use web service interfaces for controlling any type of physical device irrespective of its network technology such as Bluetooth, RF, ZigBee, RFID, WiFi, and so on. LinkSmart incorporates means for Device and Service Discovery, Semantic Model-Driven Architecture, P2P communication, and Diagnostics. LinkSmart-enabled devices and services can be secure and trustworthy through distributed security and social trust components of the middleware.
www.echelon.com/	LonWorks	LonWorks is a networking platform specifically created to address the needs of control applications. The platform is built on a protocol created by Echelon Corporation for networking devices over media such as twisted pair, power lines, fiber optics, and RF. It is used for the automation of various functions within buildings such as lighting and HVAC.
http://felix.apache.org/	Apache Felix	Apache Felix is a community effort to implement the OSGi Service Platform and other interesting OSGi-related technologies under the Apache license.
http://www.eclipse.org/equinox/	Eclipse Equinox	Equinox is an implementation of the OSGi core framework specification, a set of bundles that implement various optional OSGi services and other infrastructure for running OSGi-based systems.
http://www.knopflerfish.org/	Knopflerfish	Knopflerfish is the leading universal open-source OSGi Service Platform. Led and maintained by Makewave, Knopflerfish delivers significant value as the key container technology for many Java-based projects and products.

Smarter Home Frameworks

Frameworks are the proven enablers in the IT domain. As the developmental complexity of IT applications and services is on the climb, frameworks are being perceived to be the simplifier and streamliner. Creating and sustaining smarter home systems and networks is not an easy task, and hence frameworks are finding their relevance and root in this happening space. Here, we have listed out the prominent frameworks that go a long way in smoothening and strengthening the integration task of heterogeneous home IT products, devices, and infrastructures.

Vendor	Name	Description
Galixsys Networks http://www.galixsysnetworks.com	Andromeda-Embedded Services Framework	Andromeda can enable automated communication for devices in a variety of applications, including the following: Sensors, monitors, or controllers with automatic storage and retrieval of captured or generated data. Robotic or device artificial intelligence (AI) enhancement via server or cloud computing. Digital still cameras or video players with automatic upload or streaming of pictures and video. Remote monitors that need greater functionality or automation over web page serving.
http://www.netmf.com/	.NET Micro Framework	.NET Micro Framework helps: Easily develop powerful, interactive, and complex applications Securely connect devices over wired or wireless protocols Develop reliable solutions faster at lower cost Develop full solutions using .NET including devices, servers, and the cloud
http://restlet.org/	RESTful Web framework	The trend is that the Web is becoming ubiquitous and that REST, as the architecture style of the Web, helps to leverage all HTTP features. Restlet, the open-source REST framework, is already available on regular computers based on Java SE/EE, in Web browsers. For ubiquitous web, mobile devices have to be empowered further. With the faster commoditization of smartphones, more and more mobile users will have a usable access to the Web from their phone. So far, developers have been stuck with proprietary platforms and where lacking the productivity and portability common in the Java world. Thus, the Restlet framework is being ported to smartphones.

Vendor	Name	Description
http://www.greenpeak.com/	The Open Smart Home Framework	The Open Smart Home Framework (OSF) is an architecture that comprises the components of the ZigBee (IEEE 802.15.4) standard family that are relevant for the home and the consumer. It combines these components into an architecture that allows for an easy to install, maintenance-free, reliable, secure, and cost-effective sense and control network implementation, without any visibility for the user of the different ZigBee network layers or other underlying components that are used.
http://wosh.sourceforge.net/	WOSH Framework	WOSH (Wide Open Smart Home) is an open-source, multiplatform framework (message-oriented middleware) written in ANSI C++, designed to enable (smart) home automation. WOSH is a Service-Oriented Framework (SOF) providing a (Network) OS independent infrastructure for developing component-based software (services, aka bundles). WOSH Framework and installed services enable rapid development (RAD) and features composition. WOSH ships with many implemented services and some end-user applications (as woshsrv, WorkShop).
http://eclipse.org/smarthome/	Eclipse Smart Home Framework	Smart Home adoption will only gain momentum if the different devices can be connected into over-arching use cases, but currently the market for Smart Home systems and IoT gadgets is heavily fragmented. The only way out of this is to establish common interfaces and APIs.

Smart Education Systems Using Wearable Devices

Data is rapidly becoming the foundation for the transformation of education. Digitization is creating an opportunity to productize scalable rich-media content repositories. Education system is a strong candidate for the application of big data analytics because of the following reasons:

■ Huge amounts of educational content is available in the form of audio, instructional lectures/videos, and other types of unstructured data.

■ Digitization of content has led to a drastic increase in the availability of content repositories pertaining to potential areas of interest for a learner.

- Availability of techniques like Massive Open Online courses (MOOCs) have led to the creation of huge amounts of data about the students, which can be used to gain insights about the learning patterns of the learner. This in turn can be used for the design and delivery of personalized learning experiences for the learner using a combination of big data analytics and IoT-based wearable technologies.

Wearable learning solution is considered to be the future and promising technology that supports learning and performance. It is slowly evolving. Wearable learning is driven by wearable technology. There is a high scope that this technology can be leveraged by organizations to ensure high impact learning design for its employees based on the learning patterns of the employees, which can be tracked using the wearable devices.

Because of the data gathering ability of wearable based on biometrics, wearable devices can provide learning patterns of a learner to Artificial Intelligence (AI) systems, which in turn can learn the learning patterns and suggest appropriate learning strategies that warrantee uninterrupted and personalized learning experience for the learner. The learning patterns can be used to understand the learners' status and recommend necessary types of intervention, which in turn can lead to performance improvement.

Wearable learning solution can be implemented for practical and assessment learning. Wearable devices like GoPro can be used by learners to share the live recording of their experiments, which can be used by the trainers to evaluate and correct the behavior of the learners.

Conclusion

At the start of this chapter, use cases of IoT were divided into three broad categories, that is:

- Industry use cases
- Governance use cases
- Consumer use cases

Governance use cases focus on the governance applications of IoT. The most prominent example that comes under this category is smart city. The various aspects of smart city were discussed in this category.

Industry use cases are system centric and the applications that come under this category are generally mission or safety critical. Some examples that come under this category like smart energy systems and smart transportation systems were discussed in detail.

Consumer use cases are generally consumer centric. Some examples that come under this category like smart home/smart buildings and smart education systems were discussed at length under this category.

Some other use cases like smart healthcare systems and smart infrastructure systems like airports are discussed as separate chapters.

Reference

1. Trend Analysis: Connected Car 2015 a study by MBTech.

Chapter 12

Security Management of an IoT Ecosystem

Abstract: The IoT infrastructure in its entirety contains a wide gamut of technologies like cloud, big data, mobile devices, and Internet of Things. Each of these technological components are susceptible to various types of security vulnerabilities and threats, which can render them ineffective. It is very important to ensure that the IoT infrastructure components are adequately safeguarded from various security breaches. The crux of this chapter is the techniques to be adopted for securing the IoT platforms and technologies, which form a part of the IoT ecosystem.

The first section of this chapter examines the various security requirements for the IoT infrastructure. From next section onward, we focus on the security threats, which exist in each IoT component. Starting with cloud platform, the threats that exist for each of the underlying platform like big data and mobility are examined in detail. The various ways and means to tackle the security challenges are also discussed elaborately in this chapter.

The different types of use cases, which form a part of an IoT ecosystem, are intelligent buildings, intelligent transportation systems, intelligent water systems, intelligent grids, and so on. The security threats for some of these applications and the techniques to safeguard them are also discussed in this chapter. This chapter concludes with a framework, which can be adopted in order to build and maintain a safe and secure IT framework.

Introduction

Information and communication technology will be the key foundational component for IoT. These information and communication technological components will be closely interconnected with one another in order to facilitate efficient co-ordination among the various IoT components.

However, for this efficient communication and collaboration to happen in real time, it is very critical to ensure the safety and security of the underlying information technology infrastructure.

In this chapter, we will identify the security challenges and the security requirements to be kept in mind for the design of IoT infrastructure. In this chapter, we will identify security threats based on the four key platforms and technologies, which are used by the IoT infrastructure components. They are the following:

- Security concerns in mobile devices and platforms, which are used by IoT applications
- Security concerns in big data platforms
- Security concerns in cloud
- Security concerns in IoT platforms

We will also examine some of the techniques to be used in order to leverage the underlying technological resources in a smart manner by ensuring that there is no unintentional or malicious access to data, which is stored and accessed in the underlying IoT components.

Security Requirements of an IoT Infrastructure

The key security aspects, which need to be kept in mind for the security of information technological components, which are applicable to an IoT infrastructure, are discussed in this section.

Confidentiality, Integrity, and Availability Triad

The confidentiality, integrity, and availability (CIA) triad, which are the three fundamental requirements that need to be kept in mind during the design and development phase of the underlying IoT infrastructure, are depicted in Figure 12.1.

Confidentiality

It ensures that only authorized users will have access to the underlying information. In other words, it ensures that privacy by preventing unauthorized access to the information, which is stored and transmitted using the IoT infrastructure.

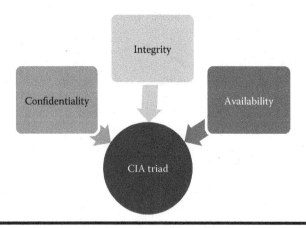

Figure 12.1   CIA triad.

Integrity

It ensures that only authorized users are allowed to modify the underlying information. It ensures that unauthorized users will not be able to alter the information in any manner. Alteration involves write, delete, and update operations.

Availability

It ensures that authorized users have access to the underlying information as and when it is required. This includes ensuring the fact that the IoT infrastructure has fault tolerance capabilities built into them. Fault tolerance can be built into the IoT infrastructure by ensuring that backup components are present for each of the IoT infrastructure components, namely, servers, storage, and networks. Server backup can be ensured by clustering the servers in order to provide a high-availability environment. It is also important to ensure that the backup server is an identical copy of the primary server and can take over the role of the primary server immediately upon the failure of the primary server. Storage backup can be ensured by using the highly scalable RAID architecture for hard disks in which same data is striped and mirrored across multiple hard disks, so that even if one hard disk fails, data will not be lost as it will stored in the other disks of the array. Fault tolerance in networks can be ensured by providing multiple switches, multiple ports, and multiple cables between the two connecting endpoints in order to ensure that the failure of any network component will not hamper the transfer of data through the network.

These components, Confidentiality, Integrity, and Availability, are commonly referred to as the CIA triad.

Authentication, Authorization, and Audit Trial (AAA) Framework

AAA framework is a security requirement, which is of paramount importance for the IoT infrastructure. The various components of the framework are described below.

Authentication

This process checks to ensure that a user's credentials are valid, so that users with invalid credentials will not be allowed to access the underlying information. The simplest way to use authentication is with the help of user names and passwords. But as hacking techniques are evolving day by day, it is very important to ensure that sophisticated authentication techniques are in place. One such authentication mechanism that is used is called multifactor authentication. Multifactor authentication is a special authentication technique, which uses a combination of parameters to verify a user's credentials. An example of multifactor authentication mechanism is described below:

First Factor: A user name and password, which will be unique for the specific user and which may be sometimes unique for the specific session as well.

Second Factor: A secret key, which is generated by a random number generator, or a secret key phrase, which is known only to the user, or answer to a secret question, which is specific to a particular user.

Third Factor: This could be any biometric parameter of the user, which could be used as the user's biometric signature. This could include aspects like iris recognition, finger print recognition, and so on.

A multifactor authentication uses a combination of all the parameters mentioned above in order to verify a user's credentials. In some cases, only two factors mentioned above may be used for authentication, and in that case, it is called two-factor authentication.

Authorization

Authorization is a process which ensures that a specific user has rights to perform specific operations on a specific object. This is generally by granting different types of permissions to different types of users based on their role in a city government. For example, a fire station executive will just be able to read the data pertaining to other city departments like water; he/she may not be able to edit it. Edit permissions may be given only to the city supervisors or executives who belong to the water department of the city. The different types of permissions for different users on different objects are mapped and stored in a table, which is called Access Control List (ACL). The different types of permissions, which are given for users, are classified as the following:

- *Read only*: The user has permission to only read the object. The user cannot delete or edit the object. These types of permissions are granted to staff who are not required to perform any alteration on the data.
- *Read and write*: The user has permission to read and alter the object. These types of permissions are granted to authorities who have the overall authority and discretion to validate the rights and access permissions of other users.

Audit Trial

Audit trial is an activity, which is conducted periodically, to assess the effectiveness of the security measures that are implemented in the IoT infrastructure. Audit trial is performed with the help of audit logs, which track the operations that are performed by different users.

Defense-in-Depth

This is a mechanism which should be used to provide high level of security to the IoT infrastructure. This mechanism ensures that multiple levels or layers of security are present within an IoT infrastructure to ensure that even if security at one level gets compromised due to some reason, security at other levels should be able to safeguard the underlying IoT infrastructure. As multiple levels of security are provided in this approach, it is also called a layered approach to security implementation. It gives enhanced security to the IoT infrastructure by providing multiple layers of security and more time to officials to react to a security breach that has happened in one layer while the other layer security measures will be working to protect it. A high-level architecture of the Defense-in-Depth approach is shown in Figure 12.2.

Trusted Computing Base (TCB)

This defines the boundary for the critical information components, which form a part of the IoT infrastructure. Any security breaches that happen within the trusted computing base (TCB) boundary will affect the entire IoT infrastructure in an adverse manner. This helps to establish a clear definition between the critical and noncritical components of the IoT infrastructure. For

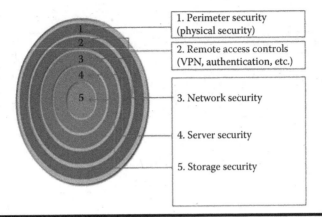

1. Perimeter security (physical security)

2. Remote access controls (VPN, authentication, etc.)

3. Network security

4. Server security

5. Storage security

Figure 12.2   Architecture of defense-in-depth.

example, if we take an example of a PC or tablet, operating system and configuration files will be a part of the TCB as any security breaches to the operating system will corrupt the entire PC. It is very important for TCB to be defined for the IoT infrastructure. It helps to provide multiple additional levels of security for the components that fall under the TCB of the IoT infrastructure.

Encryption

It is the process of converting data into a format that cannot be interpreted easily and directly by unauthorized users. It is very important to ensure that data stored in the IoT infrastructure and the data transmitted via the networks are in encrypted form. This is very helpful to prevent unauthorized deception of data by third-party agents. The process of converting the data back to its original form is called decryption. Several encryption softwares are available in the market.

PRETTY GOOD PRIVACY (PGP)

Pretty Good Privacy (PGP) is a strong data encryption and decryption program, which is widely used by federal government for protecting all types of government data like mails, files, and entire disk partitions of computers.

Apart from the security requirements mentioned above, the additional security requirement of the IoT infrastructure of an intelligent city is resilience. Resilience is the capability of an infrastructure to return back to its original state after it is disturbed due to some factors, which are internal or external.

Majority of the IoT applications will be built and deployed on cloud platforms. Hence, all security concerns of cloud platforms will pose security threats for IoT components as well. In the next section, we will examine some of the security concerns of cloud platforms.

Security Concerns of Cloud Platforms

Cloud Security architecture has three different layers: software applications layer, platform layer, and infrastructure layer. Each layer has its own set of security concerns. We will discuss some

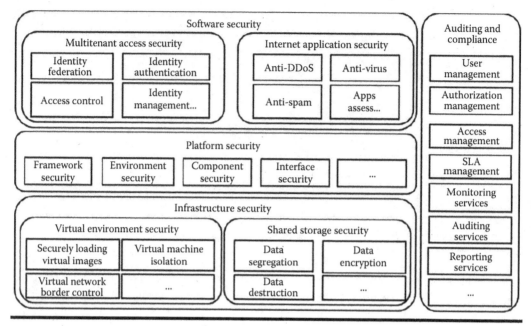

Figure 12.3   Cloud security architecture.

of them in the context of IoT components, which would mainly rely on public cloud for its IT requirements (Figure 12.3).

One of the main concerns of cloud is multitenancy. Multitenancy refers to the fact that Cloud infrastructure, because of the underlying virtualization platform, provides features to service multiple independent clients (tenants) using same set of resources. This consequently increases the risks for data confidentiality and integrity. These risks are especially more severe in case of Public Cloud environment. This is because, in Public Cloud, services can be used by competing clients as compared to Private Clouds, and also number of Cloud users are much higher in Public Clouds.

Some of the ways to overcome these concerns, which arise due to multitenancy, are as follows:

- Virtual machine segmentation
- Database segmentation
- Virtual machine introspection

Virtual Machine Segmentation

Virtualization forms the basis of most of the IaaS offerings. There are many virtualization softwares available in the market like VMware vSphere, Citrix XenServer, and Microsoft Hyper-V. These softwares provide the capability to convert a physical machine into multiple virtual machines. These virtual machines serve as databases, web servers, and file servers. These components, which run on virtual platforms, are provided to customers as a part of IaaS. The main component of virtualization platform is hypervisor, which acts as operating system for the virtual machines and provisions all the resources required for the operation of virtual machines. The major security concerns in virtualized infrastructure are due to the fact that virtual machines owned by multiple customers reside on the same physical machine. This aspect places the virtual machines in a privileged position with respect to one another. This can introduce several types of security risks like unauthorized connection, monitoring, and malware induction. In order to prevent occurrence of such security concerns, it is very important to ensure that VMs that contain confidential customer data should be segmented and isolated from one another. This process of ensuring that virtual machines are isolated or separated from one another is called virtual machine segmentation.

Database Segmentation

In IaaS, infrastructure resources are offered as a service. In SaaS, apart from software applications, database is also offered as a service. This will introduce a scenario that multiple customers will store their data in the same database as multiple rows, which are differentiated based on customer Id, which will be assigned to customers. In some situations like application code errors or access control list errors, there is a lot of risk for customer data. For controlling access to database data, there are quite a few tools and technologies available. In order to prevent the occurrence of such situations, there are many tools, which are available in the market. These tools work on the basis of a system for authentication and authorization, which ensure that some rows are only modifiable based on certain predefined security policies, which ensure that access to data is warranted. Another technique that could be used to reduce security threats in this situation is the encryption of data, which is stored in the database. This ensures that even if the security of the data is compromised, it would be difficult to decrypt it.

VM Introspection

Another important technique, which could be used to eliminate the risks of multitenancy, is VM introspection. VM introspection is a service provided by the hypervisor. This service examines the internal state of each VM, which runs on top of the hypervisor. There are many tools available in the market, which leverage the benefits of this service to provide VM segmentation and isolation. VM introspection provides following details of each VM:

- Applications and services which are present
- Configuration details

With the help of these details of VMs, it is possible to create and implement custom security policies on each VM. An example of a policy could be to ensure that no other VM should join a specific VM group until it has some matching OS configuration parameters. This ensures that in a multitenant environment, VMs remain segmented and isolated.

Distributed Denial of Service (DDoS)

In a cloud system, if a host of messages attack all nodes of the cloud system and over-utilize the server resources, making the resources unavailable for actual requirements, then it is called a distributed denial of service (DDoS) attack. There are multiple versions of DDoS attacks, which are available: simple and complex. Example of simple DDoS attack tools are X-Dos (XML-based denial of service) as well as H-Dos (HTTP-based denial of service). Example of complex DDoS attack tools are Agobot, Mstream, and Trinoo. H-DoS are used by attackers who are interested in using less complex web-based tools for attack. One additional advantage of these simple tools is the ease of implementation of attacks. DX-DoS occurs when XML-based messages are sent to a web server in such a way that it will use up all their resources. Coercive Parsing attack is an X-Dos attack in which web content is parsed using SOAP to transform it into an application. A series of open tags are used by Coercive Parsing attack to exhaust the CPU resources on the web server. In case of an H-DoS attack, a series of about 1000 plus threads are started to create HTTP simultaneous random requests to exhaust all the resources. There are several tools available in the market to detect and eliminate DDoS attacks. The Cloud Service Provider can use these tools at their discretion. One such example is discussed below.

REAL LIFE EXAMPLE OF DDOS ATTACK

Bloomberg News reported that hackers used AWS's EC2 cloud computing unit to launch an attack against Sony's PlayStation Network and Qriocity entertainment networks. The attack reportedly compromised the personal accounts of more than 100 million Sony customers.

Imperva SecureSphere Web Application Firewall to Prevent DDoS Attacks

The Imperva SecureSphere Web Application Firewall is a security appliance, which is capable of preventing DDoS attacks in a cloud infrastructure. In addition to DDoS, this software also has the capability to prevent several types of web attacks like SQL injection (Figure 12.4).

The tool uses the following features to prevent DDoS attacks on cloud infrastructure:

■ *ThreatRadar reputation*: This service keeps track of users who are attacking other websites. By using this information, it will filter off any request from those users and prevent them from getting into the cloud system.
■ *Up-to-date web attack signatures*: This service helps to monitor and keep track of bot user agents and DDoS attacks vectors.

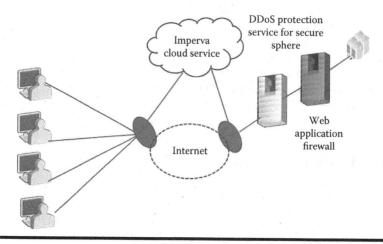

Figure 12.4   Architecture of Imperva SecureSphere.

- *DDoS policy templates*: This service helps to detect users who have the pattern of generating and sending HTTP requests with long response times.
- *Bot mitigation policies*: This service has the capability to send a JavaScript challenge to users' browsers. This JavaScript challenge has the capacity to detect and block bots.
- *HTTP protocol validation*: This service monitors and records buffer overflow attempts and other intrusion techniques.

Virtual Machine/Hypervisor-Based Security Threats

The virtual machines, which form the basis of cloud infrastructure, are also subjected to various types of vulnerabilities. These pose severe threats to the cloud infrastructure. Some of them are illustrated in Figure 12.5.

Unauthorized Alteration of Virtual Machine Image Files

Virtual machines are susceptible to security threats when they are running as well as when they are powered off. When a VM is powered off, it is available as a VM image file. This image file is exposed to several security threats like malware infections. Apart from that, if appropriate security measures are not in place, VM image files can be used by hackers to create new unauthorized VMs. It is also possible to patch these VM image files so as to infect the VMs created using these image files. VM security can be compromised even during VM migration. At the time of VM migration, the VMs are exposed to several types of network attacks like eavesdropping and unauthorized modification. One technique, which could be used to protect the VM image files, is to encrypt them when they are powered off or being migrated.

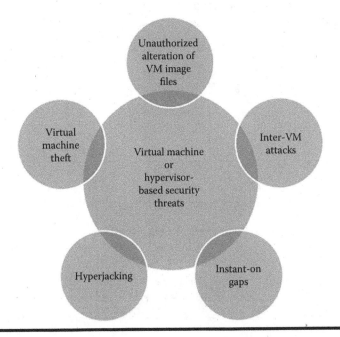

Figure 12.5   Virtual machine based security threats.

VM Theft

VM theft enables a hacker or attacker to copy or move a VM in an unauthorized manner. This is mainly made possible because of the presence of inadequate controls on VM files. These inadequate controls will allow the unauthorized copy or movement of VM files. VM theft could prove to be very fatal if the VM that is stolen contains confidential data of a customer.

One way to restrict VM theft is to impose required level of copy and move restrictions on VMs. Such restrictions effectively bind a VM to a specific physical machine in such a way that even if there is a forceful copy of the VM, it will not operate on any other physical machine. A VM with required level of copy and move restrictions cannot run on a hypervisor installed on any other physical machine.

Apart from VM theft, another threat which can happen at VM level is known as "VM escape." Normally, virtual machines are encapsulated and isolated from each other and from the underlying parent hypervisor. In normal scenarios, there is no mechanism available for a guest OS and the applications running on it to break out of the virtual machine boundary and directly interact with the hypervisor. The process of breaking out and interacting with the hypervisor is called a VM escape. Since the hypervisor controls the execution of all VMs, due to VM escape, an attacker can gain control over every other VM running on it by bypassing security controls, which are placed on those VMs.

Inter-VM Attacks

Multiple VMs run on the same physical machine. So, if the security of one VM is compromised, there is a very easy possibility for the security of other VMs running on the same physical machine to be compromised. In one scenario, it is possible for an attacker to compromise one guest VM, which can then get passed on to the other VMs, which are running on the same physical machine. In order to prevent the occurrence of such scenarios, it is very important to have firewalls and intrusion detection systems, which have the capability to detect and prevent malicious activity at the VM level (Figure 12.6).

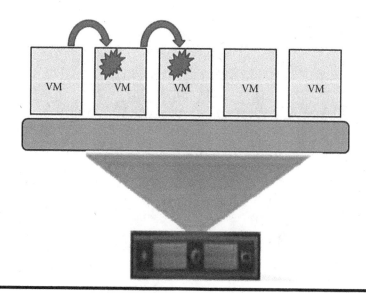

Figure 12.6   How inter-VM attacks happen.

Instant-On Gaps

Virtual machines have some vulnerabilities, which are not present in physical machines. This is mainly due to the techniques that are used to provision, use, and deprovision them. Sometimes, these cycles are repeated very frequently. This frequent activation and deactivation of VMs can pose challenges to maintain their security systems constantly updated.

After some time, these VMs can automatically deviate from their defined security baselines, and this in turn can introduce significant levels of security threats. This will give lot of options to attackers to access them. There is also a possibility that new VMs could be cloned and created out of these VMs, which have vulnerabilities. If this is done, the security threats will get passed on to the newly created VMs, and this will increase the area of the attack surface. It is very important to ensure that VMs possess a security agent, which has all the latest security configurations update.

When a VM is not online during an antivirus update, that VM will have vulnerabilities when it comes online as it would not have got the latest security updates. One solution to this problem could be to have a dedicated security VM in each physical machine to automatically update all VMs running in that physical machine with all latest security updates (Figure 12.7).

Hyperjacking

Hyperjacking enables an attacker to install a rogue hypervisor that has the capability to take complete control of the underlying physical server. This is a rootkit-level vulnerability. A rootkit is a malicious program, which is installed before a hypervisor fully boots on a physical server. In this manner, the rootkit is able to run in the server with privileged access and remains invisible to the system administrators. Once a rootkit is installed, it gives permission to an attacker to mask the ongoing intrusion and maintain privileged access to the physical server by bypassing the normal authentication and authorization mechanisms, which are employed by an OS.

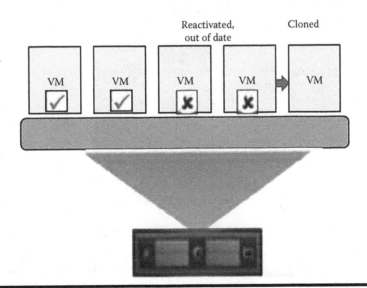

Figure 12.7   Instant-on gaps.

Using such a rogue hypervisor, an attacker can run unauthorized applications on a guest OS without the OS realizing the presence of such an application. With hyperjacking, an attacker could control the interaction between the VMs and the underlying physical server. Regular security measures are ineffective against this rogue hypervisor because of the following:

■ Guest OS is unaware of the fact that underlying server has been attacked.
■ Antivirus and firewall applications cannot detect the presence of the rogue hypervisor as it is installed directly over the server itself.

Measures against hyperjacking include the following:

■ Hardware-assisted secure launching of the hypervisor so that rootkit-level malicious programs cannot launch. This would involve designing and using a TCB for the hypervisor getting support at the hardware level.
■ Scanning hardware level details to assess the integrity of the hypervisor and locate the presence of rogue hypervisor. This scanning may include checking the state of the memory as well as registering in the CPU.

Security Threats of Big Data

Big data is huge volumes of constantly changing data which comes in from a variety of different sources. The constantly changing nature of big data introduces a variety of security threats for big data platforms. Some of the key challenges are summarized in Figure 12.8.

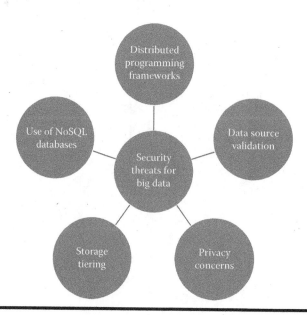

Figure 12.8   Security threats for big data.

Distributed Programming Frameworks

Many programming frameworks, which process big data, use parallel computation to process huge amounts of data quickly. One such example is the MapReduce framework, which is used for processing big data. This framework splits the data into multiple chunks. The mapper then works on each chunk of data and generates key/value pairs for each chunk. In the next step, the reducer component combines values which belong to each key and then generates a final output. In this framework, the main security threat is with regard to mappers. Mappers can be hacked and made to generate incorrect key value pairs. This in turn will lead to the generation of incorrect final results. Due to vast amounts of big data, it is impossible to detect the mapper that generated the incorrect value. This in turn can affect the accuracy of data, which may adversely affect data-rich computations. The main solution to this problem is to secure mappers using various algorithms that are available.

Use of NoSQL Databases

NoSQL databases are designed to store big data scale well to store huge amounts of data. But they do not have any security controls/policies embedded in them. The security controls are designed and incorporated into the middleware by the database programmers. There is no provision to include security practices as a part of NoSQL database design. This poses significant threat to the big data, which is stored in the NoSQL databases. A solution to this problem is that organizations should review their security policies thoroughly and ensure that appropriate levels of security controls are incorporated into their middleware.

Storage Tiering

Most of the present-day organizations have a tiered approach to store data. Tiered approach consists of multiple tiers of heterogeneous storage devices each of which vary in terms of cost, performance, storage capacity, and security policies, which are enforced. In normal scenarios, data is stored in different tiers based on their frequency of access, cost, volume, or any other parameter, which is of importance for the organization. The tiering of data is done manually. However, with the ever-increasing volumes of big data, it is becoming very difficult for the storage administrators to do tiering of such huge amounts of data manually. Hence, many organizations now have automatic storage tiering, which is done with the help of some preconfigured policies. This might ensure that some data like R&D data, which is not frequently used, may be stored in the lowest tier as it may not be frequently used as per the policy. But it might be an important data from the context of organizations, and storing such data in the lowest tier, which has less data security, may expose the data to security threats.

Data Source Validation

As per the 3V's of Big data, that is, volume, velocity, and variety, input data can be collected from diverse kinds of sources. Some sources may have data validation techniques in place and some other sources will not have data validation. This is more prominent when the input comes in from mobile devices like tablets and cell phones. Since many of the present-day organizations are promoting a bring your own device (BYOD) concept, the possibility of threats which are likely to creep in from the mobile devices are still higher. Some examples of mobile device threats are spoofed cell phone ids.

Privacy Concerns

In an attempt to perform analytics to derive insights, lot of activities of the users are being tracked without their knowledge. This data, which is tracked by organizations for deriving various types of insights, could prove to be extremely harmful for the users if it gets passed on to some untrusted third party.

> **PRIVACY CONCERN OF BIG DATA ANALYTICS**
>
> A recent event, which was news recently, is an eye opener on how big data analytics could intervene into the privacy of an individual. An analysis done by a retail organization for marketing purposes was able to inform a father about his teenage daughter's pregnancy.

Requirements of Security Management Framework for Big Data

Big data involves data of huge sizes, different types which are constantly changing in nature. In order to design a security management framework for big data, the three key parameters to be kept in mind are summarized in Figure 12.9.

Figure 12.9   Security management framework for big data.

Agile Scale-Out Infrastructure

In order to manage huge amounts of constantly changing data, the IoT infrastructure of organizations should have agility and scale-out capabilities. Apart from storing and managing huge amounts of big data, organizations also use this data to support a plethora of new delivery models like cloud computing, mobility, outsourcing, and so on. The security management infrastructure should have the capability to adapt quickly to collect and secure this type of data. The underlying security infrastructure should be able to expand and adapt easily to facilitate easy identification of new threats, which evolve continually with each new type of data and the associated delivery mechanism.

Security Analytics

Many data analytics and visualization tools exist in the market. They support analytics for wide range of activities and device types. But the number of tools that provide security analytics capabilities are limited in the market. Security management officials require many types of sophisticated analytical tools, which can provide them diverse kinds of security analysis insights and visualization capabilities. Security management in enterprises covers a wide range of functions, which include security analysis of networks, security analysis of databases, and so on. Each type of security analysis requires different types of data. For example, in order to perform security analysis of networks, logs and network information pertaining to specific sessions of activity are required. Software that supports the analytical and visualization requirements of diverse types of security personnel in an organization should be present in the organization. For example, in order to perform security analysis of log information, there are a separate category of tools available, which come under the broad umbrella called machine-to-machine (M2M) analytics.

IBM ACCELERATOR FOR MACHINE DATA ANALYTICS

Machines produce large amount of data. This data contains a wealth of actionable insights. However, in order to extract and perform analysis on such huge amount of data, tools with large-scale data extraction, transformation, and analysis capabilities are required. IBM® Accelerator for Machine Data Analytics provides a set of diverse applications, which helps to import, transform, and analyze this machine data for the purpose of identifying event and pattern correlations and use them to make informed decisions based on the data present in the log and data files.

IBM Accelerator for Machine Data Analytics provides the following key capabilities (http://www-01.ibm.com/support/knowledgecenter/SSPT3X_2.0.0/com.ibm.swg.im. infosphere.biginsights.product.doc/doc/acc_mda.html):

- Search within and across multiple log entries using text search, faceted search, or a timeline-based search in order to find specific patterns or events of interest.
- Enrich the context of log data by adding and extracting log types into the existing repository.
- Link and correlate events across systems.

Threat Monitoring and Intelligence

Diverse types of threats for data exist within an organization and outside as well. To add on to this, new types of threats are evolving every day. It is very important for organizations to stay updated on the threat environment, so that the security analysts can get a clear picture of the various types of threat indicators and the security prejudice, which is inflicted by them.

All the mobile applications and use cases of intelligent cities, which were discussed in the previous chapter, are designed with respect to smartphones. In the next section, we will examine some of the security threats for smartphones and also some mechanisms, which can be used to secure smartphones.

Security Threats in Smartphones

Smartphones have the capability to connect to various types of external systems like Internet, GPS, and other different types of mobile devices using wireless networking technology. This is the key feature of smartphone, which makes it one of the most widely used and popular device. Many IoT applications, which are run using smartphones, store personal data like address book, bank account details, meeting and appointment details, and so on in the smartphones. Proliferation of technologies like NFC for various purposes makes it very critical to ensure security of the smartphone and the data, which is stored in the smartphone. A smartphone is exposed to a lot of vulnerabilities, which can compromise its security.

The vulnerabilities in smartphones can be classified into two broad categories: internal and external. Internal vulnerabilities exist within the smartphone and external vulnerabilities creep into smartphones from the external systems to which they are connected. Some of the internal vulnerabilities are as follows:

■ *Operating system implementation error*: This error will happen due to the presence of some erroneous code in the operating system of mobile devices. Usually, these types of errors are not introduced by the end users and they creep into the mobile devices due to fault of the mobile OS owning organizations. It is very common to have such errors in the new version or version upgrades of mobile operating systems. These OS errors can easily provide lot of options to the attackers to hack the operating system and gain illegitimate access to the smartphone or install rogue applications, which can track and retrieve the details of the user from the smartphone. One way to avoid this could be by installing only version upgrades, which have been fully tested and corrected and to defer from installing beta versions of operating systems.

■ *End user unawareness error*: The smartphone end user can compromise the security by one or all of the following actions, which are mainly due to the lack of awareness of the end user. Some of the common errors introduced by the end users are the following:
  – Use untrusted wireless networks to connect to Internet.
  – Install mobile application from untrusted sources.
  – Connect to untrusted websites using mobile phones, which can inject some malware into the device.
  – Improper configuration settings in the mobile device browser.
  – Loss of mobile devices, which can pose a serious security threat for the user's personal information stored in the mobile device.

Some of the external vulnerabilities are the following:

- *Wireless network threats*: The attacker could hack the wireless network to which the smartphone is connected and thereby gain access into the mobile device of the user.
- *External websites*: If the external website to which an end user is connected is hacked by an attacker, it is also possible for the attacker to gain access to the mobile device of the user with the help of the details gathered from that specific website. It is also possible that a malware present in an external website can get automatically installed in the mobile device if security mechanisms in the mobile device are not properly configured like unavailability of antivirus software in the mobile devices.
- *Other wireless devices*: Smartphones have the capability to connect and communicate with a wide range of other wireless devices.

Security Solutions for Mobile Devices

Many measures can be adopted by the user to enhance the security of the mobile devices. But none of these measures will offer complete security to mobile devices, as threats are getting added day by day, and it is impossible to devise solutions at the pace at which threats are being created. Some of the possible security solutions, which can be adopted by the users, are as follows:

- *System add-on*: This refers to system updates, which are periodically made available to the smartphones. This will include platform updates, which will provide enhanced features and in some cases enhanced security as well. It is the responsibility of the user to ensure that the system updates are installed periodically.
- *System configuration*: This is a very expensive and time-consuming activity, as this process involves modification of the mobile OS code in order to add enhanced security features at the kernel level. This approach is rarely adopted by the users because of the huge amount of cost and time involved in it.
- *Antivirus, spam filter*: In order to protect the smartphones from virus attacks, antivirus software, is available for specific mobile OS. Also some attacks from rogue websites can be prevented by turning on the spam filter in the smartphones.
- *Cryptographic security mechanisms*: Cryptographic techniques are available to ensure confidentiality and integrity of the data, which is stored in the smartphone. Cryptography can be implemented in smartphones in two ways: mobile applications and mobile platform APIs. Cryptographic techniques use various mechanisms to ensure security of data, which is stored in the smartphone. One such mechanism is to encrypt the data, which is stored in the smartphone, so that even if it is hacked by a third party, the information cannot be deciphered without the availability of the key, which will be known only to the smartphone user. Most of the mobile platforms make several APIs for use by the developers. Some of these APIs can be used to access the mobile OS-specific security library. This way, the developers can develop specialized mobile security applications for various mobile platforms.

Apart from these methods, several mobile security applications are available in the mobile application store. It is the responsibility of the user to check and install the appropriate applications. In addition to this, in order to protect the information stored in the mobile devices, users can lock the mobile phones using strong passwords. Another option is to make a note of the International

Mobile Equipment Identity (IMEA) number of the mobile device, so that if the mobile device is lost/stolen, the IMEA number can be deactivated, which will disable all the functionalities of the mobile device automatically.

Security Concerns in IoT Components

An IoT platform will contain hundreds of sensors and other different types of devices, which are sending data to a public or private cloud or some big data platform using a wired or wireless network through a gateway as shown in the diagram, which is given below. The gateway for some devices will be present within the device itself; for some other devices, the gateway will be present externally (Figure 12.10).

In IoT platforms, all types of platforms and technologies, which were discussed previously in this chapter, are used. So the security concerns, which are present in each of them, are applicable to IoT platform as well. In addition, because of huge number and types of devices and the plethora of technologies, which are used by them for communication, it is necessary to adopt a multifaceted and multilayered approach in order to ensure appropriate security for all components, which are part of the IoT platform. The diverse aspects of this multifaceted approach should start right from the booting of the devices and should continue at each phase of the device lifecycle in order to build an IoT ecosystem, which cannot be tampered. Some of these security measures are discussed below.

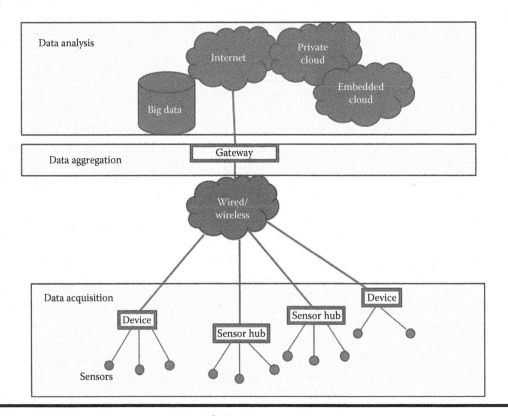

Figure 12.10   Security concerns in IoT devices.

Security Measures for IoT Platforms/Devices

In order to ensure security of various devices and platforms, which are a part of the IoT network, it is essential to ensure adopting a holistic mechanism, which spans across all the phases of a device's lifecycle. Some such mechanisms are discussed below.

Secure Booting

When a device powers on, there should be an authentication mechanism to verify that the software which runs on the device is a legitimate one. This is done with the help of cryptographically generated digital signatures. This process ensures that only authentic software which has been designed to run on the devices by the concerned parties will run on the devices. This establishes a trusted computing base for the devices upfront. But the devices still need to be protected from various kinds of run-time threats.

Mandatory Access Control Mechanisms

Mandatory access control mechanisms should be built into the operating system of the devices in order to ensure that the various applications and components will have access only to those resources, which they need for their functioning. This will ensure that if an attacker is able to gain access to any of those components/applications, they will be able to gain access to only very limited resource. This significantly reduces the attack surface.

Device Authentication for Networks

A device should get connected to some kind of a wired or wireless network in order to begin transmission of data. When a device gets connected to a network, it should authenticate itself before it starts data transmission. For some types of embedded devices (which operate without manual intervention), the authentication can be done with the help of credentials, which are maintained in a secured storage area of the device.

Device-Specific Firewalls

For each device, there should be some kind of firewall, which will filter and examine the data that is specifically sent to that device. It is not mandatory for the devices to examine all types of traffic, which traverse through the network, as that will be taken care of by the network security appliances. This is required also because of the fact that some specific types of embedded devices have custom-made protocols, which are different from the common IT protocols used by organizations for data transmission. One classic example is the smart grid, which has its own set of protocols for communication. Hence, it is very essential for the device to have firewalls or some such mechanism in place, which is intended to filter the traffic, which is intended specifically for that device.

Controlled Mechanism to Ensure Application of Security Patches and Upgrades

Once devices are connected to the networks, they start receiving security patches and upgrades. It so happens that in some situations, these patches and upgrades consume a whole lot of network bandwidth making it unavailable for other devices or applications, which are a part of the network. Operators need to ensure that patches, upgrades, and authentication of the devices should be planned in such a way that it should involve minimum bandwidth consumption, and it should not impact the functional safety of the device.

In short, for an IoT network's security, the traditional safety measures, which are typically adopted, are not sufficient. It is mandatory to inject security measures starting from the operating system of the participating devices.

Security Threats in Different Use Cases of IoT

Some of the key IoT use cases are summarized in Figure 12.11.

Next, we identify key security threats present in these IT infrastructure components along with some measures to curb them.

Security Threats in Smart Transportation Systems

Smart transportation systems enhance the quality of life by tracking and monitoring the transportation services. Sensors can capture data about the real-time status of transportation services and send the data to a centralized control center or dashboard, which can then use the data to co-ordinate transport services. Tracking and monitoring of transportation services requires a highly sophisticated IoT infrastructure and close co-ordination between the various components in order to avoid disruptions. The different types of security threats, which are possible in a smart transportation system, are the following:

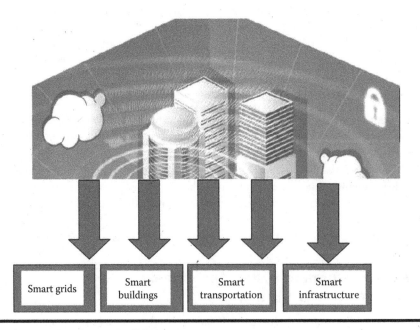

Figure 12.11 Security threats in different IoT use cases.

- Hacking the travel navigation systems to misguide vehicle drivers into wrong routes by providing erroneous information about the traffic volume at various routes.
- The data transmitted to or from mobile devices may be subjected to spoofing.
- Unencrypted traffic reports can be attacked by hackers who can inject incorrect or false traffic-related data or reports into satellite-based navigation devices.

ATTACK OF A PUBLIC TRANSPORT SYSTEM IN EUROPE

A teenager in Europe was able to attack the public transport systems with the help of a modified television remote control. He was able to cause severe traffic disruption in the city and he was even able to cause a tram derailment by forcing a vehicle to take an abrupt turn when it was traveling at high speed.

Security Threats in Smart Grids and Other IoT-Based Infrastructure Components

The different components of smart grids are the following:

- *Smart meters*: Digital meters which can track user consumption in real time and provide alerts to user end point devices.
- Networks with two-way communication capabilities.
- *Meter data acquisition and management systems*: Software which collects data from the smart meters, calculates bill value, and analyses usage metrics.

The security of each of these components can be compromised. Smart meters may be hacked to steal energy or to tamper consumption data. Meter data acquisition and management systems can be hacked by the attackers using some of the vulnerabilities, which may be present in the system, and this can severely hamper the transmission of data to the end users. White listing techniques, which can ensure that only certain applications or processes are active at specific points in time, are effective in some situations. However, there are no solutions to zero-day vulnerabilities. Zero-day vulnerabilities are those for which no security patches are available.

Networks used by smart grids and other infrastructure components can be hacked by the attackers by installing some malwares, which are capable of tracking sensitive network-related information. This sensitive information can be later used by the attackers to create DoS attacks. These network-related threats can be eliminated to a great extend by using intrusion prevention techniques combined with some robust security practices to handle aspects like browser patches, end user awareness creation, and network usage tracking.

One of the best possible ways to prevent tampering of smart meters and meter data acquisition and management system is the use of Public Key Infrastructure (PKI). PKIs can be directly implemented on smart meters. This will ensure authentication and validation of meters in a connected network. It is also important to ensure that keys and certificates pertaining to a PKI environment are guarded appropriately using an appropriate management solution.

Conclusion

The IoT infrastructure is a conglomeration of technologies like cloud, big data, mobile devices, and Internet of Things. It is very essential to ensure that each component is safe and secure in order to ensure continuous availability of services. The security requirements of the IoT infrastructure components were examined in detail in the first section of this chapter.

Each component of the IoT infrastructure is subjected to diverse types of vulnerabilities and threats. The vulnerabilities and threats, which exist in each of these platforms, were examined in detail. The techniques to safeguard the IT infrastructure components from these threats and vulnerabilities were also discussed in this chapter.

The different smart applications of IoT are smart grids, smart transport systems, smart water systems, smart buildings, and so on. The security concerns of these applications and the different ways to tackle them were also discussed in this chapter.

Bibliography

Eliminate DDoS Attacks in the Cloud and On-Premise. http://www.imperva.com/docs/SB_DDoS_Protection_Service.pdf.

http://www.symantec.com/security_response/publications/threatreport.jsp?inid=us_ghp_thumbnail1_istr-2013.

Index